Preface

Although this book shares the same title as a series of books for DOS and mainframe computers, it has been completely rewritten for SPSS Release 6.1. I hope that the many users of the earlier book will find it not just changed but improved. Its goal remains the same: to provide an unintimidating introduction both to data analysis and to SPSS. This book can be used either as a supplementary text or as the primary text in an introductory course in data analysis. It has been designed for use with SPSS for Windows and SPSS for the Macintosh, including the student versions.

These products, built around a graphical user interface, represent a substantial change from earlier versions of SPSS. Students no longer have to learn arcane commands. Classroom time no longer has to be spent on teaching students how to make things work and what to do when they don't work. There is no such thing as a job that won't run! In addition, the graphical capabilities of the software have been greatly expanded. This makes teaching and learning about data analysis easier and a lot more interesting.

Data Files

Since the best way to learn about data analysis is to actually do it, this book uses real data to solve a variety of problems. Data from the General Social Survey are analyzed in several of the chapters and in the exercises. Examples and exercises are not limited to the General Social Survey, however. The variety of data files used should make this book appealing to a broader range of students and teachers. The data files used in the chapters and in the exercises are distributed on diskette to instructors who adopt this book for classroom use. Others can purchase the data files from the publisher.

Using This Book

This book is divided into four parts: "Getting Started with SPSS," "Describing Data," "Testing Hypotheses," and "Examining Relationships." Within these parts, each chapter presents a problem and statistical techniques useful for solving it. Detailed descriptions of the SPSS procedures used are also provided. Each chapter also contains extensive exercises that use the data files described above. Instructors can choose exercises that best suit the interests and sophistication of their students.

Acknowledgments

I wish to thank the many users of the original Guide to Data Analysis for their helpful comments and suggestions. In particular, I wish to thank my students, who always made sure I knew when something I thought was admirably clear was not. I also wish to thank the reviewers of this book, especially Susan Shott, who made many valuable recommendations. Jonathan Healy, of SPSS Inc., was involved in many aspects of the preparation of this book. I am grateful for his patience and skill. Finally, I wish to thank my husband, Bruce Stephenson, for his multidimensional collaboration, and Ausra, Vytas, Daina, and Raudonis Norušis for being our friends.

Marija J. Norušis

SPSS

SPSS® 6.1
Guide to Data Analysis

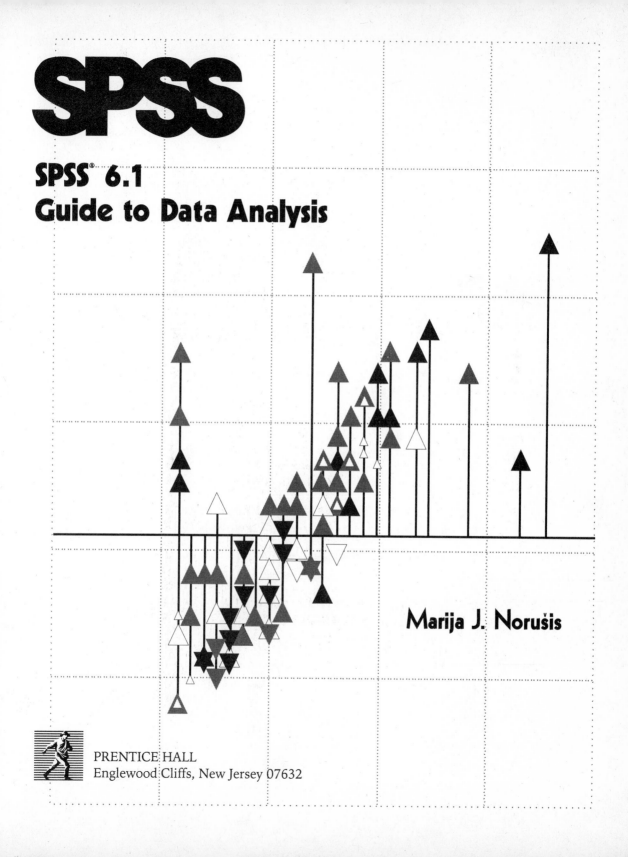

Marija J. Norušis

PRENTICE HALL
Englewood Cliffs, New Jersey 07632

For more information about SPSS® software products, please write or call

Marketing Department
SPSS Inc.
444 North Michigan Avenue
Chicago, IL 60611
Tel: (312) 329-2400
Fax: (312) 329-3668

SPSS® 6.1 Guide to Data Analysis

Published by Prentice-Hall, Inc.
A Simon & Schuster Company
Englewood Cliffs, New Jersey 07632

1 2 3 4 5 6 7 8 9 0   99 98 97 96 95

ISBN 0-13-437054-6

Contents

Part 2   Describing Data

Part 3   Testing Hypotheses

10   Evaluating Results from Samples   181

11   The Normal Distribution   197

14   Testing a Hypothesis about Two Independent Means   253

Part 4 Examining Relationships

Introduction

1

"What does it all mean?" is a question that used to be relegated to philosophy classes. But now you're probably more likely to hear it mumbled by people peering at computer screens. Gathering information has become a national pastime. Personal, corporate, and research data are comfortably lounging on disks, while their anxious keepers try to figure out how to transform them into useful conclusions and recommendations. It's unlikely that you'll be able to avoid this activity. Whether you're a corporate CEO, a zoo manager, or a research scientist, dealing with data is part of the job.

The goal of this book is to acquaint you with data analysis—the art of examining, summarizing, and drawing conclusions from data. You probably think that the word *art* is a misprint. Creativity isn't usually associated with classes in statistics or data analysis—but it should be. Data analysis is much more than knowing what some exotic terms and statistical formulas mean. Good data analysis involves a mixture of common sense, technical expertise, and curiosity. It's knowing what questions to ask and how best to answer them. Analyzing data isn't a rote activity—every data set you encounter is in some way unique.

The best way to learn about data analysis is to actually do it. In this book, you'll analyze a variety of data sets. You'll look for factors related to job satisfaction. You'll see whether marathon running alters certain chemicals found in the blood, whether a college degree makes you more likely to work longer hours and find life more interesting. You'll try to predict life expectancy for people in different countries, based on various characteristics of the countries.

Statistical software is essential for analyzing data. It lets you channel your energy into thinking about a problem instead of being preoccupied with computational details. But that doesn't mean that you need to know less about the concepts underlying data analysis. It means you must know more. Simple achievements like being able to calculate a variety of statistical tests on a pocket calculator, or being able to mimic arcane computer commands, count for little these days.

Instead, you must learn how best to harness the powerful statistical techniques at your fingertips to intelligently solve problems.

About This Book

This book is divided into four parts: "Getting Started with SPSS," "Describing Data," "Testing Hypotheses," and "Examining Relationships." In each of these parts, you're introduced to tools that you can apply to a broad range of problems. Most data analysis tasks require you to select and combine approaches from the different parts of the book. For example, examining your data values is always the first step to solving any problem, no matter how complicated or simple.

Getting Started with SPSS

The statistical program you will use to analyze data is called SPSS. While SPSS runs on a variety of platforms, this book is intended for use with SPSS for Windows and SPSS for the Macintosh. Chapters 2 and 3 provide a brief overview of how to operate the system in each of the two environments. (No need to read both! Find out which version you're running and read the appropriate chapter.) Using SPSS, you'll be able to easily produce graphical displays and statistical analyses. But the program can't do what's most important—select the appropriate procedures and interpret their results. That's left up to you.

Describing Data

The first step of any statistical analysis is displaying and summarizing the data values. How many people are satisfied with their jobs? How old are they? Where did they hear about your product? How much money do they earn? You can also look at several items together. How many men and how many women find life exciting? What are their average ages? Are college graduates more satisfied with their jobs than people without college degrees? You also identify values that appear to be unusual—ages in the 100's, incomes in the billions—and check the original records to make sure that these values are not the result of errors in coding or entering the data. You don't want to waste time analyzing incorrect data.

An important part of describing and summarizing data is making graphical displays. Some of these displays, like pie charts and bar charts, are useful for presenting your results. Other, more specialized displays help you see more complex features of the distribution of data values. As you'll learn, it can be particularly important to see these features when analyzing data.

Testing Hypotheses

Sometimes all you need to do is describe your data, since you have information available for everyone (or everything) that you're interested in drawing conclusions about. That's not usually the case, though. Instead, you want to draw conclusions about much larger groups of people or things than those for whom you have data. You want to know whether two treatments for a disease are equally effective for all people with the disease, not just for those in your study. You want to know how all the adults in your country who are satisfied with their jobs differ from all those who aren't. You don't want to restrict your conclusions to those who participated in your survey. To test hypotheses about a larger group of people or things based on the results observed in your sample, you have to learn about statistical hypothesis testing. That's what this part of this book is about.

Examining Relationships

How are sales related to marketing expenditures? Does diastolic blood pressure increase with body weight? Can you predict life expectancy for a country from its birth rate? What are good predictors of salary: education, years of work experience, job seniority, type of position? There are many different ways to study and model the relationship between variables. You can compute statistics that measure how strongly two variables are related. You can build a mathematical model to predict values of one variable from values of other variables. In the last part of the book, you'll learn about linear regression analysis, a powerful and frequently used tool for modeling relationships among variables.

Let's Get Started

Although it is possible to read through this entire book without actually attempting any of the analyses yourself, the book has been designed with a hands-on approach in mind. Each chapter provides specific instructions so that you can work along in SPSS. To get started using SPSS, turn to Chapter 2 (if you are using SPSS for Windows) or Chapter 3 (if you are using SPSS for the Macintosh). SPSS may look intimidating when you first start it up, but you'll quickly realize how easy it is to get SPSS to do the work of calculating statistical results, leaving you free to focus on the more important question: "What do the numbers mean?"

An Introductory Tour: SPSS for Windows

This chapter provides a quick, guided tour of SPSS for Windows. It applies to both the full system and the Student Version. (See Chapter 3 for a guided tour of SPSS for the Macintosh; for a more extensive guided tour, run the online tutorial that was installed along with SPSS.) In order to use SPSS, you need to know how to do the following things, all of which are included in this chapter's tour:

- Run SPSS for Windows
- Open a data file
- Run a statistical procedure and look at the results
- Generate and view a chart

The chapter concludes with an overview of three of the features that make SPSS for Windows easy to use: the toolbar, the online tutorial, and the online Help system.

To use SPSS for Windows, you need a basic understanding of Windows—how to use a mouse to select items from the Program Manager and from menus. If you don't know how to do these things, have someone show you. There's also a Windows tutorial available from the Help menu in the Windows Program Manager.

Starting SPSS for Windows

The easiest way to run SPSS for Windows is from the Program Manager. During the installation of SPSS, the Setup procedure creates an SPSS program group, as shown in Figure 2.1. (If you can't find the SPSS program group, select SPSS from the Window menu in the Program Manager.)

The SPSS program group window includes icons for the SPSS program and the SPSS tutorial, plus a sample data file and sample chart installed with the program.

Figure 2.1   SPSS program group in Program Manager

Double-click icon with left mouse button

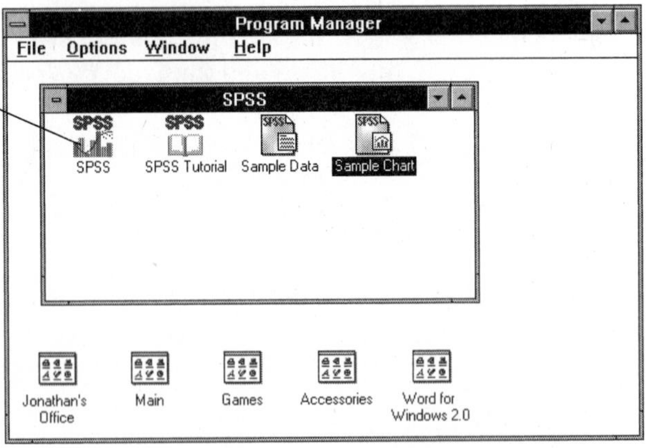

▶ To start SPSS, double-click on the SPSS icon.

Always use the left mouse button unless the right one is specifically indicated.

The SPSS application window is displayed, as shown in Figure 2.2. Inside the application window, the Data Editor and output windows are visible. You can move windows by clicking and dragging their title bars or resize them by clicking and dragging their sides or corners.

Figure 2.2   SPSS application window

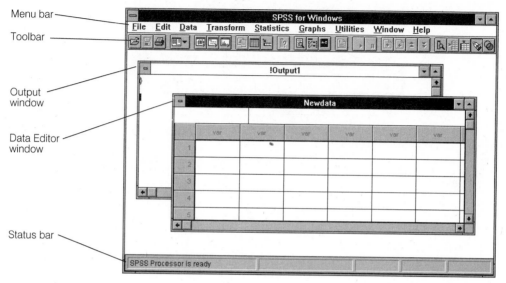

Menu bar

Toolbar

Output window

Data Editor window

Status bar

The first time you run SPSS after installing it, you might see a dialog box called Startup Preferences, with various settings in it. Don't change any of these settings unless you know what they mean. Just click on the OK button. You can always come back later and change the settings.

Opening a Data File

Students can obtain the data files used in this book from their professors. In addition, the diskette can be purchased separately from the publisher.

The SPSS Data Editor window displays your working data file. You don't have one yet—that's why the Data Editor is empty. If you have data of your own that are not in the computer yet, you can type the numbers right into the Data Editor. If the data are already in a spreadsheet or database file, you can probably read that file into SPSS. The data used in this book are already in the form of SPSS data files. To use them for the exercises, or just to follow along in the analysis, simply open the appropriate data file. To open a data file:

▶ Click the left mouse button on the word File on the SPSS menu bar, as shown in Figure 2.3.

The File menu is displayed.

▶ Click on Open ▶ in the File menu.

▶ Click on Data.

Figure 2.3 Opening a data file

Select File

Select Open

Select Data

From now on, we'll use shorthand to indicate menu selections. The following shorthand represents the steps we just took:

File
  Open ▶
    Data...

When you click on Data in the submenu, the Open Data File dialog box appears, as shown in Figure 2.4.

Figure 2.4   Open Data File dialog box

Select gss.sav

Double-click to search for the file in a different directory

Click to search for the file on a different drive

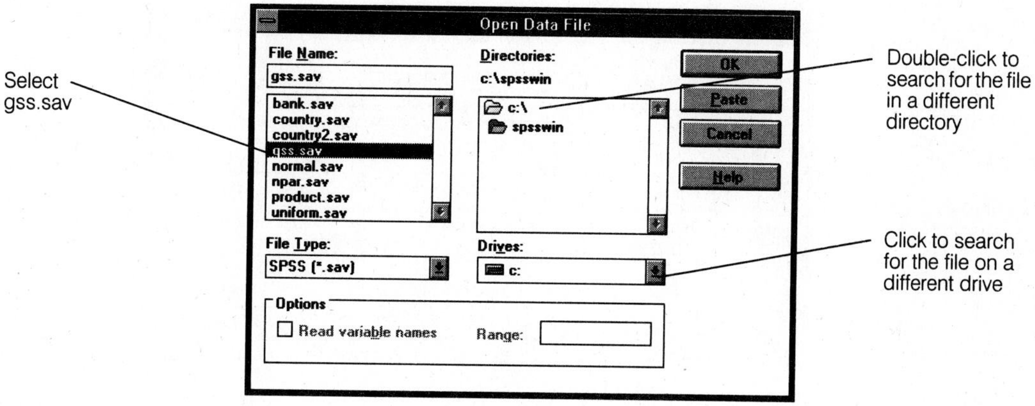

▶ Click on the *gss.sav* data file where it appears in the list.

▶ Click on OK.

What if the gss.sav file doesn't appear? Only files in the current drive and directory are listed. The file you want may either be in another directory or saved on a different drive.

To look in a parent directory (one that contains the current directory) or a subdirectory (one contained by the current directory), double-click on its name, as shown in Figure 2.4.

To look on a different drive, choose it from the drop-down list of disk drives. The list probably contains the a: and c: drives, and maybe some others, especially if your computer is on a network. ■ ■ ■

If you need further assistance using the Open Data File dialog box, click on its Help button. Help is described later in this chapter.

After SPSS has read the data file you selected, it appears in the Data Editor, as shown in Figure 2.5. This particular data file contains selected information for 1500 people who were interviewed in the 1993 General

Social Survey, which annually asks a broad range of questions to a sample of adults in the United States population.

If your screen displays all numbers rather than value labels such as Male and Female in the cells, from the menus choose:

Utilities
Value Labels

Figure 2.5 Data Editor window with GSS data

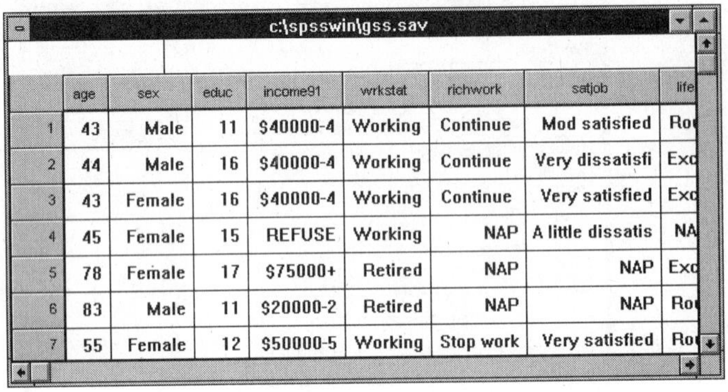

	age	sex	educ	income91	wrkstat	richwork	satjob	life
1	43	Male	11	$40000-4	Working	Continue	Mod satisfied	Ro
2	44	Male	16	$40000-4	Working	Continue	Very dissatisfi	Exc
3	43	Female	16	$40000-4	Working	Continue	Very satisfied	Exc
4	45	Female	15	REFUSE	Working	NAP	A little dissatis	NA
5	78	Female	17	$75000+	Retired	NAP	NAP	Exc
6	83	Male	11	$20000-2	Retired	NAP	NAP	Ro
7	55	Female	12	$50000-5	Working	Stop work	Very satisfied	Ro

Statistical Procedures

You can use the Frequencies procedure to summarize and display values for the variables in your data file. (Chapter 4 discusses frequency tables in detail. At this point, you'll just use Frequencies to see how SPSS procedures work.)

▶ To open the Frequencies dialog box, from the menus choose:

Statistics
  Summarize ▶
    Frequencies...

This opens the Frequencies dialog box, as shown in Figure 2.6.

Figure 2.6 Frequencies dialog box

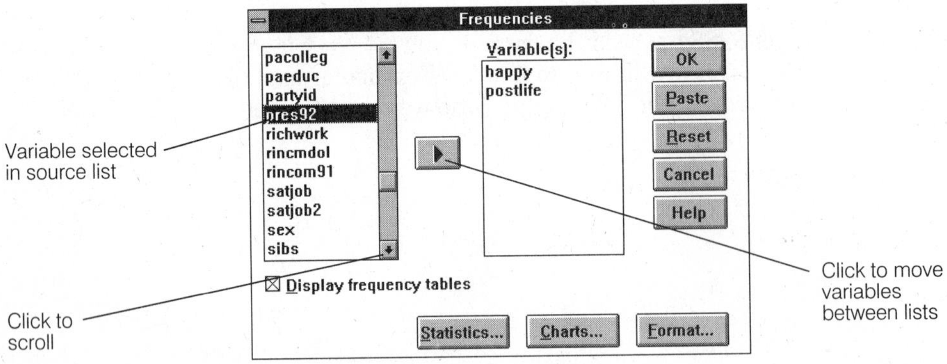

▶ Click on *happy* in the source list and then click on ▶.

This moves *happy* into the Variable(s) list.

As a shortcut to scroll the source list, click in the list and type the letter p. This scrolls to the first variable beginning with p.

▶ Scroll down the source list until you see *postlife* and move it into the Variable(s) list as well.

▶ Click on Charts.

This opens the Frequencies Charts dialog box, as shown in Figure 2.7. Here you can request charts along with your frequency tables.

Figure 2.7   Frequencies Charts dialog box

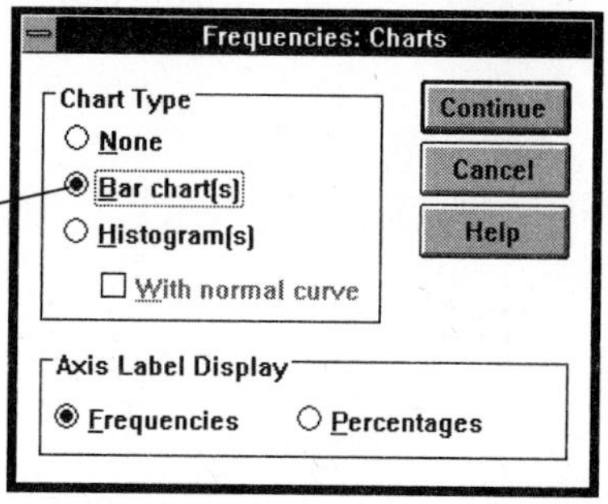

Select Bar chart(s)

▶ Select Bar chart(s), as shown in Figure 2.7.

▶ Click on Continue to close the Frequencies Charts dialog box.

▶ Click on OK.

SPSS displays the frequency tables in the output window, as shown in Figure 2.8. The SPSS Chart Carousel icon is also displayed in Figure 2.8.

The Output Window

The output window is where SPSS displays the statistics and reports—the **output**—from the analysis of your data. An SPSS output window works like a window in a simple word processor. You can scroll up and down through the output, deleting output or typing in additional comments.

Figure 2.8 shows the output for happy, one of the two frequency tables you requested. If you like, use the scroll bar to browse through the frequency tables and see if you can figure out what they mean. (See Chapter 4 if you really want to know what they mean.)

Figure 2.8 Output window and Chart Carousel icon

	SPSS for Windows	
File Edit Data Transform	Statistics Graphs Utilities	Window Help

!Output1

HAPPY   GENERAL HAPPINESS

Value Label	Value	Frequency	Percent	Valid Percent	Cum Percent
VERY HAPPY	1	477	31.8	31.9	31.9
PRETTY HAPPY	2	849	56.6	56.8	88.7
NOT TOO HAPPY	3	169	11.3	11.3	100.0
NA	9	5	.3	Missing	
		-------	-------	-------	
	Total	1500	100.0	100.0	

Hi-Res Chart # 1:Bar chart of general happiness

Click to scroll up and down

Chart Carousel icon

Chart Carousel

SPSS Processor is ready

The Chart Carousel

What about those bar charts that you requested? SPSS created them, too, and placed them in the Chart Carousel.

▶ Double-click on the Chart Carousel icon (shown in Figure 2.8) to activate the Chart Carousel.

You can also activate the Carousel by clicking on

on the toolbar.

The Chart Carousel is displayed, with the first of the bar charts you requested in the Frequencies Charts dialog box, as shown in Figure 2.9. The Carousel holds the charts you create and allows you to look at them, print them, or save them to your disk. (If you want to *modify* an

SPSS chart, you must move it out of the Carousel into a chart window. See "Modifying Charts" on p. 536 in Appendix A.)

Figure 2.9 Chart Carousel

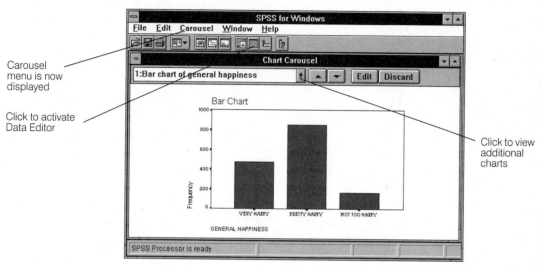

Carousel menu is now displayed

Click to activate Data Editor

Click to view additional charts

Notice that the menu bar has changed in Figure 2.9. To restore the regular SPSS menus so you can run another procedure, you need to activate the Data Editor or the output window.

▶ To activate the Data Editor, click in the Data Editor window (if it is visible) or use the toolbar, as shown in Figure 2.9.

The Data Editor Window

Let's take a closer look at the Data Editor. (See Figure 2.10.) If you've ever used a spreadsheet, the Data Editor should look familiar. It's just an array of rows and columns. In the Data Editor, each row is a case, and each column is a variable. Cases and variables are fundamental concepts in data analysis. It's time we stopped to define them.

Figure 2.10 Data Editor window

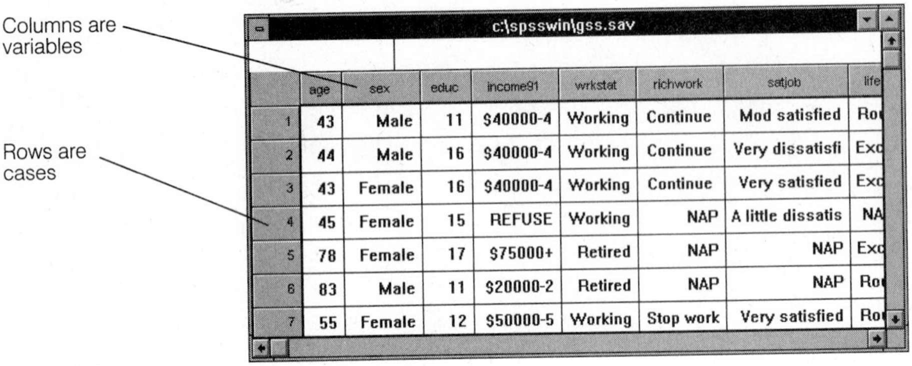

Columns are variables

Rows are cases

	age	sex	educ	income91	wrkstat	richwork	satjob	life
1	43	Male	11	$40000-4	Working	Continue	Mod satisfied	Ro
2	44	Male	16	$40000-4	Working	Continue	Very dissatisfi	Exc
3	43	Female	16	$40000-4	Working	Continue	Very satisfied	Exc
4	45	Female	15	REFUSE	Working	NAP	A little dissatis	NA
5	78	Female	17	$75000+	Retired	NAP	NAP	Exc
6	83	Male	11	$20000-2	Retired	NAP	NAP	Ro
7	55	Female	12	$50000-5	Working	Stop work	Very satisfied	Ro

Cases (rows) are the people who participate in a survey or experiment. (Another word often used is **observation**.) Actually, a case need not be a person. It can be anything. If you're doing experiments on rats, the case is the individual rat. If you're studying the beef content of hamburgers, each hamburger is a case. Generally speaking, the case is the unit for which you take measurements.

Variables (columns) are the different items of information you collect for your cases. Think about the way you conduct a survey. You ask each person for the same type of information: date of birth, sex, marital status, education, views on whatever subjects your survey is about. Each item for which you record an answer is known as a variable. The answer a particular person gives is known as the **value** for that variable. Year of birth is a variable; responses such as 1952 or 1899 are values for that variable.

The intersection of the row and the column is called a **cell**. Each cell holds the value of a particular case for a particular variable. You can edit values in the Data Editor, as follows:

▶ Click in one of the cells with the mouse.

The **cell editor** displays the value for the selected cell, as shown in Figure 2.11.

Figure 2.11 Data Editor with cell selected

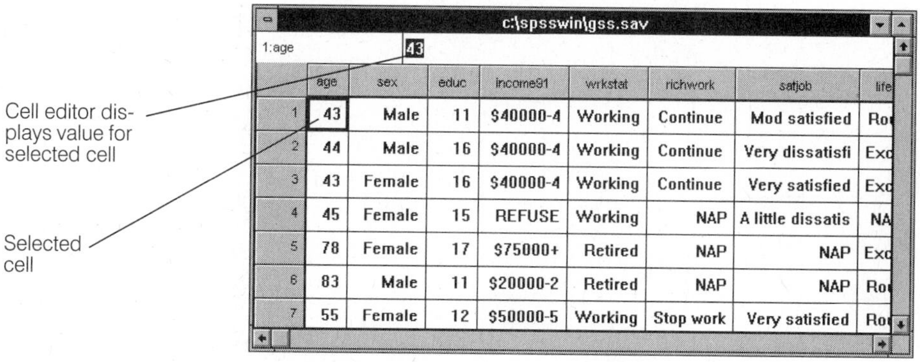

Cell editor displays value for selected cell

Selected cell

▶ Type a number to replace the existing value and press ⏎Enter.

The new value appears in the cell editor as you type it, but the value in the cell is not updated until you press ⏎Enter.

▶ Change another value in the cell editor, but instead of pressing ⏎Enter, press Esc.

When you press Esc rather than ⏎Enter, the original value in the cell remains unchanged.

Entering Non-Numeric Data

If you try to enter anything other than a number into a numeric variable cell, your computer will probably beep at you.

All of the variables in *gss.sav* are **numeric**; that is, they are made up of numbers. To enter non-numeric data into a column, you must first specify the variable type in the Define Variable dialog box.

For example, suppose you want to type the name of each respondent in the survey. To do this, you must create a new variable and define it as a **string** variable. (*String* is just a common computer term meaning that the variable contains text—words or characters—rather than numbers.)

▶ Click in any cell in the first row of the Data Editor and press End.

This scrolls the Data Editor to the last variable in the file, as shown in Figure 2.12.

Figure 2.12 Defining a new variable in the Data Editor

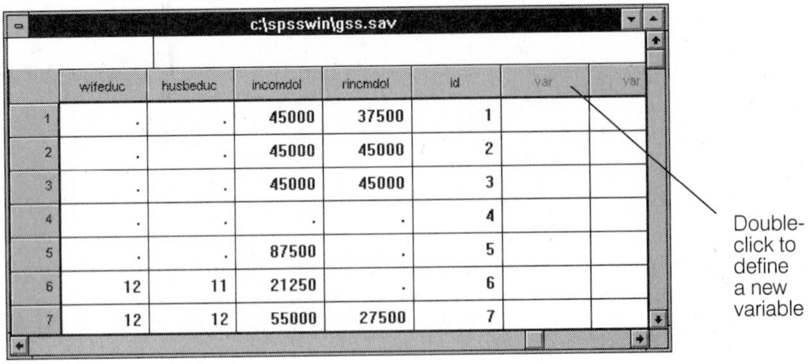

Double-click to define a new variable

▶ Double-click on *var* at the top of the empty column to define a new variable in the column.

This opens the Define Variable dialog box, as shown in Figure 2.13.

Figure 2.13 Define Variable dialog box

Click on Type

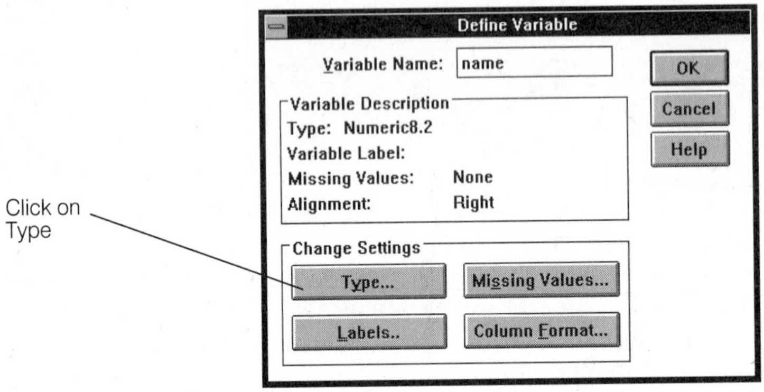

▶ In the Variable Name box, type name.

▶ Click on Type.

This opens the Define Variable Type dialog box.

▶ Select String and specify 8 for Characters.

▶ Click on Continue to close the Define Variable Type dialog box.

▶ Click on OK.

SPSS creates a new variable called *name*, which appears in the Data Editor. You can enter as many names in the column as you like.

Clearing the Data Editor without Saving Changes

You have changed some of the values in the GSS data. You don't want these changes to be permanent, because you want to get correct statistical results when you use the data again.

▶ To clear the Data Editor *without* saving your changes, from the menus choose:

File
　New ▶
　　Data...

SPSS asks if it should save the contents of the data window.

▶ Click on No.

This clears the modified GSS data from the Data Editor, so you won't forget and save it later on when you exit SPSS.

The SPSS Online Tutorial

SPSS for Windows comes with an online tutorial that shows you how to use many of the features of SPSS. To run the tutorial, select SPSS Tutorial from the Help menu or double-click on the SPSS Tutorial icon in the SPSS program group.

Figure 2.14 SPSS online tutorial main menu

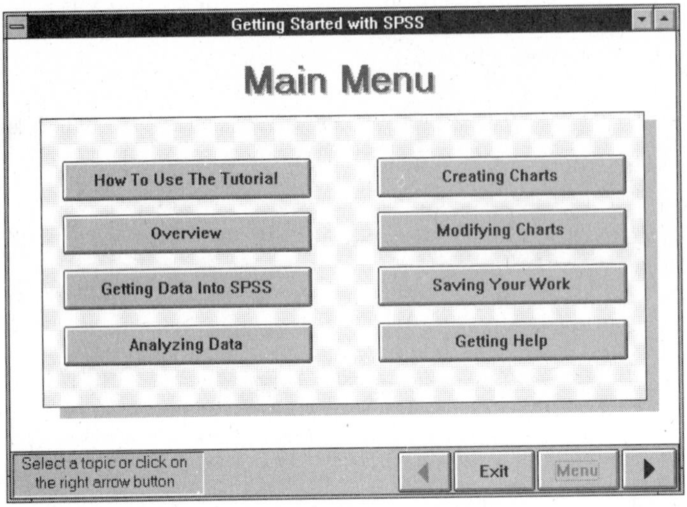

If SPSS is already running, you can start the tutorial by selecting SPSS Tutorial from the Help menu.

The tutorial is self-explanatory. It includes an overview and detailed sections on defining data, using the menus and dialog boxes, editing charts, getting help, and other topics (see Figure 2.14). You can walk through the whole tutorial, or you can choose the specific topics that interest you at the moment. If you need a more complete orientation to SPSS and how it works than this chapter can provide, the online tutorial is the best place to start.

The SPSS Toolbar

The tutorial helps you when you're getting started with SPSS. The toolbar provides shortcuts for commonly used procedures and functions. You will very likely use the toolbar more and more as you become familiar with SPSS. You may have already used it to move back and forth between the Chart Carousel and the Data Editor.

Figure 2.15 SPSS toolbar

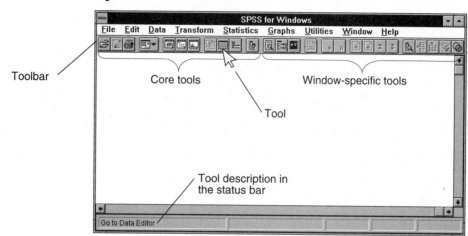

Move the pointer over any tool to display a description of what the tool does in the status bar at the bottom of your screen, as shown in Figure 2.15. You don't have to remember them all—just use the ones you find helpful.

The toolbar changes when a chart window is active, to offer chart-editing tools. You can find complete descriptions of all the tools in the online Help system. "Searching Help" on p. 21 tells you exactly where to look.

The SPSS Help System

SPSS for Windows comes with an extensive online Help system. The Help system includes topics on how to use all of the dialog boxes in SPSS; on common tasks, with step-by-step instructions; on producing all the different types of charts; and on troubleshooting. The Help system explains the SPSS for Windows software program but does not try to teach statistics. If that's what you want, though, you're in the right place—just keep reading this book!

▶ To open Help, from the SPSS menus choose:

Help
  Contents...

This opens the Help system Contents, as shown in Figure 2.16.

Figure 2.16 Help Contents

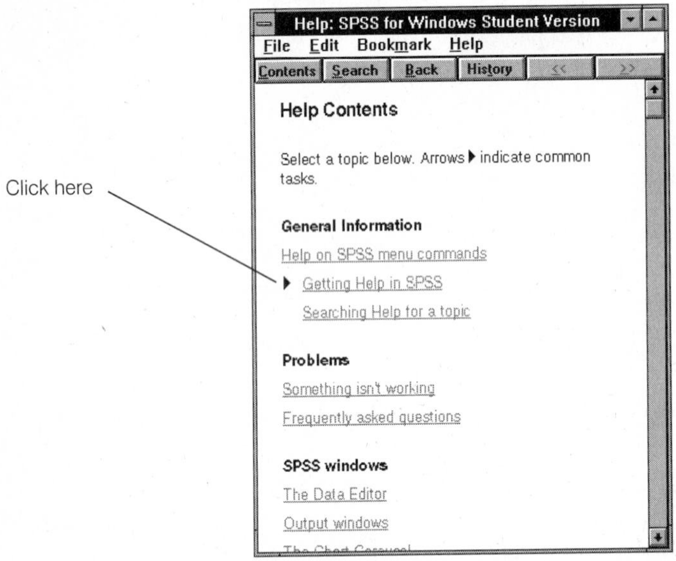

Click here

▶ Click on the highlighted phrase Getting Help in SPSS in the Help window.

You then jump to a topic about how to use the SPSS Help system.

▶ At the top of the Help window, click on the button labeled Contents.

This returns you to the Help Contents.

▶ From the Help Contents, click on the highlighted phrase Help on SPSS menu commands.

This jumps to a topic titled SPSS Menu Commands.

▶ Click on Data menu.

▶ Click on Define Variable.

A topic on the Define Variable dialog box is displayed, as shown in Figure 2.17.

Figure 2.17 Help topic

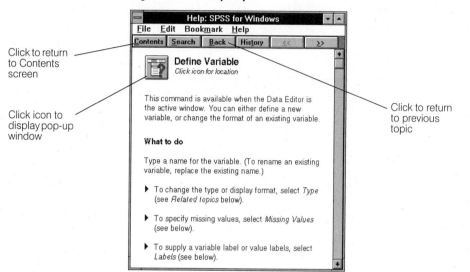

Click to return to Contents screen

Click icon to display pop-up window

Click to return to previous topic

▶ Click on the icon in the upper left corner of the Help topic, as shown in Figure 2.17.

A pop-up window is displayed, with instructions on how to open the Define Variable dialog box.

▶ Click anywhere to clear the pop-up window.

▶ Click several times on the Back button at the top of the Help window.

Each time you click on this button, you move back to the previously displayed topic, allowing you to retrace your steps.

Searching Help

Often, the quickest way to find the Help topic you want is with the Search facility. For example, to find the Help topic that describes the tools available in chart windows:

▶ Open a Help window from SPSS if one is not already open. (Click on a Help button, use the Help menu, or press F1.)

▶ Press the Search button in the Help window.

The Search dialog box appears, as shown in Figure 2.18.

Figure 2.18 Search dialog box

Type
toolbar

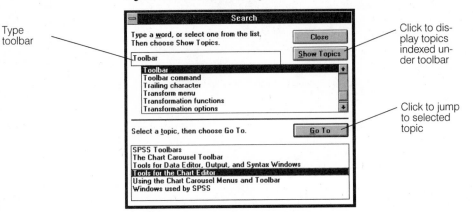

Click to dis-
play topics
indexed un-
der toolbar

Click to jump
to selected
topic

▶ Type `toolbar` and click on the Show Topics button.

▶ Select Tools for the Chart Editor and click on the Go To button.

This displays the Help topic on chart window tools, as shown in Figure 2.19. Click on any tool icon to pop up a description of that tool.

Figure 2.19 Help on chart window tools

Click any tool
icon to pop
up a descrip-
tion of the
tool

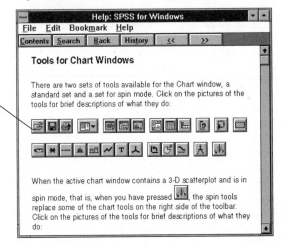

The History Window

The History window (see Figure 2.20) lists the Help topics you have visited most recently. You can return to any topic by double-clicking on its title in the History window—a good way to retrace your steps through the Help system.

Figure 2.20 History window

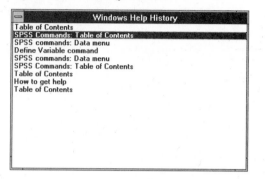

▶ To open the History window, click on the History button at the top of the Help window.

What's Next?

Once you get comfortable with the Help system, you'll find that it can tell you just about anything you need to know about how to use SPSS for Windows. To start learning how (and why) to use SPSS as a tool to solve your problems, turn to Chapter 4.

An Introductory Tour: 3
SPSS for the Macintosh

This chapter provides a quick, guided tour of SPSS for the Macintosh. It applies to both the full system and the Student Version. (See Chapter 2 for a guided tour of SPSS for Windows; for a more extensive guided tour, run the online tutorial that was installed along with SPSS.) In order to use SPSS, you need to know how to do the following things, all of which are included in this chapter's tour:

- Run SPSS for the Macintosh
- Open a data file
- Run a statistical procedure and look at the results
- Generate and view a chart

The chapter concludes with an overview of three of the features that make SPSS for the Macintosh easy to use: the toolbar, the online tutorial, and the online Help system.

To use SPSS for the Macintosh, you need a basic understanding of the Macintosh—how to use a mouse to select items from the Finder and from menus. If you don't know how to do these things, have someone show you. See your Macintosh documentation for more information.

Starting SPSS for the Macintosh

To run SPSS for the Macintosh, find the SPSS 6.1 folder on your hard disk and double-click the folder to open it. The folder contains the SPSS application and other files installed with SPSS. (See Figure 3.1.)

Figure 3.1   SPSS folder

Double-click
icon with mouse
button

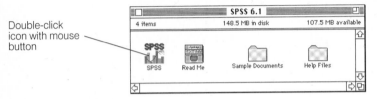

▶ To start SPSS, double-click on the SPSS icon.

It will take a while for the application to open—it's big. (Wait until the status bar at the bottom of the screen tells you SPSS processor is ready before you proceed.)

When you start SPSS, it displays the Data Editor window and the output window, as shown in Figure 3.2.

Figure 3.2   SPSS application

Menu bar

Toolbar

Output
window

Data Editor

Status bar

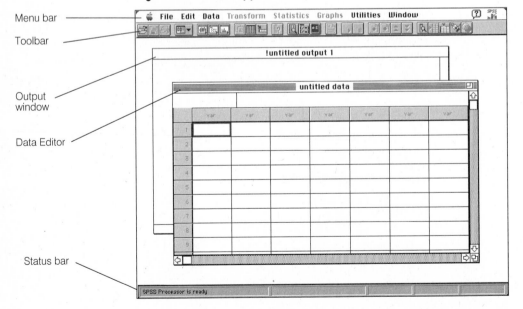

Opening a Data File

Students can obtain the data files used in this book from their professors. In addition, the diskette can be purchased separately from the publisher.

The SPSS Data Editor window displays your working data file. You don't have one yet—that's why the Data Editor is empty. If you have data of your own that are not in the computer yet, you can type the numbers right into the Data Editor. If the data are already in a spreadsheet or database file, you can probably read that file into SPSS. The data used in this book are already in the form of SPSS data files. To use them for the exercises, or just to follow along in the analysis, simply open the appropriate data file. To open a data file:

▶ Point the mouse over the word File on the menu bar, as shown in Figure 3.3.

▶ Press the mouse button and hold it down.

The File menu is displayed.

▶ Still holding the mouse button down, drag the pointer over the Open command.

▶ With Open highlighted, release the mouse button.

Figure 3.3 Opening a data file

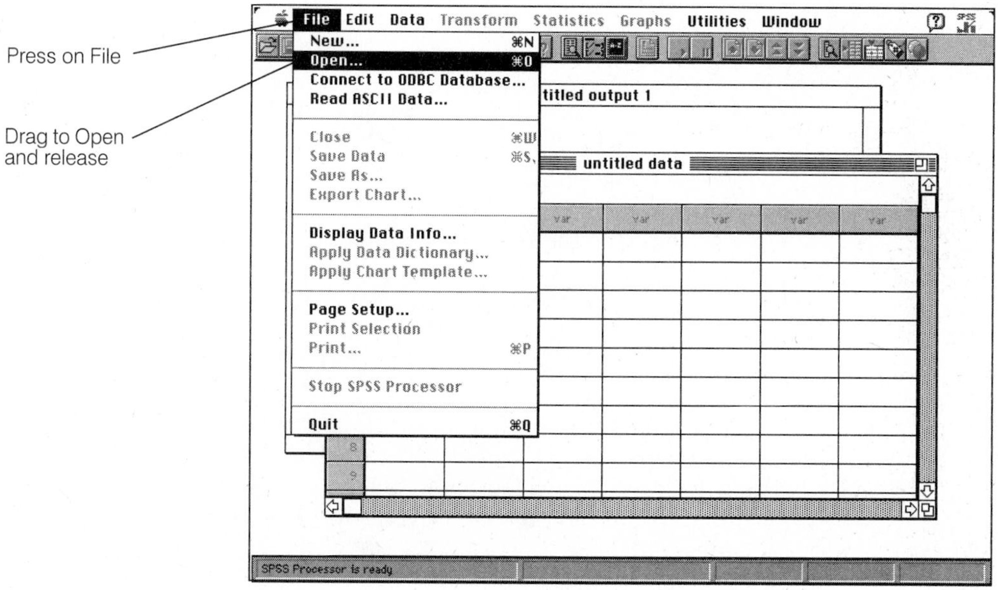

Press on File

Drag to Open and release

From now on, we'll use shorthand to indicate menu selections. The following shorthand represents the steps we just took:

File
　Open...

When you release the mouse button, a dialog box for opening files appears, as shown in Figure 3.4.

Figure 3.4   Dialog box for opening files

Select
gss.sav

Press here to
search for the file
in a different
folder

Press here and
select All Files to
see all file types
in the current
folder

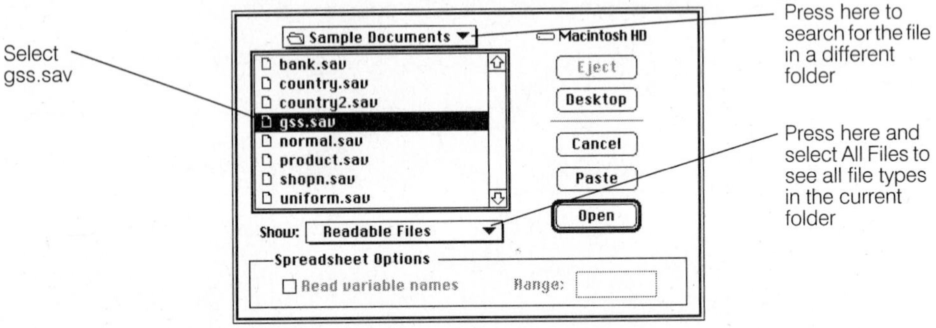

▶ Click on the *gss.sav* data file where it appears in the list.

▶ Click on Open.

?　*What if the gss.sav file doesn't appear?* The name of the current folder is shown above the list of files and folders. The file you want may be in a different folder, or it may be a file that the Macintosh does not recognize (this happens when you have copied a file from a DOS or Windows machine but haven't set its type so that the Macintosh recognizes it).

You can also
open a file or
subfolder by
double-clicking
on its name in the
list.

To look in one of the subfolders on the list, select it and click on the Open button.

To look in a parent folder (one that contains the current folder), press the mouse button on the folder name to pop up a menu of parent folders, drag to the folder you want to look at, and then release the mouse button.

To open a file that is in the current folder but doesn't appear on the list (because it is not recognized by the Macintosh), press the mouse button where it says Readable Files to pop up a menu. Move the mouse to highlight All files and release the button.　■ ■ ■

After SPSS has read the data file you selected, it appears in the Data Editor, as shown in Figure 3.5. This particular data file contains selected information for 1500 people who were interviewed in the 1993 General Social Survey, which annually asks a broad range of questions to a sample of adults in the United States population.

Figure 3.5   Data Editor with GSS data

If your screen displays all numbers rather than value labels such as Male and Female in the cells, from the menus choose:

Utilities
  Value Labels

gss.sav						
	age	sex	educ	income91	wrkstat	richwork	satjob
1	43	Male	11	$40000-49999	Working	Continue	Mod satisfied
2	44	Male	16	$40000-49999	Working	Continue	Very dissatisfied
3	43	Female	16	$40000-49999	Working	Continue	Very satisfied
4	45	Female	15	REFUSED	Working	NAP	A little dissatisfied
5	78	Female	17	$75000+	Retired	NAP	NAP
6	83	Male	11	$20000-22499	Retired	NAP	NAP
7	55	Female	12	$50000-59999	Working	Stop work	Very satisfied

Statistical Procedures

You can use the Frequencies procedure to summarize and display values for the variables in your data file. (Chapter 4 discusses frequency tables in detail. At this point, you'll just use Frequencies to see how SPSS procedures work.)

▶ To open the Frequencies dialog box, from the menus choose:

Statistics
  Summarize ▶
    Frequencies...

This opens the Frequencies dialog box, as shown in Figure 3.6.

Figure 3.6   Frequencies dialog box

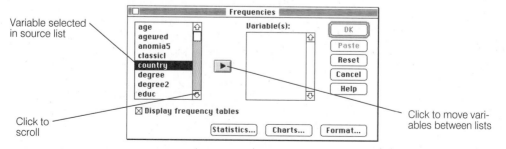

Variable selected in source list

Click to scroll

Click to move variables between lists

▶ Click on *happy* in the source list and then click on ▶.

This moves *happy* into the Variable(s) list.

Click the Help button in almost any dialog box for information about the controls in that dialog box.

▶ Scroll down the source list until you see *postlife* and move it into the Variable(s) list as well.

▶ Click on Charts.

This opens the Frequencies Charts dialog box, as shown in Figure 3.7. Here you can request charts along with your frequency tables.

Figure 3.7   Frequencies Charts dialog box

Select Bar chart(s)

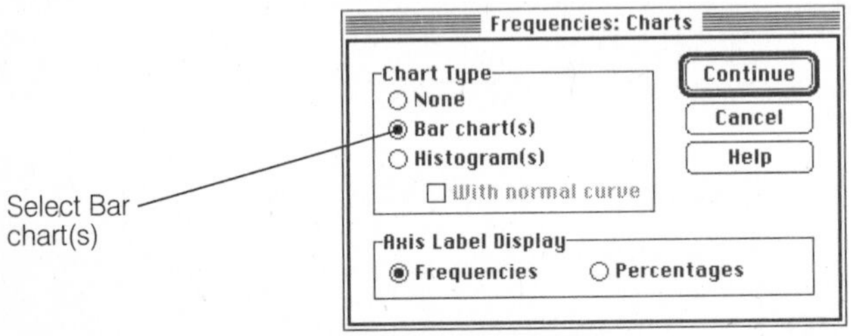

▶ Select Bar chart(s), as shown in Figure 3.7.

▶ Click on Continue to close the Frequencies Charts dialog box.

▶ Click on OK.

SPSS displays the frequency tables in the output window, as shown in Figure 3.8. The output window may be hidden behind the SPSS Chart Carousel, which displays the bar charts you requested.

The Output Window

The output window is where SPSS displays the statistics and reports—the **output**—from the analysis of your data. An SPSS output window works like a window in a simple word processor. You can scroll up and down through the output, deleting output or typing in additional comments.

In this example, you created a frequency table and a bar chart. The frequency table is displayed in the output window, which may be hidden behind the Chart Carousel window.

▶ To activate the output window, click on the Output Window tool on the toolbar, as shown in Figure 3.8.

Figure 3.8   Output window displaying frequency table

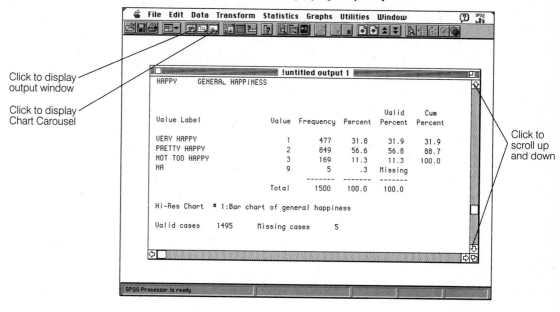

Click to display output window

Click to display Chart Carousel

Click to scroll up and down

The output window shows one of the two frequency tables you requested. If you like, use the scroll bar to browse through the frequency tables and see if you can figure out what they mean. (See Chapter 4 if you really want to know what they mean.)

The Chart Carousel

What about those bar charts that you requested? SPSS created them too, and placed them in the Chart Carousel.

▶ To activate the Chart Carousel, click on the Chart Window tool on the toolbar, as shown in Figure 3.8.

The Chart Carousel is displayed, with the first of the bar charts you requested in the Frequencies Charts dialog box, as shown in Figure 3.9. The Carousel holds the charts you create and allows you to look at them, print them, or save them to your disk. (If you want to *modify* an

SPSS chart, you must move it out of the Carousel into a chart window. See "Modifying Charts" on p. 536 in Appendix A.)

Figure 3.9   Chart Carousel

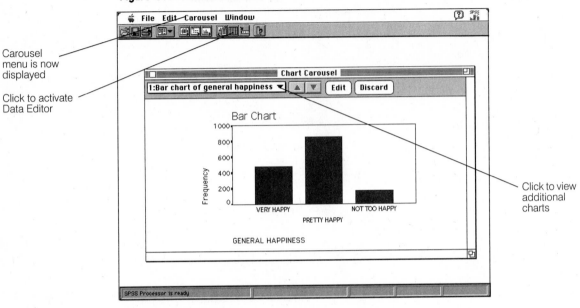

Carousel menu is now displayed

Click to activate Data Editor

Click to view additional charts

Notice that the menu bar has changed in Figure 3.9. To restore the regular SPSS menus so you can run another procedure, you need to activate the Data Editor or the output window.

▶ To activate the Data Editor, click in the Data Editor window (if it is visible) or use the toolbar, as shown in Figure 3.9.

The Data Editor Window

Let's take a closer look at the Data Editor. (See Figure 3.10.) If you've ever used a spreadsheet, the Data Editor should look familiar. It's just an array of rows and columns. In the Data Editor, each row is a case, and each column is a variable. Cases and variables are fundamental concepts in data analysis. It's time we stopped to define them.

Figure 3.10 Data Editor window

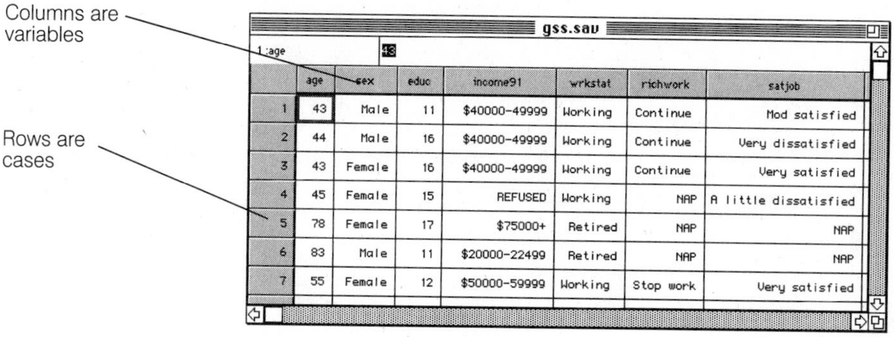

Columns are variables

Rows are cases

	age	sex	educ	income91	wrkstat	richwork	satjob
1	43	Male	11	$40000-49999	Working	Continue	Mod satisfied
2	44	Male	16	$40000-49999	Working	Continue	Very dissatisfied
3	43	Female	16	$40000-49999	Working	Continue	Very satisfied
4	45	Female	15	REFUSED	Working	NAP	A little dissatisfied
5	78	Female	17	$75000+	Retired	NAP	NAP
6	83	Male	11	$20000-22499	Retired	NAP	NAP
7	55	Female	12	$50000-59999	Working	Stop work	Very satisfied

Cases (rows) are the people who participate in a survey or experiment. (Another word often used is **observation**.) Actually, a case need not be a person. It can be anything. If you're doing experiments on rats, the case is the individual rat. If you're studying the beef content of hamburgers, each hamburger is a case. Generally speaking, the case is the unit for which you take measurements.

Variables (columns) are the different items of information you collect for your cases. Think about the way you conduct a survey. You ask each person for the same type of information: date of birth, sex, marital status, education, views on whatever subjects your survey is about. Each item for which you record an answer is known as a variable. The answer a particular person gives is known as the **value** for that variable. Year of birth is a variable; responses such as 1952 or 1899 are values for that variable.

The intersection of the row and the column is called a **cell**. Each cell holds the value of a particular case for a particular variable. You can edit values in the Data Editor, as follows:

▶ Click in one of the cells with the mouse.

The **cell editor** displays the value for the selected cell, as shown in Figure 3.11.

Figure 3.11 Data Editor with cell selected

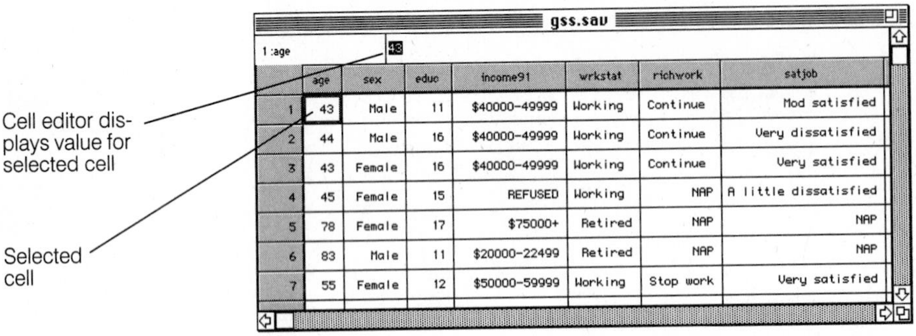

Cell editor displays value for selected cell

Selected cell

▶ Type a number to replace the existing value and press ⏎Return.

The new value appears in the cell editor as you type it, but the value in the cell is not updated until you press ⏎Return.

▶ Change another value in the cell editor, but instead of pressing ⏎Return, press Esc.

When you press Esc rather than ⏎Return, the original value in the cell remains unchanged.

Entering Non-Numeric Data

If you try to enter anything other than a number into a numeric variable cell, your computer will probably beep at you.

All of the variables in *gss.sav* are **numeric**; that is, they are made up of numbers. To enter non-numeric data into a column, you must first specify the variable type in the Define Variable dialog box.

For example, suppose you want to type the name of each respondent in the survey. To do this you must create a new variable and define it as a **string** variable. (*String* is just a common computer term meaning that the variable contains text—words or characters—rather than numbers.)

▶ Click in any cell in the first row of the Data Editor and press the command key and the right arrow key (⌘-→).

This scrolls the Data Editor to the last variable in the file, as shown in Figure 3.12.

Figure 3.12 Defining a new variable in the Data Editor

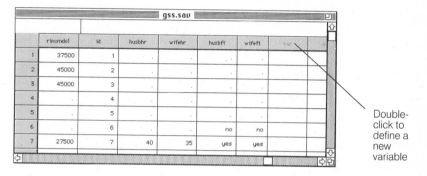

▶ Double-click on *var* at the top of the empty column to define a new variable in the column.

This opens the Define Variable dialog box, as shown in Figure 3.13.

Figure 3.13 Define Variable dialog box

▶ In the Variable Name box, type name.

▶ Click on Type.

This opens the Define Variable Type dialog box.

▶ Select String and specify 8 for Characters.

▶ Click on Continue to close the Define Variable Type dialog box.

▶ Click on OK.

SPSS creates a new variable called *name*, which appears in the Data Editor. You can enter as many names in the column as you like.

Clearing the Data Editor without Saving Changes

You have changed some of the values in the GSS data. You don't want these changes to be permanent, because you want to get correct statistical results when you use the data again.

▶ To clear the Data Editor *without* saving your changes, from the menus choose:

File
  New...

▶ In the New dialog box, select Data and click on OK.

SPSS asks if it should save the contents of the data window.

▶ Click on No.

This clears the modified GSS data from the Data Editor, so you won't forget and save it later on when you exit SPSS.

The SPSS Online Tutorial

SPSS for the Macintosh comes with an online tutorial that shows you how to use many of the features of SPSS.

▶ To run the tutorial, double-click on the SPSS tutorial icon in the SPSS application folder.

Figure 3.14 SPSS online tutorial main menu

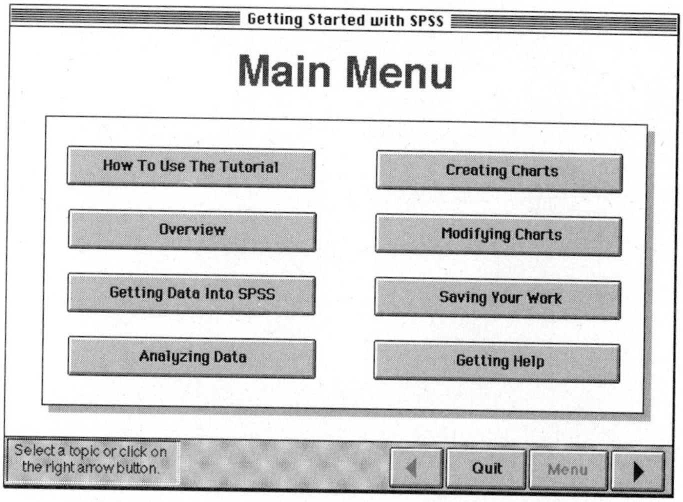

The tutorial is self-explanatory. It includes an overview and detailed sections on defining data, using the menus and dialog boxes, editing charts, getting help, and other topics. (See Figure 3.14.) You can walk through the whole tutorial, or you can choose the specific topics that interest you at the moment. If you need a more complete orientation to SPSS and how it works than this chapter can provide, the online tutorial is the best place to start.

The SPSS Toolbar

The tutorial helps you when you're getting started with SPSS. The toolbar (see Figure 3.15) provides shortcuts for commonly used procedures and functions. You will very likely use the toolbar more and more as you become familiar with SPSS. You may have already used it to move from the Chart Carousel to the Data Editor.

Figure 3.15 SPSS toolbar

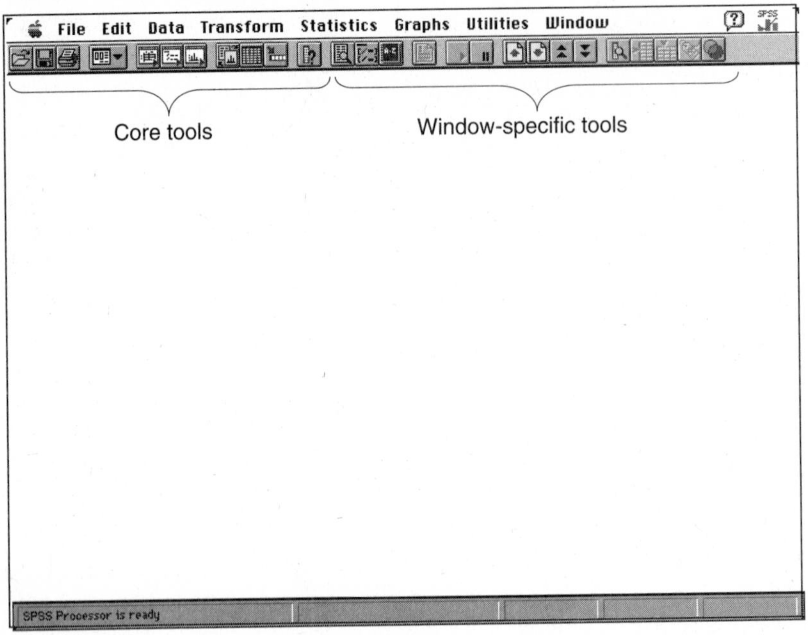

To find out what each tool does, turn on Balloon Help and then put the pointer on the tool you want to know about. The toolbar changes when a chart window is active, to offer chart-editing tools. You can find complete descriptions of all the tools in the online Help system. "Searching Help" on p. 41 tells you exactly where to look.

The SPSS Help System

SPSS for the Macintosh comes with an extensive online Help system. The Help system includes topics on how to use all of the dialog boxes in SPSS; on common tasks, with step-by-step instructions; on producing all the different types of charts; and on troubleshooting. The Help system explains the SPSS for the Macintosh software program but does not try to teach statistics. If that's what you want, though, you're in the right place—just keep reading this book!

To open the Help menu, press on

▶ To open Help, select SPSS Help from the Help menu (the balloon with the question mark in the upper right corner).

This opens the Help system Contents, as shown in Figure 3.16.

Figure 3.16 Help Contents

Click here

▶ Click on the highlighted phrase Getting Help in SPSS in the Help window.

You then jump to a topic about how to use the SPSS Help system.

▶ At the top of the Help window, click the button labeled Topics.

This returns you to the Help Contents.

▶ From the Help Contents, click on the highlighted phrase Help on SPSS menu commands.

This jumps to a topic titled SPSS Menu Commands.

▶ Click on Data menu.

▶ Click on Define Variable.

A topic on the Define Variable dialog box is displayed, as shown in Figure 3.17.

Figure 3.17 Help topic

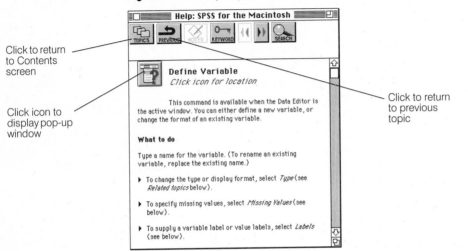

Click to return to Contents screen

Click icon to display pop-up window

Click to return to previous topic

▶ Click on the icon in the upper left corner of the Help topic, as shown in Figure 3.17.

A pop-up window is displayed, with instructions on how to open the Define Variable dialog box.

▶ Click anywhere to clear the pop-up window.

▶ Click several times on the Previous button at the top of the Help window.

Each time you click on this button, you move back to the previously displayed topic, allowing you to retrace your steps.

Searching Help

Often, the quickest way to find the Help topic you want is with the Keyword search facility. For example, to find the Help topic that describes the tools available in chart windows:

▶ Open a Help window from SPSS if one is not already open. (Click a Help button from any SPSS dialog box or use the Help menu.)

▶ Press the Keyword button in the Help window.

The Keywords window appears, as shown in Figure 3.18.

Figure 3.18 Search window

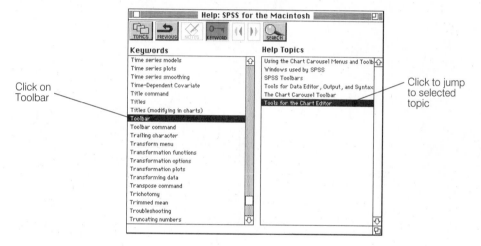

Click on Toolbar

Click to jump to selected topic

▶ Scroll the Keywords list to Toolbar.

▶ Select Toolbar in the Keywords list.

▶ Select Tools for the Chart Editor in the Help Topics list.

This displays the Help topic on chart window tools, as shown in Figure 3.19. Click on any tool icon to pop up a description of that tool.

Figure 3.19 Help on chart window tools

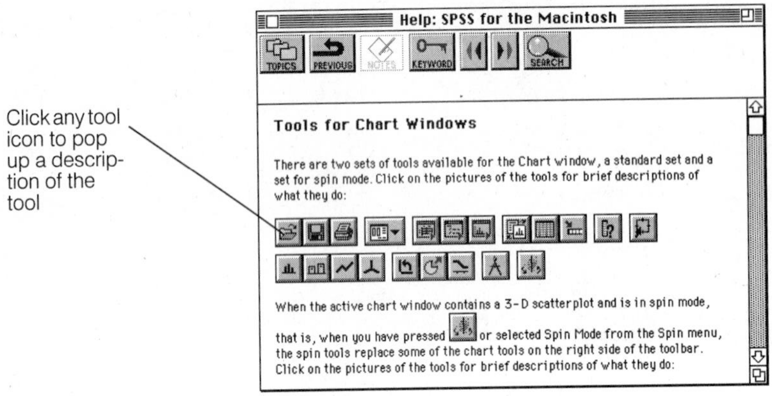

Click any tool icon to pop up a description of the tool

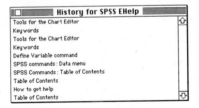

The History Window

The History window (see Figure 3.20) lists the Help topics you have visited most recently. You can return to any topic by clicking on its title in the History window—a good way to retrace your steps through the Help system.

Figure 3.20 History window

▶ To open the History window, type ⌘-H when the Help window is active.

What's Next?

Once you get comfortable with the Help system, you'll find that it can tell you just about anything you need to know about how to use SPSS for the Macintosh. To start learning how (and why) to use SPSS as a tool to solve your problems, turn to Chapter 4.

Counting Responses

How can you summarize the various responses people give to a question?

- What is a frequency table, and what can you learn from it?
- How can you tell from a frequency table if there have been errors in coding or entering data?
- What are percentages and cumulative percentages?
- What are pie charts and bar charts, and when do you use them?
- When do you use a histogram?
- What are the mode and the median?
- What do percentiles tell you?

Whenever you ask a number of people to answer the same questions, or when you measure the same characteristics for several people or objects, you want to know how frequently the possible responses occur. This can be as simple as just counting up the number of yes or no responses to a question. Or it can be considerably more complicated if, for example, you've asked people to report their annual income to the nearest penny. In this case, simply counting the number of times each unique income occurs may not be a useful summary of the data. In this chapter, you'll use the Frequencies procedure to summarize and display values for a single variable. You'll also learn to select appropriate statistics and charts for different types of data.

▶ The data analyzed in this chapter are in the *gss.sav* data file. For instructions on how to obtain the Frequencies output shown in the chapter, see "How to Obtain a Frequency Table" on p. 59.

Describing Variables

To see what's actually involved in examining and summarizing data, you'll use the nine variables from the 1993 General Social Survey described in Table 4.1. (You will use data from only 1500 respondents, since the SPSS student system is restricted in the number of cases in a data file.)

What's the General Social Survey? The General Social Survey is administered yearly by the National Opinion Research Center to a sample of about 1500 persons 18 years of age and older. The sample represents the population of non-institutionalized adults living in the United States.(College dormitories are excluded from the survey!) Questions on many different topics—from how often you pray to where you were living at age 16—are included. Data from the General Social Survey are distributed at a nominal cost and are widely used by researchers and students (Davis & Smith, 1993).

Table 4.1 Variables from the 1993 General Social Survey

Variable Name	Description
age	Age of respondent in years
sex	1=Male, 2=Female
educ	Years of education
income91	Total family income in 1993 (classified into one of 21 income categories)
wrkstat	Work status (1=Full-time work, 2=Part-time work, 3=Temporarily not working, 4=Unemployed (laid off), 5=Retired, 6=In school, 7=Keeping house, 8=Other)
richwork	"Would you continue or stop working if you became rich?" (1=Continue, 2=Stop)
satjob	Job satisfaction (1=Very satisfied, 2=Moderately satisfied, 3=A little dissatisfied, 4=Very dissatisfied)
life	"Do you find life exciting, pretty routine, or dull?" (1=Dull, 2=Routine, 3=Exciting)
impjob	"How important to your life is having a fulfilling job?" (1=One of the most important, 2=Very important, 3=Somewhat important, 4=Not too important, 5=Not at all important)

All of these variables are defined as numeric in SPSS, but in most cases the numbers are just codes for non-numeric information. Value labels for each variable specify what the codes really mean.

In SPSS, to display (or hide) value labels, from the menus choose:

Utilities
Value Labels

Start by looking at the variable *impjob,* which tells you how important a fulfilling job is to the respondent. Since there are only five possible responses, you can easily count how many people gave each of them.

A Simple Frequency Table

In Figure 4.1, you see the frequency table for the job importance variable.

Figure 4.1 Frequency table of job importance

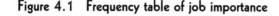

To obtain this frequency table, from the menus choose:

Statistics
Summarize ▶
Frequencies...

In the Frequencies dialog box, select the variable impjob, as shown in Figure 4.11.

```
IMPJOB    Importance to R of Having a Fulfilling Job


                                                 Valid    Cum
Value Label               Value  Frequency  Percent  Percent  Percent

One of most importan        1        316      21.1     21.4     21.4
Very important              2        833      55.5     56.3     77.7
Somewhat important          3        238      15.9     16.1     93.8
Not too important           4         62       4.1      4.2     98.0
Not at all important        5         30       2.0      2.0    100.0
DK                          8          7        .5   Missing
NA                          9         14        .9   Missing
                                    -------   -------  -------
                          Total      1500     100.0    100.0

Valid cases    1479   Missing cases     21
```

> The response "very important" was chosen by 833 people. This response is coded in the data file as the number 2.

From a frequency table, you can tell how frequently people gave each response. The first line is for the response *one of the most important* (coded in the data with the value 1). The second line is for the response *very important* (coded in the data with the number 2). Only responses actually selected by the participants are included in the frequency table. If no one selected the response *not at all important,* it would not be included in the table. Similarly, if you accidentally enter a code that does not correspond to a valid response—say a code of 0, 6, or 7 for the job importance variable—you will find it in the frequency table. That's why frequency tables are useful for detecting mistakes in the data file. If you find wrong codes in your data values, you must correct the data file before proceeding.

The last two lines of the frequency table are for the responses *don't know* and *no answer. Don't know* is used for people unwilling to commit themselves to a response. *No answer* is used when the response is illegible, lost, or not recorded by the interviewer. When the data file was defined, both *don't know* and *no answer* were identified as being missing-value codes. That is, you don't have an answer for people whose responses are coded as *don't know* or *no answer*. (In the column labeled *Valid Percent*, these values are labeled as missing.)

? *Why do you use different codes for* don't know *and* no answer? It's important to pinpoint why data values are missing. A response of *don't know* tells you that a person probably doesn't have strong feelings about the topic. It's unlikely that they find a job to be very important. A response of *no answer* doesn't tell you anything about a person's opinion of the importance of a job. The number of *no answer* responses tells you whether the survey was carefully conducted. You'll see later that if there are many cases with missing values, you may have serious problems in drawing conclusions from your data.   ■ ■ ■

In the column labeled *Value*, you see the actual code present in the data file. In the column labeled *Value Label*, you find a description of the code. If your codes are not inherently meaningful, you should assign value labels to them so that the output is easier to understand. Assigning a value label once is much easier than repeatedly having to look up the meanings of codes.

To determine how many people gave each response, look at the column labeled *Frequency*. For example, you find that 316 people find a fulfilling job to be *one of the most important* things to them, and 238 find it to be *somewhat important*. Only 30 people find having a fulfilling job *not at all important*.

From the line beneath the frequency table, you see that a total of 1500 people participated in the survey. Of these, 21 failed to select one of the five available responses; that is, their response was identified as *missing*. The other 1479 provided a valid response.

Percentages

A frequency count alone is not a very good summary of the data. For example, if you want to compare your results to those of another survey, it won't do you much good to know simply that 762 people in that survey chose the response *very important*. From the count alone, you can't tell if the other survey's results are similar to yours. To compare the two surveys, you must convert the observed counts to percentages.

From a **percentage,** you can tell what proportion of people in the survey gave each of the responses. Unlike counts, you can compare percentages across surveys with different numbers of cases. You compute a percentage by dividing the number of cases that gave a particular response by the total number of cases. Then you multiply the result by 100.

In Figure 4.1, you find percentages in the column labeled *Percent*. Note that the 316 people who gave the response *one of the most important* are 21.1% of the 1500 people in your survey. Similarly, the 238 people who gave the response *somewhat important* are 15.9% of your sample. The 7 people who *don't know* are 0.5% of the total sample. (The real percentage is 0.47%, but SPSS rounds percentages to one decimal place.) The sum of the percentages over all the possible responses, including *don't know* and *no answer*, is 100%.

Percentages Based on Valid Responses

To get the numbers in the column labeled *Percent*, you divide the observed frequency by the total number of cases in the sample and multiply by 100. Cases with codes identified as *missing* are included in the denominator. That can be a problem. For example, the General Social Survey does not ask all questions of all people. The question, Would you continue or stop working if you became rich? was asked of only two-thirds of people who were working or temporarily unemployed. Figure 4.2 shows the responses of people to this question.

Figure 4.2 Frequency table of continue working

```
RICHWORK   If Rich, Continue or Stop Working


                                              Valid     Cum
Value Label            Value  Frequency  Percent  Percent  Percent

Continue working         1       448     29.9     69.8     69.8
Stop working             2       194     12.9     30.2    100.0
NAP                      0       842     56.1   Missing
DK                       8        11      .7    Missing
NA                       9         5      .3    Missing
                              -------  -------  -------
                       Total    1500    100.0    100.0

Valid cases    642     Missing cases    858
```

The percentage of people giving the response *continue working* is 29.9. What does that mean? Does it mean that about 30% of people in the survey would continue working if they became rich? No. It means that about 30% of the people in the sample, regardless of whether they were asked the question or volunteered an answer, gave the response *continue working*. Of the 1500 people in the survey, 56.1% weren't even asked the question (recorded in the table as *NAP*, or *not applicable*). An additional 1% were asked and either gave the response *don't know* or their response was lost (*no answer*). All of these missing people are included in the denominator of the *Percent* calculation.

If you want to know what percentage of people who gave an acceptable answer selected *continue working*, look at the *Valid Percent* column. Almost 70% of people who answered the question claim that they would continue working if they struck it rich. (It's up to you whether you believe that percentage!) That's quite different from 30%. To calculate the entries in the *Valid Percent* column, you must exclude all people who gave an answer identified as *missing*. Valid percentages sum to 100 over all possible answers that are not missing. In this example, there are only two valid answers: *continue working* and *stop working*. Of the people who gave one of these answers, 69.8% selected the first, and 30.2% the second. These two percentages sum to 100.

Problems with Missing Data

Removing people who aren't asked a question from the calculation of percentages is not troublesome. They don't make interpretation of the results difficult. However, if a lot of people who are asked the question refuse to answer, that can be a problem. In Figure 4.2, you see that only 11 people gave an answer of *don't know*. They represent fewer than 2% of the 653 people who were actually asked the question. So you don't have to worry much about their impact on any conclusions you draw.

In contrast, however, consider the following situation. You conduct an employee satisfaction survey among 100 employees and find that 55 of them rate themselves as satisfied, 4 rate themselves as unsatisfied, and the remaining 41 decline to answer your question. That means that 55% of the polled employees consider themselves satisfied. However, if you exclude those who refused to answer from the denominator, 93% of the employees who answered the question consider themselves satisfied.

Which is the correct conclusion? Unfortunately, you don't know. It's possible that you have a company full of satisfied employees, many of whom don't like to answer questions. It's also possible that almost half of your employees are unhappy but are wary of voicing their dissatisfaction. When your data have many missing values because of people refusing to answer questions, it may be difficult, if not impossible, to draw correct conclusions. When you report percentages based on cases with nonmissing values, you should also report the percentage of cases that refused to give an answer.

Cumulative Percentages

There's one more percentage of interest in the frequency table. It's called the cumulative percentage. For each line of the frequency table, the **cumulative percentage** tells you the percentage of people who gave that response and any response that precedes it in the frequency table. It is the sum of the valid percentages for that line and all lines before it. Since there are only two possible valid answers for the continue working variable, the cumulative percentages in Figure 4.2 are of little interest. Instead, consider Figure 4.1 again. The cumulative percentage for *somewhat important* is 93.8. This means that over 93% of the people who answered the question said that a fulfilling job was at least somewhat important to their lives. Only 6.2% of the people rated the importance of a fulfilling job as less than *somewhat important*. Cumulative percentages are most useful when there is an underlying order to the codes assigned to a variable.

Sorting Frequency Tables

Unless you specify otherwise, SPSS produces a frequency table in which the order of the lines corresponds to the values of the codes you assign to the responses. The first line is for the smallest number found in the data values, and the last is for the largest. Codes that have been declared missing are at the end of the table. For example, if you had assigned the code 1 to *stop working*, it would have appeared first in the frequency table in Figure 4.2.

When you have several possible responses and the codes are not arranged in a meaningful order, you may want to rearrange the frequency table so that it's easier to use. You can determine the order of the lines in the table based on the frequency of values in the data. For example, Figure 4.3 shows a frequency table for the work status variable when the table is sorted in descending order of frequencies. Look at the column labeled *Frequency*. The frequencies go from largest to smallest. The column labeled *Value* no longer goes from smallest to largest.

50   **Chapter 4**

Figure 4.3   Frequency table sorted by counts

*To obtain this
output, select
Format in the
Frequencies dialog
box. Then select
Descending
counts, as shown in
Figure 4.12.*

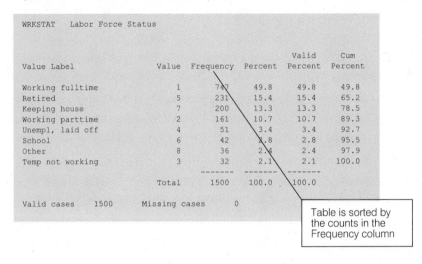

```
WRKSTAT    Labor Force Status


                                                Valid      Cum
Value Label                Value  Frequency  Percent  Percent  Percent

Working fulltime             1        747      49.8     49.8     49.8
Retired                      5        231      15.4     15.4     65.2
Keeping house                7        200      13.3     13.3     78.5
Working parttime             2        161      10.7     10.7     89.3
Unempl, laid off             4         51       3.4      3.4     92.7
School                       6         42       2.8      2.8     95.5
Other                        8         36       2.4      2.4     97.9
Temp not working             3         32       2.1      2.1    100.0
                                     -------  -------  -------
                    Total            1500     100.0    100.0

Valid cases      1500     Missing cases      0
```

Table is sorted by the counts in the Frequency column

Sorting a frequency table will usually change the values in the *Cum Percent* column, since the cumulative percentages depend on the order of the lines in the table. When the work status table is sorted by decreasing frequency, the cumulative percentage for *retired* is the percentage of people retired or working full time. In the default frequency table, however, in which the lines are sorted by the values of the codes, the cumulative percentage for *retired* is the sum of the valid percentages for codes 1 through 5.

Pie Charts

The information in a frequency table is easier to see if you turn it into a visual display, such as a bar chart or a pie chart. In Figure 4.4, you see a pie chart of the frequency table in Figure 4.3. There is a "slice" for each line of the frequency table. From the pie chart, you can easily see that almost half of your sample is *working full time.* It's also easy to see that the number of people who are *retired, keeping house,* and *working part time* are roughly equal. If you have many small slices in a pie chart, you can combine them into an *other* category. For example, Figure 4.5 is the pie chart for the same frequency table, except that all slices that have fewer than 5% of the cases (*in school, temporarily not working, unemployed,* and *other*) are combined into a single slice.

Figure 4.4 Pie chart of work status

You can obtain pie charts using the Graphs menu, as discussed in Appendix A. Select the variable wrkstat in the Pie Charts dialog box.

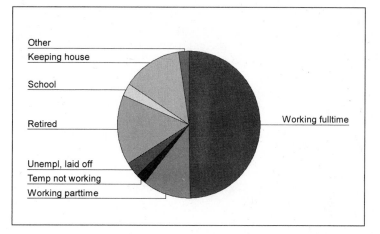

Figure 4.5 Work status with categories collapsed

You can collapse categories in a pie chart after it has been created. See "Modifying Chart Options" on p. 536 in Appendix A.

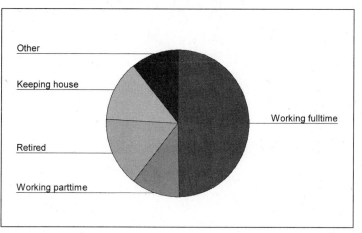

Bar Charts

In a pie chart, the size of the slice depends on the number of cases in the category. In a bar chart, the length of a bar depends on the number of cases in the category. Figure 4.6 is the bar chart for the work status variable. You have as many bars as you did slices in the pie chart. As you would expect, the tallest bar is for the *working full time* category. It's about three times as tall as the next largest bar, which represents *retired*.

Figure 4.6 Bar chart of work status

To obtain this output, select Bar chart(s) in the Frequencies Charts dialog box, as shown in Figure 4.14.

You can also obtain bar charts using the Graphs menu, as discussed in Appendix A.

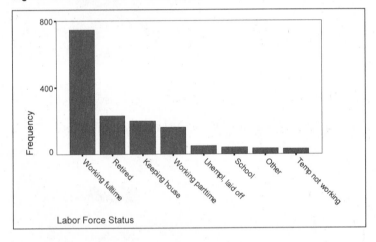

Summarizing the Age Variable

Although you can produce frequency tables for any kind of data, a frequency table becomes less useful as the number of possible responses increases. For example, you can construct a frequency table for the variable *age,* which tells you the ages of the people in your survey, but you will have as many lines in the frequency table as there are different ages in the data file. Although you can reduce the number of lines in your frequency table by using the more compact format shown in Figure 4.7, even this compact frequency table of individual values is unwieldy. (In

Chapter 7, you'll learn how to construct a frequency table in which each line corresponds to a range of values.)

What's this? Nobody in the General Social Survey sample was 90 years or older? Actually, this is just a quirk in the way ages are coded in the General Social Survey. For obscure historical reasons, the General Social Survey assigns an age of 89 to everyone with an age of 89 or older. The code 99 indicates that the age is not known. Because so few people are that old, this quirk has very little effect on analyses that use the age variable. When you design a study, record the actual age—or better yet, the birth date, since it's harder to fudge. (To remain 30 forever, you have to remember to change your birth year annually!)   ■ ■ ■

Figure 4.7   Condensed frequency table of age

To obtain this output, select Format in the Frequencies dialog box. Then select Condensed, as shown in Figure 4.12.

AGE   Age of Respondent

Value	Freq	Pct	Cum Pct	Value	Freq	Pct	Cum Pct	Value	Freq	Pct	Cum Pct
18	5	0	0	42	30	2	49	66	19	1	83
19	17	1	1	43	39	3	52	67	11	1	84
20	18	1	3	44	28	2	54	68	16	1	85
21	22	1	4	45	30	2	56	69	19	1	86
22	15	1	5	46	29	2	57	70	9	1	87
23	28	2	7	47	32	2	60	71	15	1	88
24	23	2	9	48	20	1	61	72	19	1	89
25	30	2	11	49	27	2	63	73	20	1	91
26	27	2	12	50	21	1	64	74	18	1	92
27	22	1	14	51	26	2	66	75	17	1	93
28	42	3	17	52	21	1	67	76	13	1	94
29	30	2	19	53	18	1	68	77	15	1	95
30	36	2	21	54	19	1	70	78	14	1	96
31	31	2	23	55	22	1	71	79	7	0	96
32	28	2	25	56	12	1	72	80	6	0	97
33	33	2	27	57	18	1	73	81	9	1	97
34	25	2	29	58	25	2	75	82	10	1	98
35	41	3	32	59	14	1	76	83	3	0	98
36	42	3	34	60	16	1	77	84	3	0	98
37	37	2	37	61	11	1	78	85	4	0	99
38	41	3	40	62	17	1	79	86	5	0	99
39	38	3	42	63	19	1	80	87	6	0	99
40	36	2	45	64	13	1	81	88	3	0	100
41	36	2	47	65	17	1	82	89	7	0	100

M I S S I N G   D A T A
Value   Freq

99   5

Only valid percentage is displayed

Histograms

You won't find pie charts and bar charts of the age variable to be useful either. There will be as many slices and bars as there are distinct ages. The arrangement of the values in the charts can be troublesome as well. Both bar charts and pie charts arrange bars and slices in ascending order of the values. However, if a particular age doesn't occur, an empty space is not left for it. That means that in a bar chart, the bar for 46 years may be right next to the bar for 50 years. You won't see a gap to remind you that ages 47 through 49 don't occur in your data.

A better display for a variable like *age,* for which it makes sense to group adjacent values, is a histogram. A **histogram** looks like a bar chart, except that each bar represents a range of values. For example, a single bar may represent all people in their twenties. In a histogram, the bars are plotted on a numerical scale that is determined by the observed range of your data.

Figure 4.8 Histogram of age

To obtain this output, select Charts in the Frequencies dialog box. Then select Histogram(s), as shown in Figure 4.14.

You can also obtain histograms using the Graphs menu, as discussed in Appendix A.

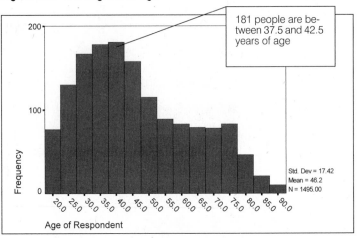

You see a histogram for the age variable in Figure 4.8. Age values are on the horizontal axis, and frequencies are on the vertical axis. The first bar represents cases with ages between 17.5 and 22.5. The middle value in this interval, the **midpoint,** is 20, which becomes the label used for the bar. From the histogram, you see that about 80 cases fall into this interval. Similarly, the second bar represents cases with ages between 22.5 and 27.5. This bar represents 130 cases.

A histogram tells you about the distribution of the data values. That is, it tells you how likely various values are. From it, you can see whether the cases cluster around a central value. You can also see whether large and small values are equally likely and whether there are values far removed from the rest. This is important not only to understand the data you've collected, but also for choosing appropriate statistical techniques for analyzing them. In Figure 4.8, you see that the age distribution has a peak corresponding to the interval 37.5 to 42.5. Additionally, you can see that the distribution of ages is not symmetric but has a "tail" extending to the older ages. That's because the General Social Survey interviews only respondents who are 18 or older.

What's a symmetric distribution? A distribution is **symmetric** if a vertical line going through its center divides it into two halves that are mirror images of each other. Figure 4.9 shows what a symmetric distribution of a hypothetical age variable might look like. Note that small and large values of age are equally likely.   ■ ■ ■

Figure 4.9   Symmetric distribution

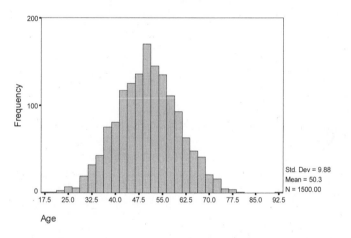

Mode and Median

You can use a variety of statistics to further summarize the information in a frequency table. In Chapter 5, you'll learn about a large number of such summary statistics. In the remainder of this chapter, you'll focus on summary measures that are easily obtained from the frequency table.

The **mode** is defined as the most frequently occurring value in your data. From the condensed frequency table in Figure 4.7, you see that two ages (28 and 36) are tied for the mode. There are 42 people with each of these ages. Although these ages occur most frequently, they represent a small percentage of the total cases. Less than 3% of the total has an age of 28. Knowing the mode tells you very little about the data.

? *What are the modes for the job importance and What if you were rich variables?* In Figure 4.1, you see that *very important* is the most frequently occurring response to the job importance question. That makes it the mode. Similarly, for the if rich variable shown in Figure 4.2, *Continue working* is the most common response, so it's the mode. ■ ■ ■

Scales on which variables are measured are discussed in Chapter 5.

If you can meaningfully order your data values from smallest to largest, you can compute additional summary measures. These measures are better than the mode, since they make use of the additional information about the order of the data values. For example, the **median** is the value that is greater than half the data values and less than the other half.

You calculate the median by finding the middle value when values for all cases are ordered from smallest to largest. If you have an odd number of cases, the median is just the middle value. If you have an even number of cases, the median is the value midway between the two middle ones. For example, the median of the five values 12, 34, 57, 92, and 100 is 57. For the six numbers 13, 20, 40, 60, 89, and 123, the median is 50, because 50 is the value midway between 40 and 60, the two middle numbers. (Add the two middle values and divide by two.)

To display the median and mode along with your frequency table, in the Frequencies dialog box, select Statistics. Then click on Median and Mode (see Figure 4.13).

You can calculate the median very easily from a frequency table. Find the first value for which the cumulative percentage exceeds or is equal to 50%. For the age variable in Figure 4.7, the median is 43. That means that half of the people in your sample are less than 43 years of age, and half are older. That's much more useful information than knowing that 28 and 36 years are tied for the mode.

? *What's the median for the work status variable?* Since there is no meaningful order of the codes assigned to the work status variable, it doesn't make sense to talk about median work status. You should use the median only when the data values can be ranked from smallest to largest. ■ ■ ■

Percentiles

When you calculate the median, you find the number that splits the sample into two equal parts. Half of the cases have values smaller than the median, and the other half have values larger than the median. You can compute values that split the sample in other ways. For example, you can find the value below which 25% of the data values fall. Such values are called **percentiles,** since they tell you the percentage of cases with values below and above them. Twenty-five percent of the cases have values smaller than the 25th percentile, and 75% of the cases have values larger than the 25th percentile. The median is the 50th percentile, since 50% of the cases have values less than the median, and 50% have values greater than the median.

Figure 4.10 Quartiles for age

To obtain this output, select Statistics in the Frequencies dialog box. Then select Quartiles, as shown in Figure 4.13.

AGE	Age of Respondent				
Percentile	Value	Percentile	Value	Percentile	Value
25.00	32.000	50.00	43.000	75.00	59.000

See "Percentiles" on p. 106 in Chapter 7 for further discussion of percentiles.

You can compute percentiles from a frequency table by finding the first value with a cumulative percentage larger than or equal to the percentile you're interested in. You can see the 25th, 50th, and 75th percentiles for the age variable in Figure 4.10. From these, you know that 25% of the cases are 32 or younger, 50% are 43 or younger, and 75% are 59 or younger. Together, the 25th, 50th, and 75th percentiles are known as **quartiles,** since they split the sample into four groups with roughly equal numbers of cases. That is, 25% of the cases are 32 years old or younger, 25% are between 32 and 43, 25% are between 43 and 59, and 25% are 59 or older.

Summary

How can you summarize the various responses people give to a question?

- A frequency table tells you how many people (cases) selected each of the responses to a question. For each code, it contains the number and percentage of the people who gave each response, as well as the number of people for whom responses are not available.

- If you find codes in the frequency table that weren't used in your coding scheme, you know that an error in data coding or data entry has occurred.

- A count can be transformed into a percentage by dividing it by the total number of responses and multiplying by 100.

- A cumulative percentage is the percentage of cases with values less than or equal to a particular value.

- Pie charts and bar charts are graphical displays of counts.

- A histogram is a graphical display of counts for ranges of data values.

- The mode is the data value that occurs most frequently.

- The median is the middle value when data values are arranged from smallest to largest.

- Percentiles are values below which and above which a certain percentage of case values fall.

What's Next?

In this chapter, you learned how to use a frequency table to summarize the values of a variable with a small number of distinct categories. You also learned about pie charts and bar charts, which are visual displays of a frequency table. You used a histogram to summarize a variable whose values can be meaningfully ordered from smallest to largest. You also saw how to use a frequency table to compute several summary statistics. In the next chapter, you'll learn about additional statistics that are useful for describing the values of a variable. You'll also learn about the scales on which variables are measured.

How to Obtain a Frequency Table

This section shows you how to use SPSS to count how frequently each value of a variable occurs in your data. The Frequencies procedure tabulates the different values that occur for a variable and produces statistics and charts based on these tabulations. In addition, the Frequencies command can:

- Calculate percentages of cases having each value of a variable.
- Calculate descriptive statistics for individual variables ("univariate" statistics).
- Produce high-resolution bar charts and histograms showing the distribution of values for individual variables.

▶ To open the Frequencies dialog box (see Figure 4.11), from the menus choose:

Statistics
　Summarize ▶
　　Frequencies...

Figure 4.11　Frequencies dialog box

Select impjob and richwork to obtain the frequency tables shown in Figure 4.1 and Figure 4.2

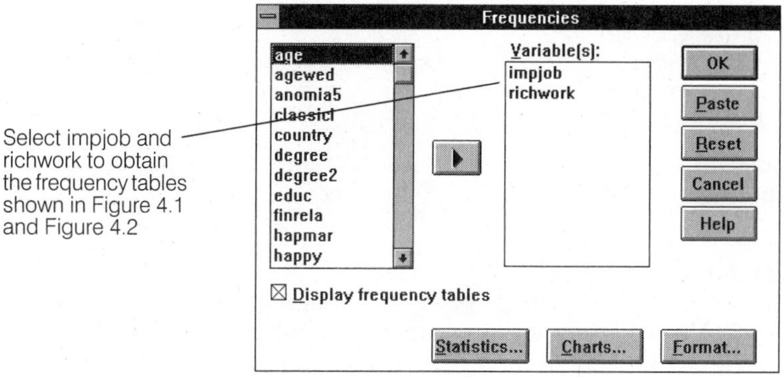

▶ In the Frequencies dialog box, select one or more variables and move them into the Variable(s) list. Make sure that the Display frequency tables option is checked, and click on OK.

This produces frequency tables like those in Figure 4.1 and Figure 4.2, showing for each value the value label; the actual value; the frequency, or count of cases; the percentages of all the cases and of all the valid (nonmissing) cases; and the cumulative percentages. The number of valid cases and the number of missing cases are displayed below the table. The Display frequency tables option lets you display or suppress the actual frequency table. Deselect this option when you are interested only in the statistics or charts and not in the tabulation. For variables with a great many different values, such as age or weight, the detailed tabulation is long and not very interesting.

Format: Appearance of the Frequency Table

In the Frequencies dialog box, click on the Format button to change the appearance of the frequency tables. The Frequencies Format dialog box (see Figure 4.12) controls the layout of the frequency table and the order in which values appear.

Figure 4.12 Frequencies Format dialog box

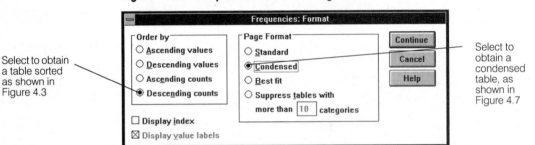

Select to obtain a table sorted as shown in Figure 4.3

Select to obtain a condensed table, as shown in Figure 4.7

Some of the available options are described below:

Order by. Choose an alternative to determine the order by which data values are sorted and displayed in a frequency table. For example, select Descending counts to see the most frequently occurring values first.

Page Format. These options give you control over the space occupied by the tables. Standard format is well suited for variables with few categories. Condensed format omits the value labels and the percentages that include missing values and rounds the remaining percentages to integers. This allows many more categories to be displayed on the page or screen. The Best fit option uses Standard format if it fits on a page, or Condensed format if not. There is also an option to suppress altogether any tables that have more than a specified number of categories.

Display index. This option is useful when you request many frequency tables at once. SPSS displays an index at the end of its output, giving the page number on which each variable's table appears.

Statistics: Univariate Statistics

In the Frequencies dialog box, click on the Statistics button. In the Frequencies Statistics dialog box, shown in Figure 4.13, you can choose any of the statistics discussed in this chapter.

Figure 4.13 Frequencies Statistics dialog box

Select to obtain the 25th, 50th, and 75th percentiles, as shown in Figure 4.10

Some of the available options are described below:

Percentiles. To request percentiles, select the Percentile(s) check box, click in the text box beside it, type a percentile (from 1 to 99), and then click on the Add button to add it to the list. Once the list has numbers in it, you can select one of them and either click on Remove to remove it from the list or change the percentile number and click on Change.

Values are group midpoints. Select if the data values represent ranges of values. For example, if the value 25 is used for all cases with values between 20 and 30, select this check box. This affects the computation of percentiles.

Charts: Bar Charts and Histograms

In the Frequencies dialog box, click on the Charts button. In the Frequencies Charts dialog box, shown in Figure 4.14, you can request bar charts or histograms for the selected variables. If you select histograms, there's an option to sketch in a normal curve over the histogram, in case you want to compare your variable's distribution to the normal distribution discussed in Chapter 11.

Figure 4.14 Frequencies Charts dialog box

Select either
Bar chart(s)
(see Figure 4.6)
or Histogram(s)
(see Figure 4.8)

This is the fastest way to get bar charts or histograms for more than one variable. As always, the new charts show up in the Chart Carousel, where you can look at them, save them as SPSS chart files, or print them. For more information about creating and editing charts, see Appendix A.

Exercises

Statistical Concepts

1. For which of the following variables would frequency tables be useful?

a. Business miles driven per year

b. Systolic blood pressure

c. Income in dollars

d. Happiness with marriage

e. Square feet of office space

f. CEO salaries

g. Region of the country

h. Cars owned

2. For which of the following variables would cumulative percentages be readily interpretable?

   a. Number of adults in a household

   b. Brand of car ownership

   c. College major

   d. Number of illnesses during the past year

3. The following data represent the number of periodicals read by 25 college students: 1, 1, 1, 1, 1, 1, 2, 2, 2, 3, 3, 3, 3, 3, 3, 4, 4, 5, 5, 5, 5, 8, 9, 9, 10.

   a. Fill in the frequency table:

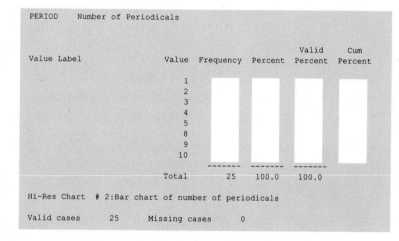

```
PERIOD     Number of Periodicals


                                                    Valid    Cum
   Value Label              Value  Frequency  Percent  Percent  Percent

                              1
                              2
                              3
                              4
                              5
                              8
                              9
                             10
                                   -------  -------  -------
                     Total          25     100.0    100.0

Hi-Res Chart  # 2:Bar chart of number of periodicals

Valid cases      25      Missing cases      0
```

   b. Using the same data, fill in the following bar chart:

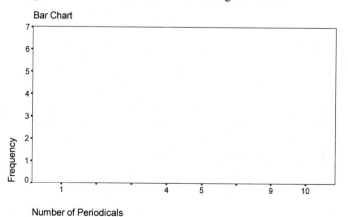

Bar Chart

c. Why are there no bars for 6 and 7 periodicals?

d. Fill in the following histogram:

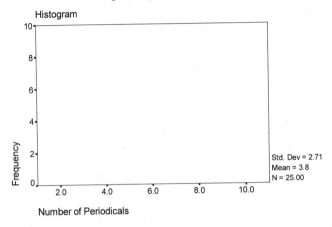

Histogram

Frequency / Number of Periodicals

Std. Dev = 2.71
Mean = 3.8
N = 25.00

e. How does the histogram differ from the bar chart?

f. What is the mode for the number of periodicals read?

g. What is the median?

4. The following table contains the results of a Harris poll of 1,254 adults (*Business Week*, 7/16/90). The question asked was: How safe is your money in a savings and loan?

```
MSAFE       Safety in Savings & Loan


                                                        Valid      Cum
Value Label                     Value  Frequency  Percent Percent  Percent

Very safe                         1       351
Somewhat safe                     2       414
Not very safe                     3       251
Not at all safe                   4       188
Not sure                          5        50
                                       -------  -------  -------
                              Total      1254    100.0    100.0

Valid cases    1254     Missing cases        0
```

a. Fill in the missing entries.

b. For the previous question, explain whether "not sure" should be considered a missing value.

c. Sketch a pie chart.

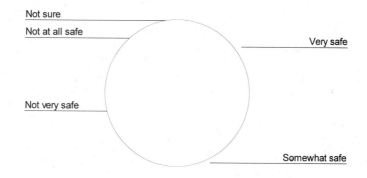

5. Without using the computer, construct a frequency table for the "gift" variable in Data Analysis question 1 (below).

Data Analysis

1. Twenty-five children were asked to sample each of three brands of cereals: Canary Crunch, Turtle Treats, and Ghostly Shadows. They were asked to choose their favorite and indicate how much they liked it (crazy about it, liked it, didn't particularly like it). They were also asked to select which of four "gifts" they'd like to find in it: a marble, a squirt gun, a whistle, or a magic ring. Here are their responses:

Child	Cereal	Like	Gift	Gender
1	Ghostly Shadows	crazy	squirt gun	M
2	Ghostly Shadows	like	squirt gun	M
3	Ghostly Shadows	not part	squirt gun	M
4	Canary Crunch	not part	ring	M
5	Turtle Treats	crazy	squirt gun	F
6	Turtle Treats	crazy	ring	F
7	Turtle Treats	crazy	squirt gun	F
8	Turtle Treats	like	ring	F
9	Ghostly Shadows	crazy	ring	M
10	Canary Crunch	not part	squirt gun	F

Child	Cereal	Like	Gift	Gender
11	Turtle Treats	crazy	squirt gun	F
12	Ghostly Shadows	like	ring	F
13	Turtle Treats	crazy	squirt gun	M
14	Turtle Treats	like	ring	M
15	Ghostly Shadows	crazy	whistle	F
16	Canary Crunch	don't know	ring	M
17	Turtle Treats	crazy	whistle	F
18	Turtle Treats	like	ring	F
19	Ghostly Shadows	like	squirt gun	F
20	Turtle Treats	crazy	can't decide	M
21	Canary Crunch	like	ring	F
22	Turtle Treats	crazy	squirt gun	M
23	Ghostly Shadows	like	ring	F
24	Turtle Treats	like	ring	F
25	Turtle Treats	crazy	ring	F

Enter the data into SPSS and use the computer to answer the following questions:

a. What percentage of the sample are males and what percentage are females?

b. Which cereal was preferred by most children?

c. Based on the sample, which gift would you include in the cereal boxes? Explain the basis for your choice.

d. What percentage of the children were crazy about their favorite cereal? Why are the percentage and valid percentage columns in the frequency tables you obtained not the same?

Use the *gss.sav* data file to answer the following questions:

2. Write a short paper describing the General Social Survey (GSS) respondents in terms of their political affiliation (variable *partyid*), whether they voted in the presidential election in 1992 (*vote92*), and for whom they voted in the 1992 presidential election (*pres92*). Include appropriate tables and charts. Don't just include the frequency tables generated by SPSS. Modify the tables so that they include only the appropriate information.

3. In the frequency table for *pres92*, why are there three different codes for missing values? Who was coded 0 (not applicable)? Are you concerned that there are so many people with this missing-value code? Do you think they affect your ability to describe the presidential preferences of your sample? Explain.

4. The variables *classicl*, *opera*, and *country* contain the opinions of the GSS respondents about each of the three types of music. Make pie charts of their responses. (To do this you must use the Graph menu and select Pie Charts.) Label each segment of the pie chart with the percentage of people giving that response. (To do this you must select Edit and then from the Chart menu select Options and check the appropriate response for Label.) Write a brief summary of the musical tastes of the GSS respondents.

5. The variable *tvhours* tells you how many hours per day GSS respondents say they watch television.

   a. Make a frequency table of the hours of television watched. Do any of the values strike you as strange? Explain. (Since you didn't conduct the survey yourself, there's no way for you to check whether the strange values are correct. You'll have to assume that they are.)

   b. Based on the frequency table, answer the following questions: Of the people who answered the question, what percentage don't watch any television? What percentage watch 2 hours or less? 5 hours or more? Of the people who watch television, what percentage watch 1 hour? What percent watch 4 hours or less?

   c. From the frequency table, estimate the 25th, 50th, 75th, and 95th percentiles. What is the value for the median? The mode?

   d. Make a bar chart of the hours of television watched. What problems do you see with this display?

   e. Make a histogram of the hours of television watched. What causes all of the values to be clumped together? Edit the histogram so that the smallest value displayed is 0 hours, the maximum is 24 hours, and the length of the interval is 1 hour. Compare this histogram to the bar chart you generated in question 5d. Which is a better display for these data?

6. Write a brief report about the age at which GSS respondents first married (*agewed*). Include appropriate charts and summary statistics.

7. How happy are GSS respondents? Write a short paper describing their responses to the following questions:

   a. Taken all together, how would you say things are these days—would you say that you are very happy, pretty happy, or not too happy (variable *happy*)?

   b. Taking things all together, how would you describe your marriage? Would you say that your marriage is very happy, pretty happy, or not too happy (*hapmar*)?

   c. In general, do you find life exciting, pretty routine, or dull (*life*)?

8. Write a short report about the educational attainment of the GSS respondents. Examine the variables *educ* (years of education) and *degree* (highest degree earned).

Use the *salary.sav* data file to answer the following questions:

9. Consider the distribution of employees within each job category (variable *jobcat*).

   a. Describe the distribution of people in each employment category.

   b. Make a pie chart that shows the percentages of employees within each job category. Modify the chart so that MBA trainees and technical employees are shown in a single slice.

   c. Make a bar chart showing the distribution of employees within job categories. Have the bars represent the percentage of employees in each category.

10. Look at the *sexrace* variable.

   a. What percentage of the bank's employees are males? White males? Minority females?

   b. Make a pie chart of the distribution of the race/gender categories.

   c. Select only clerical workers (variable *jobcat* equals 1). Make a pie chart of the distribution of the race/gender categories for clerical workers only. Does the pie chart look similar to that you obtained in question 10b? Comment on the similarities and differences.

11. Consider work experience (variable *work*).

   a. Make a bar chart and a histogram of the values. Which do you think is the better summary of the data? Why?

   b. What is the median number of years of work experience for the sample? The quartiles?

   c. What percentage of the sample had no prior work experience? Of those who did have prior work experience, what is the median number of years of experience?

Use the *electric.sav* data file to answer the following questions:

12. Make a frequency table of the first coronary heart disease event (variable *firstchd*).

   a. The sample in this file was selected in such a way that half of the 240 cases had not experienced coronary heart disease within 10 years, and half had. In the sample, what percentage of cases experienced sudden death? Either fatal or nonfatal MI?

b. Do you agree or disagree with the statement "Half of the men in the study experienced coronary heart disease within 10 years." Explain your reasoning.

c. What percentage of the deaths in your sample were attributable to fatal MI? To sudden death?

d. What percentage of men who experienced coronary heart disease experienced fatal MIs?

e. What percentage of men who experienced coronary heart disease experienced sudden death?

f. Make a bar chart that shows the distribution of type of coronary heart disease events for men who experienced coronary heart disease. (To select only men who experienced coronary heart disease, use Select Firstchd ne 1.) Write a paragraph describing your findings.

13. Make a frequency table for *firstchd* when only men who experienced coronary heart disease are selected. Explain why the percentages in this table differ from those in the table in question 12. Which percentages are more useful?

14. Make a frequency table of the number of men who died on each day of the week (variable *dayofwk*). (The day of death was obtained for all causes of death, not just for coronary heart disease.)

a. Of the men who died, what percentage died on Sunday?

b. What percentage of all men in your sample died on Sunday?

c. Explain why the percentages in questions 14a and 14b differ. Which percentage is more useful if you are studying the likelihood of deaths on different days of the week?

d. Make a pie chart of day of death. Summarize your findings.

e. What is the mode for day of death?

15. Generate the appropriate statistics and displays to summarize the distribution of cholesterol values and diastolic blood pressures in 1958 (variables *chol58* and *dbp58*). Briefly summarize your results.

a. Fifteen percent of the men had serum cholesterol values below what value? Ninety percent of men had serum cholesterol levels above what value?

b. What are the quartiles for diastolic blood pressure? Within what values did the middle 50% of the men fall?

Computing
Descriptive Statistics

How can you summarize the values of a variable?

- What are scales of measurement, and why are they important?
- How does the arithmetic mean differ from the mode and the median?
- When is the median a better measure of central tendency than the mean?
- What does the variance tell you? The coefficient of variation?
- What are standardized scores, and why are they useful?

In the previous chapter, you used frequency tables, bar charts, pie charts, histograms, and percentiles to examine the distribution of values for a variable. These are essential techniques for getting acquainted with the data. Often, however, you want to summarize the information even further by computing summary statistics that describe the "typical" values, or the **central tendency**, as well as how the data spread out around this value, or the **variability.** In this chapter, you'll learn how to use the Frequencies and Descriptives procedures to compute the most commonly used summary statistics for central tendency and variability.

▶ This chapter continues to use the *gss.sav* data file. For instructions on how to obtain the Descriptives output discussed in the chapter, see "How to Obtain Univariate Descriptive Statistics" on p. 81.

? *What's a statistic?* Often when you collect data, you want to draw conclusions about a broader base of people or objects than are actually included in your study. For example, based on the responses of people included in the General Social Survey, you want to draw conclusions about the population of adults in the United States. The people you observe are called the **sample**. The people you want to draw conclusions about are called the **population**. A **statistic** is some characteristic of the sample. For example, the median age of people in the General Social Survey is a statistic. The term **parameter** is used to describe characteristics of the population. If you had the ages of all adults in the United States, the median age would be called a parameter value. Most of the time, population values, or parameters, are not known. You must estimate them based on statistics calculated from samples. ■ ■ ■

Summarizing Data

Consider again the data described in the previous chapter. Suppose you want to summarize the data values further. You want to know the typical age for participants in the survey, or their typical status in the workplace, or typical satisfaction with their job. A unique answer to these questions doesn't exist, since there are many different ways to define "typical." For example, you might define it as the value that occurs most often in the data (the mode), or as the middle value when the data are sorted from smallest to largest (the median), or as the sum of the data values divided by the number of cases (the arithmetic mean). To choose among the various measures of central tendency and variability you must consider the characteristics of your data as well as the properties of the measures. Although the mode may be a plausible statistic to report for status in the labor force, it may be a poor selection for a variable like age.

Scales of Measurement

One of the characteristics of your data that you must always consider is the scale on which they are measured. Scales are often classified as nominal, ordinal, interval, and ratio, based on a typology proposed by Stevens (1946). A nominal scale is used only for identification. Data measured on a **nominal scale** cannot be meaningfully ranked from smallest to largest. For example, status in the work force is measured on a nominal scale, since the codes assigned to the categories, although numeric, don't really mean anything. There is no order to *retired, in* *school, keeping house,* and *other.* Place of birth, hair color, and favorite statistician are all examples of variables measured on a nominal scale.

Variables whose values indicate only order or ranking are said to be measured on an **ordinal scale**. Job satisfaction and job importance are examples of variables measured on an ordinal scale. There are limitations on what you can say about data values measured on an ordinal scale. You can't say that some one who has a job satisfaction rating of 1 (*very satisfied*) is twice as satisfied as someone with a rating of 2 (*moderately satisfied*). All you can conclude is that one person claims to be more satisfied than the other. You can't tell how much more. The variable *income91* described in Chapter 4 is also measured on an ordinal scale. That's because the income is grouped into 21 unequal categories. You can't tell exactly how much more one person earned than another.

If you record people's actual annual incomes, you are measuring income on what is called a **ratio scale**. You can tell how much larger or smaller one value is compared with another. The distances between values are meaningful. For example, the distance between incomes of $20,000 and $30,000 is the same as the distance between incomes of $70,000 and $80,000. You can also legitimately compute ratios of two values. An income of $50,000 is twice as much as an income of $25,000. Age and years of education are both examples of variables measured on a ratio scale.

An **interval scale** is just like a ratio scale except that it doesn't have an absolute zero. You can't compute ratios between two values measured on an interval scale. The standard example of a variable measured on an interval scale is temperature. You can't say that a 40°F day is twice as warm as a 20°F day. Few variables are measured on an interval scale, and the distinction between interval and ratio scales is seldom, if ever, important in statistical analyses.

Although it is important to consider the scale on which a variable is measured, statisticians argue that Stevens' typology is too strict to apply to real world data (Velleman & Wilkinson, 1993). For example, an identification number assigned to subjects as they enter a study might appear to be measured on a nominal scale. However, if the numbers are assigned sequentially from the first subject to enter the study to the last, the identification number is useful for seeing whether there is a relationship between some outcome of the study and the order of entry of the subjects. If the outcome is a variable like how long it takes a subject to master a particular task, it's certainly possible that instructions have improved during the course of a study and later participants fare better than earlier ones.

It's an oversimplification to conclude that the measurement scale dictates the statistical analyses you can perform. The questions that you want to be answered should direct the analyses. However, you should always make sure that your analysis is sensible. Using the computer, it's easy to calculate meaningless numbers, such as percentiles for place of birth or the median car color. In subsequent discussion, we'll occasionally refer to the scale of measurement of your data when describing various statistical techniques. These are not meant to be absolute rules but useful guidelines for performing analyses.

Mode, Median, and Arithmetic Average

The mode, median, and arithmetic average are the most commonly reported measures of central tendency. In Chapter 4, you saw how to compute the mode and median. You calculate the **mode** by finding the most frequently occurring value. The mode, since it does not require that the values of a variable have any meaning, is usually used for variables measured on a nominal scale. The mode is seldom reported alone. It's a useful statistic to report together with a frequency table or bar chart. You can easily find fault with the mode as a measure of what is typical. Even accompanied by the percentage of cases in the modal category or categories, it tells you very little.

If you are summarizing a variable whose values can be ranked from smallest to largest, the median is a more useful measure of central tendency. You calculate the **median** by sorting the values for all cases and then selecting the middle value. A problem with the median as a summary measure is that it ignores much of the available information. For example, the median for the five values 28, 29, 30, 31, and 32 is 30. For the five values 28, 29, 30, 98, and 190, it is also 30. The actual amounts by which the values fall above and below the median are ignored. The high values in the second example have no effect on the median.

The most commonly used measure of central tendency is the **arithmetic mean**, also known as the **average.** (For a sample, it's denoted as $\bar{X}$.) The mean uses the actual values of all of the cases. To compute the mean, add up the values of all the cases and then divide by the number of cases. For example, the arithmetic mean of the five values 28, 29, 30, 98, and 190 is

$$\text{Mean} = \frac{28 + 29 + 30 + 98 + 190}{5} = 75 \qquad \textbf{Equation 5.1}$$

Don't calculate the mean if the codes assigned to the values of a variable are arbitrary. For example, average car manufacturer and average religion don't make sense, since the codes are not meaningful.

? *Can I use the mean for variables that have only two values?* Many variables, such as responses to yes/no or agree/disagree questions, have two values. If a variable has only two values, coded as 0 or 1, the arithmetic mean tells you the proportion of cases coded 1. For example, if 5 out of 10 people answered yes to a question and the coding scheme used is 0=no, 1=yes, the arithmetic mean is 0.50. You know that 50% of the sample answered yes. ▨ ▨ ▨

Comparing Mean and Median

Figure 5.1 contains descriptive statistics from the Frequencies procedure for the age and education variables.

Figure 5.1 Mean, median, and mode for age and education

You can obtain these statistics using the Frequencies procedure, as discussed in Chapter 4. In the Frequencies Statistics dialog box (see Figure 4.12), select Mean, Median, and Mode.

```
AGE        Age of Respondent

Mean          46.227    Median      43.000    Mode        28.000


EDUC       Highest Year of School Completed

Mean          13.037    Median      12.000    Mode        12.000


Valid cases    1496     Missing cases      4
```

You see that the average age of the participants of the General Social Survey is 46.227 years. The median is somewhat lower, 43 years. The average number of years of school completed is 13.037, and the median is 12. For both of these variables, the arithmetic mean is somewhat greater than the median. The reason is that both of these variables have a "tail" toward larger values. Remember the histogram for age from Chapter 4. Since the General Social Survey is restricted to adults at least 18 years of age, young ages do not occur in the data. There is no such restriction for older ages. The older ages drive up the mean, which is based on all data values. They have no effect on the median, since it depends only on the values of the middle cases. In this example, the differences between the mean and the median are not very large. This is not always true.

Consider the following example. You ask five employees of a company how much money they earned in the past year. You get the following replies: $45,000, $50,000, $60,000, $70,000, and $1,000,000. The average salary received by these five people is $245,000. The median is $60,000. The arithmetic mean doesn't really represent the data well. The CEO salary makes the employees appear much better compensated than they really are. The median better represents the employees' salaries.

Whenever you have data values that are much smaller or larger than the others, the mean may not be a good measure of central tendency. It is unduly influenced by extreme values (called **outliers**). In such a situation, you should report the median and mention that some of the cases had extremely small or large values.

Measures of central tendency that are less affected by extreme values are discussed in Chapter 7.

Measures of Variability

Measures of central tendency don't tell you anything about how much the data values differ from each other. For example, the mean and median are both 50 for these two sets of ages: 50, 50, 50, 50, 50 and 10, 20, 50, 80, 90. However, the distribution of ages differs markedly between the two sets. **Measures of variability** attempt to quantify the spread of observations. We'll discuss the most common measures of variability in this chapter. Chapter 7 contains discussion of additional measures.

Figure 5.2 Descriptive statistics for age and education

To obtain this output, from the menus choose:

Statistics
   Summarize ▶
      Descriptives...

Select the variables age and educ, as shown in Figure 5.5.

Variable	Mean	Std Dev	Variance	Minimum	Maximum	Valid N	Label
EDUC	13.04	3.07	9.45	0	20	1496	Highest Ye
AGE	46.23	17.42	303.39	18	89	1495	Age of Res

Range

The **range** is the simplest measure of variability. It's the difference between the largest and the smallest data values. Since the values for a nominal variable can't be meaningfully ordered from largest to smallest, it doesn't make sense to compute the range for a nominal variable such as status in the work force. In Figure 5.2, you see that for the variable *age,* the smallest value (labeled *Minimum*) is 18. The largest value (labeled *Maximum*) is 89. The range is 71 years. A large value for the range tells you that the largest and smallest values differ substantially. It doesn't tell you anything about the variability of the values between the smallest and the largest.

A better measure of variability is the **interquartile range**. It is the distance between the 75th and 25th percentile values. The interquartile range, unlike the ordinary range, is not easily affected by extreme values. In Chapter 4, you calculated the 25th percentile for the age variable as 32 years, the 75th percentile as 59. The interquartile range is therefore 27, the difference between the two.

You can use the Explore procedure, described in Chapter 7, to calculate the range and the interquartile range.

Variance and Standard Deviation

The most commonly used measure of variability is the **variance**. It is based on the squared distances between the values of the individual cases and the mean. To calculate the squared distance between a value and the mean, just subtract the mean from the value and then square the difference. (One reason you must use the squared distance instead of the distance is that the sum of distances around the mean is always 0.) To get the variance, sum up the squared distances from the mean for all cases and divide the sum by the number of cases minus 1.

The formula for computing the variance of a sample (denoted s^2) is

You can obtain the variance by selecting Options in the Descriptives dialog box. See Figure 5.6.

$$\text{Variance} = \frac{\text{sum of squared distances from the mean for all cases}}{(\text{number of cases} - 1)}$$

Equation 5.2

For example, to calculate the variance of the numbers 28, 29, 30, 98, and 190, first find the mean. It is 75. The sample variance is then

$$s^2 = \frac{(28-75)^2 + (29-75)^2 + (30-75)^2 + (98-75)^2 + (190-75)^2}{4}$$
$$= 5{,}026$$

Equation 5.3

If the variance is 0, all of the cases have the same value. The larger the variance, the more the values are spread out. In Figure 5.2, the variance for the age variable is 303.39 square years; for the education variable it is 9.45 square years. To obtain a measure in the same units as the original data, you can take the square root of the variance and obtain what's known as the **standard deviation.** Again in Figure 5.2, the standard deviation (labeled *Std Dev*) for the age variable is 17.42 years; for the education variable, it is 3.07 years.

> **?** *Why divide by the number of cases minus 1 when calculating the sample variance, rather than by the number of cases?* You want to know how much the data values vary around the population mean, but you don't know the value of the population mean. You have to use the sample mean in its place. This makes the sample values have less variability than they would if you used the population mean. Dividing by the number of cases minus 1 compensates for this.   ▪ ▪ ▪

The Coefficient of Variation

The magnitude of the standard deviation depends on the units used to measure a particular variable. For example, the standard deviation for age measured in days is larger than the standard deviation of the same ages measured in years. (In fact, the standard deviation for age in days is 365.25 times the standard deviation for age in years.) Similarly, a variable like salary will usually have a larger standard deviation than a variable like height.

The **coefficient of variation** expresses the standard deviation as a percentage of the mean value. This allows you to compare the variability of different variables. To compute the coefficient of variation, just divide the standard deviation by the mean and multiply by 100. (Take the absolute value of the mean if it is negative.)

$$\text{coefficient of variation} = \frac{\text{standard deviation}}{|\text{mean}|} \times 100 \qquad \textbf{Equation 5.4}$$

The coefficient of variation equals 100% if the standard deviation equals the mean. The coefficient of variation for the age variable is 37.68%. For the education variable, the coefficient of variation is 23.54%. Compared to their means, age varies more than education.

Standard Scores

The mean often serves as a convenient reference point to which individual observations are compared. Whenever you receive an examination back, the first question you ask is, How does my performance compare with the rest of the class? An initially dismal-looking score of 65% may turn stellar if that's the highest grade. Similarly, a usually respectable score of 80 loses its appeal if it places you in the bottom quarter of the class. If the instructor just tells you the mean score for the class, you can only tell if your score is less than, equal to, or greater than the mean. You can't say how far it is from the average unless you also know the standard deviation.

For example, if the average score is 70 and the standard deviation is 5, a score of 80 is quite a bit better than the rest. It is two standard deviations above the mean. If the standard deviation is 15, the same score is not very remarkable. It is less than one standard deviation above the mean. You can determine the position of a case in the distribution of observed values by calculating what's known as a **standard score,** or **Z score.**

To calculate the standard score, first find the difference between the case's value and the mean and then divide this difference by the standard deviation.

$$\text{standard score} = \frac{\text{value} - \text{mean}}{\text{standard deviation}}$$

Equation 5.5

A standard score tells you how many standard deviation units a case is above or below the mean. If a case's standard score is 0, the value for that case is equal to the mean. If the standard score is 1, the value for the case is one standard deviation above the mean. If the standard score is –1, the value for the case is one standard deviation below the mean. (For many types of distributions, including the normal distribution discussed in Chapter 11, most of the observed values fall within plus or minus two standard deviations of the mean.) The mean of the standard scores for a variable is always 0, and their standard deviation is 1.

You can use the Descriptives procedure in SPSS to obtain standard scores for your cases and to save them as a new variable. Figure 5.3 shows descriptive statistics for the age variable as they appear in the output window. In addition, a new variable, *zage,* has been saved in the Data Editor, containing the standard scores for age (see Figure 5.4).

Figure 5.3   Descriptive statistics in the output window

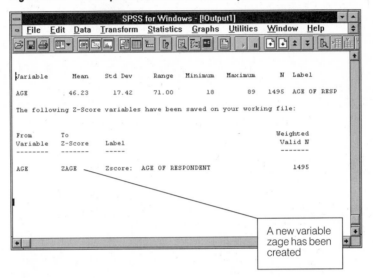

Figure 5.4   Data Editor with standard scores saved as a new variable

To save standardized scores, select Save standardized values as variables in the Descriptives dialog box, as shown in Figure 5.5.

	age	sex	zage	var	var	var
1	43	Male	-.18525			
2	44	Male	-.12784			
3	43	Female	-.18525			
4	45	Female	-.07043			
5	78	Female	1.82416			
6	83	Male	2.11122			

You see that the first case has an age of 43. From the standard score, you know that the case has an age less than average, but not very much. The age for the case is less than a quarter of a standard deviation below the mean. The fifth case has an observed age of 78, which is almost two standard deviations above the mean.

Standard scores allow you to compare relative values of several different variables for a case. For example, if a person has a standard score of 2 for income, and a standard score of –1 for education, you know that the person has a larger income than most and somewhat fewer years of education. You couldn't meaningfully compare the original values, since the variables all have different units of measurement, different means, and different standard deviations.

Summary

How can you summarize the values of a variable?

- Scales of measurement tell you about the properties of the values of a variable.

- The arithmetic mean is calculated by summing the values of a variable and dividing by the number of cases. Unlike the median and mode, the arithmetic mean uses all of the values of a variable.

- The median is a better measure of central tendency than the mean when there are data values that are far removed from the rest.

- The variance is a measure of the spread of data values around the mean. The coefficient of variation tells you the percentage the standard deviation is of the mean.

- A standardized score tells you how many standard deviation units above or below the mean an observation is.

What's Next?

In this chapter, you calculated summary statistics for all of the cases in your data file. In Chapter 6, you'll learn how to calculate summary statistics when the cases in the data file are subdivided into groups based on values of other variables.

How to Obtain Univariate Descriptive Statistics

You use the Descriptives procedure in SPSS to calculate basic univariate statistics for numeric variables. The Descriptives procedure also lets you save standardized scores (Z scores) as new variables added to your data file. The Descriptives procedure calculates statistics very efficiently, but without tabulating each individual value that occurs in the data. (Some statistics, such as the median and mode, require such tabulation, and are not available from Descriptives.)

▶ To open the Descriptives dialog box, as shown in Figure 5.5, from the menus choose:

Statistics
  Summarize ▶
    Descriptives...

Figure 5.5 Descriptives dialog box

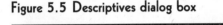

Select to save
standard scores,
as shown in
Figure 5.4

Select age
and educ to
produce the
output
shown in
Figure 5.2

▶ In the Descriptives dialog box, select one or more variables and move them into the Variable(s) list. Only numeric variables appear in the source list, because you can't calculate the mean (for example) of a string variable. When you have the variables you want in the Variable(s) list, click on OK.

This produces a default set of descriptive statistics for each of those variables, including the mean, standard deviation, minimum, and maximum. You can also choose one or more of the following:

Save standardized values as variables. Automatically creates standard scores (Z scores) for the selected variables. The standard scores show up as new variables, so that you have the choice of using either the original values or the standardized values in later analysis. SPSS displays the names of the new variables.

Display labels. Turn this option off if you want to suppress the display of variable labels.

Display index. Displays indexes showing the page number on which each variable's statistics appear. This option is useful when you calculate statistics for many variables at once, especially if you print the statistics as a reference document for your data file.

Options: Choosing Statistics and Sorting Variables

From the Descriptives dialog box, click on Options to obtain additional statistics or to specify the order in which the statistics for different variables are displayed (see Figure 5.6).

Figure 5.6   Descriptives Options dialog box

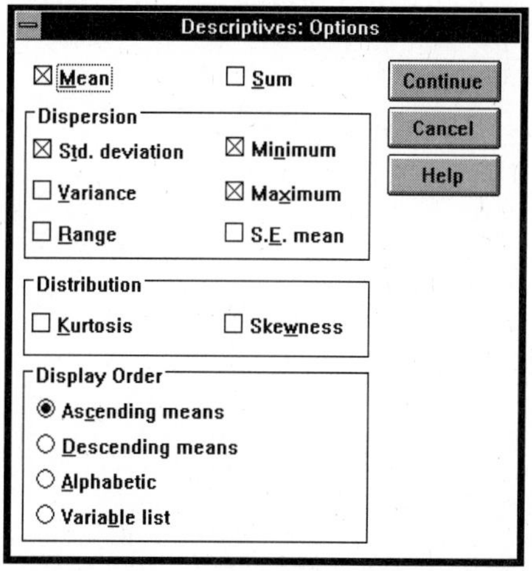

▶ Select the statistics you want with the check boxes.

You can also choose from the following group of options:

Display Order. This group lets you choose whether the statistics for different variables will appear in the order of the variables' means (either ascending or descending), in alphabetical order of the variable names, or simply in the order of the variables in the variable list.

Exercises

Statistical Concepts

1. Determine the level of measurement for each of these variables:

   a. Interest rate

   b. State in which company is incorporated

   c. Degree of satisfaction with a product

   d. Total family income

   e. Hours of television viewing

   f. Profit margin

   g. Birth order

   h. Preferred brand of gasoline

   i. Favorite music

2. A sample consists of 11 graduates of the University of Texas (coded 1), 10 graduates of the University of Michigan (coded 2), and 10 graduates of the University of Hawaii (coded 3). Which of the following statistics are appropriate for describing these data? Calculate the statistic if you think it is appropriate.

   a. Modal college attended

   b. Median college attended

   c. Mean college attended

   d. Variance of college attended

3. A sample contains 5 families who do not own a car (coded 0), 20 families who own one car (coded 1), and 10 families who own two cars (coded 2). Indicate which of the following statistics are appropriate and then calculate them.

   a. Modal number of cars owned

   b. Median number of cars owned

   c. Mean number of cars owned

   d. Variance of the number of cars owned

   e. Coefficient of variation

4. In a corporation, a very small group of employees has extremely high salaries while the majority of employees receive much lower salaries. If you were the bargaining agent for the employees, what statistic would you calculate to illustrate the low pay level for most employees, and why? If you were the employer, what statistic would you use to demonstrate a higher pay level for most employees, and why?

5. The number of dogs owned by 10 families are as follows: 0, 1, 1, 1, 2, 2, 2, 2, 2, 4. Fill in the following table based on these values:

```
Mean          _____    Std err     .335    Median      _____
Mode          _____    Std dev    1.059    Variance    _____
Range         _____    Minimum    _____   Maximum     _____


Valid cases      10     Missing cases    0
```

6. An absent-minded instructor calculated the following statistics for an examination: mean=50, range=50, number of cases=99, minimum=20, and maximum=70. She then found an additional examination with a score of 50. Recalculate the statistics, including the additional exam score.

7. Which measures of central tendency are appropriate for each of the following variables? If several can be calculated, indicate which makes most use of the available information.

   a. Number of siblings

   b. Political party affiliation

   c. Satisfaction with family

   d. Vacation days per year

   e. Type of car driven

   f. Weight of father

8. For each variable in question 7, would you make a bar chart or a histogram?

9. The number of pairs of shoes owned by seven college freshmen are 1, 2, 2, 3, 4, 4, and 5.

   a. Compute the mean, median, mode, range, and standard deviation.

   b. An eighth student, the heir to a shoe empire, is added to the sample. This student owns 50 pairs of shoes. Recompute the statistics.

   c. Which of the statistics are not much affected by the inclusion of an observation which is far removed from the rest?

   d. For all eight students, compute standardized scores for the number of shoes owned.

Data Analysis

Use the *gss.sav* data file to answer the following questions:

1. Compute descriptive statistics for the number of brothers and sisters (variable *sibs*), years of education (variable *educ*), age at first marriage (variable *agewed*), and hours worked last week (variable *hrs1*). Obtain histograms for the variables as well. For each variable compare the values of the different measures of central tendency. Indicate why and when you would prefer one measure over another.

2. Compute coefficients of variation for each variable. Which variable has the smallest coefficient of variation? Which has the largest?

3. Compute by hand the mean and median for variable *sibs* if people with 20 or more siblings are excluded. Comment on what change, if any, you see. Do you think the effect of outlying values would be different if you had a smaller sample?

4. **a.** Compute standardized scores for the number of hours of television watched per day (variable *tvhours*).

   b. Compute descriptive statistics and a histogram for the standardized variable.

   c. Does the shape of the distribution change when you compute standardized scores?

   d. In your data, what are the largest and smallest standardized scores?

   e. Compute the 5th, 25th, 50th, 75th, and 95th percentiles for the standardized scores. Does it appear that half of your cases have standardized scores greater than 0 and half less than 0? Explain why that's not the case.

   f. What's the standard score for someone who watches five hours of television a day? Someone who watches three hours? Someone who doesn't watch any television.

   g. How many hours of television does someone with a standardized score of 1 watch? With a standardized score of –1? –0.75?

5. Consider the variable *income91*. (It's called *income91* because it uses the coding scheme introduced in 1991. The variable is total family income in 1992, the year before the 1993 survey.)

   a. Make a frequency table for the variable. Does it make sense to make a histogram of the variable? A bar chart?

   b. What is the scale of measurement for the variable?

   c. What descriptive statistics are appropriate for describing this variable and why? Does it make sense to compute a mean?

d. Discuss the advantages and disadvantages of recording income in this manner. Would you record income in this way if you were doing a study? Describe other ways of recording income and the problems associated with each of them.

6. The Recode facility was used to compute a new variable named *incomdol* that is the midpoint of the income range for each value of *income91*. For example, for all cases with *income91* equal to 1, the value of *incomdol* is 500. Similarly, for cases with the value 3 for *income91,* the value of *incomdol* is 3500. For cases with the value 21 for *income91,* a value of 100,000 is used.

a. Perform appropriate analyses for the new variable. Make a histogram, if appropriate, and compute summary statistics. In the Frequencies procedure, you should check the box Values are group midpoints. This will change the calculation of some of the percentiles.

b. Do you think you know the exact income of people in your sample? Discuss the uncertainties introduced by this type of analysis.

Use the *salary.sav* data file to answer the following questions:

7. Consider beginning salary for all employees (variable *salbeg*).

a. Make a histogram. Why are all of the values bunched together?

b. Edit the histogram by going to the Chart menu and selecting Axis. Restrict the maximum value for the horizontal axis to 20,000. Compare this histogram with the one in question 7a.

c. Compute the mean, median, and mode for beginning salary. Why do you think the mean is larger than the median? Which statistic do you think better summarizes the data values?

d. Compute the quartiles for beginning salary. Within what values do the middle 50% of the salaries fall?

e. Compute the coefficient of variation for beginning salary.

8. Compute standard scores for beginning salary.

a. What are the smallest and largest standard scores?

b. How many standard deviation units from the mean is the largest score?

c. Select females only. What is their average standard score for beginning salary?

d. On average, do women earn more or less than men in the sample?

Use the *electric.sav* data file to answer the following questions:

9. Calculate the mean, median, and mode for cholesterol values and diastolic blood pressures in 1958 (variables *chol58* and *dbp58*). For each variable compare the values of these statistics. Which measure of central tendency do you think best summarizes each variable? Explain your selection.

10. Consider the number of cigarettes smoked in 1958 (variable *cgt58*). Describe the smoking habits of the men in 1958. Be sure to include what percentage of men in your sample were nonsmokers in 1958 as well as the mean and median number of cigarettes smoked by the smokers.

11. Compute the coefficient of variation for *chol58*, *dbp58*, and *cgt58*. Which has the largest? Which has the smallest?

12. Compute standardized scores for cholesterol values and diastolic blood pressure.

   a. What is the smallest standardized score for diastolic blood pressure? The largest?

   b. What is the smallest standardized score for cholesterol values? The largest?

   c. Compute the means and standard deviations of the standardized scores. What are they? Compute the quartiles for the standardized scores. Compare the quartiles for the two variables.

   d. Make histograms of the standardized and unstandardized values for diastolic blood pressure. Do the histograms differ? How?

   e. What is the standard score for a person with a diastolic blood pressure of 120? 150? 80?

Use the *schools.sav* data file to answer the following question:

13. Prepare for the Chicago Board of Education a summary of the 1993 and 1994 performance of city high schools on standardized tests. In particular, focus on the changes from 1993 to 1994. Include a summary of the demographic characteristics (variables *loinc93* and *lep93*) and graduation rates of the schools (variables *grad93* and *grad94*). Include appropriate charts.

Comparing Groups

How can you determine if the values of the summary statistics for a variable differ for subgroups of cases?

- What are subgroups of cases?
- What can you learn from calculating summary statistics separately for subgroups of cases?
- How can you graph means for subgroups of cases?

In Chapter 4 and Chapter 5, you used the Frequencies and Descriptives procedures to calculate summary statistics for all of the cases in your study. Often, however, you are interested in comparing summary statistics for different groups of cases. For example, you want to compare hours studied per week for college freshmen, sophomores, juniors, and seniors. Or you want to find the average income for people living in different geographical areas. There's no easy way with the Frequencies or Descriptives procedure to produce such information. In this chapter, you'll use the Means procedure to calculate simple summary statistics for subgroups of cases. You'll see if you can find a relationship between the average years of education and job satisfaction. You'll also see whether the relationship appears to be similar for men and women. (The Explore procedure described in Chapter 7 lets you examine the values of a variable for subgroups of cases in much greater detail.)

▶ This chapter uses the *gssft.sav* data file, which contains some of the variables in the *gss.sav* file, but for full-time workers only. (See "Case Selection" on p. 559 in Appendix B if you want to know how this smaller file was created.) For instructions on how to obtain the SPSS output discussed in this chapter, see "How to Obtain Subgroup Means" on p. 95.

Education and Job Satisfaction

In Figure 6.1, you see the average years of education and the standard deviation for people in each of four job satisfaction categories. To make comparisons easier to interpret, only people employed full time are included in the analysis.

Figure 6.1   Means output for education and job satisfaction

To obtain this output, from the menus choose:

Statistics
*   Summarize ▶*
*   Means...*

Select the variables educ and satjob, as shown in Figure 6.6.

```
                    - - Description of Subpopulations - -

Summaries of      EDUC         Highest Year of School Completed
By levels of      SATJOB       Job or Housework


Variable      Value  Label                     Mean    Std Dev   Cases

For Entire Population                        14.0375    2.7006     747

SATJOB           1  Very satisfied           14.2508    2.7943     327
SATJOB           2  Mod satisfied            13.7969    2.6008     320
SATJOB           3  A little dissatisfie     13.9189    2.7536      74
SATJOB           4  Very dissatisfied        14.6538    2.3655      26

   Total Cases = 747
```

Statistics for all cases analyzed

Statistics for individual subgroups

Looking at Figure 6.1, you see that the 747 people who are employed full time have 14.04 years of education on average, with a standard deviation of 2.70 years. These 747 people are assigned to one of four subgroups, based on their job satisfaction. The first subgroup, *very satisfied* employees, are somewhat more educated than the group as a whole, while the fourth subgroup, *very dissatisfied* respondents, are the most educated of all. People in the two subgroups in the middle—*moderately satisfied* and *a little dissatisfied* employees—have somewhat less education than the group as a whole.

Plotting Mean and Standard Deviation

A plot of the mean years of education for the four subgroups is shown in Figure 6.2. There is a bar for each of the subgroups. The height of the bar depends on the average years of education. You can easily see that the *very dissatisfied* people have the largest mean years of education. The mean years of education for the middle two satisfaction groups appear to be similar. Note, however, that the scale for the axis on which mean education is plotted doesn't start at 0. That makes even small differences in years of education look large on the plot.

Figure 6.2   Bar chart of education by job satisfaction

You can obtain bar charts using the Graphs menu, as described in Appendix A.

In the Define Simple Bar Chart Summaries for Groups of Cases dialog box, select Other summary function and select the variable educ. Select satjob for Category axis.

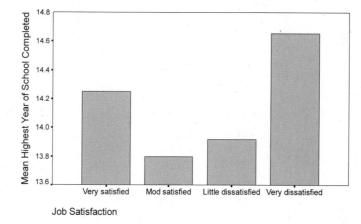

Layers: Defining Subgroups by More than One Variable

In Figure 6.1, all of the people who are employed full time are subdivided into four groups based only on their answer to the job satisfaction question. If you want to see whether the relationship between education and job satisfaction is similar for males and females, you must subdivide each of the lines of Figure 6.1 further. Figure 6.3 shows

summary statistics for full-time workers, subdivided first by job satisfaction and then by gender.

Figure 6.3   Means output for job satisfaction and gender subgroups

To obtain this
output, select the
variable sex for
layer 2 in the Means
dialog box, as
shown in
Figure 6.7.

```
              - - Description of Subpopulations - -

Summaries of      EDUC       Highest Year of School Completed
By levels of      SATJOB     Job or Housework
                  SEX        Respondent's Sex


Variable      Value  Label                Mean    Std Dev   Cases

For Entire Population                     14.0375  2.7006     747

SATJOB           1  Very satisfied        14.2508  2.7943     327
    SEX          1  Male                  14.2011  2.9970     179
    SEX          2  Female                14.3108  2.5364     148

SATJOB           2  Mod satisfied         13.7969  2.6008     320
    SEX          1  Male                  13.7110  2.6845     173
    SEX          2  Female                13.8980  2.5041     147

SATJOB           3  A little dissatisfie  13.9189    2         2
    SEX          1  Male                  14.0244    2         2
    SEX          2  Female                13.7879    2         2

SATJOB           4  Very dissatisfied     14.6538  2.3655      26
    SEX          1  Male                  15.2667  2.4044      15
    SEX          2  Female                13.8182  2.1363      11

Total Cases = 747
```

> First line in each category is the same as Figure 6.1

> Within each category, separate statistics are shown for men and women

You see that 327 people rate themselves as *very satisfied* with their job.
They have an average of 14.25 years of education. Of the 327 *very satisfied*
people, 179 are men and 148 are women. The men have an average of
14.20 years of education, while the women have 14.31 years of education. That's not much of a difference. Looking at the *moderately satisfied*
males, you see that their average years of education is about half a year
less than that of the *very satisfied* males.

One of the more interesting observations gleaned from Figure 6.3 is
that the *very satisfied* women have the highest average years of education of all the women. Women in the remaining three satisfaction categories have very similar average years of education. In contrast, the
very dissatisfied males have the highest average years of education,
15.27. (However, there are few cases in the *very dissatisfied* group, so

your conclusions are necessarily tentative.) The *moderately satisfied* males have the smallest average years of education.

> **[?]** *What if I want to see overall statistics for males and females and then statistics for each of the four subgroups of job satisfaction within the two gender groups?* That's easy to do. Just switch the order of the variables used to form the subgroups. ▪ ▪ ▪

Figure 6.4 is a bar chart that displays the results of Figure 6.3. There are four sets of bars corresponding to the job satisfaction categories. Each set of bars has separate bars for males and for females. The conclusions we reached based on the summary table are easier to see from this display. By looking at a corresponding pair of bars, you can see if the average years of education are similar for men and women within each category of job satisfaction. (Boxplots, which are a better way of comparing summary statistics for groups of cases, are described in Chapter 7.)

Figure 6.4   Bar chart of education by job satisfaction and sex

You can obtain this clustered bar chart using the Graphs menu, as described on p. 528. Select the variables educ, satjob, and sex in the Define Clustered Bar Summaries for Groups of Cases dialog box.

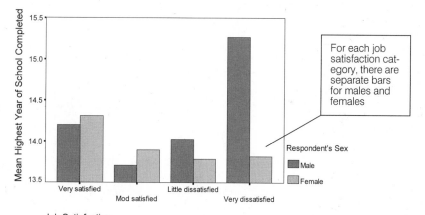

You can also group all of the bars for men and all of the bars for women together, as shown in Figure 6.5.

Figure 6.5   Bar chart of education by sex and job satisfaction

You can obtain this chart by modifying Figure 6.4, as described in "Bar Charts" on p. 538 in Appendix A. Move the chart into a chart window and from the menus choose:

Series
  Transpose...

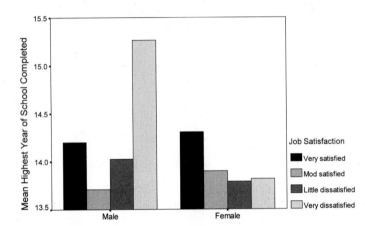

Now you have two subgroups: men and women. Within each subgroup, you see the four categories of job satisfaction. This plot makes it easy to see that the relationship between job satisfaction and education is not the same for men and women.

Means and standard deviations for groups of cases can be displayed with error bar charts. See "Error Bar Charts" on p. 541 in Appendix A.

What problems are associated with calculating statistics for subgroups of cases? As the number of subgroups you want to compare increases, the sample size in each of the subgroups diminishes. When your means are based on a small number of cases, they are not very reliable. That is, the subgroup means can change substantially if you select another sample from the same population. You'll learn more about the variability of sample means in Part 3.

Summary

> *How can you determine if the values of the summary statistics for a variable differ for subgroups of cases?*
>
> - Subgroups are formed when cases are subdivided into groups based on the values of one or more variables.
> - By calculating summary statistics separately for subgroups of cases, you can see if there is a relationship between the summary statistics and the subgroups.
> - You can make bar charts of the means of a variable for different subgroups.

What's Next?

In this chapter, you calculated basic descriptive statistics for subgroups of cases. In Chapter 7, you'll examine the distributions of values for subgroups in more detail. You'll also learn about additional summary statistics and displays.

How to Obtain Subgroup Means

This section shows how to obtain subgroup means with SPSS. In addition, the Means command can:

- Use two or more variables simultaneously to define the subgroups.
- Display statistics other than the mean for the subgroups.

The Means procedure calculates statistics for groups defined by the categories of one or more categorical variables.

▶ To open the Means dialog box (see Figure 6.6), from the menus choose:

Statistics
  Summarize ▶
    Means...

Figure 6.6 Means dialog box

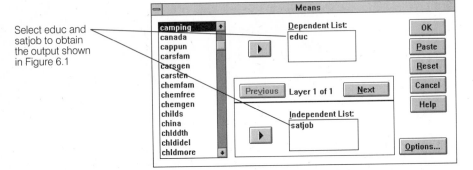

Select educ and satjob to obtain the output shown in Figure 6.1

▶ In the Means dialog box, select the variable for which you want subgroup statistics from the source variable list and move it into the Dependent List.

You can move more than one variable into the Dependent List to analyze them all with a single command.

▶ Select a categorical variable in the source variable list and move it into the Independent List at the bottom of the dialog box.

The categories of this variable define the subgroups. You can move more than one variable into this list; SPSS analyzes each set of groups separately, one after another. For example, if you move both *satjob* and *sex* into the Independent List, you will obtain two separate analyses: one for the categories of job satisfaction and one for the two categories of sex.

Layers: Defining Subgroups by More than One Variable

To use two categorical variables *simultaneously* to define the subgroups (as in Figure 6.3), move them into different layers. Notice the words Layer 1 of 1 above the Independent List in Figure 6.6. This list is really a stack of lists. Once you move a variable into Layer 1, you can click on Next to see the next layer, as shown in Figure 6.7. It will be empty until you move a variable into it; once you do, you can click on Next again to build additional layers. Or you can click on Previous to go back and add or remove variables in the previous layer. The layer controls are simple to operate, if you just keep your eye on the Layer message so you don't lose your place. What's important is to understand what layers do, so you'll know when to use them.

Figure 6.7   Means dialog box displaying Layers 1 and 2

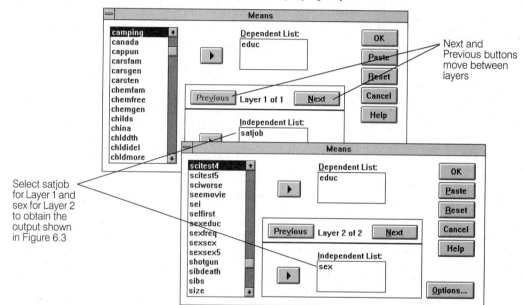

If Layer 1 of the Independent List contains one variable and Layer 2 contains another variable, SPSS uses both variables at the same time to define groups. For example, if you select *satjob* and *sex* as shown in Figure 6.7, SPSS displays statistics for each sex (the Layer 2 variable) within each job satisfaction category (the Layer 1 variable), as in Figure 6.3.

With more than one variable in any layer, SPSS analyzes the groups defined by each combination of Layer 2 variable with Layer 1 variable.

Options: Additional Statistics and Display of Labels

In the Means dialog box, click on Options. In the Means Options dialog box, shown in Figure 6.8, you can add additional information to be displayed in each cell.

Figure 6.8   Means Options dialog box

Some of the available options are:

Cell Displays. Allows you to select the subgroup statistics that are displayed. You can select any combination of one or more statistics.

Labels. Allows you to suppress value labels or variable labels.

Statistics for First Layer. Lets you request an analysis-of-variance table for testing whether in the population subgroup means are equal. Only the categories of the variable in Layer 1 are used. (Other layers, if present, are ignored.) You can also request a test for whether the differences in subgroup means vary linearly across the subgroups. These concepts are explained in Chapter 15 and Chapter 16.

Exercises

Statistical Concepts

1. A market research company is trying to decide what color to make a new brand of breath mints. They ask 100 consumers to choose among the colors white, yellow, green striped, and red striped. A research analyst assigns the codes 1 through 4 to the possible choices and uses the Means procedure to find average color preferences for men and women in each of four income categories. How would you interpret the resulting table?

2. The following table shows the mean ages of male and female Clinton, Bush, and Perot supporters.

```
- - Description of Subpopulations - -

Summaries of      AGE          Age of Respondent
By levels of      PRES92       Vote for Clinton, Bush, Perot
                  SEX          Respondent's Sex


Variable          Value  Label                    Mean      Std Dev    Cases

For Entire Population                            47.7056    16.9012     1002

PRES92              1    Clinton                 48.3318    16.8018      431
   SEX              1    Male                    48.3106    17.0691      161
   SEX              2    Female                  48.3444    16.6723      270

PRES92              2    Bush                    49.0911    17.5706      384
   SEX              1    Male                    48.4094    17.6324      171
   SEX              2    Female                  49.6385    17.5431      213

PRES92              3    Perot                   43.4171    15.0196      187
   SEX              1    Male                    44.5437    15.4163      103
   SEX              2    Female                  42.0357    14.4901       84

   Total Cases = 1006
Missing Cases = 4 or      .4 Pct
```

a. Complete the following chart of mean ages:

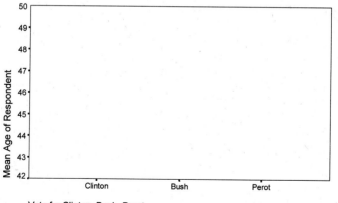

Vote for Clinton, Bush, Perot

b. Complete the following clustered bar chart of mean ages:

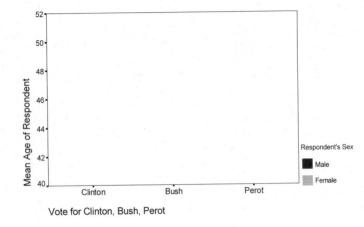

Vote for Clinton, Bush, Perot

Data Analysis

Use the *gss.sav* data file to answer the following questions:

1. What kind of people are happy people? Write a short paper which compares people that are very happy, pretty happy, and not too happy (variable *happy*) on characteristics such as age, education, hours of TV watched, and so forth. Include appropriate charts. Don't submit all of the SPSS output you produce. Instead, present only the output that supports the points you want to make. Be concise.

2. Many factors contribute to the happiness of a marriage (variable *hapmar*). Answer the question "What distinguishes people who are very happy with their marriage from those who are less content?" Write a brief report outlining your findings.

3. In the 1992 election how did Clinton, Bush, and Perot supporters differ (variable *pres92*)? Answer the following questions:

   a. Whose supporters were the oldest and by how much?

   b. Was there a relationship between years of education and candidate preference?

   c. Which candidate were wealthy people more likely to support?

   d. On average how many hours do Perot supporters watch television? Clinton supporters? Bush supporters?

4. What types of people claim that they would continue to work if they struck it rich (variable *richwork*)? Be sure to look at average education, age, income, hours worked per week.

5. There's no accounting for musical taste, but you can see how musical preferences for classical, opera, and country music (variables *classicl, opera,* and *country*) are related to variables like age, education, and so forth. Summarize your findings.

Use the *salary.sav* data file to answer the following questions:

6. Compute average beginning salaries (variable *salbeg*) for people in the different job categories (variable *jobcat*).

　　a. Which job category has the largest average beginning salary? The smallest?

　　b. Compute the coefficient of variation for each job category. What can you say about the coefficients of variation for the different categories?

　　c. Make a bar chart of average beginning salary for each job category.

7. For each job category:

　　a. Find the average beginning salaries for males and females. Summarize your findings.

　　b. Make a bar chart of average beginning salary by job category and gender. Are the differences easier to see from the table or from the chart?

　　c. What possible explanations other than gender discrimination can you offer for the observed differences?

8. Repeat the analyses in questions 6 and 7 using years of education (variable *educ*) instead of beginning salary.

Use the *electric.sav* data file to answer the following questions:

9. Examine the differences in diastolic blood pressure, cholesterol, and years of education (variables *dbp59, chol58,* and *eduyr*) for those who were alive 10 years after the study started and those who were not (variable *vital10*). Generate appropriate charts. Write a summary of your results.

10. What is the average standardized score for diastolic blood pressure for those who were alive at 10 years and those who were not? Does the difference appear to be large? What does the average standardized score tell you?

11. Compute the average diastolic blood pressure for each category of first coronary heart disease event (variable *firstchd*).

　　a. Which group has the highest average diastolic blood pressure? How many cases is this mean based on? Does the number of cases influence how much confidence you have in the mean?

　　b. What is the average diastolic blood pressure for all cases? For those with sudden death? For those with no coronary heart disease?

　　c. Does systolic blood pressure appear to be related to coronary heart disease?

12. Look at the average number of cigarettes smoked per day in 1958 (variable *cgt58*) for each category of first coronary heart disease event. Summarize your findings.

13. Calculate the average diastolic blood pressure for those alive and not alive at 10 years, separately for those with a family history of coronary heart disease and for those without (variable *famhxcvr*). Summarize your findings. Make a bar chart of your results.

Looking at Distributions

What additional displays are useful for summarizing the distribution of a variable for several groups?

- What is a stem-and-leaf plot?
- How does a stem-and-leaf plot differ from a histogram?
- What is a boxplot?
- What can you tell from the length of a box?
- How is the median represented in a boxplot?

Since most statistical analyses of data involve comparisons of groups, SPSS contains many procedures that help you to examine the distribution of values for individual groups of cases. In Chapter 6, you used the Means procedure to calculate descriptive statistics for education when the cases were subdivided on the basis of job satisfaction and gender. The output from Means is deliberately compact and basic: means, standard deviations, and numbers of cases. To examine each of the groups in more detail, you need to use the Explore procedure. That's what this chapter is about. (The statistics and displays described in this chapter are also useful for looking at the distribution of values for the entire sample.)

▶ This chapter continues to use the *gssft.sav* data file. For instructions on how to obtain the Explore output shown in the chapter, see "How to Explore Distributions" on p. 114.

Age and Job Satisfaction

In Chapter 6, you looked at the relationship between education and job satisfaction for full-time workers. You found that the average years of education did not differ much among people in the different categories of job satisfaction. Now you'll consider the relationship between age and job satisfaction for the same group of cases. You'll be able to examine the groups in considerably more detail. Consider first

103

the descriptive statistics for age among workers who rate themselves as *very satisfied* with their jobs.

Figure 7.1 Descriptive statistics for very satisfied workers

To obtain these descriptive statistics, from the menus choose:

Statistics
    Summarize ▶
       Explore...

Select the variables age and satjob, as shown in Figure 7.9.

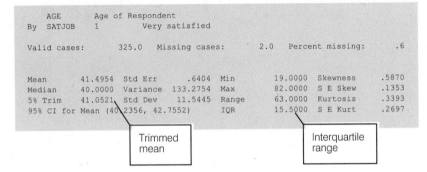

```
      AGE        Age of Respondent
By  SATJOB   1           Very satisfied

Valid cases:        325.0   Missing cases:      2.0   Percent missing:      .6


Mean         41.4954  Std Err      .6404  Min     19.0000  Skewness      .5870
Median       40.0000  Variance  133.2754  Max     82.0000  S E Skew      .1353
5% Trim      41.0521  Std Dev    11.5445  Range   63.0000  Kurtosis      .3393
95% CI for Mean (40.2356, 42.7552)         IQR     15.5000  S E Kurt      .2697
```

Trimmed mean

Interquartile range

In Figure 7.1, there are 325 cases in the *very satisfied* group for whom age is available. The number of missing cases is 2. That means that 2 *very satisfied* cases do not have a valid value for the age variable. (Since these cases represent only 0.6% of all the cases in the group, you don't have to worry about the effect of missing age values on your analysis.)

The mean of the ages in the very satisfied group is 41.5 years. The median age, 40 years, is slightly less. As you've learned in Chapter 5, one of the shortcomings of the arithmetic mean is that very large or very small values in the data can change its value substantially. The trimmed mean avoids this problem. A **trimmed mean** is calculated just like the usual arithmetic mean, except that a designated percentage of the cases with the largest and smallest values are excluded. This makes the trimmed mean less sensitive to outlying values. The 5% trimmed mean excludes the 5% largest and the 5% smallest values. It's based on the 90% of cases in the middle.

In Figure 7.1 you see that the 5% trimmed mean for age is 41.05 years. It doesn't differ much from the usual mean, since the largest age in this group (*Max*) is 82 and the smallest age (*Min*) is 19. With 325 cases in the group, you'd need a very old Roman warrior to have a real effect on the mean. The trimmed mean provides an alternative to the median when you have some data values that are far removed from the rest.

Again in Figure 7.1, you see that the variance is 133.28 squared years, and the standard deviation is 11.54 years. (The discussion of the standard error of the mean, labeled *Std Err*, and the 95% confidence interval, *95% CI for Mean*, appears in Chapter 12.) The range is 63 years (82–19); the interquartile range, labeled *IQR*, is 15.5 years. Remember, the interquartile range is the difference between the 75th and the 25th percentile values. Unlike the ordinary range, the interquartile range is not easily affected by extreme values, since the bottom 25% and the top 25% of the data values are excluded from its computation.

Identifying Extreme Values

Since many statistics are affected by data values that are much smaller or larger than most, it's always important to examine your data to see if extreme values are present. You can obtain from the Explore procedure a list of the cases with the five largest and the five smallest values in each group. Always check any suspicious values to make sure they are not the result of an error in data recording or entry. If you find a mistake, it's easy to change the values for a case using the Data Editor. If the extreme values are correct, make sure to select summary measures that are not unduly affected by these outliers.

Figure 7.2 Outliers from the very satisfied group

To obtain extreme values, select Statistics in the Explore dialog box. Then select Outliers, as shown in Figure 7.10.

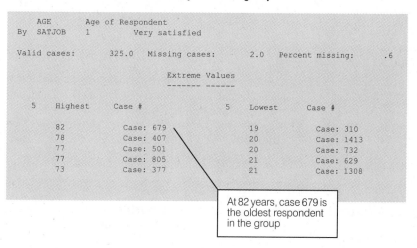

Figure 7.2 shows for the *very satisfied* group the cases with the five largest and smallest ages. The column labeled *Case #* contains the sequence number in the file for each case. That makes it easier for you to track the suspicious values. (SPSS can also show a name or any other identifier to label the cases.) You see that case 679 is the oldest, at age 82. Case 310 is the youngest, at age 19. Neither of these values is usual. Since only five cases with the smallest and largest values are listed, it's possible that not all cases with those values are listed. For example, there may be more than one 73-year-old or more than two 21-year-olds. If that's true, a note is printed beneath the table.

Percentiles

Using Explore, you can also obtain percentiles for each of the groups. Figure 7.3 shows the percentiles for age for the *very satisfied* workers.

Figure 7.3 Age percentiles for very satisfied

To obtain percentiles, select Statistics in the Explore dialog box. Then select Percentiles. (See Figure 7.10.)

```
       AGE        Age of Respondent
  By   SATJOB     1          Very satisfied

  Valid cases:        325.0   Missing cases:      2.0    Percent missing:      .6


                                     Percentiles
                                     -----------

  Percentiles          5.0000   10.0000   25.0000   50.0000   75.0000   90.0000
  Haverage            24.0000   27.0000   33.5000   40.0000   49.0000   57.4000
  Tukey's Hinges                          34.0000   40.0000   49.0000

  Percentiles         95.0000
                      61.0000
```

10th percentile: 10% of cases 27 or younger

10% are 57.4 or older

The percentiles are in the row labeled *Haverage*. **Haverage** refers to the method the Explore procedure uses to calculate percentiles. Other ways can be used, but most of the time they give pretty much the same results. You see that 10% of the cases are 27 years of age or younger (the 10th percentile) and 10% are 57.4 or older (the 90th percentile). *Tukey's Hinges*, which are quartiles (values that divide the sorted cases into four equal groups) calculated using a slightly different method, are also displayed.

How can you get different numbers for the same percentiles? Percentiles don't have a single, unique definition. For example, consider the eight numbers 25 26 27 27 27 27 30 31. What's the 25th percentile? Any number between 26 and 27 is a plausible value. One definition of percentiles gives the answer 26.5, since that's the average of 26 and 27, the interval within which the percentile falls. Another definition results in the answer 26, since that's the first value for which the cumulative percentage is equal to or greater than 25%.

For small data sets, especially when several cases have the same values, different percentiles may have the same value. For the previous example, it's possible for percentiles greater than the 25th and less than the 75th to have the value 27. For small data sets, percentile values can vary a lot for samples from the same population, so you shouldn't place too much confidence in their exact values. (You also shouldn't worry about where the "equal" goes. That is, whether 25% of the cases have values less than the 25th percentile, or whether 25% of the cases have values less than or *equal* to the 25th percentile. Statistical software packages implement arbitrary rules about where the "equal" goes.)

Grouped Frequency Tables

Whenever you have a variable that can have many different values, such as height or blood pressure, a frequency table like that described in Chapter 4 is of limited use. You'll end up with a long list of values, most of which occur with a frequency of 1. If it makes sense to group adjacent values, you can use a grouped frequency table to summarize the data. (It seldom makes sense to group adjacent groups for a nominal variable like country of birth or religious affiliation.)

Figure 7.4 contains the grouped frequency table for the age variable in the *very satisfied* group.

Figure 7.4 Grouped frequency table of age for very satisfied

To obtain a grouped frequency table, select Statistics in the Explore dialog box. Then select Grouped frequency tables. (See Figure 7.10.)

In addition, to get a grouped frequency table, you must select Plots and then select Stem-and-leaf. (See Figure 7.11.)

```
       AGE        Age of Respondent
   By  SATJOB   1          Very satisfied

   Valid cases:      325.0   Missing cases:      2.0    Percent missing:      .6


                             Frequency Table
                             --------- -----

              Bin                          Valid      Cum
            Center       Freq      Pct      Pct       Pct

              24         41.00    12.62    12.62     12.62
              34        101.00    31.08    31.08     43.69
              44         96.00    29.54    29.54     73.23
              54         66.00    20.31    20.31     93.54
              64         15.00     4.62     4.62     98.15
              74          5.00     1.54     1.54     99.69
              84          1.00      .31      .31    100.00
```

101 cases fall between ages 29 and 38.99. The midpoint is 34.

Each row in the grouped frequency table corresponds to a range of age values. The column labeled *Bin Center* tells you the middle value, or midpoint, for each interval. The length of the interval is the distance between two adjacent bin centers. In this example, the interval length is 10. The first row is for people aged 19–28.99, the next is 29–38.99 years, and so on. You see that 41 people (12.62%) in the *very satisfied* group fall within the first interval. The percentages are computed in the same way as for the ungrouped frequency table, except that missing values are not included in the grouped table, so the two percentage columns are always the same. (Sometimes in the grouped frequency table, the first and last rows are for cases with values outside of the range used in the table. For example, the Roman warrior would be in an interval labeled greater than 90 years.)

Plots

One of the easiest ways to see the distributions of your variables is literally with a picture. The Explore procedure provides several plots that let you evaluate the shape of a distribution. From these plots, you see how often different values of a variable occur in your data. As you will see in Part 3, your choice of the statistical analysis for a particular problem depends on the assumptions you are willing to make about the distributions of the variables of interest. That's why it's important to examine them.

Histograms and Stem-and-Leaf Plots

The Explore procedure can produce separate histograms for groups of cases. The histograms are identical to those produced by the Frequencies procedure, as described in Chapter 4. Figure 7.5 shows a histogram of age for the people *a little dissatisfied* with their jobs.

Figure 7.5   Age histogram for a little dissatisfied

To obtain a histogram, select Plots in the Explore dialog box. Then select Histogram, as shown in Figure 7.11.

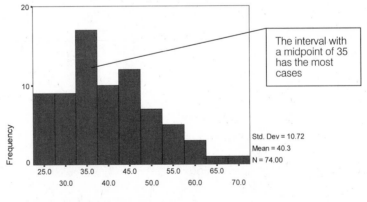

The interval with a midpoint of 35 has the most cases

Std. Dev = 10.72
Mean = 40.3
N = 74.00

Age of Respondent

Note the main peak, centered at 35 years of age, with a smaller peak at 45. From the histogram you can only tell the number of cases in each of the intervals: you don't know the actual values of the cases. For example, for the interval centered around 50, all of the cases could be 50 years old, or they could be any combination of 48-, 49-, 50-, 51- and 52-year-olds. From the histogram, you see that the distribution of age values in the groups is not symmetric. There is a tail toward larger values. You know that's because only adults are included in the General Social Survey.

? *What kinds of things should I look for in a histogram?* You already know that you should look for cases with values very different from the rest. In fact, if there are such cases, they can cause most of your data values to bunch in one or two bars of the histogram, since the horizontal axis of the histogram is selected so that all data values can be shown. You should see also whether the distribution is symmetric, since many of the statistical procedures described in Part 3 require that the distribution be more or less symmetric.

You should also look for separate clumps of data values. For example, if young men and mature women made up most of the *a little dissatisfied* group, you would see a bunch of cases with values in the 20's, perhaps, and another bunch of cases with values in the 60's. There wouldn't be many cases in between. That's an important finding, since then you know that a mean age of 40-something for the *a little dissatisfied group* is meaningless. It doesn't represent the data well. In this situation, you'd want to analyze the data for men and for women separately. ■ ■ ■

A **stem-and-leaf plot** is a display very much like a histogram. However, more information about the actual data values is preserved. Consider Figure 7.6, which is a stem-and-leaf plot for age in the group *a little dissatisfied* with their jobs. It looks like a histogram, because the length of each line corresponds to the number of cases in the interval. However, the cases are represented with different symbols. Each observed value is divided into two components—the leading digit or digits, called the **stem**, and a trailing digit, called the **leaf**. For example, the value 23 has a stem of 2 and a leaf of 3.

In a stem-and-leaf plot, each row corresponds to a stem and each case is represented by its leaf. More than one row can have the same stem. For example, in Figure 7.6 each stem is subdivided into two rows. Rows that are marked with an asterisk (*), between the stem and the leaves, are for cases with leaves of 0 through 4. Rows that are marked with a period (.) are for cases with leaves of 5 through 9.

Figure 7.6 Stem-and-leaf plot of age for a little dissatisfied

To obtain a stem-and-leaf plot, select Plots in the Explore dialog box. Then select Stem-and-leaf, as shown in Figure 7.11.

```
       AGE          Age of Respondent
  By   SATJOB   3            A little dissatisfied

  Valid cases:        74.0   Missing cases:        .0   Percent missing:        .0



  Frequency    Stem &  Leaf

      2.00       2 *   33
     13.00       2 .   5556777899999
      7.00       3 *   0123334
     18.00       3 .   555566666777788899
      7.00       4 *   0012234
     13.00       4 .   5556666677888
      5.00       5 *   02223
      5.00       5 .   55679
      3.00       6 *   013
      1.00   Extremes  (72)

  Stem width:   10
  Each leaf:        1 case(s)
```

> Multiply stem by stem width and add leaf values to get actual data values (60, 61, and 63)

Look at the row with the stem of 6 in Figure 7.6. The three leaves are 0, 1, and 3. What does this mean? In order to translate the stem-and-leaf values into actual numbers, you must look at the stem width given below the plot. In this case it's 10. You multiply each stem value by 10 and then add it to the leaf to get the actual value. The resulting age values are 60, 61, and 63. If the stem width were 100, you would multiply each stem by 100 and each leaf by 10 before adding them together. The values for the indicated row would be 600, 610, and 630.

If there are few values of the stem (for example, if most cases are in one or two decades of age), each stem can be subdivided into more than two rows. Consider, for example, Figure 7.7, which is a stem-and-leaf plot for years of education for all very dissatisfied people, regardless of their status in the work force.

> *Why all of a sudden are we looking at all people instead of full-time workers?* The data values determine the type of stem-and-leaf plot that Explore makes. To illustrate this particular version of the plot, we had to look for a set of data that would generate it. Including all cases in the *very dissatisfied* group worked. ■ ■ ■

Figure 7.7   Stem-and-leaf plot of education for very dissatisfied

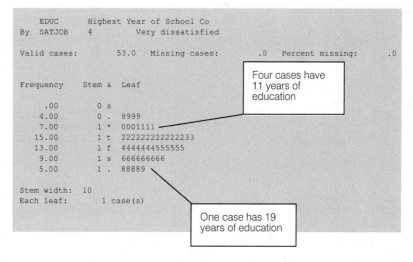

```
     EDUC        Highest Year of School Co
By  SATJOB      4              Very dissatisfied

Valid cases:         53.0    Missing cases:      .0    Percent missing:      .0

Frequency    Stem &  Leaf

    .00        0 s
   4.00        0 .  8999
   7.00        1 *  0001111
  15.00        1 t  222222222222233
  13.00        1 f  4444444555555
   9.00        1 s  666666666
   5.00        1 .  88889

Stem width:   10
Each leaf:        1 case(s)
```

Four cases have 11 years of education

One case has 19 years of education

In Figure 7.7, the stem value 1 is subdivided into five rows—each representing two leaf values. The rows identified by an asterisk are for leaves of 0 and 1, rows identified by *t* are for leaves of 2 and 3, *f* is for leaves of 4 and 5, *s* is for 6 and 7, and a period is for 8 and 9. You see that the *very dissatisfied* group is made up of people of various educational levels. Having a college degree is no guarantee of job satisfaction.

How would you make a stem-and-leaf plot of a variable like income? For a variable like income, which has many digits, it's unwieldy and unnecessary to represent each case by the last digit. (Think of how many stems you would have!) Instead, you can look at income to the nearest thousand. For example, you can take a number like 25,323 and divide it into a stem of 2 and a leaf of 5. In this case, the stem is the ten thousands, and the leaf is the thousands. You no longer retain the entire value for the case, but that's not of concern, since income differences in the hundreds seldom matter very much. The Explore procedure always displays the stem width under the plot. ■ ■ ■

Boxplots

Another display that helps you visualize the distribution of a variable is the **boxplot**. It simultaneously displays the median, the interquartile range, and the smallest and largest values for a group. A boxplot is more compact than a histogram but doesn't show as much detail. For example, you can't tell if your distribution has a single peak or if there are intervals that have no cases.

You can use the Explore procedure to produce a display that contains boxplots for all the groups of interest. Consider Figure 7.8, which is an annotated boxplot of the age of the respondent for the four categories of job satisfaction.

Figure 7.8   Boxplot of age by job satisfaction

To obtain this boxplot, select Plots in the Explore dialog box. Then select Factor levels together. (See Figure 7.11.)

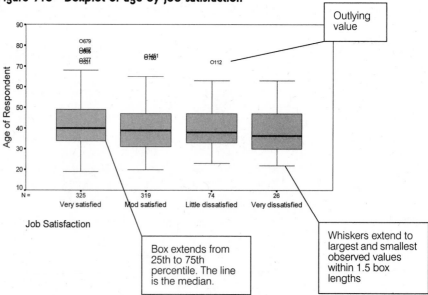

The lower boundary of the box represents the 25th percentile. The upper boundary represents the 75th percentile. (The percentile values known as Tukey's hinges are used to construct the box.) The vertical length of the box represents the interquartile range. Fifty percent of all cases have values within the box. The line inside the box represents the median. Note that the only meaningful scale in the boxplot is the vertical scale. All values are plotted on this scale. The width of a box doesn't represent anything.

In a boxplot, there are two categories of cases with outlying values. Cases with values between 1.5 and 3 box lengths from the upper or lower edge of the box are called **outliers** and are designated with (O). Cases with values more than 3 box-lengths from the upper or lower edge of the box are called **extreme values**. There aren't any such cases here, but if there were, they would be designated with asterisks (*). Lines are drawn from the edges of the box to the largest and smallest values that are outside the box but within 1.5 box lengths. (These lines are sometimes called **whiskers**, and the plot is sometimes called a **box-and-whiskers plot**.)

What can you tell about your data from a boxplot? From the median, you can get an idea of the typical value (the central tendency). From the length of the box, you can see how much the values vary (the spread or variability). If the line representing the median is not in the center of the box, you can tell that the distribution of your data values is not symmetric. If the median is closer to the bottom of the box than to the top, there is a tail toward larger values (this is also called **positive skewness**). If the line is closer to the top of the box, there is a tail toward small values (**negative skewness**). The length of the tail is shown by the length of the whiskers and the outlying and extreme points.

The Explore procedure also has more specialized charts and statistics for examining groups. These are discussed in Chapter 15 and Chapter 22.

In Figure 7.8, you see that the *very satisfied* group has the highest median age, though the differences among the groups are small. (Chapter 14 tests the hypothesis that the average age of people who are *very satisfied* is the same as the average age of those who are less than *very satisfied*.) The *very satisfied* and *moderately satisfied* groups have some large outliers. They are identified by case number in the plot. These are the satisfied old-timers who continue to work. If you specify a case label, the extreme and outlying points will be identified with this label.

? *What should I do if I find outliers and extremes on my boxplots?* Use the case numbers to track down the data points and make sure the values are correct. If these points are the results of data entry or coding errors, correct them. ■ ■ ■

Summary

What additional displays are useful for summarizing the distribution of a variable for several groups?

- A stem-and-leaf plot, like a histogram, shows how many cases have various data values. A stem-and-leaf plot preserves more information than a histogram because it does not use the same symbol to represent all cases. Instead, the symbol depends on the actual value for a case.

- A boxplot is a display that shows both the central tendency and variability of the data.

- The length of the box in a boxplot is the distance between the 25th percentile and the 75th percentile. Fifty percent of the data values fall in this range.

- The median is represented by a line in a boxplot. If the median is not in the center of the box, the distribution of values is skewed.

What's Next?

Descriptive statistics like the mean and variance are useful only for summarizing a variable that is measured on a meaningful scale. To summarize nominal variables or other variables with a small number of possible values, you can count how often various combinations of values occur. That's what the next chapter is about.

How to Explore Distributions

You can use SPSS to look at the distribution of values for a variable. The Explore procedure allows you to:

- Calculate descriptive statistics for all the cases in your data and for subgroups of cases.

- Identify extreme values. These are sometimes due to errors in collecting data or entering it into the computer. If they are correct, they can greatly influence statistical analysis, so you need to be aware of them.

- Calculate the percentiles of a variable's distribution. Again, you can do this both for all cases and for subgroups of cases.

- Display grouped frequency tables. You can display frequency tables showing the counts of cases within ranges of values.

- Generate plots. A variety of plots show graphically how data values are distributed.

▶ To open the Explore dialog box, from the menus choose:

Statistics
   Summarize ▶
      Explore...

Figure 7.9 Explore dialog box

Select age
and satjob to
obtain the
output shown
in Figure 7.1

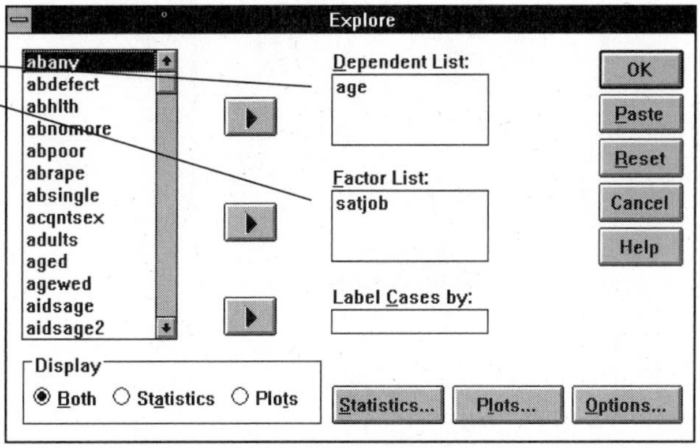

▶ In the Explore dialog box, select one or more numeric variables and move them into the Dependent List. Make sure that either the Statistics or Both radio button is selected in the Display group at the bottom left.

▶ If you want to calculate these statistics for subgroups of cases, such as those that are *very satisfied, moderately satisfied,* and *a little dissatisfied* with their jobs, you must specify a factor variable.

A factor variable is simply a variable that distinguishes groups of cases. All the cases in each group have the same value for the factor variable. If you want to specify a factor variable, select it and move it into the Factor List in Figure 7.9. You can move more than one variable into the Factor List. If you do, the calculations of subgroup statistics are done separately for the categories of each factor.

▶ If you want to label the five largest and smallest values on the outlier list, or identify points on the boxplot, specify the variable used as the label in the Label Cases by box.

Explore Statistics: Outliers and Grouped Frequency Tables

From the Explore dialog box, click on Statistics to open the Explore Statistics dialog box (see Figure 7.10), where you can request outliers, grouped frequency tables, and additional statistics. (The Descriptives check box is selected by default. That's why SPSS calculated descriptive statistics in Figure 7.1, even when you didn't change anything on the Explore Statistics dialog box.)

Figure 7.10 Explore Statistics dialog box

Select to display descriptive statistics, as shown in Figure 7.1

Select to display outliers, as shown in Figure 7.2

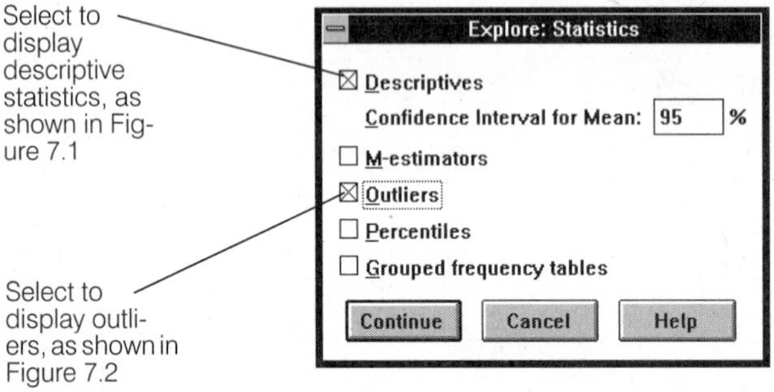

At least one statistic must be selected. In addition to descriptive statistics, you can select from the following:

M-estimators. Statistics that resemble the mean but give weights to observations depending on their distance from a central point.

Outliers. SPSS displays the five highest and five lowest values of the dependent variable. They are identified by case number, or sequential position in the data file, as in Figure 7.2.

Percentiles. Displays the 5th, 10th, 25th, 50th, 75th, 90th, and 95th percentiles. The 25th, 50th, and 75th percentiles are called **quartiles**; they divide the cases into four equal groups based on the values of the dependent variable.

Grouped frequency tables. Displays frequency tables like those shown in Figure 7.4. Here frequency counts are displayed not for each distinct value but for ranges of values called **bins**. When a variable has many values, and it is sensible to group adjacent values, a grouped frequency table is useful.

Graphical Displays

The Explore procedure offers several graphical ways of seeing the distribution of variables. By default, it displays boxplots and stem-and-leaf plots of all dependent variables for each category of each factor variable. To suppress display of specific plots, or to request additional ones, select Plots in the main Explore dialog box. This opens the Explore Plots dialog box, as shown in Figure 7.11.

Figure 7.11 Explore Plots dialog box

For more information about creating and editing charts in SPSS, see Appendix A.

Select to obtain stem-and-leaf plots and histograms, as shown in Figure 7.5 and Figure 7.6

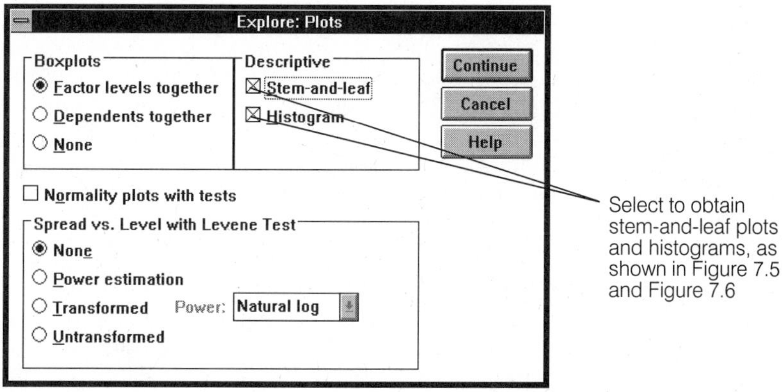

The following groups of options are available:

Boxplots. The Boxplots control group lets you rearrange the display of multiple boxplots or suppress them entirely. The first two alternatives are for situations when you have more than one dependent variable, and you have at least one factor variable. If you're interested primarily in comparing distributions across categories of the factors, select Factor levels together. If you're more concerned about whether the dependent variables are distributed differently within each factor category, select Dependents together. For example, if you have three variables that are IQ scores for the same children measured at ages 5, 7, and 10 and want to see the distributions of the three variables on the same plot, select Dependents together. On the other hand, if you want to look at differences between males and females at each age, select Factor levels together. This will produce for each variable male and female scores on the same display. If you don't want to see boxplots at all, select None in this group.

Descriptive. The Descriptive control group lets you suppress the stem-and-leaf plots or histograms (see "Histograms and Stem-and-Leaf Plots" on p. 108).

Spread vs. Level with Levene Test. Many statistical procedures, such as those discussed in Chapter 15 and Chapter 16, are dependent on the assumption that a dependent variable has about the same variance ("spread") for the cases with each level of a factor variable. If this assumption doesn't hold, you can sometimes transform the dependent variable so that the assumption does. When you have specified a factor variable, you can request Untransformed spread-versus-level plots to determine whether the dependent variable has the same variance within each factor level. If not, you can request Power estimation, which determines the best transformation to use. Once you know this, you can request Transformed spread-versus-level plots, using the Power drop-down list to indicate the desired transformation. After applying a transformation, you should make a stem-and-leaf plot of the data values to see what effect the transformation has.

The following check box is also available:

Normality plots with tests. Select this check box if you want to test whether the sample comes from a population that has a normal distribution. This causes SPSS to display the normality plots and tests shown in "Examining Normality" on p. 245 in Chapter 13, allowing you to test the null hypothesis that your data are from a normal distribution.

Options

The Explore Options dialog box lets you control the way in which missing data are handled by the Explore procedure. From the Explore dialog box, click on Options to open the Explore Options dialog box, as shown in Figure 7.12.

Figure 7.12 Explore Options dialog box

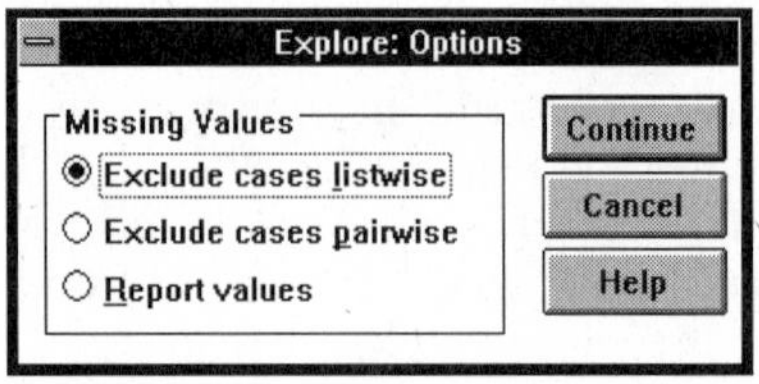

You can choose from the following alternatives:

Exclude cases listwise. When this is selected, cases with a missing value for any of the variables in the Dependent list or the Factor list in the Explore dialog box are omitted from all calculations and plots.

Exclude cases pairwise. When this is selected, each statistic or plot uses all the cases that have non-missing information for the variables actually needed for it. Cases with a missing value for one dependent variable are still used to calculate statistics for other dependent variables. This option uses all available data in the computations, but not all of the output is necessarily based on the same cases.

Report values. When this is selected, missing values for a factor variable are treated as a category of the factor. Statistics and plots contain a group of cases that have the factor variable declared missing. Missing values for a dependent variable are included in any frequency tables you request, but not in the calculation of statistics.

Exercises

Statistical Concepts

1. Consider the following twenty ages: 21, 22, 22, 22, 25, 28, 30, 31, 32, 34, 35, 35, 35, 35, 38, 39, 40, 40, 41, and 80.

   a. Complete the following stem-and-leaf plot for them:

   ```
   Frequency    Stem &  Leaf

       4.00        2 *
       2.00        2 .
       4.00        3 *
       6.00        3 .
       3.00        4 *
       1.00 Extremes

   Stem width:        10
   Each leaf:      1 case(s)
   ```

b. Complete the following histogram:

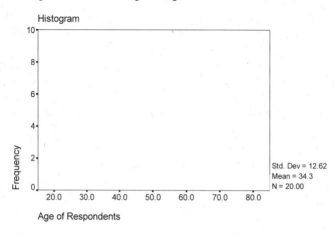

Histogram

Std. Dev = 12.62
Mean = 34.3
N = 20.00

Age of Respondents

c. Compared to a histogram, what are the advantages of a stem-and-leaf plot?

2. Answer the following questions based on the boxplot below. The plots represent the time it took to ship products from three warehouses.

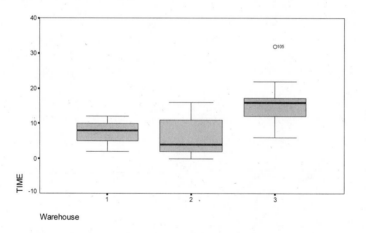

Warehouse

a. Estimate the median for warehouse 1.

b. Estimate the interquartile range for warehouse 2.

c. For warehouse 3, what is the largest value that is not an outlier?

d. Which warehouse has the most variability?

e. If you were to choose one of the warehouses to ship your product, which warehouse would you select and why?

3. Based on the following stem-and-leaf plot, complete the frequency table below.

```
Frequency    Stem &  Leaf

    5.00     15 .  03469
    8.00     16 .  11235788
    4.00     17 .  0022
    2.00     18 .  08
    1.00     19 .  0
    1.00     20 .  4
    1.00     21 .  5
    3.00     22 .  228

Stem width:     10.00
Each leaf:       1 case(s)
```

```
                        Frequency Table
                        --------- -----

                Bin                        Valid      Cum
                Center    Freq     Pct      Pct        Pct

                155.00
                165.00
                175.00
                185.00
                195.00
                205.00
                215.00
                225.00
```

4. Based on the summary statistics shown in the table below, sketch a boxplot of age.

Mean	56.6923	Std Err	.5280	Min	37.0000	Skewness	-.2528
Median	57.0000	Variance	36.2457	Max	76.0000	S E Skew	.2124
5% Trim	56.7906	Std Dev	6.0204	Range	39.0000	Kurtosis	.8720
95% CI for Mean	(55.6476, 57.7370)			IQR	8.0000	S E Kurt	.4218

```
                        Percentiles
                        -----------
```

Percentiles	5.0000	10.0000	25.0000	50.0000	75.0000	90.0000
Haverage	45.5500	48.0000	53.0000	57.0000	61.0000	64.0000
Tukey's Hinges			53.0000	57.0000	61.0000	

Data Analysis

Use the *gss.sav* data file to answer to following questions:

1. Compute descriptive statistics and obtain a stem-and-leaf plot of age separately for people in each of the categories of variable *vote92*.

   a. Look at the stem-and-leaf plot for people who were ineligible. List all of their ages.

   b. Compare the shapes of the stem-and-leaf plots for people who voted and those who did not. What differences and similarities can you see?

   c. Look at the boxplot for voters and nonvoters. Based on the boxplot, summarize all that you can about the distribution of age in the two groups.

2. Look at the relationship between age and fondness for opera (variable *opera*). Obtain boxplots of age for each group.

   a. Which group has the most variability? Indicate what criterion of variability you are using.

   b. Do you think the age distribution is symmetric for each group?

   c. For each group, below what value of age do 25% of the ages fall? Above what value do 25% of the ages fall?

   d. What are the medians for each group?

   e. What can you conclude about the relationship between fondness for opera and age?

3. In Chapter 6, you saw that the variable *tvhours* had some unusual values, including one person who claimed to watch television 24 hours per day. To assess the impact of the unusual values on the average hours of television watched, run the Examine procedure and compare the arithmetic mean, the 5% trimmed mean, and the median. Look at a histogram for television variable again. Which of the measures of central tendency do you think best describe the television-viewing habits of the General Social Survey respondents?

Use the *salary.sav* data file to answer the following questions:

4. The job seniority variable indicates the length of time an employee has been on the job (variable *time*). Make a stem-and-leaf plot of this variable.

   a. How would you characterize the shape of the distribution? Does it have a single peak around which values are concentrated?

   b. What are the five shortest job seniorities? The five longest?

5. Make a boxplot of average time on the job for workers in the four gender/race categories (variable *sexrace*). Write a brief description of the plot.

6. Make a grouped frequency table of the job seniority variable.

    a. What values fall within the first interval of the table?

    b. Roughly what percentage of employees fall into each interval?

    c. Estimate the median for job seniority based on the grouped frequency table.

Use the *electric.sav* data file to answer the following questions:

7. Compute descriptive statistics and make a stem-and-leaf plot and a boxplot of average diastolic blood pressure (variable *dbp58*).

    a. Describe the distribution. Does it have a single peak? Does the distribution look symmetric? If it has a tail, is it toward large or small values?

    b. From the stem-and-leaf plot, what are the three largest diastolic blood pressure values? What are the values for the cases with the 10 smallest values?

    c. Look at the boxplot. Is the median in the middle of the box? What does that tell you? Are there outliers or extreme observations in the data values? Within what range do the middle 50% of the data values fall? What is the interquartile range for the data?

8. Make a grouped frequency table of average diastolic blood pressure.

    a. What diastolic blood pressure values fall in the first bin? How many cases are there with these values?

    b. What percentage of men have diastolic blood pressures less than 95? Less than 115?

    c. From the grouped frequency table estimate the 70th percentile.

    d. Can you tell from the grouped frequency table exactly what the smallest and largest observed values are? The observed smallest value can't be less than what value? The largest value can't be larger than what value?

9. Select a variable from the *electric.sav* file and use the Examine procedure to study its distribution for men who were alive 10 years after the study started and in men who were not alive (variable *vital10*). Write a short summary of results, including appropriate graphs.

Counting Responses for Combinations of Variables

How can you study the relationship between two or more variables that have a small number of possible values?

- Why is a frequency table not enough?
- What is a crosstabulation?
- What kinds of percentages can you compute for a crosstabulation, and how do you choose among them?
- What's a dependent variable? An independent variable?
- What if you want to examine more than two variables together?
- How can you use a chart to display a crosstabulation?

The Means and Explore procedures described in Chapter 6 and Chapter 7 are useful only when statistics such as the mean and standard deviation are appropriate measures for the variable whose values you want to summarize. You can't use Means or Explore to look for relationships between color of car driven and region of the country, since it doesn't make sense to compute an average color or region. When you want to look at the relationship between two variables that have a small number of values or categories (sometimes called **categorical variables**), you may want to use a **crosstabulation**, a table that contains counts of the number of times various combinations of values of two variables occur. For example, you can count how many men and how many women are in each of the job satisfaction categories, or you can see the distribution of car colors for various regions of the country.

In this chapter, you'll use a crosstabulation to look at the relationship between job satisfaction and total family income, measured on a four-point scale.

▶ This chapter continues to use the *gssft.sav* file. For instructions on how to obtain the crosstabulation output shown in this chapter, see "How to Obtain a Crosstabulation" on p. 137.

Income and Job Satisfaction

In the General Social Survey, respondents are asked to select the range of values into which their annual family income falls. There are 21 categories, ranging from under $1,000 (assigned a code of 1) to $75,000 and over (assigned a code of 21). To look at the relationship between income and job satisfaction for full-time employees, you'll use four income groups with roughly the same number of cases. That is, you will use quartiles of income. (The variable *income4* contains the income data recoded into quartile categories.) You see from Figure 8.1, which shows a frequency distribution of the four categories of income, that as expected, roughly 25% of the people fall into each of the income groupings.

Figure 8.1 Frequency table for income quartiles

To obtain this frequency table, select the variable income4 in the Frequencies dialog box. See Chapter 4 for information on frequency tables.

```
INCOME4    Total Family Income


                                                    Valid      Cum
Value Label                  Value  Frequency  Percent  Percent  Percent

24,999 or less                1.00       174     23.3     23.3     23.3
25,000 to 39,999              2.00       194     26.0     26.0     49.3
40,000 to 59,999              3.00       156     20.9     20.9     70.1
60,000 or more                4.00       223     29.9     29.9    100.0
                                       -------  -------  -------
                             Total       747    100.0    100.0


Valid cases      747     Missing cases      0
```

To examine the relationship between income and job satisfaction, you want to count how many *very satisfied, moderately satisfied, a little dissatisfied,* and *very dissatisfied* people there are in each of the income categories. Figure 8.2 contains this information. The income groups make up the columns of the table. The rows are the job satisfaction categories. A cell appears in the table for each combination of values of the two variables. The first cell, at the top left of the table, is for *very satisfied* people in the lowest income group. You see that 53 people fall into this cell. The cell in the second row of the first column is for *moderately satisfied* people in the lowest income category. There are 93 people in this cell. Similarly, the last cell of the table tells you that there are 7 *very dissatisfied* people in the highest income group.

Figure 8.2 Crosstabulation of job satisfaction by income

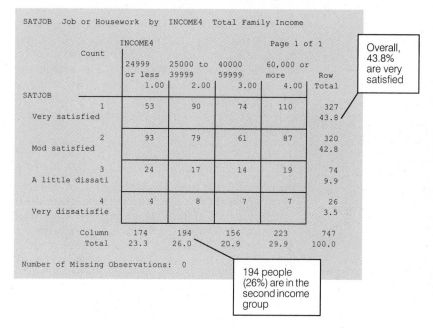

To obtain this crosstabulation, from the menus choose:

Statistics
   Summarize ▶
      Crosstabs...

In the Crosstabs dialog box, select the variables satjob and income4, as shown in Figure 8.9.

To the right and at the bottom of the table are totals—often called **marginal totals** because they are in the table's margin. The margins of the table show the same information as frequency tables for each of the two variables. In the right margin, labeled *Row Total*, you have the total number of people who gave each of the job satisfaction answers. The right margin also shows what percentages these counts are of the total sample. For example, the first row total, 327, is the number of *very satisfied* people. These 327 people are 43.8% of the total of 747 people. Similarly, the first column total of 174 is the number of people in the lowest income category. The lowest income category contains 23.3% of the sample.

Will the marginal totals and percentages that I get in a crosstabulation table always be the same as those I would get from frequency tables for the variables individually? Not if you have missing values for either of the two variables in the crosstabulation. For example, the crosstabulation in Figure 8.2 includes only cases that have nonmissing values both for job satisfaction and for income. The marginal totals for income are therefore based on cases that have nonmissing values for both income and job satisfaction. When you make a frequency table for income, the only cases excluded from the valid percentages are those with missing values for income.   ■ ■ ■

If you look at the counts in the crosstabulation, you see that 53 people from the lowest income category said they are *very satisfied* with their jobs, 90 from the second income category, 74 from the third income category, and 110 from the highest income category. Can you tell from the counts just what the relationship is between income and a high level of job satisfaction? Of course not, since you can't just compare the counts when there are different numbers of people in the four income groups. To compare the groups you must look at percentages instead of counts. That is, you must look at the percentage of people in each of the income groups who gave each of the job satisfaction responses.

Row and Column Percentages

Figure 8.3 contains both the counts and the column percentages. From the row totals, you see that, overall, 43.8% of the sample are *very satisfied* with their jobs. You also see that 30.5% of the lowest income group, 46.4% of the second income group, 47.4% of the third income group, and 49.3% of the highest income group are *very satisfied* with their jobs. It appears that the lowest income people are less likely than average to be *very satisfied*, while the high income people are more likely than average to be *very satisfied*.

Figure 8.3 Crosstabulation showing column percentages

To obtain column percentages, select Cells in the Crosstabs dialog box. Then select Column, as shown in Figure 8.11.

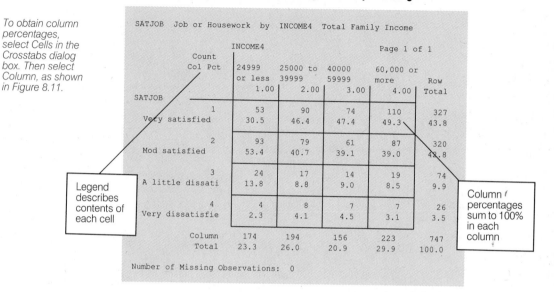

Legend describes contents of each cell

Column percentages sum to 100% in each column

The percentages you used to make comparisons are known as **column percentages**, since they express the number of cases in each cell of the table as a percentage of the column total. That is, for each income group, they tell you the distribution of job satisfaction. The column percentages sum up to 100% for each of the columns.

You can also calculate row percentages for the table. **Row percentages** tell you what percentage of the total cases of a row fall into each of the columns. For each job satisfaction category, they tell you the percentage of cases in each income category. (You can also compute what are called **total percentages**. The count in each cell of the table is expressed as a percentage of the total number of cases in the table.) Figure 8.4 contains counts and row percentages for our example. There is a description of the contents of each cell of the table in the legend at the top left of the table.

Figure 8.4 Crosstabulation showing row percentages

To obtain row percentages, select Cells in the Crosstabs dialog box. Then select Row. (See Figure 8.11.)

```
SATJOB  Job or Housework  by  INCOME4  Total Family Income

                       INCOME4                         Page 1 of 1
             Count
             Row Pct  24999    25000 to  40000    60,000 or
                      or less  39999     59999    more        Row
                        1.00 |    2.00 |   3.00 |    4.00 |  Total
       SATJOB       ---------------------------------------
                1       53        90       74       110        327
       Very satisfied  16.2      27.5     22.6      33.6       43.8

                2       93        79       61        87        320
       Mod satisfied  29.1       24.7     19.1      27.2       42.8

                3       24        17       14        19         74
       A little dissati 32.4     23.0     18.9      25.7        9.9

                4        4         8        7         7         26
       Very dissatisfie 15.4     30.8     26.9      26.9        3.5

            Column     174       194      156       223        747
            Total      23.3      26.0     20.9      29.9

       Number of Missing Observations:  0
```

Legend

Row percentages sum to 100% across each row

From the row percentages, you see that 16.2% of the *very satisfied* respondents are in the lowest income group, 27.5% are in the second income group, 22.6% in the third income group, and 33.6% in the fourth income group. The four row percentage values sum to 100 for each of the rows. In this example, the row percentages aren't very helpful, since you can't make much sense of them without taking into account the overall percentages of cases in each of the income categories. That is, you can't tell whether the percentage of high income cases in the *very satisfied* category is due to a large number of high income cases in your sample or to high satisfaction rates in that category.

For a particular table, you must determine whether the row or column percentages answer the question of interest. This can be done easily if one of the variables can be thought of as an independent variable and the other as a dependent variable. An **independent variable** is a variable that is thought to influence another variable, the **dependent variable**. For example, if you are studying the incidence of lung cancer in smokers and nonsmokers, smoking is the independent variable. Smoking influences whether people get cancer, the dependent variable. Similarly, if you are studying the income categories of men and women, gender is the independent variable since it might influence how much you get paid.

If you can identify one of your variables as independent and the other as dependent, then you should compute percentages so that they sum to 100 for each category of the independent variable. In other words, what you want to see is the same number of people in each of the categories of the independent variable. Having the percentages sum to 100 for each category of the independent variable is the equivalent of having 100 cases in each category. For example, you want 100 smokers and 100 nonsmokers. Then you can compare the incidence of lung cancer in the two groups. In the current example, income category is the independent variable and job satisfaction is the dependent variable. That means you'd like to see 100 people in each of the income categories. Since income is the column variable in Figure 8.3, you use column percentages that sum to 100 for each category of income.

Can't you analyze these data using the Means procedure? The General Social Survey codes income in unequal intervals. For example, the interval from $8,000 to $9,999 is coded 8, but the interval $60,000 to $74,999 is coded 20. So you don't want to compute means for these codes. Instead, if you want to compute average family income, you must change the coding scheme so that the code for a case is the midpoint of the appropriate income interval. For example, an income anywhere in the range of $8,000 to $9,999 would be assigned a code of $9,000. Similarly, incomes in the range of $60,000 to $74,999 would be assigned a code of $67,500, the midpoint of the interval. You can then compute descriptive statistics for the recoded incomes. Of course, the means won't be the same as those you would get if you had the exact income for each person, but they're the best you can do given the limitations of the data.

Bar Charts

You can display the results of a crosstabulation in a clustered bar chart. Consider Figure 8.5, which is a bar chart of family income by job satisfaction. The length of a bar tells you the number of cases in a category.

Figure 8.5   Bar chart of income by job satisfaction

You can obtain this bar chart using the Graphs menu, as described in "Bar Charts" on p. 538 in Appendix A. In the Clustered Bar Summaries for Groups of Cases dialog box, select the variables income4 and satjob.

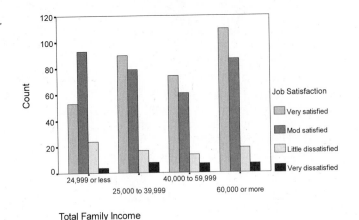

There is a cluster of bars for each of the four income categories. Within each cluster, there is a bar for each of the job satisfaction categories. Since there are unequal numbers of people in the income categories, comparing bar lengths across income categories presents the same problem as looking at simple counts in a crosstabulation. All you can really do with this bar chart is compare bar lengths within a cluster and see whether the patterns are the same across clusters.

Figure 8.6   Stacked bar chart

You can obtain this chart by modifying Figure 8.5, as described in "Bar Charts" on p. 538 in Appendix A. Move the chart into a chart window and from the menus choose:

Gallery
  Bar...

In the Bar Charts dialog box, select Stacked.

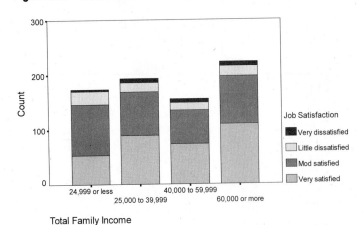

Stacked Bar Charts

You can stack the bars in a clustered bar chart one on top of the other. The result is the stacked bar chart in Figure 8.6. Now it's easier to see for each income category the proportion of people in each of the job satisfaction categories. However, the lengths of the bars aren't equal for the four income categories, so that still gets in the way.

Ideally, you want each of the bars to be of the same length, so you can easily compare the areas across bars. What you'd really like to see is a plot of the column percentages from Figure 8.3. You can do this by turning the counts in each bar into percentages, as shown in Figure 8.7. Now each of the bars has the same length—100%—and you can easily compare the job satisfaction distributions across bars. You see that people in the lowest income group are least likely to be *very satisfied* with their jobs. They are also least likely to be *very dissatisfied*. The distribution of job satisfaction categories seems to be very similar for the other three income groups. The proportion of *very satisfied* people doesn't increase with income for these three groups. You can also see that the sum of the percentages for *very satisfied* and *moderately satisfied* is very similar for the four groups.

Figure 8.7 Stacked bar chart with percentage scale

You can obtain this chart by modifying Figure 8.6 as described in "Bar Charts" on p. 538 in Appendix A. Move the chart into a chart window and select Change scale to 100% in the Bar/Line/Area Options dialog box.

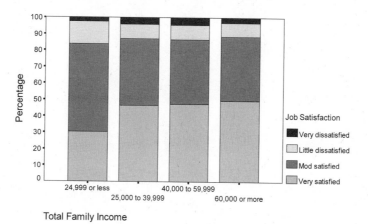

Adding Control Variables

So far, you've considered the relationship between income and job satisfaction for the entire sample. It's possible that if you consider additional variables, the relationship you've seen between the two variables may change. For example, it may be that the relationship between income and job satisfaction is different for men and women. To test this, you can make separate tables of income and job satisfaction for men and for women. Gender is then called a **control variable**, since its effect is removed, or "controlled" for, in each of the separate tables. Figure 8.8 shows separate crosstabulation tables for men and women.

Figure 8.8 Job satisfaction by income for men and women

To obtain these separate— or layered— crosstabulations, select sex as a layer variable, as shown in Figure 8.10.

```
SATJOB  Job or Housework  by  INCOME4  Total Family Income
Controlling for..
SEX  Respondent's Sex  Value = 1  Male
```

		INCOME4			Page 1 of 1	
	Count Col Pct	24999 or less 1.00	25000 to 39999 2.00	40000 59999 3.00	60,000 or more 4.00	Row Total
SATJOB						
Very satisfied	1	30 34.9	51 47.2	41 45.6	57 46.0	179 43.9
Mod satisfied	2	44 51.2	44 40.7	36 40.0	49 39.5	173 42.4
A little dissati	3	10 11.6	10 9.3	7 7.8	14 11.3	41 10.0
Very dissatisfie	4	2 2.3	3 2.8	6 6.7	4 3.2	15 3.7
Column Total		86 21.1	108 26.5	90 22.1	124 30.4	408 100.0

```
SATJOB  Job or Housework  by  INCOME4  Total Family Income
Controlling for..
SEX  Respondent's Sex  Value = 2  Female
```

		INCOME4			Page 1 of 1	
	Count Col Pct	24999 or less 1.00	25000 to 39999 2.00	40000 59999 3.00	60,000 or more 4.00	Row Total
SATJOB						
Very satisfied	1	23 26.1	39 45.3	33 50.0	53 53.5	148 43.7
Mod satisfied	2	49 55.7	35 40.7	25 37.9	38 38.4	147 43.4
A little dissati	3	14 15.9	7 8.1	7 10.6	5 5.1	33 9.7
Very dissatisfie	4	2 2.3	5 5.8	1 1.5	3 3.0	11 3.2
Column Total		88 26.0	86 25.4	66 19.5	99 29.2	339 100.0

As you can tell from the cell contents at the top left of the table, the cell entries are counts and column percentages. An interesting difference emerges between the two tables. For women, job satisfaction seems to increase with income. Almost twice as many women in the highest income category (53.5%) are very satisfied compared to women in the lowest income category (26.1%). For men, the difference is not as striking. Almost 35% of men in the lowest income category are *very satisfied*, compared to 46% of the men in the highest income category.

Summary

How can you study the relationship between two or more variables that have a small number of possible values?

- A crosstabulation shows the numbers of cases that have particular combinations of values for two or more variables.
- The number of cases in each cell of a crosstabulation can be expressed as the percentage of all cases in that row (the row percentage) or the percentage of all cases in that column (the column percentage).
- A variable that is thought to influence the values of another variable is called an independent variable.
- The variable that is influenced is called the dependent variable.
- If there is an independent variable, percentages should be calculated so that they sum to 100% for each category of the independent variable.
- When you have more than two variables, you can make separate crosstabulations for each of the combinations of values of the other variables.
- Bar charts can be used to display a crosstabulation graphically.

What's Next?

So far, you've only used crosstabulations to summarize the relationship between two variables. In Chapter 17, you'll learn how to compute statistical tests to determine whether the two variables in a crosstabulation are related. In Chapter 19, you'll compute statistics that measure the strength of the relationship between the two variables in a crosstabulation. In Chapter 9, you'll see how scatterplots can be used to display the values of two variables that are measured on a meaningful numeric scale.

How to Obtain a Crosstabulation

This section shows how to obtain crosstabulations of two or more variables with SPSS. The Crosstabs procedure tabulates the different combinations of values that occur for two or more variables. You should use crosstabulations only if your variables have a small number of distinct values. In addition, the Crosstabs command can:

- Display percentages, expected counts, and residuals within each cell.
- Calculate tests of statistical independence and measures of association for pairs of variables ("bivariate" statistics).
- Control some aspects of the table format.

▶ To open the Crosstabs dialog box (see Figure 8.9), from the menus choose:

Statistics
  Summarize ▶
    Crosstabs...

Figure 8.9 Crosstabs dialog box

Select satjob and income4 to obtain the crosstabulation shown in Figure 8.2

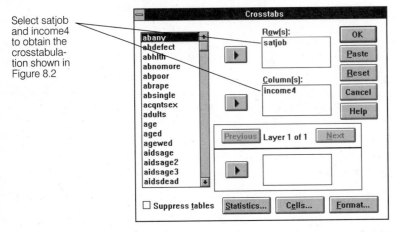

▶ In the Crosstabs dialog box, select a categorical variable and move it into the Row(s) list. Select another categorical variable and move it into the Column(s) list.

This produces a single table with the categories of the first variable down the left side, defining the rows, and the categories of the second variable across the top, defining the columns. Each cell contains the number of cases with the corresponding values for the two variables.

▶ Move several variables into the Row(s) list or the Column(s) list or both to obtain multiple bivariate crosstabs.

SPSS displays a table for each combination of row and column variables. If one list has two variables and the other list has three, six tables are displayed.

The following option is also available:

Suppress tables. Lets you suppress the display of the actual tables in case you are interested in only the statistics (see "Bivariate Statistics" on p. 140).

Layers: Three or More Variables at Once

You can obtain a different bivariate crosstabulation for each category of a control variable (as in Figure 8.8, which shows a crosstabulation with *sex* as a control variable).

▶ To specify a control variable, select the variable and move it into the Layer 1 of 1 list, as shown in Figure 8.10. As with row and column variables, you can move more than one variable into this list.

Figure 8.10 Selecting a layer variable

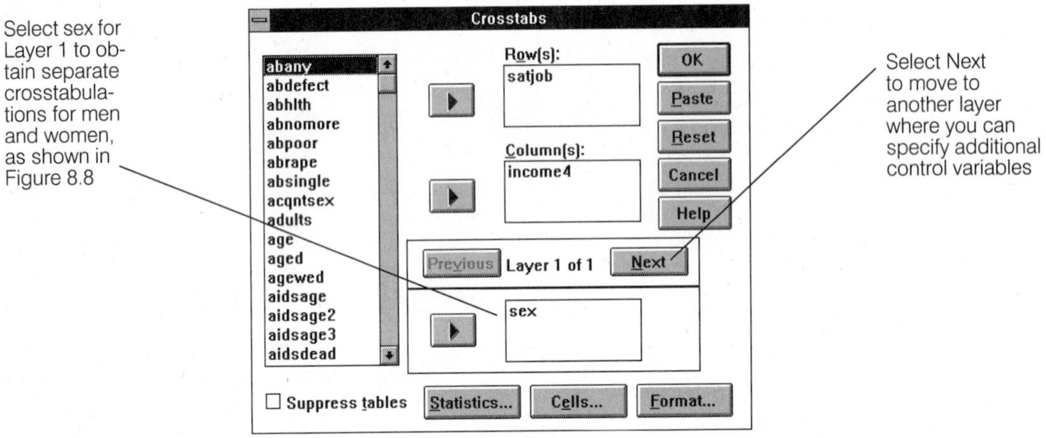

Select sex for Layer 1 to obtain separate crosstabulations for men and women, as shown in Figure 8.8

Select Next to move to another layer where you can specify additional control variables

SPSS displays all of the bivariate crosstabulations for each category of the first control variable, then for each category of the second control variable, and so on through the list.

▶ Optionally, you can click on Next to specify additional layers of control variables.

If you move one or more variables into the Layer 2 list, SPSS displays all of the bivariate crosstabulations for each category of the Layer 1 variables, combined with each category of the Layer 2 variables. After you have a Layer 2 list, you can continue to click on Next and build additional layers. Or you can click on Previous to go back and add or remove variables in the previous layer.

Cells: Percentages, Expected Counts, and Residuals

From the Crosstabs dialog box, click on Cells to open the Crosstabs Cell Display dialog box, as shown in Figure 8.11. Here you can add additional information to the observed case count that is displayed by default in each cell.

Figure 8.11 Crosstabs Cell Display dialog box

Select Column to display column percentages, as shown in Figure 8.3

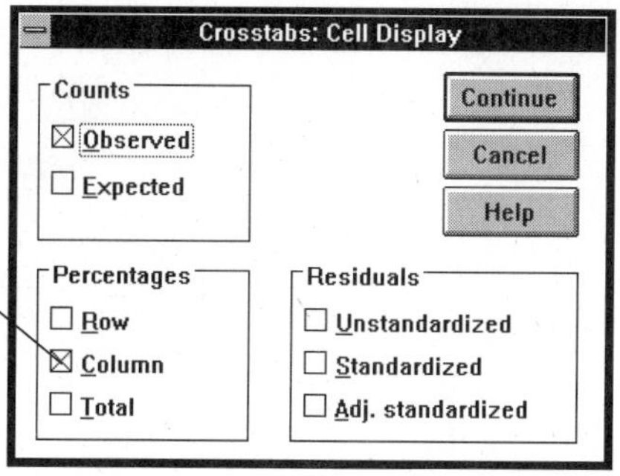

The following groups of options are available:

Counts. The observed count is the number of cases in the cell. The expected count is the number of cases that would be in the cell if the row and column variables were statistically independent.

Percentages. Row percentages sum to 100% across each row of the table. Column percentages sum to 100% down each column. Total percentages sum to 100% over the table as a whole.

Residuals. Residuals are the difference between observed and expected cell counts.

Bivariate Statistics

From the Crosstabs dialog box, click on Statistics to open the Crosstabs Statistics dialog box (see Figure 8.12), which allows you to choose statistics to be displayed along with your crosstabulation. (You will learn more about these statistics in Chapter 17 and Chapter 19.)

Figure 8.12 Crosstabs Statistics dialog box.

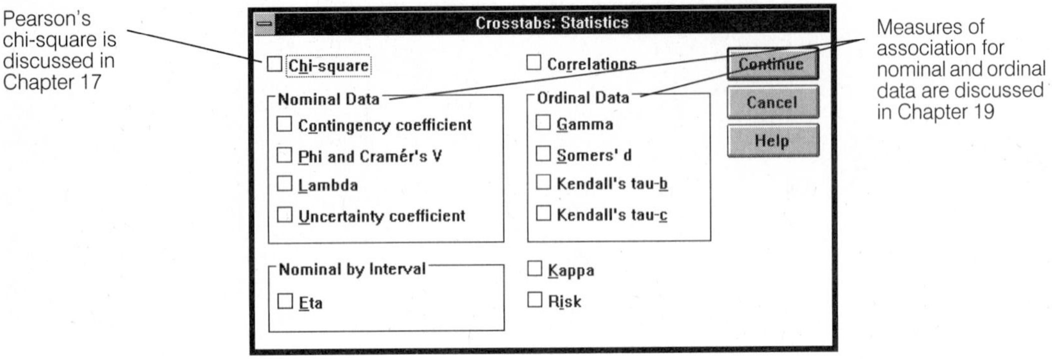

Pearson's chi-square is discussed in Chapter 17

Measures of association for nominal and ordinal data are discussed in Chapter 19

Format: Adjusting the Table Format

From the Crosstabs dialog box, click on Format to open the Crosstabs Table Format dialog box (see Figure 8.13), which allows you to modify the format of the tables.

Figure 8.13 Crosstabs Table Format dialog box

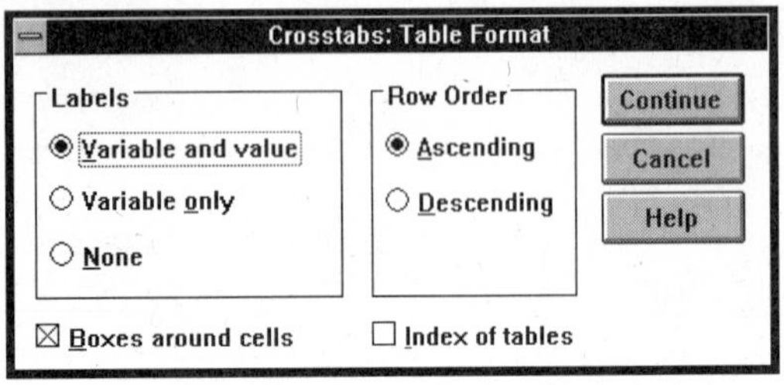

The following groups of options are available:

Labels. These alternatives allow you to suppress the labels defined for the variables in the tables.

Row Order. Determine whether the rows of the table are listed in ascending or descending order of the categories of the row variable.

Boxes around cells. Deselect to suppress the drawing of boxes around the cells.

Index of tables. Generate an index of all the tables generated by this execution of Crosstabs.

Statistical Concepts

1. Indicate whether you would use procedure Frequencies, Crosstabs, or Means to find the following:

a. The average age of purchasers of different brands of a product

b. The number of married, single, widowed, divorced, and never-married purchasers of different brands of a product

c. The number of purchasers of each brand

d. The average age of male and female purchasers of each brand

e. The number of men and women in each of the marital categories who purchase each brand

2. Identify the dependent and independent variables, if possible, for each of the following pairs of variables:

a. Satisfaction with job and race

b. Belief in life after death and gender

c. Astrological sign and excitement with life

d. Mother's highest degree and daughter's highest degree

e. Happiness with one's marriage and belief in life after death

3. If you construct a crosstabulation for each of the pairs of variables in the previous question, with the first variable forming the rows of the table and the second variable forming the columns, should you calculate row or column percentages? Answer for all five pairs.

4. The following table indicates whether each of twenty people owns or rents a home (1=own, 2=rents) and how satisfied they are with city services (1=not satisfied, 2=satisfied, 3=very satisfied).

Person	Owner	Satisfied
1	1	1
2	1	1
3	1	1
4	1	1
5	1	1
6	1	2
7	1	3
8	1	3
9	2	2
10	2	2
11	2	3
12	2	3
13	2	3
14	2	3
15	2	3
16	2	3
17	2	3
18	2	3
19	2	3
20	2	3

a. Summarize the data by filling in the values for the cell counts and marginals of the following crosstabulation.

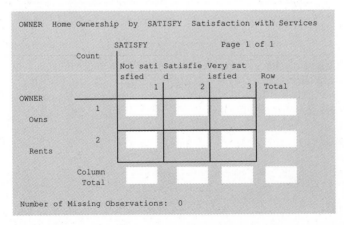

b. Calculate the row and column percentages.

c. What percentage of the sample are homeowners?

d. What percentage of the sample are very satisfied with city services?

e. What percentage of homeowners are very satisfied with city services? Of non-owners?

5. Fill in the missing information in the following table:

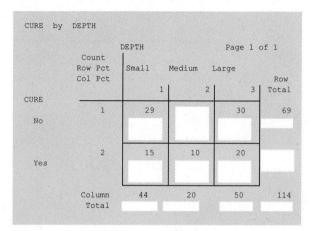

CURE by DEPTH

	DEPTH			Page 1 of 1
Count Row Pct Col Pct	Small	Medium	Large	Row Total
	1	2	3	
CURE				
1 No	29		30	69
2 Yes	15	10	20	
Column Total	44	20	50	114

6. Your local newspaper's Sunday supplement contains an article on job satisfaction and marital status. The article contains the following table. The authors conclude that marriage makes people more satisfied with their jobs, since 62% of the very satisfied people are married, while only 17% have never been married. Comment on the conclusions from the study.

```
MARITAL  Marital Status  by  SATJOB  Job or Housework

                       SATJOB                          Page 1 of 1
              Count
              Col Pct   Very sat  Mod sati  A little  Very dis
                        isfied    sfied     dissati   satisfie   Row
                            1         2         3         4      Total
MARITAL       ─────────
              1           302       257        58        28       645
    MARRIED               61.6      54.4      45.7      52.8      56.5

              2            26        19         5         1        51
    WIDOWED                5.3       4.0       3.9       1.9       4.5

              3            66        77        20        11       174
    DIVORCED              13.5      16.3      15.7      20.8      15.2

              4            12        14         7         1        34
    SEPARATED              2.4       3.0       5.5       1.9       3.0

              5            84       105        37        12       238
NEVER MARRIED             17.1      22.2      29.1      22.6      20.8

           Column        490       472       127        53      1142
           Total         42.9      41.3      11.1       4.6     100.0

Number of Missing Observations:  358
```

7. Below is a crosstabulation of belief in life after death and highest degree earned. Calculate the appropriate percentages, and write a few sentences summarizing the table.

```
POSTLIFE  Belief in Life After Death  by  DEGREE  RS Highest Degree

                       DEGREE                          Page 1 of 1
              Count
                        Less      High      Junior    Bachelor Graduate
                        than HS   school    college                       Row
                            0         1         2         3         4     Total
POSTLIFE      ─────────
              1           132       392        45       110        52      731
    YES                                                                    80.7

              2            37        82        12        29        15      175
    NO                                                                     19.3

           Column        169       474        57       139        67      906
           Total         18.7      52.3       6.3      15.3       7.4     100.0

Number of Missing Observations:  594
```

8. For which of the following pairs of variables do you think a crosstabulation would be appropriate?

a. Weight in pounds and daily intake in calories

b. Number of cars and highest degree earned

c. Body temperature in degrees and survival after an operation

d. Eye color and undergraduate grade point average

9. You are interested in studying the relationship between highest degree earned by a person in school, the person's marital status, and several other variables. Which SPSS procedure would you use to investigate the relationship of these two variables and

a. The number of hours of television watched per week

b. Religious affiliation

c. Job satisfaction

d. Number of siblings

e. Zodiac sign

Data Analysis

Use the *gss.sav* data file to answer the following questions:

1. Make a crosstabulation to examine the relationship between highest degree earned (variable *degree*) and a person's perception of life (variable *life*).

a. How many people without a high-school diploma find life exciting?

b. What percentage of people without a high-school diploma find life exciting?

c. Of the people who find life exciting, what percentage do not have a high-school diploma?

d. If *degree* is the column variable and *life* is the row variable, what kind of percentages should you compute for the table?

e. Summarize the relationship, if any, between perception of life and highest degree earned.

2. What kinds of people claim that they will continue to keep working if they strike it rich (variable *richwork*)? Use the Crosstabulation procedure to examine the relationship between *richwork* and characteristics such as gender, education, job importance, and perception of life (variables *sex*, *degree*, *impjob*, and *life*). Write a brief report summarizing your findings. Use graphical displays when appropriate.

3. Belief in life after death (variable *postlife*) may be related to characteristics such as age, education, income, marital status, and so forth. How many characteristics can you identify that are associated with belief in life after death? Write a short report about your findings.

4. Look at the relationship between a person's highest degree (*degree*) and their general happiness (*happy*). Does there seem to be a relationship between the two variables?

5. Repeat the analysis you did in question 4 separately for men and women. Does the relationship between the two variables appear to be similar for males and for females? Explain how you reached your conclusion.

6. How many characteristics can you identify that distinguish people who voted in 1992 from those who did not (variable *vote92*)? For example, are degree, gender, and marital status related to the likelihood of voting?

7. You've been hired to do a "postmortem" on the election of 1992. Write a short paper describing what types of people voted for each of the candidates (variable *pres92*).

Use the *salary.sav* data file to answer the following questions:

8. Consider the relationship between the gender/race categories (variable *sexrace*) and job category (variable *jobcat*).

   a. How many white males are employed as clerical workers? What percentage of white males are clerical workers? Of clerical workers, what percentage are white males?

   b. If you make a crosstabulation table in which *sexrace* is the column variable and *jobcat* is the row variable, would you compute row or column percentages? Why? Make such a table and write a short paragraph summarizing your results.

9. In the Transform menu use the Recode facility to create a new variable named *degree*. Compute it in the following way from years of education (variable *edlevel*):

edlevel	degree	Value label
0–11	1	Less than high school
12	2	High-school diploma
13–15	3	Some college
16+	4	College degree

   You can assign the value labels in the Data Editor after the variable is computed.

   a. What percentage of white males have college degrees? White females? Non-white males and females?

b. Write a paragraph summarizing the relationship between education and the gender/race categories. Do the categories seem to differ in educational attainment?

Use the *electric.sav* data file to answer the following questions:

10. Use a crosstabulation to look at the relationship between vital status at 10 years (variable *vital10*) and family history of coronary heart disease (variable *famhxcvr*).

   a. What percentage of men without a family history were alive 10 years after the study started? What percentage of those with a family history were alive?

   b. If *famhxcvr* is the column variable, would you compute row or column percentages? If *famhxcvr* is the row variable, would you compute row or column percentages?

11. Using the *cgt58* variable (number of cigarettes smoked per day in 1958), compute a new variable called *smoke* that has the value 0 if the person did not smoke at the start of the study and a value of 1 if they did. (Use the Recode facility in the Transform menu to do this.) Make a crosstabulation that shows the relationship between smoking status and vital status after 10 years (variable *vital10*). What percentage of smokers are alive after 10 years? What percentage of non-smokers?

12. Using the *eduyr* variable, create a new variable called *degree* that has the following coding scheme:

eduyr	degree	Value label
0–8	1	Grammar school or less
9–11	2	Some high school
12	3	High-school graduate
13–15	4	Some college
16	5	College graduate

You can assign the value labels in the Data Editor after the variable is computed.

   a. Use a crosstabulation to examine the relationship between *degree* and *vital10*. What percentage of people with less than a high-school diploma are alive? What percentage of people with a high-school diploma or more are alive?

   b. Look at the relationship between *degree* and *smoke*. Write a short paragraph summarizing your results.

Plotting Data

How can you display the relationship between two variables that are measured on a scale with meaningful numeric values?

- What is a scatterplot, and why is it useful?
- What is a scatterplot matrix?
- How can a scatterplot be used to identify unusual observations?
- What can you learn from a three-dimensional plot?

In previous chapters, you've used a variety of graphical displays to summarize your data. You've made pie charts, bar charts, histograms, and boxplots. All of these plots show the distribution of the values of a single variable. In this chapter, you'll learn how to display the values of two variables that are measured on a meaningful scale. Using **scatterplots**, you can look at the relationships of pairs of variables, like beginning salary and college GPA; weight and cholesterol; or the compensation of CEO's and corporate profits.

A scatterplot is one of the best ways to look for relationships and patterns among variables. It is simple to understand, yet it conveys much information about the data. In Part 4 of this book, you'll learn methods for summarizing and describing relationships, but these methods are no substitute for plots. You should always plot the data first and then think about appropriate methods for summarizing them.

▶ This chapter uses demographic data from a sample of 122 nations (The World Almanac and Book of Facts, 1994). To work along in SPSS, use the *country.sav* data file. For specific instructions on how to create scatterplots, see "How to Obtain a Scatterplot" on p. 164. For an overview of creating and modifying charts in SPSS, see Appendix A.

149

Examining Population Indicators

You'll learn about scatterplots by looking at the relationships between female life expectancy, birthrate per 1000 population, and percentage of population living in urban areas for a sample of 122 countries. (Most values are for 1992. When 1992 data were unavailable, prior year data were used.) Birthrates as well as life expectancies have traditionally been related to economic prosperity. Better education, better health, and increasing urbanization led to declining birthrates in Western nations. Recent studies of developing nations (Robey, Rutstein, & Morris, 1993) suggest, however, that birthrates are declining in the absence of economic improvement. Changes in cultural values and availability of family planning have resulted in declining fertility rates, though not necessarily in increasing life expectancy.

Simple Scatterplots

Figure 9.1 is a scatterplot of female life expectancy and birthrate. Life expectancy, the average number of years a newborn female is expected to live, is plotted on the vertical axis (the *y*-axis), and the birthrate per 1000 population is plotted on the horizontal axis (*x*-axis). Consider the circled point. It represents Indonesia, with a female life expectancy at birth of 64 years and a birthrate of 26 births per 1000 population. (Dotted lines are drawn from the point to the axes to help you see what the values for the point are.)

Figure 9.1 Scatterplot of life expectancy with birthrate

To create this scatterplot, from the menus choose:

*Graphs
  Scatter...*

See "Obtaining a Simple Scatterplot" on p. 165 for details.

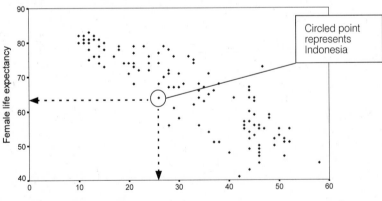

> *Does it matter which variable I plot on the Y axis and which variable I plot on the X axis?* If one of the two variables that you're plotting is considered a dependent variable and the other an independent variable, it's traditional to plot the dependent variable on the *Y* axis. For example, if you're plotting salary and years of education, plot the salary on the *Y* axis, since salary may well depend on years of education.■ ▨ ▨

What can you tell from the scatterplot shown in Figure 9.1? First of all, you see that the points are not randomly scattered over the grid. There seems to be a pattern. The points are concentrated in a band from the top left of the plot to the bottom right. As the birthrate increases, life expectancy decreases. In fact, the relationship appears to be more or less linear. That is, a straight line might be a reasonable summary of the data.

From a scatter plot, you can also see if there are cases that have unusual combinations of values for the two variables. In this plot, there aren't any cases that are really far removed from the overall pattern. However, if there were a country with a birthrate of 10 per 1000 and a female life expectancy of 50, that would be an unusual point that should be scrutinized to ensure that it is correct. Individually, the values for the two variables are not unusual. Neither would stand out on a stem-and-leaf plot or a histogram. There are many countries with a birthrate of around 10. There are also many countries with a life expectancy of around 50 years. What would be unusual is the combination of these two values.

Labeling the Points

From Figure 9.1, you can't tell which point represents which country. Identifying points can be important. If you find unusual points, you can investigate them more easily. If points represent entities such as car brands, companies, or countries, by examining the labels, you can identify types of cars or companies on the plot. For example, you can see if all of the European countries or African countries cluster together on the plot.

Figure 9.2 is the same plot as Figure 9.1, with some of the countries labeled. You see that Niger has the highest birthrate of all the countries in the plot and one of the lowest female life expectancies. The United States (and Canada) are in the upper left corner of the plot. They have low birthrates and relatively high life expectancies. Jordan sticks out somewhat in the plot. It has a higher life expectancy than other countries with similar birthrates.

? *Won't labeling the points cause the plot to be unreadable, since there will be labels all over?* SPSS has a special point-identification capability that lets you click on a particular point for the label to appear (see "Case Identification" on p. 173). If you click on the point again, the label disappears. That means that you can look at the points as much as you want and not worry about the plot becoming unreadable. ■ ■ ■

Figure 9.2 Life expectancy with birthrate showing labels

To display country labels, select the variable country for Label Cases by, as shown in Figure 9.15. You can then display case labels, as described in "Case Identification" on p. 173.

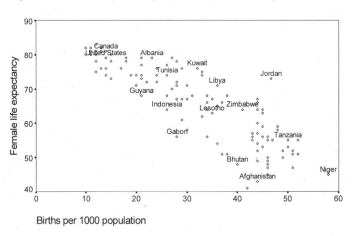

Identifying Different Groups

Often, when you look at the relationship between two variables, you are interested in how other factors affect the relationship. For example, if you're looking at the relationship between salary and years of experience, you may want to know if it's similar for males and females. Or if you're looking at the relationship between blood pressure and weight, you may want to see if it's similar for smokers and nonsmokers. An easy way to see whether different groups of cases behave similarly is to identify each point with a marker that indicates what group it's in. Sometimes the variable whose values determine the marker is called a **control variable**, because when you identify the point with its value, you "control" for the effect of the variable.

For example, if you want to see whether the relationship between birthrate and life expectancy is similar for developing nations and for those considered developed, you can identify each of the points in Figure 9.1 as belonging to a developing or developed country.

Figure 9.3   Life expectancy with birthrate by development status

To identify points by development status, select develop for Set Markers by, as shown in Figure 9.15.

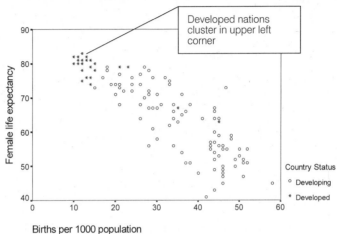

Figure 9.3 is the same plot as Figure 9.1. The only difference is that points are identified with two different markers, depending on whether a country is considered developed or developing. (Membership in the Group of 77, an organization of developing countries, was the primary criterion for determining development status. A couple of exceptions were made to this rule for clearly developing countries that are not members.)

You see that most of the developed nations cluster in the upper left corner of the plot. They have low birthrates and high life expectancies. The developing countries have a large spread in values for birthrate and life expectancy. For example, their birthrates range from 15 per 1000 all the way to almost 60 per 1000. The developing countries take up most of the plot.

? *What happens if I have two points with the same values for life expectancy and birthrate but one is developed and one is developing?* If you have data in which points overlap (cases have identical or very similar values for the two variables) but the cases have different values for the variable that determines the marker used, only one of the markers will appear. If that happens often, you'll have difficulty interpreting the plot. This can be a serious problem for large data sets. It's not much of a problem in Figure 9.3, since the developed and developing countries are well-separated on the plot.

Sunflower Plots

In Figure 9.3, you see a lot of points that are close to one another. In fact, some of them are overlapping, but you can't tell, because when two points overlap only one point is visible. (Figure 9.3 has 112 visible points to represent 122 countries, since 10 points overlap.)

When you have many points, it's helpful to represent overlapping or nearly overlapping points with **sunflowers**. The idea is simple. You divide the entire plotting grid into equal-sized regions (cells) and count the number of points that fall into each region. The count in each cell is represented by a sunflower symbol. If a cell contains only one point, it is represented by a small circle. If a cell has more than one point, each point is represented by a short line (a "petal") originating from the circle. (If you like, you can specify an integer larger than 1 for the number of cases represented by each petal.)

Figure 9.4 Sunflower plot of life expectancy and birthrate

To display sunflowers, select Show sunflowers in the Scatterplot Options dialog box after creating the chart. See "Scatterplot Options" on p. 169.

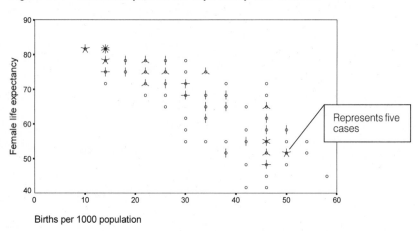

Figure 9.4 is a sunflower plot of the life expectancy and birthrate data. The solitary circles represent individual points. Note that many of the sunflowers with the largest number of petals are in the upper left corner of the plot. That's because most of the developed nations have very similar birthrates and life expectancies.

Am I supposed to count the petals on the sunflowers? No. Just let the density of the petals show you how the cases cluster. With sunflowers, you can easily distinguish between areas of the scatterplot that have many cases and few cases. That's all you want to do. ■ ■ ■

Scatterplot Matrices

So far, you've looked at the relationship between life expectancy and birthrate. What if you want to see how these variables relate to another variable, say percentage of urban population? You can certainly make additional plots of birthrate against percentage urban and of life expectancy against percentage urban. However, when you are interested in the relationships between several pairs of variables, you can make a scatterplot matrix of all of the variables of interest. A **scatterplot matrix** is a display that contains scatterplots for all possible pairs of variables.

Figure 9.5   Birthrate, life expectancy, and percentage urban

To obtain this scatterplot matrix, select the Matrix icon in the initial Scatterplot dialog box (see Figure 9.14). Then select the variables, as shown in Figure 9.17.

Scan first row to see how birthrate is related to the other variables

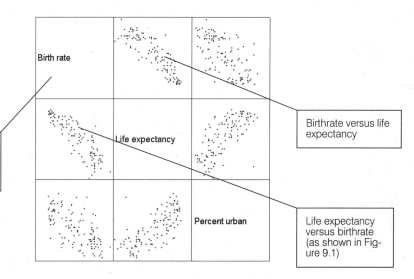

Birthrate versus life expectancy

Life expectancy versus birthrate (as shown in Figure 9.1)

Look at Figure 9.5, which is a scatterplot matrix of birthrate, life expectancy, and percentage urban. A scatterplot matrix has the same number of rows and columns as there are variables. In this example, you see three rows and three columns. Each cell of the matrix is a plot of a pair of variables. The labels in the diagonal cells tell you which variables are plotted in the other cells. For example, the first diagonal cell contains the label *Birth rate*. This tells you that, for all plots in the first row, the birthrate per 1000 population is plotted on the *Y* axis (the vertical axis). For all plots in the first column, the birthrate is plotted on the *X* axis (the horizontal axis). Similarly, the label *Life expectancy* in the second diagonal cell tells you that the life expectancy is plotted on the vertical axis for all plots in the second row and on the horizontal axis for all plots in the second column.

Look at the first plot in the first row. It's a plot of birthrate with life expectancy. This plot differs from the one you see in Figure 9.1, since female life expectancy is now on the horizontal axis instead of the vertical axis. (The first plot in the second row is the same as Figure 9.1.) In a scatterplot matrix, plots for all possible pairs of variables are displayed. The plots above the diagonal are the same as the plots below the diagonal. The only difference is that the variables are flipped. That is, the variables that are on the horizontal axis above the diagonal are on the vertical axis below the diagonal, and vice versa.

What's the easiest way to read a scatterplot matrix? Try to scan across an entire row or column. For example, by reading across the first row, you see how birthrate relates first to life expectancy and then to urbanization. Similarly, the last row tells you how urbanization relates to birthrate and then to life expectancy at birth. The easiest way to identify an individual plot in a scatterplot matrix is to look up or down to find which variable is on the horizontal axis, and look right or left to find out which variable is on the vertical axis. ▪ ▪ ▪

From the scatterplot matrix, you see that the strongest relationship appears to be between life expectancy and birthrate. There is a negative relationship between the two variables. As the birthrate decreases, the life expectancy increases. The birthrate also decreases with increasing urbanization, but not as strongly. That's not surprising, since urban dwellers are usually better educated than their rural counterparts. They also have less of an economic need for children than do people in agricultural areas. Life expectancy and urbanization are positively related. As urbanization increases, so does life expectancy. There's a strange point in the urbanization and life expectancy plots that you'll examine in the section "Identifying Unusual Points" on p. 162.

You can identify points in a scatterplot matrix in the same way as in a scatterplot. The point is labeled in all of the plots.

Overlay Plots

The scatterplots you've looked at so far show the values of a single pair of variables. One of the variables is plotted on the horizontal axis, and the other is plotted on the vertical axis. Sometimes it's informative to plot several pairs of variables on the same axes. For example, if you want to study the relationship between high school GPA and the percentile ranks on standardized tests of math skills and of verbal skills, you can make two plots: math percentile against GPA and verbal percentile against GPA. Since the scales for the variable pairs are the same for both plots, you can literally put one plot on top of the other. That's what an **overlay plot** does.

Figure 9.6 Overlay scatterplot of birth and death versus urbanization

To create this overlay scatterplot, select the Overlay icon in the initial Scatterplots dialog box (see Figure 9.14). Then select the variables, as shown in Figure 9.16.

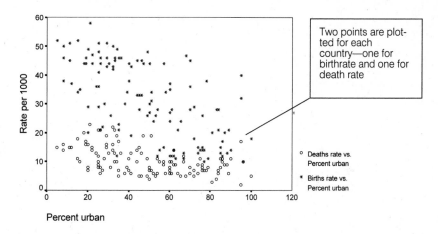

Look at Figure 9.6, which is an overlay plot of birthrate against percentage urban and death rate against percentage urban. The marker tells you whether the point is a birthrate or a death rate. Each country appears twice on the plot, once with its birthrate plotted against percentage urban and once with its death rate plotted against percentage urban.

How did this plot differ from the one in which you identify members of different groups by different markers? Although the plots might look similar, since several different markers are used to identify the points, the plots are completely different. Figure 9.3 plots two variables, with a third variable used to classify each country as developing or developed. Figure 9.6, the overlay scatterplot, plots two separate *pairs* of variables—really it's two scatterplots on top of one another. That means each country appears not once, but twice, in the overlay plot. The marker tells you which pair of variables is being plotted.

Figure 9.6 has a lot of points. You may have some difficulty seeing the relationships between the two pairs of variables. To make it easier to sort out what's going on, you can draw summary curves for each pair of variables. Look at Figure 9.7. It's the same as Figure 9.6, but there are now two curves, called lowess smooths, on the plot.

Figure 9.7 Overlay plot with lowess smooths

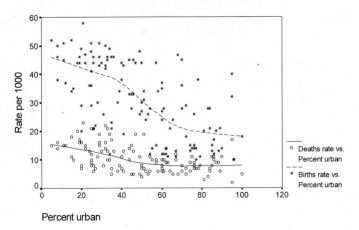

To display lowess smooths, select Total in the Scatterplot Options dialog box. Then select Fit Options to specify the lowess method (see "Scatterplot Options" on p. 169).

From the legend, you can tell which curve is for birthrate and which is for death rate. Now it's easier to see that both death rates and birthrates decrease as urbanization increases. The highest birthrates and death rates are for countries with little urbanization. You also see that birthrates decline more steeply than do death rates. Although the curves on the plot are not straight lines, they're not too far from being linear. That is, you could straighten out the curves and they would still be fairly good summaries of the relationships. In Part 4 of this book, you'll see how to fit straight lines that summarize points in a scatterplot.

Where did the curves come from? The curves drawn on the plots are called lowess smooths. (In case you haven't already guessed, that's an abbreviation for *locally weighted regression scatterplot smoothing!*) A lowess smooth doesn't make assumptions about the mathematical form of the relationship between the two variables. It just looks at cases that have similar values for the *X* variable and, using an intricate mathematical algorithm, figures out where a reasonable average *Y* value for them might be. By looking at a lowess smooth of a plot, you can get an idea of the relationship between the two variables. If your plot has areas with few points, the lowess smooth may not be good for them, since it depends on having points with similar *X* values. Lowess smoothing requires many computations, especially for large data sets, so it may take a while for your plots to be drawn.

You should use an overlay plot only when the plots that are being super-imposed have similar scales. You don't want to overlay plots of per capita domestic product against urbanization and birthrate against urbaniza-tion. Per capita domestic product and birthrate have very different val-ues, and plotting both of them on the same axis will result in a useless plot. The axis that shows both per capita GDP and birthrate will have a wide range, since it must accommodate numbers in the thousands. You'll be unable to see differences in birthrates on such a scale, since they will be bunched together. (If you want to plot variables with differ-ent scales on the same plot, you may want to standardize the variables. Then they will both have a mean of 0 and a standard deviation of 1.)

Three-Dimensional Plots

All the scatterplots you've looked at so far plotted the values of cases on two axes, the horizontal (X) axis and the vertical (Y) axis. The cases were represented in two dimensions. You can also plot data in three di-mensions. For example, you can make a scatterplot that shows simul-taneously the values of female life expectancy, urbanization, and birthrate.

Figure 9.8   3-D plot of life expectancy, birthrate, and urbanization

To create this 3-D scatterplot, select the 3-D icon in the Scatterplot dialog box (see Figure 9.14). Then select the variables, as shown in Figure 9.18.

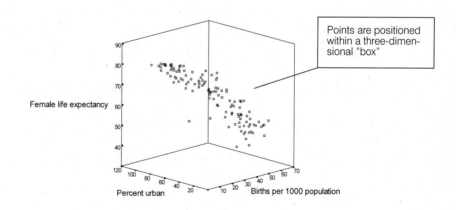

Look at Figure 9.8. Instead of a plot that looks flat, like a sheet of paper, you see what looks like a box. You now have three axes instead of two on which to plot the values of the variables. (The additional axis is not unexpectedly called the *Z* axis.) The SPSS 3-D Scatterplot procedure calls the axis on which life expectancy is plotted the *Y* axis, the axis on which percent urban is plotted the *X* axis, and the axis on which birthrate is plotted the *Z* axis. (From this plot you see that there are several points that are far removed from the rest. We'll examine them later.)

Figure 9.9   3-D plot with spikes

To draw spikes to the floor, select Floor for Spikes in the 3-D Scatterplot Options dialog box, as shown in Figure 9.22.

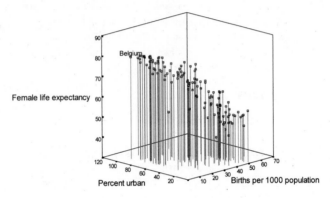

To make it easier to tell where the points are located, you can draw what are called **spikes**. Figure 9.9 is the same plot as Figure 9.8 with spikes drawn to the floor of the plot. The height of the spike tells you a point's value for the *Y* variable. By looking at the position of the bottom of the spike, you can see the values for the *X* and *Z* variables.

Look at the spike labeled *Belgium* in Figure 9.9. If you compare its height to the *Y* axis, you see that the value for life expectancy is around 80 years. Now look at the bottom of the spike. It's position on the percentage urban axis is about 95. On the birthrate axis, its position is about 10.

How did you get those numbers? Reading the numbers off a 3-D plot is tricky. Look at Figure 9.10. The point represents a case with values $Y=63$, $X=25$, and $Z=42$. To read the values for the point from the axes, you have to follow the arrows. The bottom of the spike indicates the position of the point in the XZ plane; to tell what the point's values are, you must draw lines perpendicular to the axes that define that plane, as shown. Similarly, to estimate the Y coordinate, you must first draw your own spike to visualize the position of the point within the XY plane (also shown). Remember, everything is in three dimensions. ■ ■ ■

Figure 9.10 Reading a 3-D scatterplot

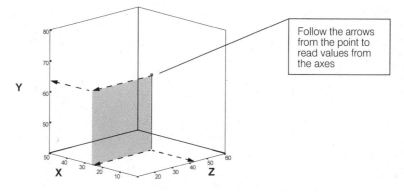

Follow the arrows from the point to read values from the axes

If you look at the heights of the spikes in Figure 9.9 you see that the tall spikes, which indicate long life expectancy, are for countries with low birthrates and high urbanization. Similarly, the shortest spikes are for countries with high birthrates and low urbanization. There is a transition from high to low spikes over the range of birthrates and urbanization.

Figure 9.11 3-D plot with countries identified by status

To identify countries by status, in the 3-D Scatterplot dialog box, specify develop for Set Markers by, as shown in Figure 9.18.

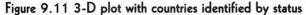
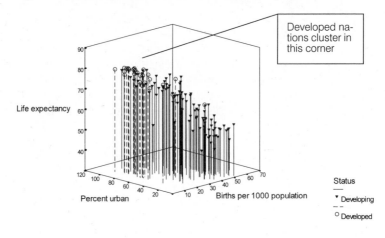

You can identify the points in Figure 9.8 as corresponding to developed or developing nations. This scatterplot is shown in Figure 9.11. Note how the developed countries cluster together in the corner that corresponds to high urbanization and low birthrates.

Identifying Unusual Points

You can identify unusual points in Figure 9.11 by looking for short spikes in the midst of tall ones. However, it's easier to spot unusual points when they're not obscured by a bunch of spikes. Figure 9.12 shows the original 3-D scatterplot with some of the points labeled.

Figure 9.12 3-D scatterplot with points labeled

To display country labels, select the country variable for Label Cases by, as shown in Figure 9.18. You can then display case labels as described in "Case Identification" on p. 173.

For information on locating a case in the Data Editor, see p. 175.

The point farthest removed from the rest is *Bhutan*. Instead of trying to read its values from the plot, you can select the point and then go to the Data Editor, where SPSS selects the case representing Bhutan. In the Data Editor, you see that the female life expectancy for Bhutan is 48 years. The birthrate is 40 per 1000 population, and the percentage urban is 95. Individually, none of these values is strange. There are a lot of countries with birthrates in the 40's, life expectancies in the 40's, or urban percentages in the 90's. What's strange about Bhutan is the combination of 95 for urban percentage and 48 for life expectancy. (You can also see the point as an outlier in the scatterplot matrix of life expectancy and percentage urban.)

Since you know that Bhutan is a tiny Himalayan kingdom, you should immediately suspect problems with the data. It's unlikely that the explanation is an intriguing sociological phenomenon at play. Sure enough, Bhutan is 95% rural, not 95% urban. So the value for percentage urban should be only 5.

? *What should I do now that I've found a problem with the data?* Fix it. Go into the Data Editor, and change the percentage urban value for Bhutan from 95 to 5. Then save the data file. If you don't do this, you won't get the correct answers in the subsequent chapters that use the *country.sav* data file. ■ ■ ■

Rotating 3-D Scatterplots

It's easy to examine a two-dimensional plot. You see the exact position of all the points. There aren't any surprises. Examining a three-dimensional plot is considerably more complicated. You can rotate it in all directions and get different views of the same plot. You can see if, in some views, the points cluster together, indicating a relationship among the three variables. SPSS has extensive facilities for rotating three-dimensional plots.

Figure 9.13 Rotated 3-D scatterplot

To rotate a 3-D scatterplot, click on

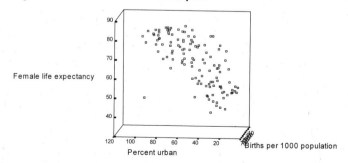

For a simple example of a 3-D rotation, look at Figure 9.13. The axes have been rotated so that you get an almost two-dimensional view of life expectancy and percentage urban. That's the same plot you see in the scatterplot matrix, except that the scale for urban goes from large to small.

Summary

How can you display the relationship between two variables that are measured on a scale with meaningful numeric values?

- A scatterplot displays the values of two variables for each case.
- A scatterplot matrix displays scatterplots of all possible pairs of variables.
- You can identify unusual points in a scatterplot by looking for points that are far removed from the rest.
- A 3-D scatterplot shows the values of three variables at once.

What's Next?

In this chapter, you constructed a variety of scatterplots that are essential for examining the relationships between variables. In Part 4 of this book, you'll learn how to quantify the strength of the relationship between two variables. You'll also learn ways to predict the values of one variable from those of other variables. In Chapter 10, which starts Part 3, you'll learn how to test hypotheses about the population based on results observed in samples.

How to Obtain a Scatterplot

The Scatterplot procedure displays two-dimensional plots or three-dimensional plots (as seen in perspective) of the actual values of two or more variables. You can easily produce bivariate scatterplots (with or without control variables), overlay scatterplots, scatterplot matrices, and 3-D scatterplots. Once you have generated a plot, you can use the Chart Editor to enhance it with such things as sunflowers or a best-fitting line or curve.

Note: This section provides information specific to creating and modifying scatterplots. For a general overview of the SPSS charting facility, see Appendix A.

Obtaining a Simple Scatterplot

▶ To open the Scatterplot dialog box (see Figure 9.14), from the menus choose:

Graphs
  Scatter...

Figure 9.14 Scatterplot dialog box

Select the icon for the chart type you want

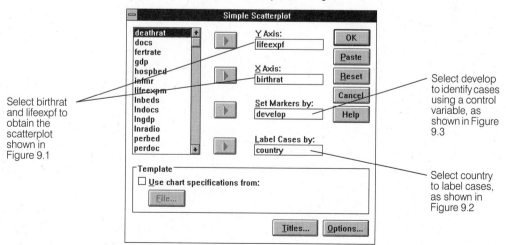

▶ Choose the icon for the chart type you want, and then click on Define.

This opens a dialog box where you can choose variables and options for the scatterplot (see Figure 9.15).

Figure 9.15 Simple Scatterplot dialog box

Select birthrat and lifeexpf to obtain the scatterplot shown in Figure 9.1

Select develop to identify cases using a control variable, as shown in Figure 9.3

Select country to label cases, as shown in Figure 9.2

▶ Select numeric variables for the vertical (Y) and horizontal (X) axes and move them into the appropriate boxes. You can request only one simple scatterplot at a time.

▶ Click on OK to produce the plot.

Optionally, you can move a case-label variable into the Label Cases by box in the Simple Scatterplot dialog box. The values of this variable can then be displayed as case labels in the plot. (See "Case Identification" on p. 173.)

If you wish, choose a chart template or specify Titles and Options, as described in Appendix A.

Scatterplot with Control Variable

In a simple, matrix, or 3-D scatterplot, you can specify a control variable whose value determines the plot symbol that is used for each case (see Figure 9.3).

▶ To specify a control variable, move a variable into the Set Markers by box, as shown in Figure 9.15.

Obtaining an Overlay Scatterplot

In the initial Scatterplot dialog box (see Figure 9.14), select the Overlay icon and click on Define to open the Overlay Scatterplot dialog box, as shown in Figure 9.16.

Figure 9.16 Overlay Scatterplot dialog box

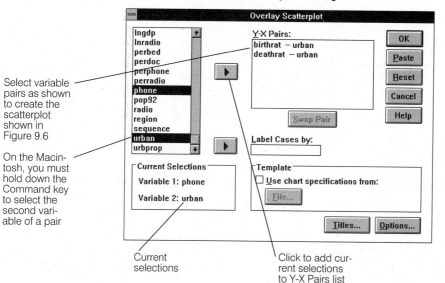

Select variable pairs as shown to create the scatterplot shown in Figure 9.6

On the Macintosh, you must hold down the Command key to select the second variable of a pair

Current selections

Click to add current selections to Y-X Pairs list

▶ Select two numeric variables in the source variable list and move the pair into the *Y-X* Pairs list. Until you select two variables, you won't be able to move into that list. If you select more than two variables in the source list, only the first two are used.

Notice that the list of variable pairs is described as *Y-X* Pairs. The first variable is going to be on the *Y* (vertical) axis, and the second on the *X* (horizontal) axis.

▶ If this is the reverse of what you want, select the pair of variables in the *Y-X* Pairs list and click on Swap Pair.

You can move a variable into the Label Cases by box, as discussed in "Simple Scatterplots" on p. 150. If you wish, choose a chart template or specify Titles and Options, as described in Appendix A. Click on OK to produce the plot.

Obtaining a Scatterplot Matrix

In the Scatterplot dialog box (see Figure 9.14), select the Matrix icon and click on Define to open the Scatterplot Matrix dialog box, as shown in Figure 9.17.

Figure 9.17 Scatterplot Matrix dialog box

Select birthrat, lifeexpf, and urban as shown to create the scatterplot matrix shown in Figure 9.5

▶ Select three or more numeric variables and move them into the Matrix Variables list. (Remember that you are requesting a matrix of plots; if you move six variables into the matrix, you will get 36 tiny plots on your screen.)

You can move a variable into the Label Cases by box, and you can move a control variable into the Set Markers by box. (These specifications apply to all plots in the matrix.) If you wish, choose a chart template or specify Titles and Options, as described in Appendix A. Click on OK to produce the plot.

Obtaining a 3-D Scatterplot

In the Scatterplot dialog box (see Figure 9.14), select the 3-D icon and click on Define to open the 3-D Scatterplot dialog box, as shown in Figure 9.18.

Figure 9.18 3-D Scatterplot dialog box

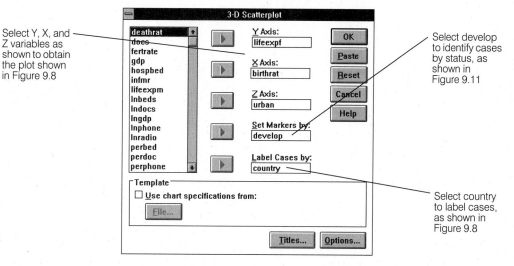

Select Y, X, and Z variables as shown to obtain the plot shown in Figure 9.8

Select develop to identify cases by status, as shown in Figure 9.11

Select country to label cases, as shown in Figure 9.8

▶ Select three or more numeric variables and move them into the *Y*, *X*, and *Z* axis boxes. The *y*-axis is vertical in the initial orientation of the plot, although you can rotate it as you please in the Chart Editor.

You can move a variable into the Label Cases by box, and you can move a control variable into the Set Markers by box. If you wish, choose a chart template or specify Titles and Options, as described in Appendix A. Click on OK to produce the plot.

Scatterplot Options

Scatterplot options allow you to display or suppress case labels, specify display of sunflowers, or add one or more fit lines to the chart.

Note: Before you can open the Options dialog box for a scatterplot (or modify any chart in any way), you must move the chart from the Chart Carousel, where it first appears, into a chart window. (See Appendix A to learn about the difference between the Chart Carousel and a chart window.)

Figure 9.19 Moving a chart from the Chart Carousel into a chart window

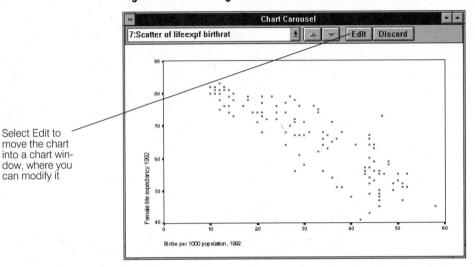

Select Edit to move the chart into a chart window, where you can modify it

▶ To move the chart into a chart window, select Edit on the Chart Carousel toolbar, as shown in Figure 9.19.

The chart window menus and toolbar are now displayed, as shown in Figure 9.23 on p. 174.

▶ From the menus choose:

Chart
  Options....

This opens a dialog box in which you can change options for the scatterplot. The exact appearance of the dialog box will vary depending on the type of scatterplot (see Figure 9.20 and Figure 9.22).

Options for 3-D Scatterplots

Figure 9.22 shows the 3-D Scatterplot Options dialog box. (See "Scatterplot Options" on p. 169 for instructions on how to open the dialog box.)

Figure 9.22 3-D Scatterplot Options dialog box

Select Floor to display spikes, as shown in Figure 9.9

The dialog box has several options specific to 3-D scatterplots (see "Options for Simple and Matrix Scatterplots" on p. 171 for descriptions of other options):

Spikes. Displays a line from each data point as specified by one of the following options:

    Floor. Spikes extend to the floor, or *XZ* plane (see Figure 9.9).

    Origin. Spikes end at the origin (0,0,0,).

    Centroid. Spikes are displayed from each point to the centroid of all the points.

Wireframe. Select an icon to specify what type of frame is displayed.

Case Identification

In scatterplots and boxplots, you can display case labels for all points in your chart, or for selected points.

Note: Before you can display case labels, you must first create the chart and move it into a chart window. (See Figure 9.19 to learn how to move a chart into a chart window.)

Displaying Labels for Selected Points

You display labels for selected cases using Point Selection mode.

Figure 9.23 Scatterplot in a chart window

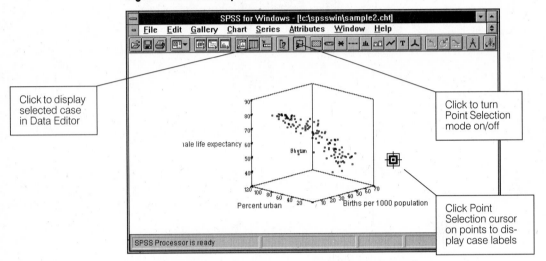

▶ To turn on Point Selection mode, click on the Point Selection tool on the chart window toolbar, as shown in Figure 9.23.

The cursor changes to the Point Selection cursor.

▶ Click on any point in the chart to display a label for that point.

The type of label depends on previous specifications. If you selected a variable to label cases when creating the chart (see Figure 9.15), the value label (or the value) of that variable will be displayed. If you didn't specify a label variable, the case number will be displayed. To turn off Point Selection mode, click on the Point Selection tool again.

Displaying Labels for All Points

If you have only a small number of points, you may want to display case labels for all points. You can do this easily by selecting On for Case Labels in the Scatterplot Options dialog box (see Figure 9.20).

Locating a Case in the Data Editor

If you select a point in a chart and then click on the Data Editor tool (see Figure 9.23), the Data Editor becomes the active window, and the selected point is highlighted, as shown in Figure 9.24.

Figure 9.24 Data Editor with selected case highlighted

c:\spsswin\country.sav

83:country   Bhutan

	country	pop92	urban	gdp	perradio	perphone	lifeexprn	lifeexpf	b
80	Vietnam	68.964	20	230	10.0	544.0	63	67	
81	Afghanistan	16.095	18	220	11.0	443.0	45	43	
82	Bangladesh	119.000	24	200	24.0	572.0	55	54	
83	Bhutan	1.660	95	199	64.0	675.0	50	48	
84	India	886.362	28	380	15.0	200.0	57	58	

Rotating a 3-D Scatterplot

On the chart window toolbar, click on the 3-D Scatterplot Rotation tool to open the 3-D Rotation dialog box, as shown in Figure 9.25.

Figure 9.25 3-D Rotation dialog box

To open this dialog box, click on

▶ Click the rotation icons to rotate the wireframe as desired. Then click on Apply to apply the change to the actual scatterplot.

You can rotate the plot in any of three dimensions: around a horizontal line, a vertical line, or a line perpendicular to the screen (coming right out of the screen toward you). To restore the wireframe to its original position before any change has been applied, click on Reset.

Spin Mode

*To turn spin
mode on and
off, click on*

You can also rotate a 3-D scatterplot using spin mode. In spin mode, the six rotation icons are displayed on the toolbar, allowing you to see the actual plotted points as you rotate the chart.

Exercises

Statistical Concepts

1. Indicate whether you would use the Crosstabs procedure, the Means procedure, or scatterplots to display the relationship between the following pairs of variables:

   a. Job satisfaction (measured on a scale of 1–4) and income in dollars

   b. Likelihood of buying a product and marital status

   c. Current stock price and profit-to-earning ratio

   d. Car color preference of husband and car color preference of wife

   e. Miles per gallon and weight in pounds for a car

   f. Hours studied for an examination and letter grade on the exam

   g. Job satisfaction and income measured in dollars

   h. Race and marital status

   i. Systolic blood pressure and age

   j. Husband's highest degree and wife's highest degree

2. The following table contains the age at first marriage, years of education, and gender for five people. Plot these values, identifying whether each is for a male or female.

agewed	educ	sex
18	12	M
22	13	F
30	16	M
16	10	M
25	18	F

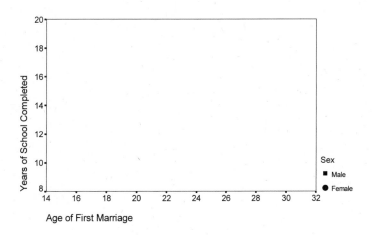

Data Analysis

Use the *gss.sav* data file to answer the following questions:

1. For the married couples in the General Social Survey, make a scatterplot of years of husband's education (*husbeduc*) against years of wife's education (*wifeduc*).

   a. Write a sentence describing the relationship.

   b. Go into the Chart Editor and edit the plot so that negative years of education do not appear on the axes.

   c. Change the scatterplot to a sunflower plot. Do you think the sunflower plot makes it easier to see what's going on?

   d. Identify each of the points on the scatterplot by how exciting the respondent perceives life to be (variable *life*). What problems do you see with this plot?

   e. Using point selection mode, identify by ID number the cases that have the value 0 for husband's or wife's education.

2. Make a scatterplot matrix of the respondent's education (*educ*), the respondent's mother's education (*maeduc*), and the respondent's father's education (*paeduc*).

   a. What can you tell from the plot about the relationships of the variables?

   b. Do the variables appear to be positively or negatively related?

c. By default, points that do not have valid values for all variables in the scatterplot matrix are excluded from the plot. Does that exclude any particular group of people from your plot? What type of people are excluded if you make a scatterplot of *husbeduc, wifeduc, paeduc,* and *maeduc*?

3. Make an overlay plot of the following two plots: hours worked (variable *hrs1*) and respondent's income (variable *rincmdol*); and hours of television watched per day (variable *tvhours*) and respondent's income. Describe the problems you see with this plot.

4. Make a three-dimensional plot of *educ, maeduc,* and *paeduc*. From this plot identify three cases that are outliers. Click on one of the points so that the ID is displayed. Then rotate the plot. Pay attention to how the identified point moves as you spin the plot in different directions. Do the points appear randomly scattered or do you see a pattern?

Use the *salary.sav* data file to answer the following questions:

5. Make a scatterplot with current salary (variable *salnow*) on the vertical axis and beginning salary (variable *salbeg*) on the horizontal axis.

a. Describe the relationship between the two variables.

b. Identify each of the points by gender. Does this help you see anything interesting in the data?

c. Turn the plot into a sunflower plot. Comment on the useful features of this kind of plot.

6. Make a scatterplot matrix of beginning salary, current salary, and educational level (variable *edlevel*). Comment on the relationships between pairs of these variables.

Use the *electric.sav* data file to answer the following questions:

7. Make a scatterplot of weight (variable *wt58*) on the vertical axis and height (variable *ht58*) on the horizontal axis.

a. Does there appear to be a relationship between the two variables? Describe it.

b. Edit the chart so that sunflowers are used to represent the points. What advantage, if any, do you see to this type of plot?

8. Plot weight against height, this time identifying each point by the respondent's vital status at 10 years (variable *vital10*). Does the relationship between height and weight appear to be different for those who are alive and for those who are not?

9. Make a scatterplot matrix of height, weight, and diastolic blood pressure (variable *dbp58*). Write a brief summary of what you see.

Use the *schools.sav* data file to answer the following question:

10. Using the plots available on the Graphs menu, examine the relationship between percentage of low income students (*loinc93*), percentage of limited English proficiency students (*lep93*), graduation rates (*grad93*), and the school performance variables. Write a report based on your observations. Include appropriate graphs.

Use the *country.sav* data file to answer the following questions:

11. Plot birthrate (variable *birthrat*) against infant mortality rate (variable *infmr*), identifying countries by their development status (variable *develop*). Edit the plot to draw a Lowess smooth. Use point selection mode to identify the countries that are different from the rest. Summarize the relationship between the two variables.

12. Make a scatterplot matrix of birth rate, infant mortality rate, and the number of doctors per 10,000 population (variable *docs*). Identify the country with the largest number of doctors per 10,000 population. Which country has the smallest? Describe the different relationships between the three pairs of variables.

13. Make a three-dimensional plot of birthrate, infant mortality rate, and the number of doctors. Click to identify one of the points which is removed from the rest. Spin the plot, looking at how the labeled point moves. Are there views in which the points cluster together more tightly than in others? Do different points appear to be outliers as you rotate the plot?

Use the *buying.sav* data file to answer the following questions:

14. Make a scatterplot of wives' buying scores and husbands' buying scores (variables *wsumbuy* and *hsumbuy*). Does there appear to be a relationship between the two variables?

15. Make a plot of wives' influence scores and husbands' influence scores (variables *wsuminf* and *hsuminf*). Does there seem to be a relationship between the scores?

Evaluating Results from Samples

What can you say about a population, based on the results observed in a random sample?

- Are the results you observe in a sample identical to the results you would observe from the entire population?
- What is the sampling distribution of a statistic?
- How is it used to test a hypothesis about the population?
- What factors determine how much sample means vary from sample to sample?
- What is an observed significance level?
- What is the binomial test, and when do you use it?

In previous chapters, you've answered questions like "What percentage of survey respondents are very satisfied with their jobs?" or "What is the relationship between job satisfaction and education?" All you did was describe the results you found in the General Social Survey (GSS). Nothing more.

In this section of the book, you'll begin to look at the problems you face when you want to draw conclusions about a larger number of people or objects than those actually included in your study. You'll learn how to draw conclusions about the population based on the results observed in a sample.

▶ This chapter uses generated computer data in the file *simul.sav.* For information on how to obtain the binomial test results shown in the chapter, see "Binomial Test" on p. 354 in Chapter 18.

From Sample to Population

In the General Social Survey sample, almost 44% of people employed full time rated themselves as being *very satisfied* with their jobs. Unless errors have been made while recording or entering the data, you know this for a fact. Similarly, you know exactly how old the people in the sample are, how much education they have, and so on. You can describe in great detail and with much certainty the results observed in this sample. Unfortunately, that's not really what's of interest. What you really want to do is draw conclusions about the larger group that the people in the GSS represent, the **population**.

The participants in the GSS are a sample from the population of adults in the United States. Based on the results you observe from the participants, you want to draw conclusions about *all* adults in the United States. You want to be able to say, for example, that in the United States, highly paid workers are more satisfied with their jobs than those paid less.

On first thought, that might not seem too complicated. Why not assume that what's true for the sample is also true for the population? That would certainly be simple. But would it always be correct? Do you really believe that, since 43.8% of the full-time workers in your sample are *very satisfied* with their jobs, that's exactly the percentage of *very satisfied* people in the population? Common sense tells you that it's very unlikely that the results you see in a sample are identical to those you would obtain if you made measurements or inquiries of the entire population of interest. If that were the case, one quick poll before an election would eliminate the need to even hold elections.

What's true instead is that different samples give different results, and it's highly unlikely that any one sample will hit the population results on the nose. To see what you can conclude about the population based on a sample, you must consider what results are possible when you select a sample from a population.

A Computer Model

Although we could use mathematical arguments to derive the properties of samples and populations, it's less intimidating and more fun to discover them for yourself. You can use the computer to keep drawing random samples from the same population and see how much the results change from sample to sample. This process is known as a **computer simulation**.

> *What's a random sample?* A **random sample** gives every member of the population (animal, vegetable, mineral, or whatever) the same chance of being included in the sample. No particular type of creature or thing is systematically excluded from the sample, and no particular type is more likely to be included than any other. Each member is also selected independently; including one particular member doesn't alter the chance of including another.
>
> A sample is **biased** if, for example, rich people have a better chance of being included than poor people, or healthier people are more likely to be selected than sick people. You can't draw correct conclusions about the population based on the results from such a sample. ▪ ▪ ▪

Let's use the computer to solve the following problem. A Noted Physician claims that she has a better treatment for the Disease of Interest. Of 10 patients who received her new treatment, 70% were cured. Extensive literature on the topic indicates that nationwide, only 50% of patients with this disease are cured. Based on the results of her experiment, can you tell if the physician has really made inroads into the treatment of this disease?

Are the Observed Results Unlikely?

To evaluate the physician's claim, you have to ask yourself the question, Are the results she observed (7 out of 10 cures) unlikely if the true population cure rate is 50%? You know that if half of all people with a disease can be cured, that doesn't mean that any time you select 10 patients, exactly 5 will be cured by the treatment. Consider a coin-tossing analogy. You know that if a coin is fair, heads and tails are equally likely. If you flip a fair coin ten times, however, you don't expect to see exactly 5 heads every 10 flips. Sometimes you get more heads, sometimes more tails. (Try flipping a coin 10 times and see how many heads—cures—you get. Record your results. Repeat this as many times as you have the patience for and then make a stem-and-leaf plot of the results. You can compare your results with those you'll see in this chapter.)

To evaluate the Noted Physician's claim, instead of spending the afternoon flipping a coin, you can use the computer to construct a population in which half of the patients are cured and half are not. That's the situation if the physician's claim is not true. Then you can have the computer take a random sample of 10 patients and record the percentage that are cured. Have it repeat this procedure 500 times.

The reason you're doing this is to see what kind of sample results are possible if the new treatment is not different from the standard one. You can then determine whether finding 70% cured in a sample of 10 patients is an unusual finding when the true cure rate is 50%.

A stem-and-leaf plot of the results of the 500 experiments is shown in Figure 10.1.

Figure 10.1 Stem-and-leaf plot of percentage cured for sample size 10

You can obtain stem-and-leaf plots using the Explore procedure, as described in Chapter 7. Select the variable cured10 in the Explore dialog box.

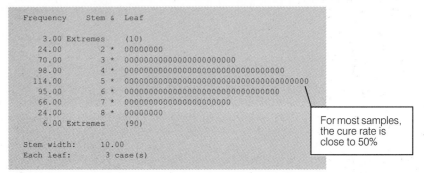

```
Frequency      Stem &  Leaf

    3.00 Extremes    (10)
   24.00       2 *   00000000
   70.00       3 *   0000000000000000000000000
   98.00       4 *   0000000000000000000000000000000000
  114.00       5 *   00000000000000000000000000000000000000
   95.00       6 *   0000000000000000000000000000000
   66.00       7 *   0000000000000000000000
   24.00       8 *   00000000
    6.00 Extremes    (90)

Stem width:     10.00
Each leaf:       3 case(s)
```

For most samples, the cure rate is close to 50%

From this plot, you can tell approximately how often you would expect to see various outcomes in samples of size 10. The distribution of all possible sample outcomes for a statistic (such as the percentage cured) is called the **sampling distribution** of the statistic.

? *Exactly what is a statistic anyhow?* A **statistic** is some characteristic of a sample. The sample mean and variance are both examples of statistics. The term **parameter** is used to describe the characteristics of the population. For example, the average height of people in your sample is a statistic. If you measured the heights of all people in the population of interest, that would be called a parameter of the population. Parameters are usually designated (by statisticians, at least) with Greek symbols. For example, the mean of a population is called μ (mu), while the mean of a sample is called $\bar{X}$. Similarly, the standard deviation of the population is called σ (sigma), while the value for a sample is called s. Most of the time, population values, or parameters, are not known. You must estimate them based on statistics calculated from samples. ■ ■ ■

The sampling distribution is usually calculated mathematically. In this case, you're using a computer to give you some idea of what it looks like. In Figure 10.1, you see that for most samples, the percentage of cures is close to 50%. In fact, 307 out of the 500 experiments resulted in cure rates of 40%, 50%, or 60%. The further you move from 50%, in either direction, the fewer samples you see. Although various outcomes are possible, the outcomes are not equally likely. For example, only 6 experiments out of 500 resulted in a cure rate of 90% or greater.

You can calculate descriptive statistics for the data summarized in Figure 10.1. These summary statistics are shown in Figure 10.2. The values range from a minimum of 10% to a maximum of 90%, but the mean is very close to 50%. (In fact, for the mathematically computed sampling distribution, the mean value is exactly 50%, the mean of the population from which the samples are being drawn.) The standard deviation of the percentages, labeled *Std Dev* in Figure 10.2, is 16.22%. The standard deviation tells you how much the percentage cured varies in samples of size 10. (The standard deviation of the distribution of all possible values of a statistic is called the **standard error** of the statistic. For example, the standard deviation of all possible values of a sample mean is called the standard error of the mean.)

Figure 10.2 Descriptive statistics for samples of size 10

You can obtain these statistics using the Descriptives procedure, as described in Chapter 5.

```
Number of valid observations (listwise) =        500.00

                                                    Valid
Variable       Mean    Std Dev   Minimum   Maximum      N   Label

CURED10       50.02     16.22     10.00     90.00     500
```

What's the difference between a standard deviation and a standard error? Standard deviation refers to the variability of the observations in a sample. The term standard error is used when you are talking about the variability of a statistic. For example, if you have a sample of 10 systolic blood pressures, you can calculate their mean, variance, and standard deviation in the usual way. From the standard deviation of the 10 blood pressure measurements, you can also estimate how much *average* blood pressures calculated from samples of 10 people vary. That's the standard error of the mean for samples of this size. Figure 10.2 contains descriptive statistics for 500 means for samples of size 10. The standard deviation of these 500 means is an estimate of the standard error of the mean for samples of size 10. ■ ■ ■

Using Figure 10.1 as a guideline, you can estimate whether the physician's results are unusual if the true cure rate is 50%. You see that 96 out of 500 simulated experiments (19.2%) resulted in cure rates of 70% or more. That indicates that even if the new treatment is no better than the standard, you would expect to see cure rates at least as large as those observed by the physician almost 1 out of 5 times you repeated the experiment. (In fact, it is possible to calculate mathematically that the probability of obtaining 7 or more cures in a sample of 10 is close to 17% when the true cure rate is 50%.)

Of course, it's always possible that the new treatment is really *less* effective than the usual treatment. So if you want to test the hypothesis that the new treatment is not different from the standard treatment, you must evaluate the probability of results as extreme as the one observed in either direction—increasing or decreasing the cure rate. You can estimate from Figure 10.1 that the probability of 30% or fewer cures and the probability of 70% or more cures is $(96 + 97) / 500 = 38.6\%$.

Based on this, you have little reason to believe that the Noted Physician is really onto something. Her results are certainly not incompatible with samples selected from a population in which the true cure rate is 50%.

? *Why look at cure rates of 70% or more* and *cure rates of 30% or less?* Consider the following analogy. Your friend gives you a coin and claims it is not fair. That is, heads and tails are not equally likely. Your friend wants your opinion. What outcomes will make you suspicious of the coin? Obviously, too many, or too few heads (or tails) will cause you to be suspicious. You have to consider both possibilities if you don't know whether the coin is biased in favor of heads or tails. On the other hand, if you know that the coin would only be rigged in favor of heads, because that's what the coin's owner always bets on, you can ignore the possibility of getting too few heads.

Returning to the Noted Physician example, you are interested in both possibilities—too few and too many cures. That's because it's possible that the new treatment may work worse than the standard, and you want to know that. If there is a reason why the new treatment can't be worse—for example, if it involves adding meditation to the standard treatment, you can restrict your attention to cure rates at least as large as the one observed. ▪ ▪ ▪

The Effect of Sample Size

As you saw above, when the true cure rate is 50%, there's a good chance that anywhere from 3 to 7 patients could be cured in a sample of 10. Most of the outcomes that can occur would not be considered unusual, because they could reasonably occur if the true cure rate is 50%. What's more, if the new treatment results in a cure rate of 60% or 70%, you probably would not detect the improvement, since many sample rates that are compatible with true rates of 60 or 70% are also compatible with the 50% rate. That means that based on a sample of only 10 patients, it's very difficult to evaluate a new treatment.

Can you ever tell from a sample of just 10 patients that a new treatment is better? Yes. Since the existence of one little green man could convince you that there's life on Mars, similarly, 10 cures of a previously incurable disease could convince you that it's worth pursuing your treatment. It all depends on how unlikely your results are.   ■ ■ ■

To see what effect sample size has on your ability to evaluate the Noted Physician's claim, consider what happens if you take samples of 40 patients, instead of just 10, from the same population with a cure rate of 50%. The results of this computer experiment are shown in Figure 10.3. (Note that each stem in the plot is now divided into two rows.) When you compare Figure 10.3 with Figure 10.1, you see that the values are much closer to 50% than before. Values greater than 60% or less than 40% are now noticeably less likely. These rates were not particularly unusual when you had samples of 10 patients. Based on Figure 10.3, you would estimate your chance of finding a sample rate of 70% or more or 30% or less when the true rate is 50% to be about 3 in 500, 0.6%. That means that only about 1 in 200 times would such a cure rate occur if the new treatment doesn't differ from the standard treatment.

In summary, when you have samples of 40 cases, an observed rate of 70% or more, or 30% or less, is possible, but not very likely when the true population rate is 50%. If the physician sees the same cure rate of 70% based on a sample of 40 patients, you would be more likely to believe that perhaps she's onto something. Her results really would be unusual when the true cure rate is 50%.

? *Just how unusual does "unusual" need to be?* The rule of thumb that is usually used to characterize results as unusual is a probability of 5% or less. That is, if results as extreme or more extreme than those observed are expected to occur in 5 (or fewer) samples out of 100, the results are considered unusual, or statistically significant. ■ ■ ■

Figure 10.3 Stem-and-leaf plot of percentage cured for sample size 40

To obtain this stem-and-leaf plot, select the variable cured40 in the Explore dialog box.

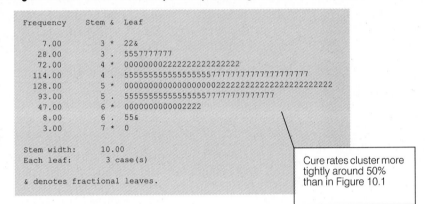

```
    Frequency     Stem &  Leaf

        7.00        3 *  22&
       28.00        3 .  5557777777
       72.00        4 *  0000000022222222222222222
      114.00        4 .  5555555555555555577777777777777777777777
      128.00        5 *  0000000000000000000222222222222222222222222
       93.00        5 .  5555555555555555577777777777777777
       47.00        6 *  0000000000002222
        8.00        6 .  55&
        3.00        7 *  0

    Stem width:    10.00
    Each leaf:      3 case(s)

    & denotes fractional leaves.
```

Cure rates cluster more tightly around 50% than in Figure 10.1

Larger samples improve your chances of detecting a difference in the cure rates (if in fact there is one) because there is less variability in the possible outcomes. Consider Figure 10.4, which contains descriptive statistics for the distribution shown in Figure 10.3. The mean value is again close to 50%. The standard deviation, however, is much smaller than for samples of size 10. It is now 7.29%, compared to the standard deviation of 16.22% in Figure 10.2. There's a pattern in the way that sample size affects the variance of the sampling distribution of means. If you increase the sample size by a factor of four, the variance decreases by a factor of four. Since the standard deviation is the square root of the variance, it decreases by a factor of two.

Figure 10.4 Descriptive statistics for samples of size 40

```
Number of valid observations (listwise) =        500.00


                                              Valid
Variable      Mean    Std Dev   Minimum   Maximum      N   Label

CURED40      49.84      7.29     30.00     70.00      500
```

The standard error of the mean is much smaller than for samples of size 10

The Binomial Test

In the previous example, you estimated the probability of various outcomes of an experiment from a stem-and-leaf plot obtained by repeated samples from the same population. The reason for doing it this way is to show you that when you take a sample from a population, the value you calculate for a statistic such as the mean is one of many possible values you can obtain. The possible values have a distribution—the sampling distribution of the statistic. Results vary from sample to sample, and you must take this variability into account when drawing conclusions about the population based on results observed from a sample.

Fortunately, in most situations, you don't need to personally determine the possible outcomes and their likelihoods by performing computer experiments. These can be mathematically calculated for you by SPSS. For example, you can use the **binomial test** to determine whether an observed cure rate is unlikely if the true rate is 50%. Your goal is to compare your experiment's success rate to a standard or usual rate. You observe the outcome of interest for a sample of subjects or objects.

To use the binomial test, your experiment or study must have only two possible outcomes, such as cured/not cured, pass/fail, buy/not buy, defective/not defective, and so on. All of the observations must be independent, and the probability of success must be the same for each member of the sample population.

? *What do you mean by independent?* For observations to be **independent**, one subject's response can't influence that of another. For example, if students collaborate on an exam, their scores are not independent. One student's results influence those of another. If you make multiple observations on the same subject, the observations are similarly not independent. Curing the same patient from 10 bouts of a disease is not equivalent to curing 10 patients from 1 bout. The 10 observations from a single patient are not independent. ■ ■ ■

Figure 10.5 shows the results of the binomial test for the 10-subject experiment. You see that there are 10 cases, 7 of which are coded 1, indicating a cure, and 3 of which are coded 0, indicating no cure. The population value that you want to test against (0.5) is labeled *Test Prop.* The proportion of successes in the sample, 0.7, is labeled *Obs. Prop.* The probability of obtaining results as extreme or more extreme than the ones you observe in your sample, when the true probability of a cure is 0.5, is labeled *2-Tailed P.* (*P* is for *probability*.) This probability has a special name: it's called the **observed significance level**.

The observed significance level tells you that the probability of obtaining a cure rate of 70% or greater or 30% or less, when the true cure rate is 50%, is 0.3438. (Note how close this exact probability is to your estimated probability of 0.386 from Figure 10.1.) Since the observed significance level is larger than 0.05, the usual frame of reference, you don't have enough evidence to believe that the physician has achieved a cure rate different from 50%. The sample with an observed cure rate of 70% is not particularly unusual if the true population cure rate is 50%. In fact, more than 34% of samples from this population are as unusual as the one sample the physician observed.

Figure 10.5 Binomial test: sample size 10

*For instructions
on how to obtain
a binomial test,
see p. 354 in
Chapter 18.*

```
      Cases
                            Test Prop. =   .5000
        7    = 1            Obs. Prop. =   .7000
        3    = 0
        ---                 Exact Binomial
       10   Total           2-Tailed P =   .3438
```

There is a 34% chance of observing a cure rate as extreme as 70% when the true rate is 50%

The results from the 40-patient experiment are shown in Figure 10.6. There are now 28 cases with the response of 1, and 12 cases with the response of 0, giving the same observed proportion of 0.70. The test proportion is unchanged at 0.50. The observed significance level is 0.0177. That means that, with samples of size 40, you would expect to see samples as unusual as the one observed less than 2% of the time. (Again, this value is reasonably close to the empirical estimate of 0.6% from Figure 10.3.) If the physician finds a 70% cure rate based on 40 patients, you're much more likely to believe that the physician is doing better than the usual 50%.

Figure 10.6 Binomial test: sample size 40

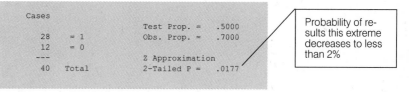

```
Cases
                     Test Prop. =   .5000        Probability of re-
   28    = 1         Obs. Prop. =   .7000        sults this extreme
   12    = 0                                     decreases to less
                                                 than 2%
   ---               Z Approximation
   40    Total       2-Tailed P =   .0177
```

Would you embrace her cure based only on these results? Of course not. A statistical analysis is useless if a study is poorly designed. Here are some important concerns: How were patients selected for inclusion in her study? Is there something about them that would make them more likely to be cured than those in the population at large? Were there objective criteria for establishing a cure, or was it a subjective judgment? Did the evaluator and/or the patient know that a new drug was being used?

The correct way to conduct an evaluation of a new treatment is to allocate patients randomly to two treatment groups. One receives the standard treatment, and the other receives the new one. Ideally, neither the patient nor the physician knows which treatment the patient is receiving. Evaluation is done, based on well-established criteria, by physicians who are unaware of which patients received which treatment. These precautions help to ensure that the results of the study measure what they were intended to measure.

Summary

What can you say about a population, based on the results observed in a random sample?

- When you take a sample from a population, you won't get the same results as you would if you had data for the entire population.
- The sampling distribution of a statistic tells you, for a particular sample size, about the distribution of all possible sample values of that statistic.
- From the sampling distribution of a statistic, you can tell if observed sample results are unusual under particular circumstances.
- As the sample size increases, the variability of statistics calculated from the sample decreases.
- The observed significance level is the probability of observing a sample difference at least as the large as the one observed, when there is no difference in the population.
- A binomial test is used to test the hypothesis that a variable comes from a binomial population with a specified probability of an event occurring. The variable can have only two values.

What's Next?

In this chapter, you saw that the results you observe when you perform an experiment or conduct a survey are only one of many possible outcomes. Different samples from the same population give different results. You also saw how sampling distributions can be used to determine how likely or unlikely various sample results are. In Chapter 11, you'll learn more about testing hypotheses about a population, based on results observed in a sample. You'll also learn about the importance of the normal distribution in hypothesis testing.

Exercises

Statistical Concepts

1. In a large university, there is a proposal to drop statistics as a requirement for graduation. Each of the 500 professors at the university commissions a survey to gauge student support for the proposal. Each survey contains a random sample of 50 students. The results are summarized in the following table and stem-and-leaf plot:

```
Valid cases:        500.0   Missing cases:        .0   Percent missing:      .0


Mean        40.6153  Std Err       .2887  Min      18.2073  Skewness    -.1179
Median      40.7617  Variance   41.6639  Max      57.3425  S E Skew     .1092
5% Trim     40.6620  Std Dev     6.4548  Range    39.1352  Kurtosis     .2157
95% CI for Mean (40.0481, 41.1824)        IQR       8.1217  S E Kurt     .2180


Frequency     Stem &  Leaf

      6.00 Extremes    (18), (21), (22), (24)
      2.00      2 f  5
      7.00      2 s  677
      8.00      2 .  899
     24.00      3 *  00000011111
     21.00      3 t  2222333333
     40.00      3 f  44444444455555555555
     61.00      3 s  6666666666666677777777777777777
     58.00      3 .  8888888888888888889999999999
     68.00      4 *  0000000000000000011111111111111111
     58.00      4 t  2222222222222222333333333333
     53.00      4 f  4444444444444455555555555555
     30.00      4 s  66666667777777
     22.00      4 .  88888899999
     20.00      5 *  000001111
     10.00      5 t  22233
     10.00      5 f  4445
      1.00      5 s  &
      1.00 Extremes    (57)

Stem width:      10.00
Each leaf:      2 case(s)


& denotes fractional leaves.
```

Based on the stem-and-leaf plot and summary statistics:

a. What is your best guess for the percentage of students favoring the proposal?

b. When the 500 professors presented their results to the president, she was aghast that the results of all of the surveys were not similar. She is considering censuring the professors whose polls were far removed from the average value. She thinks that they "rigged" their polls to support their own viewpoints. How would you defend the professors at their hearing?

c. Based on the stem-and-leaf plot, if the true percentage favoring the proposal is 40%, what's the probability that a poll will estimate the value to be 25% or greater? 55% or greater? Less than 35%?

2. As superintendent of Chicago schools, you are interested in seeing whether average ACT scores have improved between 1993 and 1994. You obtain a sample of 56 schools and find that scores have improved in 19 and worsened in 37.

a. How can you tell if your observed results are plausible if there has been no change in average ACT scores?

b. From the binomial test, you find that the observed significance level is 0.0231. Does this support the claim that ACT scores have improved?

c. Explain to the mayor whether it's possible that average ACT scores have not really changed?

d. What's the probability that you would see results as extreme as the ones observed when average ACT scores have not changed?

Data Analysis

Use the *gss.sav* data file to answer the following questions:

1. A social science researcher claims that half of the adults in the United States are male and half are female. Assume that the General Social Survey respondents are a random sample of the United States population.

a. What percentage of the sample are males? Females?

b. If the adult population is really half male and half female are your observed results unusual?

c. What do you think about the researcher's claim in light of the General Social Survey data?

2. A sociologist claims that half of adults in the United States believe in a life after this one.

a. Analyze the variable *postlife* and write a brief commentary on the sociologist's claim.

b. What if the sociologist claimed that 3 out of 4 adults believe in life after death? Based on the data, would you believe his claim?

3. Your mother wants you to change your college major from opera to statistics. She claims that only 1 out of 5 people like opera (codes of 1 or 2 for variable *opera*), whereas everyone likes statistics. Use the binomial test to see if you can dispute your mother's claim about opera. (You know she's right about statistics.) Write a letter to your mother explaining your findings. (Or e-mail her!)

The Normal Distribution

What is the normal distribution, and why is it important for data analysis?

- What does a normal distribution look like?
- What is a standard normal distribution?
- What is the Central Limit Theorem, and why is it important?

In Chapter 10, you learned how to evaluate a claim about the mean of a variable that has two possible values. Using the binomial test, you calculated the probabilities of getting various sample results when the probability of a success was assumed to be known. In this chapter, you'll learn how to test claims about the mean of a variable that has more than two values. You'll also learn about the normal distribution and the important role it plays in statistics.

▶ This chapter examines data on serum cholesterol levels from the *electric.sav* data file. In addition, some figures use simulated data sets included in the file *simul.sav*. The histograms and output shown can be obtained using the SPSS Graphs menu (see Appendix A) and the Descriptives procedure (see Chapter 5).

The Normal Distribution

You may have noticed that the shapes of the two stem-and-leaf plots in Chapter 10 are similar. They look like bells (on their sides). The same data are displayed as histograms in Figure 11.1 and Figure 11.2, where a bell-shaped distribution with the same mean and variance as the data is superimposed. You can see that most of the values are bunched in the center. The farther you move from the center, in either direction, the fewer the number of observations. The distributions are also more or less symmetric. That is, if you divide the distribution into two pieces at the peak, the two halves of the distribution are very similar in shape, but mirror images of each other. (The theoretical bell distribution is perfectly symmetric.)

Figure 11.1 Simulated experiments: sample size 10

You can obtain histograms using the Graphs menu, as described in Appendix A.

In the Histograms dialog box, select the variables cured10 and cured40.

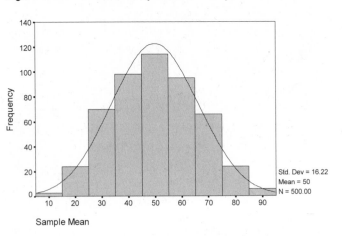

Figure 11.2 Simulated experiments: sample size 40

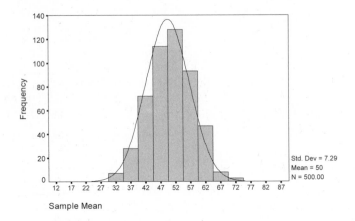

Many variables—such as blood pressure, weight, and scores on standardized tests—turn out to have distributions that are bell-shaped. For example, look at Figure 11.3, which is a histogram of cholesterol levels for a sample of 239 men enrolled in the Western Electric study (Paul et al., 1963). Note that the shape of the distribution is very similar to that in Figure 11.2. That's a pretty remarkable coincidence, since Figure 11.2 is a plot of many sample means from a distribution that has only two values (1=cured, 0=not cured), while Figure 11.3 is a plot of actual cholesterol values.

Figure 11.3 Histogram of cholesterol values

*To obtain this
histogram, open
the electric.sav
data file and
select chol58 in
the Histograms
dialog box.*

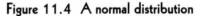

Std. Dev = 52.59
Mean = 264
N = 240.00

Serum Cholesterol (mg/dl)

The bell distribution that is superimposed on Figure 11.1, Figure 11.2, and Figure 11.3 is called the **normal distribution**. A mathematical equation specifies exactly the distribution of values for a variable that has a normal distribution. Consider Figure 11.4, which is a picture of a normal distribution that has a mean of 100 and a standard deviation of 15. The center of the distribution is at the mean. The mean of a normal distribution has the same value as the most frequently occurring value (the mode), and as the median, the value that splits the distribution into two equal parts.

Figure 11.4 A normal distribution

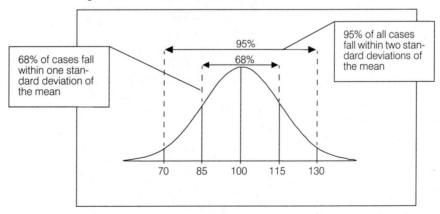

If a variable has exactly a normal distribution, you can calculate the percentage of cases falling within any interval. All you have to know are the mean and the standard deviation. Suppose that scores on IQ tests are normally distributed, with a mean of 100 and a standard deviation of 15, as was once thought to be true. In a normal distribution, 68% of all values fall within one standard deviation of the mean, so you would expect 68% of the population to have IQ scores between 85 (one standard deviation below the mean) and 115 (one standard deviation above the mean). Similarly, 95% of the values in a normal distribution fall within two standard deviations of the mean, so you would expect 95% of the population to have IQ scores between 70 and 130.

Since a normal distribution can have any mean and standard deviation, the location of a case within the distribution is usually given by the number of standard deviations it is above or below the mean. (Recall from Chapter 5 that this is called a standard score or Z score.) A normal distribution in which all values are given as standard scores is called a **standard normal distribution**. A standard normal distribution has a mean of 0, and a standard deviation of 1. For example, a person with an IQ of 100 would have a standard score of 0, since 100 is the mean of the distribution. Similarly a person with an IQ of 115 would have a standard score of +1, since the score is one standard deviation (15 points) above the mean, while a person with an IQ of 70 would have a standard score of –2, since the score is two standard deviation units (30 points) below the mean.

Figure 11.5 The standard normal distribution

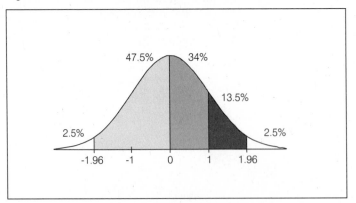

Some of the areas in a standard normal distribution are shown in Figure 11.5. Since the distribution is symmetric, half of the values are greater than 0, and half are less. Also, the area to the right of any given positive score is the same as the area to the left of the same negative score. For example, 16% of cases have standardized scores greater than +1, and 16% of cases have standardized scores less than –1. Appendix D gives areas of the normal distribution for various standard scores. The exercises show you how to use SPSS to calculate areas in a normal distribution.

If you're more than 2 standard deviations from the mean on some characteristic, does that mean you're abnormal? Not necessarily. For example, pediatricians often evaluate a child's size by finding percentile values. They may tell the parents that their child is at the 2.5th percentile, or 97.5th percentile for height. (For a normal distribution, these percentiles correspond to standardized scores of –2 and +2.) The small or large percentile values don't necessarily indicate that something is wrong. Even if you took a group of healthy children and looked at their height distribution, some of them would be more than two standard deviations from the mean. Somebody has to fall into the tails of the normal distribution. This also leads to a convincing argument against grading on the curve. Even in a brilliant, hard-working class, some students will receive scores more than 2 standard deviations below the mean. Does that make their performance unacceptable? Not necessarily. ■ ■ ■

Samples from a Normal Distribution

If you look again at Figure 11.3, you'll see that the normal distribution that is superimposed on the cholesterol data doesn't fit the data values exactly. The observed data are not perfectly normal. Instead, the distribution of the data values can be described as approximately normal. That's not surprising. Even if you assume that cholesterol values have a perfect normal distribution in the population, you wouldn't expect a sample from this distribution to be exactly normal. You know that a sample is not a perfect picture of the population. You expect that samples from a normal population would appear to be more or less bell shaped, but it would be unrealistic to expect that every sample is exactly normal. In fact, even the population distribution of most variables is not exactly normal. Instead, it's usually the case that the normal distribution is a good approximation. Slight departures from the normal distribution have little effect on statistical analyses that assume that the distribution of data values is normal.

Means from a Normal Population

Since we've established that the normal distribution is a reasonable representation of the distribution of data values for many variables, we can use this information in testing statistical hypotheses about such variables. For example, suppose you want to test whether highly paid CEO's have average cholesterol levels which are different from the population as a whole. In 1991, *Forbes* sent out a survey to the 200 most highly compensated CEO's requesting their cholesterol levels. The 21 CEO's who responded had an average cholesterol of 193 mg/dL. Assume that, in the population, cholesterol levels are normally distributed with a mean of 205 and a standard deviation of 35. Based on this information, how would you determine if the CEO's differ from the rest of us not only in their net worth but in average cholesterol as well?

To answer this question, you need to know whether 193 is an unlikely sample value for the mean, when the true population value is 205. To arrive at this information, you'll follow the same procedure as you did in Chapter 10. However, instead of taking samples from a population in which only two values can occur, you'll take repeated samples from a normal population.

Figure 11.6 Distribution of 500 sample means

To obtain this histogram, open the simul.sav file and select the variable normal21 in the Histograms dialog box.

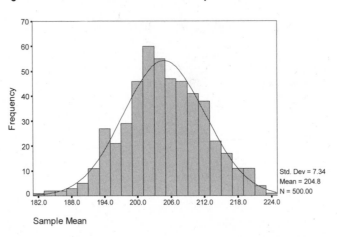

Figure 11.6 shows the distribution of 500 sample means from a normal distribution with a mean of 205 and a standard deviation of 35. Each mean is based on 21 cases. As you can see, the distribution of sample means is also approximately normal. That's always the case when you calculate sample means for data from a normal population.

The mean of the sample means is very close to 205, the population value. In fact, for the theoretical sampling distribution of the means, the value is exactly 205. (Remember, the theoretical distribution of sample means is mathematically derived and tells you precisely what the distribution of the sample means is for all possible samples of a particular size.) In Figure 11.6, the standard deviation of the means, also known as the **standard error of the mean**, is 7.34.

Standard Error of the Mean

You saw in Chapter 10 that the standard error of the mean tells you how much sample means from the same population vary. It depends on two things: how large a sample you take (that is, the number of cases used to compute the mean) and how much variability there is in the population. Means based on large numbers of cases vary less than means based on small numbers of cases. Means calculated from populations with little variability vary less than means calculated from populations with large variability.

If you know the population standard deviation (or variance) and the number of cases in the sample, you can calculate the standard error of the mean by dividing the standard deviation by the square root of the number of cases. In this example, the population standard deviation is 35 and the number of cases is 21, so the standard error of the mean is:

$$\frac{35}{\sqrt{21}} = 7.64 \qquad\qquad \textbf{Equation 11.1}$$

Note that the value we calculated based on the 500 samples with 21 hypothetical CEO's in each sample was not exactly 7.64, but very close. What we obtained was an *estimate* of the true value. That's because we did not take all possible samples from the population, but restricted our attention to 500.

> **?** *Will the standard error of the mean always be smaller than the standard deviation of the data values?* Yes. It's always the case that the standard error of the mean is smaller than the standard deviation of the data values. That makes sense if you think about it. When you calculate a mean, it falls in between the smallest and largest sample values. It's not as extreme as the actual data values in your sample. Thus the mean has less variability than the original observations. The larger the sample that you take, the more you smooth out the variability of the individual data values when you calculate the mean. ■ ■ ■

Are the Sample Results Unlikely?

Now that you know about the important properties of the sampling distribution of the mean from a normal population, let's return to the cholesterol levels of the CEO's. Figure 11.6 gives you a rough idea of how often you can expect various values for sample means when cholesterol is normally distributed in the population, with a mean of 205 and a standard deviation of 35. It's easy to see that the observed sample value of 193 is not a particularly unusual value.

You can use the characteristics of the normal distribution to calculate *exactly* how often you would expect to see, based on 21 cases, a sample mean of 193 (12 less than the population mean) or less, or 217 or greater (12 more than the population mean). You're interested in both large and small cholesterol values, since you don't know in advance whether CEO values will be larger or smaller than those of the general population. It may be that the *foie gras* on Parisian business trips raises their cholesterol levels. Or that exercising in swanky health clubs while the rest of us work decreases their cholesterol levels.

First, you must calculate a standard score for the observed mean. You calculate it in the usual way: subtract the population mean from the observed mean and then divide by the standard deviation. The only trick to remember is that since you're dealing with a distribution of means, you must use the standard deviation of the means (the standard error of the mean), not the standard deviation of the sample values themselves. In our example, the standard score is

$$Z = \frac{193 - 205}{7.64} = -1.57$$

Equation 11.2

Look at Figure 11.7 for a summary of the situation.

Figure 11.7 How unlikely is a sample mean of 193?

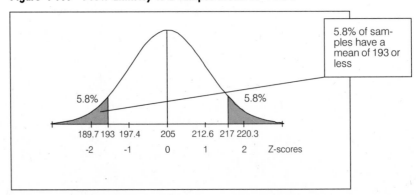

You see that the distribution of all possible sample means of 21 cases is normal, with a mean of 205 mg/dL and a standard error of 7.64 mg/dL. The observed sample mean of 193 has a standard score of −1.57. In a normal distribution, 11.6% of the cases have standardized values less than −1.57 or greater than +1.57. Based on this, you don't have enough evidence to conclude that CEO cholesterol levels are different from those in the general population. (The observed significance level of 0.116 is larger than 0.05, the usual criterion for unusual.)

> *Since only 21 out of 200 CEO's responded, shouldn't you be concerned about the results from a survey that has a response rate of 10.5%?* Absolutely. There are many reasons why those who responded to the survey may differ from those who did not. It may be that CEO's with low cholesterol levels are more likely to volunteer this information than CEO's with high cholesterol levels. Or it may be that CEO's who have experienced medical problems are more likely to know, and perhaps to volunteer, their cholesterol levels than CEO's who are healthy. Our analysis was based on the rather shaky assumption that CEO's who responded don't differ from those who didn't. We also made the simplifying assumption that middle-aged males have the same cholesterol distribution as the general population. If this isn't the case we'd have to compare CEO values to those for middle-aged males. (Unfortunately, all results were from middle-aged males.) Our analysis also assumes that the CEO's reported their correct current cholesterol values. Anyone who has read an annual report to shareholders knows that CEO's can cast any kind of data in the best possible light.

Testing a Hypothesis

In the previous example, you used statistical methods to test a hypothesis about the population based on results observed in a sample. Here's a summary of the procedure you followed:

1. You wanted to see if the average cholesterol levels of highly paid CEO's differ from those of the general population. You obtained a sample of cholesterol values from 21 such highly paid CEO's.

2. You calculated the average cholesterol value for the 21 CEO's in your sample to be 193 mg/dL.

3. You used the normal distribution with a mean of 205 and a standard error of 7.64 to determine how often you would expect to see average cholesterol values less than 193 or greater than 217, when the population mean is 205.

4. You found that sample means as unusual as the one you observed are expected to occur in about 11.6% of samples from the population, so you didn't have enough evidence to conclude that average cholesterol levels for CEO's are different from those of the population.

Means from Non-Normal Distributions

You probably weren't too surprised that the distribution of sample means from a normal population is also normal. That makes a certain amount of sense. But it is surprising that the distributions of means shown in Figure 11.1 and Figure 11.2 at the beginning of this chapter also appear to be normal.

Remember that these are not means of a variable that has a normal distribution. The cure variable has only two equally likely values—0 for not cured and 1 for cured. This remarkable finding is explained by what's called the Central Limit Theorem. The **Central Limit Theorem** says that for samples of a sufficiently large size, the distribution of sample means is approximately normal. The original variable can have any kind of distribution. It doesn't have to be bell shaped at all.

? *Sufficiently large size? What does that mean?* How large a sample you need before the distribution of sample means is approximately normal depends on the distribution of the original values of a variable. For a variable that has a distribution not too different from the normal, sample means will have a normal distribution even if they're based on small sample sizes. If the distribution of the variable is very far from normal, larger sample sizes will be needed for the distribution of sample means to be normal. The important point is that the distribution of means gets closer and closer to normal as the sample size gets larger and larger—regardless of what the distribution of the original variable looks like. ■ ■ ■

Means from a Uniform Distribution

As an example of the Central Limit Theorem, let's see what the distribution of sample means looks like if cholesterol values had a uniform distribution in the population. In a uniform distribution, all values of a variable are equally likely. Figure 11.8 shows a histogram of 5000 values from a uniform distribution with a range of 135 to 275. All of the bars representing values from 135 to 275 are of approximately equal length.

Figure 11.8 A uniform distribution

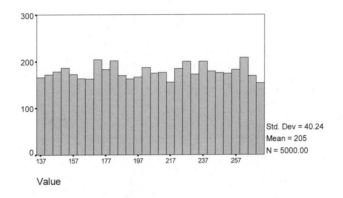
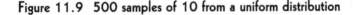

Value

Let's see what happens if we take a sample of 10 cases from the distribution and compute their mean. Figure 11.9 shows the histogram of 500 such sample means.

Figure 11.9 500 samples of 10 from a uniform distribution

To obtain this histogram, open the simul.sav file and select the variable unif10 in the Histograms dialog box.

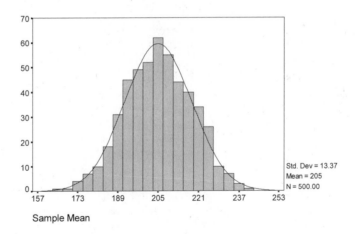

Sample Mean

What is amazing is that the distribution of sample means looks nothing like the original distribution of values. The distribution of means is approximately normal, even when the distribution of a variable is not, provided that the sample size is large enough. This remarkable fact explains why the normal distribution is so important in data analysis. If the variable you're studying does have a normal distribution, then the distribution of sample means will be normal for samples of any size. The more unlike the normal distribution the distribution of your variable is, the larger the samples have to be for the distribution of means to be approximately normal. You'll be able to use the properties of the normal distribution to test a variety of hypotheses about population means based on the results observed in samples.

Summary

What is the normal distribution, and why is it important for data analysis?

- A normal distribution is bell shaped. It is a symmetric distribution in which the mean, median, and mode all coincide. In the population, many variables, such as height and weight, have distributions that are approximately normal.

- Although normal distributions can have different means and variances, the proportional distribution of the cases about the mean is always the same.

- A standard normal distribution has a mean of 0 and a standard deviation of 1.

- The Central Limit Theorem states that for samples of a sufficiently large size, the distribution of sample means is approximately normal. (That's why the normal distribution is so important for data analysis.)

What's Next?

In this chapter, you performed a very simple statistical test. You tested whether a sample might be coming from a population with a known mean and standard deviation. You used the properties of the normal distribution to help you evaluate whether your sample results were unusual. In the chapters that follow, you will learn how to test a variety of hypotheses. The basic idea will not change, just some of the details.

Exercises

Statistical Concepts

1. You are interested in estimating the mean vacancy rate on Saturday night at hotels in major metropolitan areas. Let's assume that in the population of all hotels in major metropolitan areas, the distribution of vacancy rates is approximately normal with a mean of 50 and a standard deviation of 15. That is, the distribution of vacancy rates for individual hotels looks like the following stem-and-leaf plot:

```
Frequency    Stem &   Leaf

    6.00 Extremes    (0), (6), (9), (10), (12)
    4.00        1 .  6&
    9.00        2 *  0124&
   22.00        2 .  5667788899
   23.00        3 *  0012223444
   43.00        3 .  555666667778888899999
   67.00        4 *  0000001111112222222333333444444
   67.00        4 .  555555556666666677788888999999
   78.00        5 *  0000001111112222222223333333444444444
   61.00        5 .  555556666667777788888888999999
   42.00        6 *  00000011112222233334
   27.00        6 .  5555666777789
   25.00        7 *  00011112344
   14.00        7 .  55668&
   10.00        8 *  1113&
    1.00        8 .  &
    1.00 Extremes    (88)

Stem width:     10.00
Each leaf:       2 case(s)


& denotes fractional leaves.
```

a. Based on the figure, approximately what percentage of all hotels have vacancy rates within one standard deviation of the mean. Within two standard deviations?

b. How do the values you estimated from the figure compare to the values shown in Appendix D?

c. The stem-and-leaf plot above is based on 500 values from a normal distribution with a mean of 50 and a standard deviation of 15. How would you expect the distribution of values to change if you took 1000 values from the same normal distribution?

2. Consider what would happen if you took a random sample of five hotels and calculated the average vacancy rate. Would you expect the rate to be 50? Would you expect the standard deviation to be 15? Explain your answer.

3. If you repeated taking a random sample of five hotels and computing their average vacancy rate 500 times you would get a distribution of means that looks like the following:

```
Frequency     Stem &  Leaf

    5.00 Extremes     (29), (31), (32)
    7.00      3 f  555&
   13.00      3 s  666777
   15.00      3 .  8888999
   21.00      4 *  0000111111
   37.00      4 t  2222222223333333333
   33.00      4 f  4444444555555555
   55.00      4 s  666666666666667777777777777
   55.00      4 .  888888888888888899999999999
   69.00      5 *  0000000000000000000011111111111111
   59.00      5 t  222222222222222233333333333333
   50.00      5 f  4444444444444445555555555
   35.00      5 s  66666666667777777
   20.00      5 .  8888888999
   11.00      6 *  00011
    8.00      6 t  223
    3.00      6 f  4&
    2.00      6 s  6
    2.00 Extremes     (68)

Stem width:     10.00
Each leaf:       2 case(s)


& denotes fractional leaves.
```

a. What's similar and what's different about the above distribution and the distribution of individual values shown in question 1? Be sure to comment about the means and standard deviations of the two distributions.

b. Estimate the standard deviation of the above distribution based on the relationship between the standard deviation and the standard error of the mean.

4. You're interested in buying a hotel. The seller assures you that the average vacancy rate for Saturday night is 50%, just like that for all hotels in the area. You take a sample of five Saturdays and compute the average vacancy rate to be 75%. What would you conclude about the seller's claim? How often would you expect to see a rate of 75% or more if the seller's claim is correct?

a. The seller is unhappy with your statistics. He tells you that five Saturdays are much too few for you to draw meaningful conclusions. He recommends you examine a random sample of 40 Saturdays instead. In this situation, what is the hypothesis that you are interested in testing?

b. Sketch what you would expect the sampling distribution of the mean based on samples of size 40 to be, if the null hypothesis is correct. Be sure to indicate what the mean and standard deviation are for the distribution.

c. On the basis of the sample of size 40, you find the average vacancy rate to be 60%. The seller is noticeably relieved, since he is sure that a value of 60% is close enough to 50% for you to believe his claim. Do you? Explain your answer.

5. Explain why you agree or disagree with each of the following statements:

a. It's better to include a small number of subjects in a study than a large number.

b. All samples from the same population give the same results.

c. How much the mean varies from sample to sample depends on both the size of the sample and the variability in the population.

d. Both variables and statistics have distributions.

6. If you are told that in the population of adults in the United States, nostril width is normally distributed with a mean of 0.9 inches and a standard deviation of 0.2 inches, list all the facts about nostril width that you can deduce from the statement.

7. If grades on an examination are approximately normally distributed with an average of 70 and a standard deviation of 10, what percentage of the students:

a. Received grades less than 70?

b. Received grades greater than 70?

c. Received grades less than 60?

d. Received grades less than 50?

e. Received grades less than 50 or greater than 90?

f. Received grades less than the median?

8. Two researchers are studying the effect of positive thinking on recovery time after surgery. Both take a sample of 25 persons about to undergo surgery, teach them how to think positively, and then examine how long they stay in the hospital.

a. The first researcher calculates the average stay to be 12 days and the standard deviation to be 3 days. He reports these results in the *Journal of Positive Living*. The second researcher calculates the average stay to be 12.5 days. He reports the standard error of the mean to be 0.6 days. When he submits his results to the same journal, the editors question his findings. They want to know why his measure of variability is so much less than the first researcher's. Explain to the editors of the journal the difference between the two statistics. Indicate the relationship of the two statistics as well.

b. What would be the standard error of the mean if the standard deviation remained at 3, but the sample size was increased to 50? What if it was decreased to 10?

9. In this exercise, you will use SPSS to compute areas under the normal curve. Assume that scores on a test are normally distributed in the population with a mean of 100 and a standard deviation of 15. You have seven people with scores of 55, 70, 85, 100, 115, 130, and 145. You want to tell them what proportion of people in the population have scores less than or equal to theirs.

a. First, use the Data Editor to enter the seven scores into a data file. Call the variable *score*.

b. Next, compute standardized scores (Z scores) for the seven data values. You can't use the Descriptives procedure to do this, since Descriptives will standardize the scores using the mean and standard deviation of the seven scores in your file. You want to standardize the scores using the population mean of 100 and the population standard deviation of 15. To do this you must use the Compute facility in the Transform menu. Compute a variable named *zscore* equal to the following expression:

(score − 100) / 15

Then look at the Data Editor to make sure you have the correct Z score for each value of *score*.

c. In the Compute Variable dialog box, there is a function called CDFNORM(zvalue). You supply a standardized score (Z value) and it tells you what proportion of cases in a standard normal distribution have values less than equal to your standardized score. Compute a variable *cumprob* equal to the following expression:

cdfnorm (zscore)

The variable *cumprob* is the proportion of cases in a normal distribution with standardized scores less than or equal to *zscore*.

d. In the Data Editor, you now have three variables: *score*, *zscore*, and *cumprob*. Double-click the column heading for *cumprob*. In the Define Variable dialog box, click on Type. Change the number of decimal places displayed for *cumprob* to 4.

e. Based on the values of *cumprob*, indicate the areas in the following drawings:

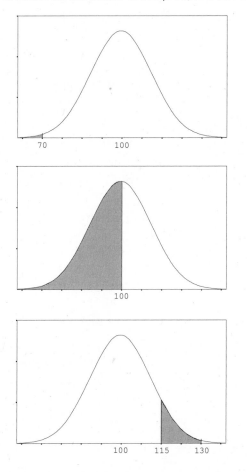

10. Using the CDFNORM function described above and simple arithmetic, you can calculate any area in the normal distribution. For example, if you want to know the proportion of cases in a standard normal distribution with standardized scores in absolute value at least as large as the one you observed, you would compute a variable (call it *twotailp*) using the following expression:

$$2 \times (1 - \text{cdfnorm}(\text{abs}(z\text{score})))$$

Here's what the expression does. Consider a standard score of +2. To calculate the proportion of cases with standardized scores greater than +2, you have to subtract the proportion of cases with values less than 2 from the total area under the curve, which equals 1. For example, in a normal distribution, 97.72%

of cases have standardized scores less than or equal to 2. The percentage with standardized scores greater than 2 is then

$$100\% - 97.72\% = 2.28\%$$

Since the normal distribution is symmetric, scores less than –2 and scores greater than +2 are equally likely. You can therefore get the probability of obtaining a score less than –2 or greater than +2 by doubling the probability of a score greater than +2. Thus, the probability of obtaining a standard score at least 2 in absolute value is 2 times 0.0228, or 0.0456. The absolute value function abs(zscore) ensures that you'll get the same two-tailed probability for negative Z scores (such as –2) and positive Z scores (such as +2).

a. Using the Compute facility calculate the variable *twotailp* for the Z scores in your data file. Increase the number of decimal places displayed to 4.

b. Based on the results you obtained in question 10a, answer the following: What's the probability that a person has a test score less than 85 or greater than 115? What's the probability that a person has a test score greater than 145? Less than 100? Less than 55 or greater than 145? Between 55 and 145?

11. Modify the expression in question 10 to compute the probability of a standardized score at least as large as the one observed and of the same sign. Call the new variable *onetailp*.

a. What's the relationship between *onetailp* and *twotailp*?

b. If a person asks you, "What percentage of people in the population scored at least as well as I did?" which probability would you quote?

c. If a person asks you, "What percentage of people in the population scored as 'weird' as I did?" which probability would you quote?

d. What percentage of people have standardized scores greater than –2? Greater than +3?

Data Analysis

Use the *gss.sav* file to answer the following questions:

1. Make histograms of *age*, *educ*, *tvhours*, and *hrs1*. Superimpose a normal curve on them. Do any of these distributions appear approximately normal? Describe how each of the distributions is different from the normal distribution.

2. Generate a fake, normally distributed IQ score for each case in the file. To do this, use the Compute facility and place the following expression into the dialog boxes:

IQ = norm (15) + 100

These instructions generate a random sample from a normal distribution with a mean of 100 and a standard deviation of 15.

a. Make a histogram of IQ and superimpose the normal curve on it

b. If IQ is exactly normally distributed, what percentage of cases should have values between 70 and 130? What percentage of cases in your sample have IQ's in this range?

c. What percentage of the cases would you expect to have IQ's of 115 or more if IQ is exactly normally distributed? What percentage of cases in your sample have IQ's greater than 115?

d. What percentage of cases in your sample have IQ's less than 85? What would you expect if the distribution is exactly normal?

3. Compute standard scores for the IQ variable. Make a histogram with a normal curve superimposed.

a. What is the mean of this distribution? The standard deviation?

b. From Appendix D, what percent of the cases would you expect to have standard scores between –1 and +1? Between 0 and 1.5? Greater than +2? Less than –2?

c. Compute the quartiles of the standardized variable. How do your observed quartiles compare to the quartiles of a normal distribution?

Use the *electric.sav* data file to answer the following questions:

4. Make histograms of *chol58, dbp58, ht58, cgt58,* and *wt58.* Superimpose a normal distribution with the same mean and variance on each one. Does the distribution of any of these variables appear to be approximately normal?

5. Standardize each of the variables in question 4. For the standardized variables compute the 5th, 16th, 50th, 84th, and 95th percentiles. How do your observed percentiles compare to those that would be expected if the distributions were exactly normal?

Testing a Hypothesis about a Single Mean

How can you test the hypothesis that a sample comes from a population with a known mean?

- What's a one-sample *t* test?
- Why are confidence intervals useful?
- What is a null hypothesis? An alternative hypothesis?

In Chapter 11, you learned how to test whether a sample comes from a population with a known mean. Your test was based on the fact that if you select samples from a population that has a normal distribution, the distribution of the sample means will be normal as well. You also saw that for sufficiently large sample sizes, the distribution of sample means will be normal even if the population from which you select your sample is not normal.

To use the normal distribution to test whether your sample comes from a particular population, you have to know the population mean and standard deviation. For example, to see if the cholesterol levels of the CEO's appear to be unusual, you had to know the mean and standard deviation of the cholesterol values in the general population. Often, however, you don't know the standard deviation of the population values and instead must estimate it from the sample. In this chapter, you'll learn how to use a distribution closely related to the normal, the **t distribution**, to test whether a sample comes from a population with a specified mean when you don't know the population standard deviation.

▶ This chapter uses the *gssft.sav* data file, which includes data for full time workers only. You must select people with college degrees to run the analysis. For instructions on how to obtain the *t* test output shown in this chapter, see "How to Obtain a One-Sample t Test" on p. 231. For instructions on how to restrict your analysis to people with college degrees, see "Example: Selecting College Graduates" on p. 562 in Appendix B.

The Mythical Work Week

The 40-hour work week is an established standard for full-time employees. Work less, and you feel guilty for not putting in a full week. Work more, and you feel that you're performing beyond expectation. How realistic is the notion that the average college graduate who is employed full time works a 40-hour week? In this chapter, you'll use data from the General Social Survey to test the hypothesis that the average work week for college graduates is 40 hours.

Examining the Data

The first step in analyzing data is examining a plot of the data values. From a frequency table, stem-and-leaf plot, or histogram, you can see if there are any strange data values. You can also see whether the distribution of data values looks approximately normal. If the distribution of data values looks not too far from normal, you can be confident that the distribution of means will be normal, even for small sample sizes.

Figure 12.1 Hours worked for college graduates

You can obtain stem-and-leaf plots using the Explore procedure, as described in Chapter 7. Select the variable hrs1 in the Explore dialog box.

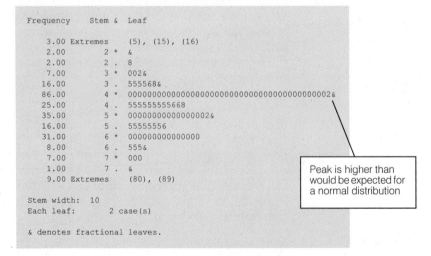

```
   Frequency     Stem &  Leaf

       3.00  Extremes    (5), (15), (16)
       2.00       2 *   &
       2.00       2 .   8
       7.00       3 *   002&
      16.00       3 .   555568&
      86.00       4 *   00000000000000000000000000000000000000000002&
      25.00       4 .   555555555668
      35.00       5 *   00000000000000002&
      16.00       5 .   55555556
      31.00       6 *   000000000000000
       8.00       6 .   555&
       7.00       7 *   000
       1.00       7 .   &
       9.00  Extremes    (80), (89)

   Stem width:   10
   Each leaf:        2 case(s)

   & denotes fractional leaves.
```

Peak is higher than would be expected for a normal distribution

Figure 12.1 is a stem-and-leaf plot of the hours worked the previous week for the 248 college graduates in your sample. You see that the distribution of the data values is not quite normal. The peak at 40 hours is higher than you would expect for a normal distribution. There is also a tail toward larger values of hours worked. It appears that people are more likely to work a long week than a short week. Since the sample size is quite large and the distribution is somewhat bell-shaped you can count on the Central Limit Theorem to ensure that the sampling distribution of the means is approximately normal.

In Figure 12.2, you see that the average work week is 47.73 hours, and the standard deviation is 12.52 hours.

Figure 12.2 Descriptive statistics for hours worked

You obtain these descriptive statistics as part of the one-sample t test output. See Figure 12.4.

```
One Sample t-tests


                                    Number
    Variable                        of Cases      Mean         SD    SE of Mean

    HRS1  NUMBER OF HOURS WORK        248       47.7298     12.521         .795
```

You know that even if college graduates work an average of 40 hours a week, you don't expect a random sample of 248 of them to hit the norm on the head. You know that means calculated from samples from the same population vary. How much they vary depends on the size of the sample and the standard deviation of the values in the population.

If you know the population value for the standard deviation of the number of hours worked per week, you can use the procedure described in Chapter 11 to determine whether the observed sample mean of 47.73 is unlikely if the population mean for number of hours worked is 40.

? *How would you go about determining if 47.73 is an unlikely value if you know the standard deviation?* First, find the difference between the observed sample mean and the hypothetical population mean. The difference is $47.73 - 40$, or 7.73 hours. Then you calculate the standard error of the mean, which is the population standard deviation divided by the square root of the sample size. Let's assume that you know that the population standard deviation is 12.5 hours. The standard error is then $12.5/(\sqrt{248}) = 0.79$.

Next, you have to figure out the standard score for your observed mean. You do this by dividing the difference between the observed and hypothetical mean by the standard error. For this example, the standard score is $7.73/0.79 = 9.78$. Since 99% of the cases in a normal distribution have standardized values between -2.6 and $+2.6$, you know that a standard score of 9.78 is extremely unusual. ■ ■ ■

The t Distribution

It may seem reasonable that if you don't know the value for the population standard deviation, you should just substitute the sample standard deviation and proceed as before to base your test on the normal distribution. For small sample sizes, that's not a good idea. Here's why. You've already seen that when you take a sample from a population and calculate the sample mean, it's very unlikely that the sample mean will be the same as the population mean. The same is true for the sample variance. If you take a sample from a population and calculate the variance, it is very unlikely that the sample variance will be the same as the population variance. Sample variances, just like sample means, have sampling distributions. That is, if you take repeated samples of the same size from a population and calculate their variances, these variances will spread out into a distribution. (The distribution will not be normal, however. If the samples are from a normally distributed population, the distribution of sample variances has what's called an *F* distribution. This distribution is discussed in Chapter 15.)

If you use the sample standard deviation instead of a known population value in the computation of the standard score, you introduce additional uncertainty into the result. For example, if your sample standard deviation is smaller than the population value, the resulting standard score will be too large. If the observed sample standard deviation is too large, the standard score will be too small. That's why, when you don't know the population standard deviation but estimate it from the sample, the distribution of standard scores is no longer normal. Instead, it follows what's called the *t* distribution. The *t* distribution takes into account the fact that, by using the sample standard deviation instead of the population standard deviation, you're introducing error into the computation of the standard score. The *t* distribution looks like a normal distribution but it has more area in the tails. That's because large standard scores can result not only from sample means that are far from the population mean but also from poor estimates of the population standard deviation.

Another way that the *t* distribution differs from the normal distribution is that its shape depends on the number of cases in your sample. On first reflection, this may seem odd, but it's not. You know that if you estimate a population standard deviation based on a sample of 4 cases, the possible results will have much more variability than if you estimate the population standard deviation based on 4000 cases. You're much more confident that the estimate based on the larger sample size is closer to the true value than the estimate based on the smaller sample size. If you have a large sample size, the fact that you don't know the population standard deviation becomes much less important than if you have a small sample size.

Look at Figure 12.3, which shows the *t* distribution for degrees of freedom of 3, 10, and 50. (It is customary to identify a *t* distribution not by the actual number of cases in the sample, but by what's called the degrees of freedom. In this example, it's just the number of cases in the sample minus 1.)

Figure 12.3 t distribution for 3, 10, and 50 degrees of freedom

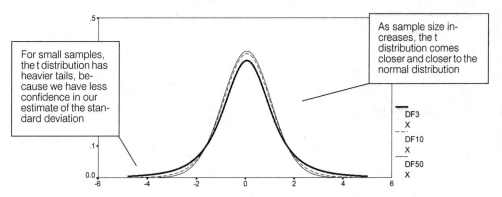

In Figure 12.3, you see that as the degrees of freedom increase, the *t* distribution becomes more peaked. That is, the percentage of the total area in the tails decreases. For 50 degrees of freedom, the *t* distribution and the normal distribution are indistinguishable. For small degrees of freedom, the tails of the *t* distribution are heavier than those of the normal distribution. When you have to estimate the population standard deviation, you'll find more seemingly large deviations from the population mean than you would if you knew the standard deviation.

? *What do the Guinness Brewery in Dublin and the* t *distribution have in common?* W. S. Gosset, of course. Gosset was a chemist who worked for Guinness in the early 1900's. Since he carried out experiments based on small sample sizes, he worried about the consequences of using a sample value for the standard deviation when testing hypotheses about the mean. Standard practice was to just use the normal distribution. Gosset derived the *t* distribution and published his results under the pseudonym Student. That's why the *t* distribution is often called Student's *t*. ▪ ▪ ▪

Calculating the t Statistic

To test the hypothesis that a sample comes from a population with a known mean but an unknown standard deviation, you calculate what's called a *t* **statistic**. The calculations are exactly the same as for the standard score, except that the value of the sample standard deviation is used in place of the population value in calculating the standard error of the mean.

For this example, the value for the *t* statistic is

$$t = (47.73 - 40) / 0.795 = 9.72$$ **Equation 12.1**

The observed significance level is obtained from the *t* distribution with 247 degrees of freedom. (Since the number of cases in your sample is quite large, the *t* distribution and the normal distribution will give the same observed significance levels.) The observed *t* value is so large, that you know the observed significance level is very close to 0.

Figure 12.4 One-sample t test

To obtain this output, from the menus choose:

Statistics
  Compare Means ▸
    One-Sample T Test...

Select the hrs1 variable and specify 40 for Test Value, as shown in Figure 12.8.

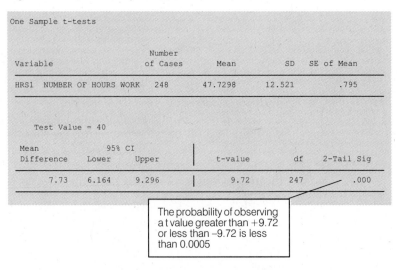

Figure 12.4 contains the value for the *t* statistic as well as additional output from the SPSS One-Sample T Test procedure. You see that the difference between the observed mean and the hypothetical population mean of 40 (labeled *Test Value*) is 7.73. For your sample, the average work week was 7.73 hours longer than the hypothesized 40 hours.

The probability of observing a sample t value greater than +9.72 or less than –9.72 is given by the entry labeled *2-Tail Sig*. Since the observed significance level is less than 0.0005, SPSS displays it as 0.000. This does not mean that the probability is 0. It is less than 0.0005. Based on the observed significance level, you can conclude that it's quite unlikely that college graduates work a 40-hour week on average. They seem to work much more.

The probability given on the output is called "two-tailed" because it the sum of the areas in both tails of the t distribution: the area less than –9.72, and the area greater than 9.72. You're interested in both of these areas since the average number of hours worked by college graduates can be either less than 40 hours or greater than 40 hours. Both alternatives are possible and of interest.

? *When should I use the One-Sample T Test procedure?* You should use the One-Sample T Test procedure if you have a single sample of data and want to test whether your sample comes from a population with a known mean. For example, you can use the One-Sample T Test procedure to see whether 16-ounce boxes of cereal really weigh 16 ounces on average, or to test whether children who are born prematurely have an average IQ of 100. In both of these examples, you have a single set of data—cereal boxes that you weighed, and premature babies whom you tested. You want to compare your sample means to known population values. Your test values are not estimated from another set of data. They are known values. If you have two samples of data, for example, CEO's and non-CEO's, or premature and full-term infants, and you want to compare their means, you should *not* use the one-sample t test. Instead, you'll probably want to use the independent-samples t test described in Chapter 14. ▪ ▪ ▪

Confidence Intervals

From the results of the t test, you're reasonably confident that the average work week for college graduates is not 40 hours. What do you think it is? Based on your sample, your best guess is 47.73 hours, but you know that it's most unlikely that the true population value for all college graduates is actually equal to the value found in your sample.

Let's see how, based on the normal distribution, you can obtain useful information about a plausible range of values for the population mean.

Figure 12.5 Sampling distribution of means

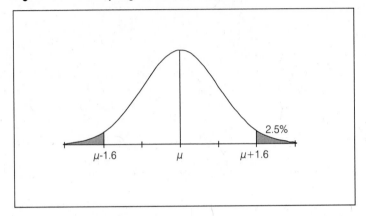

First consider Figure 12.5, which is the distribution of all possible sample means for samples of 248 college graduates. (For simplicity, we've assumed that the population standard deviation is 12.5 hours, so the standard error of the mean is about 0.8 hours.) The first thing that should strike you about this distribution is that you don't know its mean. You only know the average hours worked for one sample of 248 college graduates. In Figure 12.5, the unknown population mean is identified by the Greek symbol μ (mu), the common abbreviation for the population mean (well, common if you read statistics books...).

Although you don't know the value for the mean of the sampling distribution of means, we're supposing that you do know the standard deviation of the distribution—the standard error. It's about 0.8 hours. If the sample means are normally distributed, you also know that approximately 95% of the sample means should be within about two standard errors, or 1.6 hours, of the unknown population mean. (More precisely, within about 1.96 standard errors.) Only 5% of the sample means fall in the shaded region of Figure 12.5.

Based on the previous information, you can calculate a range of values—an interval—that should include the population mean 95% of the time. You calculate the lower limit of this interval by subtracting 1.96 times the standard error from your sample mean. You calculate the upper interval by adding 1.96 times the standard error to the sample mean. For this example, the interval is from 47.73 – 1.57 to 47.73 + 1.57; that is, from 46.16 to 49.30 hours. This interval has a special name. It's called a **95% confidence interval** for the population mean.

> **?** *If the population standard deviation isn't known—if it must be estimated from the sample—how does that change the computation of the confidence interval?* The only difference is that you must use values from the *t* distribution instead of the normal distribution. For example, if you have a sample of 10 cases, instead of using the value 1.96 in the computation of the 95% confidence interval, you must use the value 2.26, because 95% of the values in a *t* distribution with 9 degrees of freedom are between –2.26 and 2.26. ■ ■ ■

It may help you to understand the idea behind confidence intervals if you identify a possible sample mean in Figure 12.5 and calculate the confidence interval. Consider first a sample mean that is 1.5 standard errors above the population mean. It's shown in Figure 12.6, as is the 95% confidence interval based on it.

Figure 12.6 Sample mean 1.5 standard errors above population mean

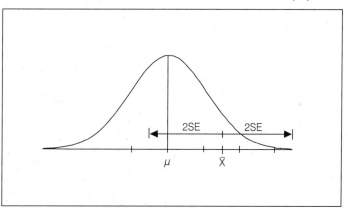

Does the confidence interval include the unknown population value? Sure it does. The confidence interval extends for two standard errors below the sample mean, while the population mean is only 1.5 standard errors less than the sample mean. Now look at Figure 12.7, which shows a sample mean 1 standard error below the population mean. Again, the 95% confidence interval includes the population value.

Figure 12.7 Sample mean 1 standard error below population mean

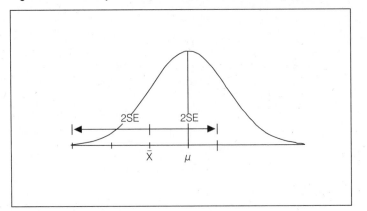

The only time the confidence interval won't include the population value is when your sample mean falls into the shaded region of Figure 12.5. The shaded region corresponds to the 5% of the distribution that is more than two standard error units from the population mean. Unfortunately, you can never tell whether your particular sample mean is one of the unlucky ones in the shaded region. All you can do is calculate the 95% confidence interval and hope that your sample is one of the 95-out-of-100 for which the confidence interval includes the population value.

Am I correct in saying that the probability is 95% that the population mean for the average hours worked by college graduates is in the range of 46.16 hours to 49.30 hours? Not quite. Once you go and actually compute the confidence interval based on a sample mean, the resulting interval either contains the population mean or it doesn't. The correct statement is that you're 95% *confident* that the interval contains the population mean.

The following analogy may make the idea clearer (and might make this book a *New York Times* best-seller). Before a baby is conceived, the probability that it will be a girl is roughly 50%. Once the deed is done, the baby is either a boy or a girl. The same is true for confidence intervals. Before you conduct your survey or experiment, you know that 95 times out of 100, the 95% confidence interval based on your sample mean will include the population mean. Once you've calculated the interval, it either does or it doesn't include the population value. ■ ■ ■

Other Confidence Levels

Although the 95% confidence interval is the most commonly reported, you can calculate intervals for any confidence level. What changes is the width of the interval. For example, to construct a 99% confidence interval, for a large sample you use the value 2.57 instead of 1.96. That's because 99% of sample means are within 2.57 standard error units of the unknown population mean. The 99% confidence interval for the average number of hours worked by college graduates is from 45.67 hours to 49.79 hours. Although you're more confident that this interval contains the population mean, the interval is wider than before. A wide interval is less useful than a narrower one. For example, if you are confident that a drug prolongs life by 5 to 6 years, that's more useful than knowing that the drug prolongs life from 1 month to 15 years. Whenever you compute a confidence interval, you trade off the degree of confidence and the interval width—the higher the confidence level, the wider the interval.

How can I get SPSS to compute confidence intervals for me? The easiest way to get a confidence interval for a mean is to run the Explore procedure. A 95% confidence interval is part of the default output. You can change the confidence level as described in "Explore Statistics: Outliers and Grouped Frequency Tables" on p. 116 in Chapter 7. SPSS also computes confidence intervals as part of the output in other procedures.

Confidence Interval for a Difference

You can easily convert the observed confidence interval for the average hours worked in a week by college graduates into a confidence interval for the difference between the population mean and the hypothesized value of 40. All you have to do is subtract the value 40 from the lower and upper bounds of the confidence interval for the population mean. This gives you a 95% confidence interval from 6.16 to 9.30 hours. You are 95% confident that the difference between the number of hours actually worked by the average college graduate and the mythical 40 hour work week is between 6.16 and 9.30 hours. It appears likely that the average college graduate works quite a bit more than 40 hours (or inflates the hours worked when asked). The 95% confidence interval for the population mean difference is shown in Figure 12.4.

When you run the one-sample *t* test, you can calculate a confidence interval at whatever level you want. For example, the 99% confidence interval for the difference from 40 hours extends from 5.67 to 9.79

hours. As you expect, it is wider than the 95% confidence interval. That's because the only way you can be more certain that you're trapping the population value is to increase the range of values included in the interval.

Confidence Intervals and Hypothesis Tests

If you look at the 95% confidence interval for the difference between the hours actually worked and 40 hours, you will notice that the value 0 is not included in the interval (the interval ranges from 6.16 to 9.30). That tells you that 0 is not a plausible population value. It appears unlikely that the true difference between the average hours worked and 40 hours is 0. There's a close relationship between hypothesis tests and confidence intervals: If a value is not included in a 95% confidence interval for the difference, you can reject the hypothesis that it's a plausible value for the population difference, using a 5% criterion for unusual.

From the confidence interval, you can conclude that the true difference is unlikely to be smaller than 6.16 hours or larger than 9.30 hours. If you did a one-sample t test and set your hypothetical week to be less than 46.16 hours or greater than 49.30 hours, the two-tailed probability level for that t test would be less than 0.05. If you set the hypothetical value to be between 46.16 and 49.30, the observed significance level would be greater than 0.05. Similarly, if you calculate a 99% confidence interval, and it does not contain a particular value, then the corresponding t test for that hypothetical value will have an observed significance level of less than 0.01.

Null Hypotheses and Alternative Hypotheses

In the last few chapters, you've learned how to test a hypothesis statistically. You tested whether a new drug has the same cure rate as the standard treatment, whether CEO's have the same average cholesterol levels as the general population, and whether college graduates work a 40-hour week. You followed the same steps for testing all three hypotheses, although the statistic on which you based your conclusion differed. (For the cure rate example, you used a binomial test; for the CEO cholesterol levels, a test based on the normal distribution; and for the work week, a test based on the t distribution.) The statistical test you use depends on the hypothesis of interest and the type of data available.

In each of the three situations, there are two hypotheses or claims of interest. The first one is that there is nothing going on: the new drug is as effective as the standard, CEO's have the same average cholesterol levels as the general population, and college graduates really do work a 40-hour week. In statistical terms these are called **null hypotheses**. (Notice that each null hypothesis is precise. It describes a hypothetical but exact state of affairs.) The **alternative hypothesis** describes the situation when the null hypothesis is false. The following are all alternative hypotheses: the new treatment changes the cure rate, CEO's have different cholesterol levels than the general population, and college graduates don't work a 40-hour week.

When you statistically test a hypothesis, you assume that the null hypothesis correctly describes the state of affairs. The null hypothesis is the frame of reference against which you'll judge your sample results. You assume that the cure rate is the population value of 50%. You assume that the CEO's have average cholesterol levels of 205. You assume that college graduates work a 40-hour week. The null hypothesis describes a well-defined situation. If the population cure rate is 50%, you can determine how often you expect to see various possible sample outcomes, such as 12 cures or more in a sample of size 20. If the true cholesterol value is 205 mg/dL, you can calculate how often you would expect to see samples of size 21 with average cholesterol levels of 193 mg/dL or less. If the true work week is 40 hours, you can determine how often a sample of 248 people would have an average work week as long as 47.7 hours.

You must state the null hypothesis so that it perfectly describes a single situation. The null hypothesis cannot state that college graduates don't work a 40-hour week. That statement cannot serve as a frame of reference for evaluating sample results, since it describes many possible outcomes. (On the other hand, college graduates working the same number of hours as people who haven't graduated from college is a perfectly acceptable null hypothesis. It describes a situation that can be used as a frame of reference for evaluating your observed sample results.)

Most of the time when you perform an experiment or conduct a study, the null hypothesis claims the opposite of what you would like to be true. If you've synthesized a new compound that you think improves memory, the null hypothesis would state that it does not. If you think that men and women are not equally satisfied with their jobs, the null hypothesis would state that they are.

An alternative hypothesis can specify the direction of the difference that you expect to observe. If you know that the cure you are touting cannot be worse than the standard, your alternative hypothesis can claim that your cure rate is better than the standard. However, the direction of your alternative hypothesis must be stated in advance. You can't look at the data values and then decide on the direction. The reason for this is that if you know the direction in advance your observed significance level can be restricted to include possible outcomes only in the direction of interest. That will make your observed significance level smaller than if you consider both alternatives. For example, if you know that your treatment can only be better, you can calculate the probability of getting sample results as extreme as the ones you observed in a positive direction. If your treatment can help or hinder, than you must consider differences at least as large as the ones observed in either direction.

? *How can I get the correct observed significance level for an alternative hypothesis that specifies a direction?* If you are using a statistical test that calculates the observed significance level from a symmetric distribution, like the normal or the *t* distribution, you can divide the two-tailed observed significance level by 2. That will give you a one-tailed significance level. It's called one-tailed, since it's based on the area in only one tail of the distribution. ■ ■ ■

Rejecting the Null Hypothesis

Since the null hypothesis serves as the frame of reference against which sample results are evaluated, if your sample results appear to be unlikely when the null hypothesis is true, you reject the null hypothesis. That is, if the probability of obtaining sample results as extreme as the ones you've observed (the observed significance level) is small, usually less than 0.05, you are entitled to reject the null hypothesis. In the previous example, you rejected the null hypothesis that college graduates work a 40-hour week. You did not reject the null hypothesis that CEO's have an average cholesterol value that is the same as that of the general population. In the chapters that follow, you'll learn more about what you can and can't conclude when you reject or don't reject the null hypothesis.

Summary

How can you test the hypothesis that a sample comes from a population with a known mean?

- A one-sample *t* test is used to test the null hypothesis that a sample comes from a population with a particular mean.
- A confidence interval is a range of values which, with a designated likelihood, includes the unknown population value.
- The null hypothesis is the frame of reference used to evaluate a claim about a population.
- The alternative hypothesis specifies the situation if the null hypothesis is false.

What's Next?

In this chapter, you used the one-sample *t* test to test the null hypothesis that a sample comes from a population with a given mean. You identified the null and alternative hypotheses. You assumed that the null hypothesis was true and calculated the observed significance level, which told you how often you would expect to see sample results as extreme as the ones you observed, if in fact the null hypothesis is true. If this observed significance level was small, you rejected the null hypothesis.

In this chapter, you were interested in drawing conclusions based on a single sample of data. In Chapter 13, you'll learn how to apply the techniques described in this chapter to testing hypotheses about two related samples.

How to Obtain a One-Sample t Test

This procedure tests the null hypothesis that a sample comes from a population with specified mean. It also displays a confidence interval for the difference.

▶ To open the One-Sample T Test dialog box, from the menus choose:

Statistics
    Compare Means ▶
        One-Sample T Test...

Figure 12.8   One-Sample T Test dialog box

Select hrs1
and specify 40
to produce the
output shown
in Figure 12.4

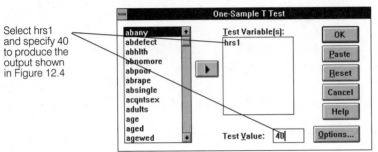

▶ In the One-Sample T Test dialog box, select in the source variable list the variable you want to test and move it into the Test Variable(s) list. You can move more than one variable into the list to test all of them against the specified test value.

▶ Enter a number into the Test Value box and click on OK.

For each variable selected, SPSS calculates the *t* statistic and its observed significance level.

Options: Confidence Level, Labels, and Missing Data

To change the confidence level for which SPSS displays the confidence interval for the difference between the population mean and the test value, or to control the handling of cases with missing values, click on

Options in the One-Sample T Test dialog box. This opens the One-Sample T Test Options dialog box, as shown in Figure 12.9.

Figure 12.9 One-Sample T Test Options dialog box

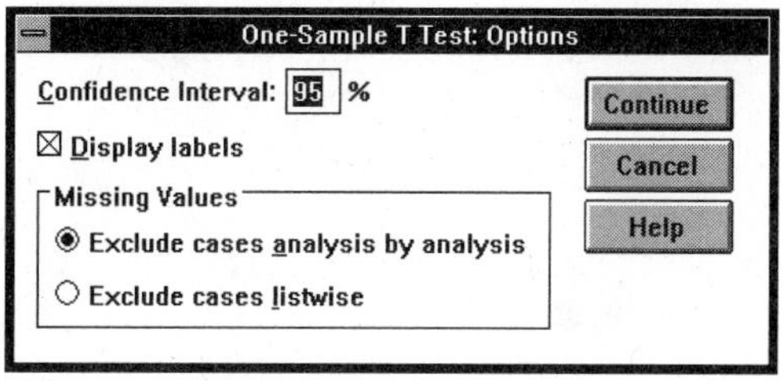

Available options include:

Confidence Interval. Allows you to specify a confidence level between 1 and 99.

Display labels. Deselect to suppress the display of variable labels.

Missing Values. Two alternatives control the treatment of missing data for multiple test variables:

Exclude cases analysis by analysis. Uses all cases that have valid data for each variable in the statistics for that variable.

Exclude cases listwise. Uses only the cases that have valid data for all specified test variables. This ensures that all of the tests are performed using the same cases.

Exercises

Statistical Concepts

1. You suspect that your favorite candy bar manufacturer's 8-ounce candy bars weigh less than advertised. You go out and buy 200 candy bars from different stores. You find that their average weight is 7.75 ounces, with a standard deviation of 0.5 ounces. Do you have enough evidence to believe that you are being shortchanged? Explain.

2. Your local pizza chain claims that the delivery time of their pizzas is normally distributed with a mean of 30 minutes and a standard deviation of 10 minutes.

  a. You order a single pizza and it arrives in 42 minutes. Do you have reason to disbelieve the chain's claim?

  b. Twenty of your friends in different locations order pizzas. The average delivery time is 42 minutes. Do you have reason to disbelieve the chain's claim? How often would you expect an average delivery time of 42 if the chain's claim is correct?

  c. Compute a 95% confidence interval for the true average delivery time based on the results in question 2b.

  d. Compute a 95% confidence interval for the true difference based on the results in question 2b.

3. For which of the following situations is a one-sample t test appropriate:

  a. You want to know if the average salary for males is the same as the average salary for females. You have available a sample of male salaries and female salaries.

  b. You want to know if the average difference in systolic blood pressure in a standing and reclining position is 0. You have values for differences for 54 people.

  c. You want to know if the average ACT score for your school is 18.

  d. You want to know if two schools have the same average ACT scores.

Data Analysis

The *gssft.sav* file contains data from the General Social Survey for full-time employees only. Use this file to answer the following questions:

1. In this chapter, you tested the hypothesis that college graduates who work full time work a 40-hour work week. Now test the hypothesis that for all full-time workers the population value for average hours worked is 40 hours (variable *hrs1*).

  a. What assumptions do you need to use the one-sample t test? Do you think the data meet the assumptions?

  b. What is the null hypothesis that you want to test? The alternative hypothesis?

  c. Test the hypothesis and write a brief summary of your conclusions.

  d. Explain the difference between 11.27, the standard deviation of your sample, and 0.414, the standard error of the mean.

e. If your sample size were doubled, how would you expect the value of the standard deviation to change? How would the value of the standard error of the mean change? Estimate both the standard deviation and the standard error for a sample twice as large.

f. What is the 95% confidence interval for the average number of hours per week by full-time workers? How does it differ from the 95% confidence interval for the difference?

g. Based on the 95% confidence interval for the mean difference, can you reject the null hypothesis that the average population value for hours worked is 43 hours? Explain.

h. Based on the confidence interval for the mean, what is a plausible range of population values for the average hours worked? .

2. Repeat the analysis in question 1 for women who work full time (use the Select Cases facility to analyze only cases where variable *sex* equals 2). Summarize your conclusions.

Use the *gss.sav* file to answer the following questions:

3. The variable *sibs* is the respondent's number of siblings.

a. Make a histogram of the variable. Do you think its distribution is normal? Is it symmetric? Explain why it looks the way it does.

b. Assume that the sample size is large enough for the Central Limit Theorem to hold. Test the null hypothesis that the average number of siblings is 2.5. Summarize your conclusions.

c. Without running the One-Sample T Test procedure, test the null hypothesis that the average number of siblings is 3. Indicate what procedure you followed.

4. Since the General Social Survey contains people of all ages, you can't conclude anything about the average size of today's family. To get a better idea of current family size, use the Select Cases facility to restrict your analysis only to respondents who are 21 years of age or younger. Test the null hypothesis that the average number of siblings they have is 2.5. Write a short summary of your results.

5. Based on the output you generated for question 4, answer the following questions:

a. What is the probability that the null hypothesis is true?

b. What is the probability that the null hypothesis is false?

c. Have you proved that the average number of siblings for people 21 or younger is 2.5?

d. What does the two-tailed significance level tell you?

Use the *electric.sav* data file to answer the following questions:

6. Use the Select Cases facility to select only men with coronary heart disease (variable *chd* equals 1). Test the hypothesis that they come from a population in which the average serum cholesterol is 205 mg/dl (variable *dbp58*).

    a. State the null and alternative hypotheses.

    b. What do you conclude about the null hypothesis based on the *t* test?

    c. What is the difference between your sample mean and the hypothetical population value?

    d. How often would you expect to see a sample difference at least this large in absolute value if the null hypothesis is true?

    e. Give a range of values that you are 95% confident include the population value for the mean cholesterol of men with coronary heart disease. Does that interval include your test value of 205?

    f. What is the range of values that you are 95% confident include the true difference between 205 and the average cholesterol for the population of men with coronary heart disease?

7. Select only men without coronary heart disease (variable *chd* equals 0).

    a. Is it plausible that they are a sample from a population in which the average weight is 175 pounds (variable *wt58*)? Explain your reasoning.

    b. What is the 99% confidence interval for the population value for average weight for men without coronary heart disease?

    c. On the basis of the confidence interval you computed in question 7b, can you reject the null hypothesis that the population value is 180 pounds?

Use the *schools.sav* data file to answer the following question:

8. The leader of the Chicago schools claims that dramatic improvements have occurred between 1993 and 1994. Look at the variables that show the change in the percentage of schools meeting or exceeding state standards (*mathch94, readch94,* and *scich94*). Test the hypothesis that the true change in the percentage meeting state standards is 0. Write a short report to the mayor detailing your findings.

Testing a Hypothesis about Two Related Means

How can you test the null hypothesis that the average difference between a pair of measurements is 0?

- What are paired experimental designs, and what are their advantages?
- What types of problems can occur when you use paired designs?
- What is a paired *t* test?
- What are Type 1 and Type 2 errors?
- Why do you use a normal probability plot?

In Chapter 12, you used the one-sample *t* test to test whether the average work week for college graduates is 40 hours. You were interested in drawing conclusions about one group of people only—college graduates who work full time. For each person in your analysis, you had a single measurement: the number of hours worked the previous week. In this chapter, you'll learn about a closely related test—the paired-samples *t* test. You can use the **paired-samples *t* test** to analyze the results of experiments when the same person or animal is observed under two different conditions, or studies in which you have a pair of subjects (or measurements) that are matched in some way. One type of such study is the "before and after" design. For example, you might obtain a student's pulse rate before and after completing an exam, or you might record the blood pressure of a patient before and after a treatment.

▶ This chapter uses the *endorph.sav* data file. For instructions on how to obtain the paired-sample *t* test output shown, see "How to Obtain a Paired-Samples t Test" on p. 248.

Marathon Runners in Paired Designs

Dale, Fleetwood, Weddell, and Ellis (1987) investigated the possible role of β-endorphins in the collapse of runners. (β-endorphins are morphine-like substances manufactured in the body.) They measured plasma β-endorphin concentrations for 11 runners before and after they participated in a half-marathon run. The question of interest was whether average β-endorphin levels changed during a run. The authors postulated that runners were able to continue running despite pain and discomfort because β-endorphin levels increased and produced a sense of well-being. Since the same variable, β-endorphin level, was measured twice on each subject, this study is an example of a paired design.

The advantage of a paired design is that it makes it easier to detect true differences when they exist. When the same person is measured before and after a marathon, observed differences in β-endorphin levels are more easily attributable to running. If you obtain values for two separate groups of people, one group before the race and another group after, some of the observed difference between the two means might be the result of inherent differences between people in the two groups. For example, the "before" people might have naturally lower levels of β-endorphin than the "after" people.

Paired designs are not restricted to situations in which the same person or object is measured under two different conditions. If you are interested in whether sons are taller than their fathers, you can create father-son pairs. Or if you are interested in whether wives spend more time on household chores than husbands do, you can form wife-husband pairs. The important consideration is that the two members of a pair are matched in some way. In the housework example, if you obtain values from spouses, you're controlling for some of the factors that might be associated with time spent working around the house. For example, the number and ages of children, socioeconomic class, and the size of the house are the same for spouses. You can rule them out as possible explanations for any observed differences between men and women.

> ❓ *What if my matched pairs of cases don't really match?* If it turns out that the pairs of subjects are not really similar, then a paired design will actually make it harder for you to detect true differences than if you didn't pair the subjects but used two independent groups of subjects. For example, if you arbitrarily create pairs of students and then assign each member of a pair to one of two teaching programs, you'll be worse off than if you randomly assigned students to the two teaching programs. The same is true if the characteristics you use to create pairs aren't related to the variable being measured. For example, if you match students on the basis of height when you're studying methods of teaching reading, the pairing will not do you any good. Analyzing the data with a paired *t* test will hinder your ability to detect a true difference between the teaching methods.   ■ ■ ■

Looking at Differences

Whenever you have a paired design, you are primarily interested in the difference between the two measurements for the same individual or for the matched pair. The sign of the difference is important since it tells you the direction of the change. If you subtract the *before* value from the *after* value and the result is positive, that means the values after some event are larger than the values before the event. If the result is negative, the values after the event are smaller than those before the event. If there has been no change, then you expect to have roughly the same number of positive and negative signs.

Figure 13.1 β–endorphin levels for 11 runners

You can obtain a listing like this one by choosing:

Statistics
Summarize ▸
List Cases...

```
    BEFORE     AFTER      DIFF

     4.30     29.60      25.30
     4.60     25.10      20.50
     5.20     15.50      10.30
     5.20     29.60      24.40
     6.60     24.10      17.50
     7.20     37.80      30.60
     8.40     20.20      11.80
     9.00     21.90      12.90
    10.40     14.20       3.80
    14.00     34.60      20.60
    17.80     46.20      28.40


Number of cases read:  11    Number of cases listed:  11
```

Figure 13.1 shows the data values and the difference between the *after* and *before* values for the 11 runners. You can see the stem-and-leaf plot of the difference in Figure 13.2.

Figure 13.2 Stem-and-leaf plot of differences in β—endorphin levels

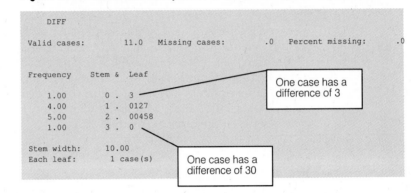

You can obtain stem-and-leaf plots using the Explore procedure, as described in Chapter 7.

See "Examining Normality" on p. 245 for tests that can be used to check for normality.

The first row of the display in Figure 13.2 represents a case with a difference of 3, while the last row represents a case with a difference of 30. (The stem width is 10, which means that the stem values must be multiplied by 10 before adding them to the leaf values.) As you can see in both figures, all of the differences are positive. That is, the *after* values are always greater than the *before* values. The stem-and-leaf plot doesn't suggest any obvious departures from normality, although when you have so few observations, it's hard to tell if the data come from a population that has a normal distribution. (In the section titled "Examining Normality" on p. 245, you'll learn about statistical tests that can be used to check for normality.) The paired-samples *t* test, like the one-sample *t* test to which it's closely related, requires the differences to be a random sample from a normal population, or the sample size to be large enough so that you can rely on the Central Limit Theorem to make the distribution of sample mean differences normal.

? *Isn't it usually impractical to get a random sample from a population?* Yes, in practice that's seldom possible. A large-scale survey like the General Social Survey can draw a random sample of most of the population of the United States, while an investigator who wants to study β–endorphins probably can't take a random sample of American marathon runners. What's possible and important is to make sure that the sample you select is not in some way biased. That is, it should not differ from the population in any important way. For example, if you're studying a new treatment, your patients should not be healthier or sicker than the diseased population of interest. All statistical procedures are based on the assumption that the selected sample is fair. ■ ■ ■

Is the Mean Difference Zero?

The null hypothesis for a paired design is that there is no difference between the average values for the two members of a pair in the population. In other words, the average population difference is 0. The alternative hypothesis is that there is a difference in the average values.

How would you go about statistically testing the hypothesis that the sample comes from a population where the average difference is 0? Just as in the previous chapters, you have to determine if your sample results are unlikely if the null hypothesis is true. That is, you want to know how often you would expect to see a mean difference at least as large as the one you've observed in your sample if the real population difference is 0.

? *What if I want to test whether the two means are equal?* Testing whether the average difference is 0 is the same as testing whether the two means are equal. For example, testing whether the average blood pressure before treatment is the same as the average blood pressure after treatment is the same as testing whether the average difference in the before and after blood pressure values is 0. ■ ■ ■

Two Approaches

If you think about it, you'll realize that you already know how to solve this problem. It's identical to the one you solved in Chapter 13. Once you've calculated the difference between the pair of measurements, you have one sample of differences, and you want to know if it comes from a population with a mean of 0. Instead of testing whether the average *work week* is 40 hours, you want to test whether the average *difference* between the two measurements is 0. You can obtain the answer from SPSS in one of two ways: you can compute the differences and run the One-Sample T Test procedure, or you can run the Paired-Samples T Test procedure, which automatically computes the differences for you.

? *When does it makes sense to use the paired-samples* t *test?* You should use the paired-samples *t* test only when you have measurements for the same variable on two different occasions for the same subject, or when you have values for the same variable for matched pairs of cases. You can't use a paired-samples *t* test to compare average height and weight, for instance, because those are entirely different variables. ■ ■ ■

Computing the One-Sample T Test

See Appendix B for information on computing variables in SPSS.

To use the One-Sample T Test procedure in SPSS to solve this problem, you first compute a new variable that is the difference between the *after* value and the *before* value. (You don't have to do this if you have a variable that is the difference.)

The output from the One-Sample T Test procedure is shown in Figure 13.3. You see that the average difference between the *after* and *before* marathon values is 18.74 picomoles per liter. The standard deviation of the difference is 8.33 pmol/l. The 95% confidence interval for the average difference is between 13.14 and 24.33 pmol/l. Since the confidence interval does not include the value of 0, you can reject the null hypothesis that the average difference between the two measurements is 0, in the population. It's unlikely that you would see a sample difference at least as large as 18.74, for samples of 11 pairs, when the true difference is 0. An equivalent way of testing the hypothesis is to look at the *t* value and its associated two-tailed significance level. As you expect, the significance level is small ($p < 0.0005$), leading you to reject the null hypothesis. It appears that β-endorphin levels rise during a marathon run. (In fact, the authors found that the median β-endorphin level for a sample of people who collapsed during the run was

110 pmol/l. That was significantly different from the median levels for the runners who did not collapse.)

Figure 13.3 Output from the One-Sample T Test procedure

You can obtain this output using the One-Sample T Test procedure, as described in Chapter 12.

```
One Sample t-tests


                                      Number
        Variable                     of Cases        Mean          SD      SE of Mean

        DIFF                            11         18.7364        8.330       2.512



           Test Value = 0

        Mean               95% CI
        Difference     Lower     Upper   |    t-value       df     2-Tail Sig

           18.74      13.140    24.332   |      7.46         10       .000
```

> Since the confidence interval does not include 0, you can reject the null hypothesis that the average difference is 0

How do I fill in the One-Sample T Test dialog box for this kind of test? It's easy. The Test Variable is the variable that contains the differences between the two values of a variable for a pair. The Test Value remains at 0, its default, since you're interested in testing whether the test variable comes from a population with a mean of 0. ■ ■ ■

The Paired-Samples t Test

To use the one-sample *t* test to test a hypothesis about the mean difference between pairs of observations, you have to compute the differences between the pair of values for each case. You can skip that step if you use the Paired-Samples T Test procedure. This procedure automatically calculates the differences. Figure 13.4 is output from the Paired-Samples T Test procedure for the same problem.

Figure 13.4 Output from the Paired-Samples T Test procedure

To obtain this output, from the menus choose:

*Statistics
Compare Means ▶
Paired-Samples...*

Select the before and after variables, as shown in Figure 13.7.

```
t-tests for Paired Samples

                    Number of          2-tail
Variable              pairs    Corr    Sig       Mean        SD      SE of Mean

AFTER                                          27.1636      9.678      2.918
                       11      .515    .105
BEFORE                                          8.4273      4.248      1.281


           Paired Differences
    Mean        SD     SE of Mean  |   t-value        df      2-tail Sig

  18.7364     8.330     2.512      |    7.46          10        .000
  95% CI (13.140, 24.332)         |
```

Results in the lower part of table are the same as in Figure 13.3

You see that there are separate summary statistics for the *after* and *before* measurements. The average value for the β-endorphins after running is 27.16 pmol/l, while before running it is 8.43. (The statistic labeled *Corr* measures how strongly the *before* and *after* values are related. This statistic is discussed further in Chapter 20.)

Statistics for the differences between the two measures are shown in the second part of the table. You see that the statistics in this part of the table are identical to those in Figure 13.3. That's because the same analysis is being performed with both procedures.

Are You Positive?

Based on the paired-samples *t* test, you concluded that β-endorphin levels appear to change during a half-marathon run. Can you be absolutely certain of this conclusion? The answer is no. Whenever you reject the null hypothesis, there is a chance that you are wrong. That's because you reject the null hypothesis when the observed sample results appear to be unlikely, not impossible. The observed significance level even tells you the probability that you would see results as extreme as the ones you observed *when the null hypothesis is true*. If your null hypothesis is true, and you decide to reject it whenever the observed significance level for a sample is less than 0.05, you will be rejecting a perfectly good null hypothesis 5% of the time.

Statisticians creatively call this type of error—rejecting the null hypothesis when it is true—a **Type 1 error**. The other error—failing to reject the null hypothesis when it is false—is called a **Type 2 error**. You would make a Type 2 error if you conclude that running doesn't change β-endorphin levels when in fact it does. Table 13.1 summarizes what can happen when you test a null hypothesis.

Table 13.1 Testing a Null Hypothesis

	The null hypothesis is:	
Your action	True	False
Reject	Type 1 error	You are correct
Not reject	You are correct	Type 2 error

In Chapter 14, you'll learn more about the factors that contribute to Type 1 and Type 2 errors.

Some Possible Problems

When you have a paired design in which the same person is studied under two different conditions, poor experimental design may also cause you to reject the null hypothesis when it true. When you use a paired design, you should keep in mind the following caveats:

- If you want to compare two treatments on the same person, you must make sure that enough time passes between treatments so that one treatment wears off before the other begins. Otherwise, you won't be able to separate the effects of the two interventions. For example, if you want to study the effect of two different tasks on pulse rate, you must make sure the subject's pulse returns to normal before the second task is begun.

- If you have subjects repeat the same task or test twice, they may do better the second time because of the learning effect. That's why you should be wary of experiments in which the same (or a similar) test is administered before and after an intervention. Even if the intervention is ineffective, the learning effect may cause a change in the two sets of scores.

See Chapter 18 for information about nonparametric tests, which do not require the assumption of normality.

Examining Normality

Since a paired-samples *t* test is fundamentally the same as a one-sample *t* test, the same assumptions are required for its use. The differences should come from a normal population, or the sample size should be large enough so that the distribution of sample mean differences is approximately normal. In Figure 13.2 you see that there are no strange or outlying values. Although the sample size is small, the observed data may well be from a normal distribution.

Although you can examine a histogram or a stem-and-leaf plot to see if the data appear to come from a normal distribution, there are special plots and statistics that make it easier for you to assess normality. One such plot, called a **normal probability plot**, or **Q-Q plot**, is shown in Figure 13.5. For each data point, the Q-Q plot shows the observed value and the value that's expected if the data are a sample from a normal distribution. The points should cluster around a straight line if the data are from a normal distribution. The normal probability plot of the difference variable is more or less linear, so the assumption of normality appears to be reasonable.

Figure 13.5 Q-Q plot for β-endorphin differences

You can obtain normal Q-Q charts using the Graphs menu, as described in Appendix A. Select the variable diff in the Normal Q-Q dialog box.

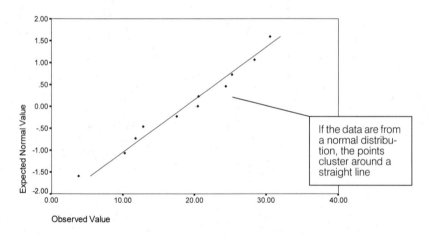

If the data are from a normal distribution, the points cluster around a straight line

There are also formal statistical tests that you can use to test the null hypothesis that the data are a sample from a normal distribution. If the observed significance levels for the tests are small, you have reason to doubt the assumption of normality. Two commonly used tests are shown in Figure 13.6.

Figure 13.6 Shapiro-Wilk's and K-S Lilliefors tests for normality

Normality tests can be obtained using the Explore procedure, as described in Chapter 7.

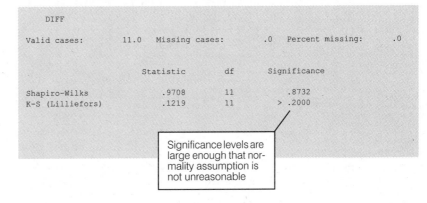

Their observed significance levels are reasonably large, indicating that normality is not an unreasonable assumption. Of course, for small sample sizes, you may be unable to reject the normality assumption even if it's wrong. If the assumption of normality appears suspect and the sample size is small, you should consider transforming the data values—for example by taking logs or square roots—to make the distribution more normal. If this is unsuccessful, you can use a statistical test that does not require the assumption of normality. Such tests are described in Chapter 18.

Should I not use the t test if the significance level for the test of normality is small? It depends upon your sample size. If you have a large sample, even small differences from normality may result in a small observed significance level for the tests of normality. This is just another example of the fact that when samples are large, even small differences may be statistically significant, though not necessarily of any practical importance. So if your sample is large and the distribution of values is not extremely far from normal, you don't really have to worry. The *t* test does not by any means require that the sample come from a perfectly normal population. ■ ■ ■

Summary

How can you test the null hypothesis that the average difference between a pair of measurements is 0?

- In a paired design, the same subject is observed under two conditions, or data are obtained from a pair of subjects that are matched in some way.

- Paired designs help to make the two groups being compared more similar. Some of the differences between subjects are eliminated.

- If you observe the same subject under two conditions, you must make sure that the effect of one treatment has worn off before the other one is given.

- You can compare two related means using a paired-samples *t* test.

- A Type 1 error is made when you reject a null hypothesis that is true. A Type 2 error is made when you don't reject a null hypothesis that is false.

- The normal probability plot is used to examine the assumption of normality.

What's Next?

In this chapter, you learned how to test hypotheses about two means when the data are obtained from matched pairs of observations. You saw that the paired *t* test is the same as a one-sample *t* test of the differences. In Chapter 14, you'll learn how to test hypotheses about two independent means.

How to Obtain a Paired-Samples t Test

The Paired-Samples T Test procedure tests the null hypothesis that the difference in means of two related variables is 0. It also displays a confidence interval for the difference between the population means of the two variables.

▶ To open the Paired-Samples T Test dialog box (see Figure 13.7), from the menus choose:

Statistics
  Compare Means ▶
    Paired-Samples T Test...

Figure 13.7 Paired-Samples T Test dialog box

Select before and after to produce the output shown in Figure 13.4. On the Macintosh, you must hold down ⌘ as you select the second variable in a pair.

Click to add current selections to list

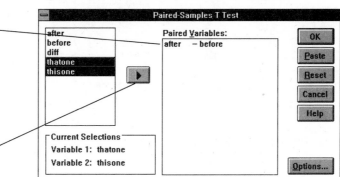

To compare means between two groups of cases for one or more variables, see Chapter 14.

▶ In the Paired-Samples T Test dialog box, click on each of the two variables whose means you want to compare. Make sure that their names appear in the Current Selections box, then click the usual button to move them into the Paired Variables list.

If you click on a variable by mistake but have not yet moved the pair into the Paired Variables list, simply click it again to remove it from the Current Selections box. If you add an incorrect pair to the Paired Variables list, select it in that list and move it back out.

▶ Click on OK.

You can select more than one pair of variables if desired. For each pair of variables, SPSS calculates a *t* statistic and its observed significance level.

Options: Confidence Level, Labels, and Missing Data

In the Paired-Samples T Test Options dialog box, Figure 13.8, you can change the confidence level for which SPSS displays the confidence interval for the difference between the population means of the pair of variables.

▶ In the Paired-Samples T Test dialog box, click on Options to open the Paired-Samples T Test Options dialog box.

Figure 13.8 Paired-Samples T Test Options dialog box

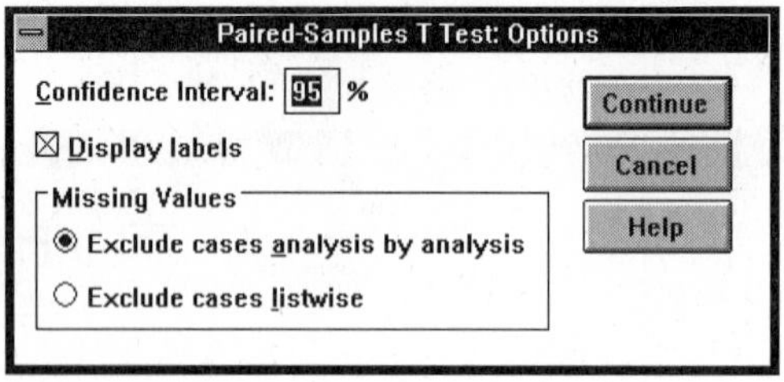

Confidence Interval. Specify a value (such as 90 or 99) in this text box.

Display labels. This check box lets you suppress the display of variable labels.

Missing Values. Two alternatives control the treatment of missing data for multiple pairs of variables:

Exclude cases analysis by analysis. Uses all cases that have valid data for the two variables in a pair in the test for that pair.

Exclude cases listwise. Uses only the cases that have valid data for all variables in any of the pairs. This ensures that all of the tests are performed using the same cases.

Exercises

Statistical Concepts

1. An investigator wants to test the hypothesis that children who drink orange juice before class will be more attentive than children who drink milk. He selects a classroom of children and obtains an alphabetical list of the students. He assigns the first child to orange juice therapy, the next to milk therapy, and so on down the list. He wants to analyze the experiment using the paired *t* test, since he has formed pairs of children based on the alphabetic list. Suggest to him how he might analyze his data. Do you think this is a paired experiment? If not, give an example of a paired design for this question.

2. Studies sometimes use twins who have been raised separately to investigate questions like, "What are the roles of parental influence and genetic heritage in

children's intellectual development?" Discuss the advantages and disadvantages that you see in using twins for studies of this nature.

3. Discuss any problems you see in the following studies:

a. Anxiety often affects performance on tests. A psychologist has developed a new method for reducing stress during statistics exams. To evaluate the new method he tests each of 50 students under two conditions. He gives each student the final exam before stress-reduction training and then again after the training. He then compares the two sets of scores.

b. A market researcher wants to study consumer preferences for five brands of pizza. He invites 250 people to a pizza party. Each person is instructed to make sure that he or she eats a piece of all five brands. As they are leaving, each participant fills out a questionnaire evaluating the five brands of pizza.

c. As a drug manufacturer you're interested in studying the effectiveness of a new drug for headache relief. You place an ad in the newspaper recruiting "headache sufferers" who want to volunteer for the study. At the beginning of the study you question each participant about the frequency and duration of headaches. Then you send the sufferers home with a week's supply of new medicine. A week later, you ask each participant the same questions about their headaches.

d. You want to compare two methods for weight reduction. You recruit 123 people who are interested in losing weight. You instruct everyone to use the first method until they have lost 10 pounds, and then use the second method until they have lost 10 more. You then compare the length of time it takes to lose the first 10 pounds to the length of time it takes to lose the next 10 pounds.

Data Analysis

Use the *gss.sav* data file to answer the following questions:

1. Use the Compute facility to create a new variable that is the difference between a husband's and wife's years of education (variables *husbeduc* and *wifeduc*).

a. Make a histogram of the difference. What should you look for in the histogram?

b. Make a Q-Q plot of the differences. How does the distribution differ from the normal distribution?

c. Identify the outlying points using point selection mode and go to the Data Editor to look at their values. Record the values. Are they believable?

d. Since the sample size is quite large, it's reasonable to believe that the distribution of mean differences is normal. Perform a paired *t* test using the Paired-Samples T Test procedure. Write a brief summary of your results. Be sure to state your null and alternative hypotheses.

e. Run a one-sample t test on the difference variable. Compare your results to those from the paired t test. In what ways are the two tests different?

2. Now consider differences between the parents' years of education (variables *paeduc* and *maeduc*). Is there a statistically significant average difference between fathers' and mothers' years of education? Summarize your findings.

Use the *gssft.sav* data file to answer the following questions:

3. You are studying the work habits of spouses. You want to know whether husbands and wives who are both employed full time (variable *bothft* equals 1) work the same average number of hours per week (variables *husbhr* and *wifehr*). Perform the appropriate analyses and write a short summary of your results.

4. Based on the analyses you performed in question 3, is it reasonable to conclude that women who work full time on average work fewer hours than men who work full time? Explain your reasoning.

Use the *electric.sav* data file to answer the following question:

5. Make histograms and Q-Q plots of *dbp58, cgt58, wt58, chol58,* and *ht58.* Describe for each variable the types of departures from normality that you see.

Use the *schools.sav* data file to answer the following question:

6. Look at the changes between 1993 and 1994 in graduation rates (variables *grad93* and *grad94*), ACT scores (variables *act93* and *act94*), and percentages of students taking ACT tests (variables *pctact93* and *pctact94*). Does it look like the Chicago school system is improving? Which schools appear to be "outliers?"

Use the *renal.sav* data file to answer the following question:

7. For patients who developed acute renal failure (variable *type* equals 1), determine if there was a statistically significant change in average BUN and creatinine at admission (variables *admbun* and *admcreat*) and average BUN and creatinine at discharge (variables *finbun* and *fincreat*). For all patients see if there was a statistically significant change in creatinine between the time of admission (variable *admcreat*) and the time of surgery (variable *precreat*).

Use the *country.sav* data file to answer the following question:

8. Test the null hypothesis that the average life expectancy for males is the same as the average life expectancy for females (variables *lifeexpm* and *lifeexpf*). Look at the distribution of the differences. Summarize your conclusions.

Use the *buying.sav* data file to answer the following question:

9. Test the following hypotheses: husbands' and wives' average buying scores are equal (variables *hsumbuy* and *wsumbuy*); wives' average buying scores and their husbands' prediction of them are equal (variables *wsumbuy* and *hpredsum*); husbands' average buying scores and their wives' prediction of them are equal (variables *hsumbuy* and *wpredsum*); average influence scores assigned by husbands and wives are equal (variables *hsuminf* and *wsuminf*). Be sure to look at the distribution of differences. Summarize your results.

Testing a Hypothesis about Two Independent Means

How can you test the null hypothesis that two population means are equal, based on the results observed in two independent samples?

- Why can't you use a one-sample *t* test?
- What assumptions are needed for the two independent-samples *t* test?
- Can you prove the null hypothesis is true?
- What is power, and why is it important?

You know how to test whether a single sample of data comes from a population with a known mean. You've tested whether the average cholesterol level for CEO's is the same as the average for the general population, whether college graduates work a 40-hour week on average, and whether the average change in β-endorphin values is 0 during a half-marathon run. In Chapter 13, although you had pairs of observations, you analyzed the differences between the two values and tested the hypothesis that these differences come from a population with a mean of 0.

In this chapter, you'll learn how to test whether two population means are equal based on the results observed in two independent samples—one from each of the populations of interest. You'll use a statistical technique called the **two independent-samples t test**. You can use the two independent-samples *t* test to see if, in the population, men and women have the same scores on a test of physical dexterity or if two treatments for high cholesterol result in the same mean cholesterol levels.

▶ This chapter uses the *gssft.sav* data file, which includes only cases for people holding full-time jobs. For instructions on how to obtain the independent-samples *t* test output shown in this chapter, see "How to Obtain an Independent-Samples t Test" on p. 271.

Looking at Age Differences

In Part 2 of this book, you examined the relationship between job satisfaction, age, and education for full-time employees. You saw that the average values of age and education vary among the different job satisfaction groups. That isn't surprising, since you know that even if the average ages and educational levels in the population are the same for all job satisfaction groups, the sample means will not be equal. Different samples from the same population result in different sample means and standard deviations. To determine if any of the observed sample differences among groups might be real, that is, not simply the result of the usual variability of sample means from a single population, you need to determine if the observed sample means would be unusual when the population means are equal.

Let's consider what happens if you form two independent groups of people—those who are very satisfied with their jobs and those who are not. You want to determine whether the population values for average age and average education are the same for the two groups. First we'll look at age.

What do you mean by independent groups? Samples from different groups are called **independent** if there is no relationship between the people or objects in the different groups. For example, if you select a random sample of males and a random sample of females from a population, the two samples are independent. That's because selecting a person for one group in no way influences the selection of a person for another group. The two groups in a paired design are not independent, since either the same people or closely matched people are in both groups.

Since you have means from two independent groups, you can't use the one-sample t test to test the null hypothesis that two population means are equal. That's because you now have to cope with the variability of two sample means: the mean for *very satisfied* people and the mean for the *not very satisfied* people. When you test whether a single sample comes from a population with a known mean, you only have to worry about how much individual means from the same population vary. The population value to which you compare your sample mean is a fixed, known number. It doesn't vary from sample to sample. You assumed that the value of 205 mg/dL for the cholesterol of the general population is an established norm based on large-scale studies. Similarly, the value of 40 hours for a work week is a commonly held belief.

The two independent-samples *t* test is basically a modification of the one-sample *t* test that incorporates information about the variability of the two independent-sample means. The standard error of the mean difference is no longer estimated from the variance and number of cases in a single group. Instead, it is estimated from the variances and sample sizes of the two independent groups.

Descriptive Statistics

Look at Figure 14.1, which shows descriptive statistics for the age variable, when full-time workers are classified into one of two distinct groups—the *very satisfied* and the *not very satisfied*.

Figure 14.1 Descriptive statistics for age by job satisfaction category

You can obtain these statistics using the Explore procedure, which is described in Chapter 7. Select the variables age and satjob2 in the Explore dialog box.

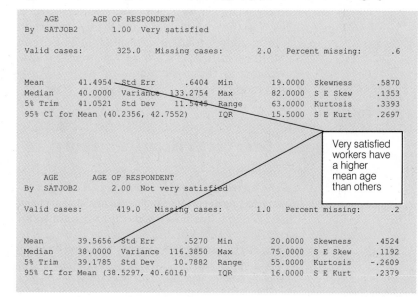

```
        AGE       AGE OF RESPONDENT
By  SATJOB2       1.00  Very satisfied

Valid cases:      325.0   Missing cases:      2.0   Percent missing:      .6


Mean       41.4954  Std Err      .6404  Min     19.0000  Skewness       .5870
Median     40.0000  Variance  133.2754  Max     82.0000  S E Skew       .1353
5% Trim    41.0521  Std Dev    11.5445  Range   63.0000  Kurtosis       .3393
95% CI for Mean (40.2356, 42.7552)      IQR     15.5000  S E Kurt       .2697
```

Very satisfied workers have a higher mean age than others

```
        AGE       AGE OF RESPONDENT
By  SATJOB2       2.00  Not very satisfied

Valid cases:      419.0   Missing cases:      1.0   Percent missing:      .2


Mean       39.5656  Std Err      .5270  Min     20.0000  Skewness       .4524
Median     38.0000  Variance  116.3850  Max     75.0000  S E Skew       .1192
5% Trim    39.1785  Std Dev    10.7882  Range   55.0000  Kurtosis      -.2609
95% CI for Mean (38.5297, 40.6016)      IQR     16.0000  S E Kurt       .2379
```

You see that the average age of the *very satisfied* group is 41.5 years, while the average age of the *not very satisfied* group is 39.6. The standard deviation of the *very satisfied* group, 11.5 years, is slightly larger than the standard deviation of the *not very satisfied* group, 10.8 years. In the General Social Survey sample the *very satisfied* people are on average 1.9

years older than those less content with their jobs. Based on these sample results what can you reasonably conclude about the population of American adults who are employed full time? Can you conclude that there is a difference in average ages between the two groups?

Distribution of Differences

To answer this question, you have to determine if your observed age difference would be unusual if the two populations have the same average age. In the previous chapters, you answered similar questions by looking at the distribution of all possible means from a population. Now you'll look at the distribution of all possible *differences* between sample means from two independent groups.

Fortunately, the Central Limit Theorem works for differences of sample means as well as for individual means. So if your data are samples from approximately normal populations, or your sample size is large enough so that the Central Limit Theorem holds, the distribution of differences between two sample means is also normal. It's always a good idea to obtain stem-and-leaf plots or histograms for each of the two groups. From these, you can tell what the distribution of values looks like.

Standard Error of the Mean Difference

If two samples come from populations with the same mean, the mean of the distribution of differences is 0. However, that's not enough information to determine if the observed sample results are unusual. You also need to know how much the sample differences vary. The standard deviation of the difference between two sample means, the **standard error of the mean difference**, tells you that. When you have two independent groups, you must estimate the standard error of the mean difference from the standard deviations and the sample sizes in each of the two groups.

? *How do I estimate the standard error of the difference?*
The formula is

$$S_{\bar{X}_1 - \bar{X}_2} = \sqrt{\frac{S_1^2}{n_1} + \frac{S_2^2}{n_2}}$$

where S_1^2 is the variance for the first sample and S_2^2 is the variance for the second sample. The sample sizes for the two samples are n_1 and n_2. If you look carefully at the formula, you'll see that the standard error of the mean difference depends on the standard errors of the two sample means. You square the standard error of the mean for each of the two groups. Next you sum them, and then take the square root. ■ ■ ■

Computing the t Statistic

Once you've estimated the standard error of the mean difference, you can compute the *t* statistic the same way as in the previous chapters. You divide the observed mean difference by the standard error of the difference. This tells you how many standard error units from the population mean of 0 your observed difference falls. That is,

$$t = \frac{\left(\bar{X}_1 - \bar{X}_2\right) - 0}{S_{\bar{X}_1 - \bar{X}_2}}$$

Equation 14.1

If your observed difference is unlikely when the null hypothesis is true, you can reject the null hypothesis.

? *How is this different from the one-sample* t *test?* The idea is exactly the same. What differs is that you now have two independent-sample means, not one. So you estimate the standard error of the mean difference based on two sample variances and two sample sizes. ■ ■ ■

Output from the Two Independent-Samples t Test

Look at Figure 14.2, which shows the results from SPSS of testing the null hypothesis that in the population the average age of *very satisfied* full-time workers and *not very satisfied* full-time workers is the same.

Figure 14.2 Independent-samples t test of age by job satisfaction

To obtain this
output, from
the menus
choose:

Statistics
  Compare Means ▶
    Independent
    Samples...

Select the variables
age and satjob2,
as shown in
Figure 14.8.

```
t-tests for Independent Samples of SATJOB2    Job Satisfaction


                              Number
Variable                     of Cases      Mean         SD    SE of Mean

AGE   AGE OF RESPONDENT

Very satisfied                  325     41.4954      11.544        .640
Not very satisfied              419     39.5656      10.788        .527


      Mean Difference = 1.9298

      Levene's Test for Equality of Variances: F= .377    P= .540


        t-test for Equality of Means                            95%
Variances   t-value      df    2-Tail Sig   SE of Diff    CI for Diff

Equal        2.35       742       .019         .822      (.315, 3.544)
Unequal      2.33     672.44      .020         .829      (.301, 3.558)
```

The mean age for the two samples differs by 1.93 years

There is only a 1.9% chance of observing a mean difference at least this large if the null hypothesis is true

In the output, there are two slightly different versions of the *t* test. One makes the assumption that the variances in the two populations are equal; the other does not. This assumption affects how the standard error of the mean difference is calculated. You'll learn more about this distinction later in this chapter.

Consider the row labeled *Equal*. You see that for the observed difference of 1.93 years, the *t* statistic is 2.35. (To calculate the *t* statistic, divide the observed difference of 1.93 by 0.822, the standard error of the difference estimate when the two population variances are assumed to be equal.) The degrees of freedom for the *t* statistic are 742, the sum of the sample sizes in the two groups minus 2.

The observed two-tailed significance level is 0.019. This tells you that only 1.9% of the time would you expect to see a sample difference of 1.93 years or larger, when the two population means are equal. Since 1.9% is less than 5%, you reject the null hypothesis that the two groups of workers come from populations with the same average age. Your observed results are unusual if the null hypothesis is true.

Confidence Intervals for the Mean Difference

Take another look at Figure 14.2. The 95% confidence interval for the true difference is from 0.315 years to 3.544 years. This tells you it's likely that the true mean difference is anywhere from a third of a year to slightly more than three and one-half years. Since your observed significance level for the test that the two population means are equal was less than 5%, you know that the 95% confidence interval will not contain the value of 0. (Remember, only likely values are included in a confidence interval. Since you found 0 to be an unlikely value, it won't be included in the confidence interval.)

To calculate a 99% confidence interval, specify 99 in the T Test Options dialog box (see Figure 14.10).

? *If I compute a 99% confidence interval for the true mean difference, will it also not include 0?* The 99% confidence interval for the mean difference extends from –0.194 to 4.053. This interval does include the value of 0. That's because your observed significance level is greater than 1%. If your criterion for unusual is 1 in a 100 or less, you cannot reject the null hypothesis based on the *t* test or on the corresponding 99% confidence interval for the mean difference. ■ ■ ■

Another Way of Looking at It

You found a small, but statistically significant, age difference between people who are *very satisfied* with their jobs and those who aren't. Since the observed sample difference is less than two years, it's tempting to dismiss this finding as not particularly interesting. However, there are many different ways you can look at the relationships between the two variables. Sometimes uninteresting information can become more interesting when looked at in another way.

Figure 14.3 Crosstabulation of job satisfaction and age

You can obtain
crosstabulations
using the
Crosstabs
procedure, as
discussed in
Chapter 8.

```
AGECAT4  by  SATJOB2   Job Satisfaction

                        SATJOB2         Page 1 of 1
             Count
             Row Pct  Very sat Not very
                      isfied    satisfi   Row
                        1.00      2.00 |  Total
AGECAT4      ─────────────────────────────
             1.00        46        91     137
18-29                  33.6      66.4     18.3

             2.00       112       131     243
30-39                  46.1      53.9     32.5

             3.00        89       121     210
40-49                  42.4      57.6     28.1

             4.00        80        77     157
50+                    51.0      49.0     21.0

           Column       327       420     747
           Total       43.8      56.2   100.0
```

33.6% of people less than 30 are very satisfied with their jobs

51% of people age 50 and over are very satisfied

```
   Chi-Square              Value       DF      Significance
──────────────────────  ───────────   ────    ────────────

Pearson                   9.77330       3         .02059
Likelihood Ratio          9.89026       3         .01952
Mantel-Haenszel test for  5.91108       1         .01505
   linear association

Minimum Expected Frequency -   59.972
```

Look at Figure 14.3, which is a crosstabulation of the two categories of job satisfaction and four categories of age. From the row percentages, you see that only 33.6% of people less than 30 are *very satisfied* with their jobs, while over 50% of people age 50 and over are *very satisfied*. Overall, 43.8% of full-time workers claim to be *very satisfied* with their jobs. The crosstabulation provides findings that are more interesting and easier to interpret. (In Chapter 17, you'll learn how to test hypotheses that the two variables in a crosstabulation are independent, and you'll learn how to interpret the statistics along the bottom of Figure 14.3.)

Testing the Equality of Variances

You saw that there are two different *t* values in Figure 14.2. That's because there are two different ways to estimate the standard error of the difference. One of them assumes that the variances are equal in the two populations from which you are taking samples, the other one does not.

In Figure 14.1, you see that the observed standard deviations in the two samples are fairly similar. You can test the null hypothesis that the two samples come from populations with the same variances using the Levene test, which is shown in Figure 14.4. If the observed significance level for the Levene test is small, you can reject the null hypothesis that the two population variances are equal.

For this example, you can't reject the equal variances hypothesis, since the observed significance level for the Levene test is 0.54. That means you can use the results labeled *equal variances* in Figure 14.4.

Figure 14.4 Levene test for equality of variances

To obtain this output, select the variables age and satjob2 in the Independent-Samples T Test dialog box, as shown in Figure 14.8.

```
t-tests for Independent Samples of SATJOB2     Job Satisfaction


                                Number
Variable                        of Cases      Mean         SD    SE of Mean

AGE   AGE OF RESPONDENT

Very satisfied                     325      41.4954     11.544        .640
Not very satisfied                 419      39.5656     10.788        .527


       Mean Difference = 1.9298

          Levene's Test for Equality of Variances: F= .377    P= .540


        t-test for Equality of Means                            95%
Variances   t-value      df    2-Tail Sig    SE of Diff       CI for Diff

Equal        2.35       742        .019          .822       (.315, 3.544)
Unequal      2.33     672.44       .020          .829       (.301, 3.558)
```

You don't reject the hypothesis that the two population variances are equal based on the Levene test

If the Levene test leads you to reject the null hypothesis that the two population variances are equal, or if you are unsure, you should use the results from the row labeled *Unequal* in Figure 14.4. Notice that the estimate of the standard error of the difference is not the same in the two rows. This affects the *t* value and confidence interval. When you use the unequal variance estimate of the standard error of the difference, the degrees of freedom for the *t* statistic are no longer the sum of the two sample sizes minus two. They are calculated based on both the sample sizes and the standard deviations in each of the groups. In this example, the *Equal* and *Unequal* variance *t* tests give very similar results, but that's not always the case.

? *Why do you get different numbers for the standard error of the mean difference depending on the assumptions you make about the population variances?* If you assume that the two population variances are equal, you can compute what's called a pooled estimate of the variance. The idea is similar to that of averaging the variances in the two groups, taking into account the sample size. The formula for the pooled variance is

$$S^2 = \frac{(n_1 - 1) S_1^2 + (n_2 - 1) S_2^2}{(n_1 - 1) + (n_2 - 1)}$$

It's this pooled value that is substituted for both S_1^2 and S_2^2 in the equation on p. 257. If you don't assume that the two population variances are equal, the individual sample variances are used in the equation on p. 257. ■ ■ ■

Comparing Education

From the previous analysis, you concluded that there appears to be a difference in average ages between those who are *very satisfied* with their jobs and those who are not. Younger people tend to be less satisfied with their jobs than older people. Now consider education. As always, your first step should be to look at the data values in the two groups. Look at the distributions, and try to see if there's anything unusual going on. For small sample sizes, see if the distribution of data values is approximately normal.

Figure 14.5 contains the descriptive statistics for the two groups. You see that the very satisfied people are somewhat better educated (or at least went to school longer) than those who are *not very satisfied*. The difference is slightly more than a third of a year. Figure 14.6 shows the distribution of education graphically. From the boxplot, you see that the variability of the two groups is similar. Since the median for the *very satisfied* group is in the middle of the box, the distribution of values for the group is more or less symmetric. One case stands out in the plot. That's the person who claims no formal education. For the *not very satisfied* group, the median is close to the bottom edge, indicating that there is a tail toward higher educational levels. If your sample is small, and the departures from normality are severe, you may want to substitute one of the nonparametric tests described in Chapter 18 for the independent-samples *t* test. In this case, the sample sizes are large, so the independent-samples *t* test should work just fine.

Figure 14.5 Descriptive statistics for education by job satisfaction

You can obtain these statistics using the Explore procedure, as discussed in Chapter 7.

```
      EDUC        HIGHEST YEAR OF SCHOOL CO
By  SATJOB2         1.00  Very satisfied

Valid cases:         327.0  Missing cases:        .0  Percent missing:      .0


Mean         14.2508  Std Err     .1545  Min       .0000  Skewness    -.3084
Median       14.0000  Variance  7.8081  Max     20.0000  S E Skew     .1348
5% Trim      14.2830  Std Dev   2.7943  Range   20.0000  Kurtosis    1.6528
95% CI for Mean (13.9468, 14.5548)      IQR      4.0000  S E Kurt     .2689


      EDUC        HIGHEST YEAR OF SCHOOL CO
By  SATJOB2         2.00  Not very satisfied

Valid cases:         420.0  Missing cases:        .0  Percent missing:      .0


Mean         13.8714  Std Err     .1277  Min      6.0000  Skewness     .1828
Median       13.0000  Variance  6.8474  Max     20.0000  S E Skew     .1191
5% Trim      13.8651  Std Dev   2.6168  Range   14.0000  Kurtosis    -.1983
95% CI for Mean (13.6204, 14.1224)      IQR      4.0000  S E Kurt     .2376
```

Figure 14.6 Boxplot of education by job satisfaction

You can obtain this boxplot using the Explore procedure, as discussed in Chapter 7.

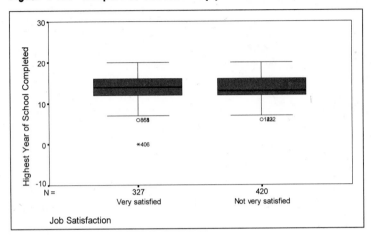

Based on the Levene test in Figure 14.7, there is no reason to doubt that the population variances are equal, so you can use the *t* value in the row labeled *Equal* to test the null hypothesis that in the population, the average years of education are the same for those who are *very satisfied* with their jobs and those who are not. The two-tailed significance level is 0.057, so you don't reject the null hypothesis. As expected, the 95% confidence interval for the mean difference includes the value of 0.

Figure 14.7 Independent-samples t test of education by job satisfaction

To obtain this output, select the variables educ and satjob2 in the Independent-Samples T Test dialog box. See Figure 14.8.

```
t-tests for Independent Samples of SATJOB2    Job Satisfaction


                            Number
                          of Cases      Mean       SD   SE of Mean
Variable

EDUC   Highest Year of School Completed

Very satisfied              327       14.2508     2.794      .155
Not very satisfied          420       13.8714     2.617      .128


       Mean Difference = .3793

       Levene's Test for Equality of Variances: F= .261    P= .609


          t-test for Equality of Means                          95%
Variances    t-value      df    2-Tail Sig    SE of Diff    CI for Diff

Equal         1.91       745      .057          .199       (-.011, .770)
Unequal       1.89     677.43     .059          .200       (-.014, .773)
```

Can You Prove the Null Hypothesis?

You may have noticed that when phrasing the results of a hypothesis test, we've always been careful to say that you either rejected the null hypothesis or not rejected it. The phrase, "You've proved the null hypothesis is true" has never been used. The reason for that is that you can't prove that the null hypothesis is true. Think about it. Do you really believe that you've shown that the average years of education are exactly the same for people who are *very satisfied* with their jobs and those who are not? Of course not. Your sample results are compatible with many values besides 0 for the population difference. Even if you observed a sample difference of 0, that wouldn't tell you that the true difference is 0. Sample differences of 0 are compatible with values other than 0 for the true population difference.

From the 95% confidence interval, you see that values anywhere in the range of –0.011 to 0.770 years are plausible. If you increase your sample size, your confidence interval will become shorter; that is, it will include fewer "plausible" values, but it will never exclude all values except 0. What all this means is that based on the results of a hypothesis test, you should never claim that you've shown that the null hypothesis is really true. All you can claim is that your sample results are not unusual if the null hypothesis is true.

Sometimes a legal analogy is drawn to statistical hypothesis testing. The null hypothesis is compared to the presumption of innocence in a legal case. Failure to find a defendant guilty doesn't prove innocence. All it says is that there was not enough evidence to establish guilt.

Interpreting the Observed Significance Level

When the observed significance level is small, you reject the null hypothesis and conclude that the two population means appear to be unequal. However, you know that there's a chance that your conclusion is wrong. It's possible that the null hypothesis is true, and your observed difference is one of the remote events that can occur. In fact, that's what the observed significance level tells you—how often you would expect to see a difference at least as large as the one you observed when the null hypothesis is true.

When your observed significance level is too large for you to reject the null hypothesis that the means are equal, two explanations are possible. The first explanation is that really there is no difference between the two population means (a conjecture you can't prove), or that there is a small difference, and you can't detect it. For example, if there really is an average difference of 30 days of education between the *very satisfied* and *not very satisfied* groups, it's of little consequence that you can't identify it. Differences of $10 in annual income or 1 point on a standardized test are rarely important.

The second explanation is more troublesome: there is an important difference between the two groups, but you did not detect it. How can this happen? One reason you did not reject the null hypothesis when it is false may be that the sample size is small and the observed result doesn't appear to be unusual. Remember, when the sample size is small, many outcomes are compatible with the null hypothesis being true. For example, if you flip a coin only three times, you'll never be able to exclude the possibility that it is a fair coin.

> *Why not?* If a coin is fair and you flip it three times, the probability of observing three heads or three tails is 0.25. That means that one out of four times when you flip a fair coin three times, you will get all heads or all tails. So even if you're flipping a coin that has two heads or two tails, the results you get (all heads or all tails) are compatible with the null hypothesis that the coin is fair.

Even if there is a large difference in education between the *very satisfied* and *not very satisfied* groups, you may not be able to detect it if you have five cases in each of the two groups. That's because the observed sample difference may be compatible with many population values, including 0.

Your ability to reject the null hypothesis when it is false also depends on the variability of the observed values. If your observed values have a lot of variability, the range of plausible values for the true population difference will be broad. For the same sample size, as the variability decreases, the range of plausible population values does, too. Remember, when you calculate a t statistic, you divide the observed difference by the standard error of the difference. The standard error of the difference depends on both the sample variances and the sample sizes.

Power

Power is the statistical term used to describe your ability to reject the null hypothesis when it is false. It is a probability that ranges from 0 to 1. The larger the power, the more likely you are to reject the null hypothesis when it is false. Power depends on how large the true difference is, your sample size, the variance of the difference and the significance level at which you are willing to reject the null hypothesis. Although detailed discussion of power is beyond the scope of this book, since power is so important in data analysis, let's consider a simple example.

? *Why does power depend on all these factors?* All these factors are involved in the computation of the *t* statistic, which is what determines whether you reject the null hypothesis. You'll have a large *t* statistic if the numerator is large and the denominator is small. The numerator of the *t* statistic is the difference between the two sample means. So, the larger the population difference, the more likely it is that you will have a large numerator for the *t* statistic. The denominator of the *t* statistic depends on the variances of the groups and the number of cases in each group. You'll have a small denominator if the sample variances are small and the sample sizes are large. ■ ■ ■

Monitoring Death Rates

You're the CEO of a large hospital chain that is under increasing pressure to monitor quality. Insurance companies and business coalitions want to see if you're doing a good job before they sign contracts with your organization. Although there are many components that contribute to hospital quality, death rates of hospitalized patients are of major concern to all involved. Since death rates depend on type of disease, you have to examine death rates separately for patients with different diseases. Assume that a 10% death rate is the norm for the condition you want to study. In order to compare your hospital's performance to the norm, how many hospitalized cases of the disease should you include in your sample?

? *Is it fair to compare a hospital's observed mortality rate to a national or state norm?* Comparing mortality rates is tricky. However, with the increasing emphasis on cost and quality of medical care, it's being done more and more often. If hospitals have different patient mixes—that is, if sicker or more complicated cases are concentrated in particular types of hospitals—then it's not fair to expect all hospitals to have the same mortality rates. Sophisticated statistical techniques are used to adjust observed mortality rates for differences in patient characteristics. ■ ■ ■

To answer the sample size question, look at Table 14.1. Each of the columns of the table corresponds to a possible true death rate for your hospital. That's the value you would get if you looked at all patients with the diagnosis of interest treated at your hospital chain. It's not the same as the death rate you observe in a sample of patients. Each of the rows of the table corresponds to a different sample size. The entry in each of the cells of the table is the power, that is, the probability that you reject the null hypothesis that the true rate for your hospital is 10%, the norm. The criterion used to reject the null hypothesis is a two-tailed observed significance level of 0.05 or less.

Table 14.1 Probability of rejecting the null hypothesis[†] using a two-tailed significance level of 0.05

	Your hospital's true death rate					
Sample size	2%	5%	15%	20%	30%	40%
20	.35	.16	.10	.24	.60	.89
50	.71	.32	.17	.52	.94	.99
80	.89	.48	.24	.72	.99	*
100	.94	.56	.29	.81	*	*
160	.99	.77	.43	.95	*	*
200	*	.85	.52	.98	*	*
300	*	.96	.69	.99	*	*
400	*	.99	.81	*	*	*
500	*	*	.89	*	*	*
800	*	*	.98	*	*	*

With a true 2% death rate and a sample size of 20, you have only a 35% chance of rejecting the false null hypothesis

[†]The null hypothesis is that the death rate is 10%.

*Indicates probabilities > 0.99.

? *What is the null hypothesis that I'm testing here?* The null hypothesis is that your hospital's death rate for a particular condition is the same as the norm—10%. The norm is not a value you estimate. It's a value that was established previously on the basis of large-scale studies. This is the same situation as in Chapter 10 where you tested whether a new treatment for a disease has the same cure rate as the established treatment. You can use the same binomial test to test this hypothesis. ■ ■ ■

Look at the column labeled 2%. If your hospital's true mortality rate is 2% and you count the number of deaths in a random sample of 20 cases, there is only a 35% chance that you will correctly reject the null hypothesis that the true mortality rate for your hospital is 10%, using an observed significance level of 0.05 or less for rejecting the null hypothesis. That means that two out of three times you will fail to reject the null hypothesis when in fact it's false. You'll fail to identify your hospital as an exceptional performer when it really is. If you increase the sample size to 80, there is almost a 90% chance that you will correctly reject the null hypothesis. With a sample size of 80, you're much more likely to detect your hospital's good performance. As you can see in Table 14.1, for each of the hypothetical hospital rates (the columns), as you increase your sample size, your power increases.

Now look at the row that corresponds to a sample size of 100. You see that the power is 94% when the true hospital value is 2%. That means that 94% of the time when you take a sample of 100 cases and your hospital's true death rate is 2%, you will correctly reject the null hypothesis that your hospital's true rate is 10%. However, if your true value is 5%, meaning that your hospital's mortality is half of the national average, your probability of detecting that difference is only 56%. Similarly, if your true hospital rate is 15%, a 50% increase over the population rate, with a sample size of 100, you stand only a 29% chance of detecting it. (With a sample of 500 patients, you stand almost a 90% chance of detecting it.) From the table, you see that the larger the difference from the population rate, the easier it is to detect.

? *How come the power values aren't the same for 5% and 15% true death rates? They are both 5% different from the hypothetical rate of 10%.* The reason for this is that if you have a population in which only 5% of the cases die, the variability of the sample death rates will be smaller than if you have a population in which 15% of the cases die. If the population probability of dying is 0, whenever you take a sample, there's only one possible outcome—everyone's alive. You're not going to see any variability from sample to sample. If the population probability of dying is 5%, you'll see somewhat more variability, but not that much more. Regardless of the sample size that you take, your sample will consist of mostly living people. If the probability of dying increases to 15%, the variability of possible sample outcomes increases as well. The population isn't as homogeneous as before. In fact, at 50%, you'll have the largest possible variability, since that's when your population is most diverse. You expect to see all kinds of sample values. ■ ■ ■

In summary, when you fail to reject the null hypothesis, you should be cautious about the conclusions you draw. In particular, if your sample size is small, you may be failing to detect even large differences. That's why, when you design a survey or experiment, you should make sure to include enough cases so that you have reasonable power to detect differences that are of interest.

Does Significant Mean Important?

In Table 14.1, you see that as you increase your sample size, you are able to detect smaller and smaller discrepancies from the null hypothesis. For example, if your sample size is 10,000 cases, you might be able to detect that your hospital rate is really 10.1%, compared to the norm of 10%. Or you might reject the null hypothesis that there is no difference in β-endorphin levels before and after running, based on a very small change. Just because you are able to reject the null hypothesis doesn't mean you've uncovered an important or large difference. For very large sample sizes, even very small differences may cause you to reject the null hypothesis. Before you conclude that you've found something important, evaluate the observed difference on its own merits. Is a difference of one month of education really a worthwhile finding? Does a difference of one point in a test score really tell you anything?

Summary

How can you test the null hypothesis that two population means are equal, based on the results observed in two independent samples?

- The one-sample *t* test is appropriate only when you want to test hypotheses about one population mean.
- For the independent-samples *t* test, you must have two unrelated samples from normal distributions, or the sample size must be large enough to compensate for non-normality.
- You can't prove that the null hypothesis is true.
- Power is the probability of correctly rejecting a false null hypothesis. If you have small sample sizes, you may be unable to detect even large population differences.

What's Next?

Now that you know how to test hypotheses about two independent means, you're ready to consider a somewhat more complicated problem. How can you tell if *more* than two means are different from each other? That's what Chapter 15 is about.

How to Obtain an Independent-Samples t Test

The SPSS Independent-Samples T Test procedure tests the null hypothesis that the population mean of a variable is the same for two groups of cases. It also displays a confidence interval for the difference between the population means in the two groups.

To obtain an independent-samples *t* test, you must indicate the variable(s) whose means you want to compare, and you must specify the two groups to be compared.

▶ To open the Independent-Samples T Test dialog box (see Figure 14.8), from the menus choose:

Statistics
  Compare Means ▶
    Independent-Samples T Test...

Figure 14.8   Independent-Samples T Test dialog box

Make these selections to obtain the output shown in Figure 14.2

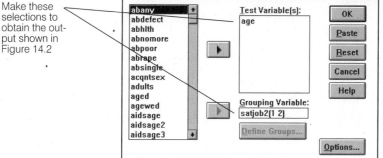

In the Independent-Samples T Test dialog box:

▶ Select the variable whose mean you want to test and move it into the Test Variable(s) list. You can move more than one variable into the list to test all of them between two groups of cases.

▶ Select the variable whose values define the two groups and move it into the Grouping Variable box. Click on Define Groups and indicate how the groups are defined.

▶ Click on OK.

For each test variable, SPSS calculates a *t* statistic and its observed significance level.

Define Groups: Specifying the Subgroups

After you move a variable into the Grouping Variable box, click on Define Groups to open the Define Groups dialog box, as shown in Figure 14.9.

Figure 14.9 Independent-Samples T Test Define Groups dialog box

Values correspond to codes used in variable satjob2:
1 = very satisfied
2 = not very satisfied

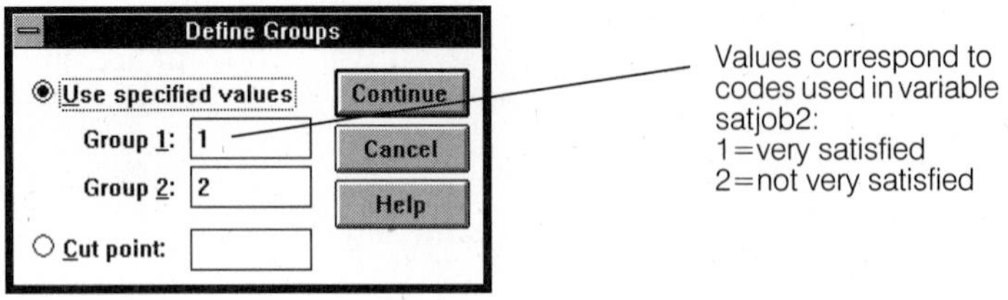

For a numeric grouping variable, you have the following alternatives:

Use specified values. If each group corresponds to a single value of the grouping variable, select this option and enter the values for group 1 and group 2. Other values of the grouping variable are ignored.

Cut point. If one group corresponds to small values of the grouping variable and the other group to large values, select this option and enter a value that separates the groups. Cases that exactly equal the cut point are included in the second group. (If you don't want to remember that, enter a cut point that doesn't occur in your data. To compare codes 1 and 2 with codes 3 and 4, enter a cut point of 2.5 and be sure.)

String Grouping Variable

For a string grouping variable, a cut point isn't available. The Define Groups dialog box simply asks for the two values that identify the groups you want to compare.

Options: Confidence Level, Labels, and Missing Data

In the Independent-Samples T Test dialog box, click on Options to open the Independent-Samples T Test Options dialog box, as shown in Figure 14.10. This dialog box allows you to change the confidence level for the confidence interval for the population difference between the means of the two groups, and to control the handling of missing values.

Figure 14.10 Independent-Samples T Test Options dialog box

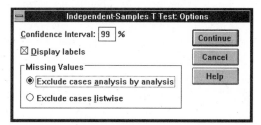

Confidence Interval. Defines the desired confidence interval (usually 95 or 99).

Display labels. Suppresses the display of variable labels.

Missing Values. Two alternatives control the treatment of missing data for multiple test variables.

> **Exclude cases analysis by analysis.** All cases that have valid data for the grouping variable and a test variable are used in the statistics for that test variable.

> **Exclude cases listwise.** Only the cases that have valid data for the grouping variable and all specified test variables are used. This ensures that all of the tests are performed using the same cases, but doesn't necessarily use all of the available data for each test.

Statistical Concepts

1. For the following studies, indicate whether an independent-samples or paired *t* test is appropriate:

   a. You want to study regional differences in consumer spending. You randomly select a sample of consumers in the Midwest and the East and track their spending patterns.

   b. You want to study differences in the spending habits of teenage boys and girls. You select 100 brother-sister pairs and study their spending behavior.

   c. You want to compare error rates for 20 employees before and after they attend a quality improvement workshop.

d. Weight is obtained for each subject before and after Dr. Nogani's new treatment. The hypothesis to be tested is that the treatment has no effect on weight loss.

e. The Jenkins Activity Survey is administered to 20 couples. The hypothesis to be tested is that husbands' and wives' scores do not differ.

f. Subjects are asked their height and then a measurement of height is obtained. The hypothesis to be tested is that self-reported and actual heights do not differ.

g. You want to compare the durability of two types of socks. You have people wear one type of sock on one foot and another type of sock on the other. You see how long it takes for a hole to appear. (Assume they wash them periodically!)

2. You want to compare the average ages of people who buy and who don't buy a product. Suppose you obtain the following results:

```
t-tests for Independent Samples of BUY


                              Number
Variable                     of Cases        Mean        SD    SE of Mean

AGE

No                              100         29.4478     15.559     1.556
Yes                             100         38.0009     15.493     1.549


        Mean Difference = -8.5530

        Levene's Test for Equality of Variances: F= .052    P= .820


           t-test for Equality of Means                             95%
Variances   t-value      df    2-Tail Sig    SE of Diff        CI for Diff

Equal        -3.90      198       .000         2.196       (-12.883, -4.223)
Unequal      -3.90    198.00      .000         2.196       (-12.883, -4.223)
```

a. Write a short paragraph summarizing your findings.

b. Have you proved that in the population the two groups have different mean ages?

c. What is a plausible range for the true difference?

d. What would happen to the observed significance level if the difference and the standard deviations in the two groups remained the same but the sample sizes were tripled?

3. A market research analyst is studying whether men and women find the same types of cars appealing. He asks 150 men and 75 women to indicate which one of the following types of cars they would be most likely to buy: two-door with trunk, two-door with hatchback, convertible, four-door with trunk, four-door with hatchback, or station wagon. Each of the possible responses is assigned a code number. The analyst runs a t test and finds that the average value for males and females appears to differ ($p=0.008$). He doesn't know how to interpret his output, so he comes to you for advice. Explain to him what his results mean.

4. You are interested in whether the size of a company, as measured by the number of employees, differs between companies that offer pension plans and those that don't. You select a random sample of 75 companies and obtain information about the number of employees and availability of a pension plan. You run a two-independent-samples t test and find that there is not a statistically significant difference between the two types of companies ($p=0.237$). A colleague of yours conducts a similar study. She polls 200 companies and finds a similar difference in the number of employees between the two types of companies. However, she claims that she found a significant difference ($p=0.002$). Is this possible? Explain.

5. You are interested in whether average family income differs for people who find life exciting and for those who don't. You take a sample of people at a local museum on Sunday afternoon and find that there is a $5,000 difference in income between the two groups. You do a t test and find the observed significance level to be 0.03.

   Your friend is also studying the same problem. She takes a sample of people in a department store on Saturday afternoon. She finds a $10,000 difference in family income between the two groups. But when she does a t test, she finds an observed significance level of 0.2.

   Discuss these studies, their shortcomings, and possible reasons for the contradictory results.

Data Analysis

Use the *gss.sav* data file to answer the following questions:

1. Perform the appropriate analyses to test whether the average number of hours of daily television viewing (variable *tvhours*) is the same for men and women. Write a short summary of your results, including appropriate charts to illustrate your findings. Be sure to look at the distribution of hours of television viewed separately for men and women.

   a. Based on the results you observed, is it reasonable to conclude that in the population men and women watch the same amount of television?

b. If you found a statistically significant difference between average hours watched by men and women, would you necessarily conclude that men and women do not watch the same amount of television? What other nonstatistical explanations are possible for your findings?

2. Now restrict the analysis in question 1 to men and women who are employed full time (variable *wrkstat* equals 1). Again, test the null hypothesis that the average hours of television viewing are the same for males and females. Summarize your findings.

3. Translate the average difference between men's and women's television viewing into minutes. Translate the confidence interval from hours to minutes (just convert 0.06 hours to minutes). Do you think there is a large difference between the genders? How accurately do you think you can estimate the number of hours of television you watch a day? Do you think you can estimate it to the nearest 10 minutes? Based on these data, do you think there is an important difference in the average number of hours of television viewing by men and women?

4. Discuss the possible advantages of a paired design to analyze differences between men's and women's television viewing. Discuss the drawbacks as well.

5. You want to know what kinds of people like opera, classical, and country music so that you can target your advertising better. For each of the three types of music (variables *opera*, *classicl*, and *country*), form two independent groups of people: those who like it very much or like it (codes 1 and 2), and all others. See if you can identify differences in age, education, television viewing, and so on. Write a paper summarizing your findings. Be sure to include appropriate charts.

6. Some people claim that they would continue to work if they struck it rich, and others say that they would not (variable *richwork*). Use the two-independent-samples *t* test to identify possible differences between the groups in age, education, television viewing, and so on. Write a paper summarizing your findings.

7. What distinguishes people who believe in life after death from those who do not (variable *postlife*)? Use the available data to identify differences between the two groups. Write a short paper summarizing your results.

Use the *salary.sav* data file to answer the following questions:

8. Use the Select Cases facility to restrict the analysis to clerical workers only (variable *jobcat* equals 1).

   a. Test the assertion that male and female clerical workers have the same average starting salaries. Summarize your findings.

   b. You are 95% confident that the true difference in average beginning salaries for male and female clerical workers is in what range?

c. How often would you expect to see a difference at least as large in absolute value as the one you observed if, in fact, male and female clerical workers have the same beginning salaries?

d. Evaluate how well your data meet the assumptions needed for a two-independent-sample t test.

9. The bank claims that male clerical workers are paid more than female clerical workers because they have more formal education. Do the data support this assertion? Explain.

10. Consider office trainees (variable *jobcat* equals 2). The women trainees have hired you to show that the bank discriminates again women office trainees by paying them less. Analyze the data, and prepare a summary of your findings.

11. The bank has now hired you to refute the claim that they discriminate against women office trainees. What evidence can you come up with to support the bank's position? Write a summary of your findings on behalf of the bank.

Use the *electric.sav* data file to answer the following questions:

12. Write a short report discussing the claim that average diastolic blood pressure in 1958 (variable *dbp58*) is the same for men who were alive in 1968 and for men who were not (variable *vital10*). Include appropriate summary statistics and charts.

13. There is one man with a diastolic blood pressure of 160 mm Hg. Rerun the independent-samples t test excluding him from the analysis. How does your conclusion change? What can you conclude about the effect of outliers on the results of a t test?

14. Test the null hypothesis that average diastolic blood pressure is the same for men who smoke and for men who don't smoke. Write a paragraph summarizing your conclusions. Include appropriate charts. Be sure to consider the effect of the outlier on your results.

Use the *schools.sav* data file to answer the following question:

15. Look at schools that are above and below the median percentage of low income for all Chicago schools (variable *medloinc*). Are there differences between the two groups in the school performance variables? Summarize your results.

Use the *renal.sav* data file to answer the following question:

16. Use the independent-samples t test to identify differences between cardiac surgery patients who developed acute renal failure (variable *type* equals 1) and those who did not (variable *type* equals 0). Identify the variables in the data file for which a t test is appropriate. Summarize your findings.

Use the *buying.sav* data file to answer the following question:

17. Test the null hypothesis that the family buying score (variable *famscore*) is the same when pictures are shown and when they are not (variable *picture*). Test the null hypothesis that the average buying score for the husband (variable *hsumbuy*) is the same with and without pictures. Repeat for the average buying score for wives (variable *wsumbuy*). Summarize your results.

One-Way Analysis of Variance

How can you test the null hypothesis that several population means are equal?

- What is analysis of variance?
- What assumptions about the data are needed to use analysis-of-variance techniques?
- How is the *F* ratio computed, and what does it tell you?
- Why do you need multiple comparison procedures?

You've already learned how to test hypotheses about two population means using the paired-samples *t* test and the independent-samples *t* test. Often, however, you want to compare more than two population means. For example, if you are studying four methods for teaching mathematics, you want to compare average test scores for all four groups. Or, if you are testing seven different treatments for lowering cholesterol, you may want to compare the average final cholesterol levels for all seven methods. In this chapter, you'll learn how to test the null hypothesis that several independent population means are equal. The technique you'll use is called **analysis of variance**, usually abbreviated as ANOVA.

▶ This chapter uses the *gssft.sav* data file, which includes only people holding full-time jobs. For instructions on how to obtain the One-Way ANOVA output shown in the chapter, see "How to Obtain a One-Way Analysis of Variance" on p. 294.

Hours in a Work Week

In Chapter 12, you looked at the average number of hours worked in a week by college graduates. Based on the results from the General Social Survey, you rejected the null hypothesis that the average work week is 40 hours. You found the 95% confidence interval for the population value for the average number of hours worked to be from 46.16 hours to 49.30 hours. So it's not inconceivable that the average college graduate works almost an extra 8-hour day each week.

An obvious question that arises is whether it's just college graduates who suffer from the expansion of the work week, or is everyone, regardless of educational background, working more? Using the General Social Survey, you can look at the average number of hours worked by full-time employees of various educational backgrounds.

Describing the Data

You see in Figure 15.1 that the average work week for all full-time employees is 46.29 hours. (It's the entry in the row labeled *Total*.) The average work week ranges from a low of 43.69 hours for people without a high school diploma to a high of 50.27 hours for people with graduate degrees.

Figure 15.1 Descriptive statistics for hours worked

To obtain this
output, from
the menus
choose:

Statistics
  Compare Means ▶
    One-Way ANOVA...

Select the variables
hrs1 and degree, as
shown in Figure 15.5.

In the One-Way
ANOVA Options
dialog box, select
Descriptive, as shown
in Figure 15.8.

Group	Count	Mean	Standard Deviation	Standard Error	95 Pct Conf Int for Mean		
Less tha	52	43.6923	8.7235	1.2097	41.2637	TO	46.1209
High sch	387	45.7728	10.5769	.5377	44.7155	TO	46.8297
Junior c	54	45.8704	11.6636	1.5872	42.6868	TO	49.0539
Bachelor	162	46.3827	12.8909	1.0128	44.3826	TO	48.3828
Graduate	86	50.2674	11.4382	1.2334	47.8151	TO	52.7198
Total	741	46.2888	11.2691	.4140	45.4761	TO	47.1015

GROUP	MINIMUM	MAXIMUM
Less tha	20.0000	70.0000
High sch	8.0000	80.0000
Junior c	25.0000	80.0000
Bachelor	5.0000	89.0000
Graduate	34.0000	89.0000
TOTAL	5.0000	89.0000

The average work week ranges from 43.69 hours to 50.27 hours

In the column labeled *Standard Deviation*, you see that the smallest variability in hours worked is for people with less than a high school diploma, while the largest is for people with bachelor's degrees. The next column, labeled *Standard Error*, tells you how much the sample means vary in repeated samples from the same population. For each group, it's the standard deviation divided by the square root of the sample size. The smallest standard error is for high school graduates, since they are the largest group.

Confidence Intervals for the Group Means

In the last two columns of Figure 15.1, you see for each group the 95% confidence interval for the population value of the average hours worked per week. You are 95% confident that the true work week for those with less than a high school diploma is between 41.26 and 46.12 hours. For those with a graduate degree, you are 95% confident that work week is between 47.82 and 52.7 hours.

Figure 15.2 Plot of sample means and 95% confidence intervals

You can obtain this error bar chart using the Graphs menu, as described in "Error Bar Charts" on p. 541 in Appendix A.

In the Define Simple Error Bar Summaries for Groups of Cases dialog box, select the variables hrs1 and degree.

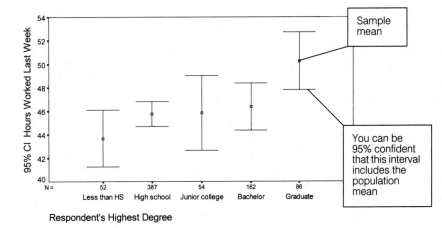

Plots of the means and confidence intervals are shown in Figure 15.2. You see that the 95% confidence interval for high school graduates is the narrowest. That's because there are so many of them in the sample. Many of the confidence intervals in Figure 15.2 overlap. That tells you that some of the values that are plausible for the true work week in one group are also plausible for the true work week in the others. The exception is the confidence interval for those with graduate degrees. It doesn't overlap the confidence interval for those with less than a high school education, nor the interval for those with a high school education.

? *Can you tell from the plot if the 40-hour work week is a reasonable guess for the true hours worked per week?* Sure. Remember, if a value doesn't fall in the 95% confidence interval for the mean, you can reject the hypothesis that it's a plausible population value. You see in Figure 15.2 that the value 40 is not included in any of the confidence intervals. That means you can reject the hypothesis that it's a reasonable value for any of the groups. It appears that the 40-hour work week may be a thing of the past, regardless of your education level. ■ ■ ■

Testing the Null Hypothesis

The descriptive statistics and plots suggest that there are differences in the average work week among the five education groups. Now you need to figure out whether the observed differences in the samples may be attributed to just the natural variability among sample means or whether there's reason to believe that some of the five groups have different values in the population for average hours worked.

The null hypothesis says that the population means for all five groups are the same. That is, there is no difference in the average hours worked for people in the five education categories. The alternative hypothesis is that there is a difference. The alternative hypothesis doesn't say which groups differ from one another. It just says that the groups means are not all the same in the population; at least one of the groups differs from the others.

The statistical technique you'll use to test the null hypothesis is called analysis of variance (abbreviated ANOVA). It's called analysis of variance because it examines the variability of the sample values. You look at how much the observations within each group vary as well as how much the group means vary. Based on these two estimates of variability, you can draw conclusions about the population means. If the sample means vary more than you expect based on the variability of the observations in the groups, you can conclude that the population means are not all equal.

SPSS contains several different procedures that perform analysis of variance. In this chapter, you'll use the One-Way ANOVA procedure. It's called one-way analysis of variance because cases are assigned to different groups based on their values for one variable. In this example, you form the groups based on the values of the *degree* variable. The variable used to form groups is called a **factor**. In Chapter 16, you'll learn how to test hypotheses when cases are classified into groups based on their values for two factors.

Assumptions Needed for Analysis of Variance

Analysis of variance requires the following assumptions:

- Independent random samples have been taken from each population.
- The populations are normal.
- The population variances are all equal.

The Kruskal-Wallis test, described in Chapter 18, requires more limited assumptions about the data.

Independence. The independence assumption means that there is no relationship between the observations in the different groups and between the observations in the same group. For example, if you administer four different treatments to each individual, you cannot use the one-way analysis-of-variance procedure to analyze the data. Observations from the same individual appear in each of the groups, so they are not independent. (In this situation, you must use an extension of the paired-samples *t* test. It's called repeated measures analysis of variance, a topic not covered in this book.) Observations within a group are also not independent if conditions are changing with time. For example, if you are explaining a task to subjects and your instructions get better with time, early subjects may not perform as well as later subjects. In this situation, the response of the subject depends on the point in time he or she entered into the study. Consecutive subjects will be similar to each other.

Normality. The normality assumption in analysis of variance can be checked by making histograms or normal probability plots for each of the groups. In practice, the analysis of variance is not heavily dependent on the normality assumption. As long as the data are not extremely non-normal, you do not have to worry. (If your sample sizes in the groups are small, you should be aware of the impact of unusual observations, which can have a big effect on the mean and standard deviation. You can rerun the analysis without the unusual point to make sure that you reach the same conclusions.)

Equality of Variance. The equality of variance assumption can be checked by examining the spread of the observations in the box plot. You can also compute the Levene test for equality of variance, which is available in the Explore and One-Way procedures. In practice, if the number of cases in each of the groups is similar, the equality of variance assumption is not too important.

What should I do if I suspect that my data violate the necessary assumptions? Well, it depends on which assumption is being violated. For example, if you're worried about the normality or equal-variance assumptions, sometimes you can transform your data so that the distribution of values is more normal or the variances in the groups are more similar. Taking logarithms or square roots of the data values is often helpful. If this fails, you can use a statistical test that makes fewer assumptions about the data. In particular, you may want to use the Kruskal-Wallis test described in Chapter 18.

The situation is considerably more complicated if you're worried about whether the groups are somehow biased. That is, you're concerned that one or more of your samples differs in some important way from the population of interest. For example, if you want to compare four medical treatments, and the participating physicians have assigned the sickest patients to a particular group, you've got a real problem. You may not be able to draw any correct conclusions from your data. That's why it's very important when comparing several treatments or conditions, to make sure that the subjects are randomly assigned to the different groups. *Randomly* doesn't mean *haphazardly*. It means that you must have a well organized system for random assignment of cases. ■ ■ ■

Analyzing the Variability

In analysis of variance, the observed variability in the sample is divided (partitioned, in statistical lingo) into two parts: variability of the observations *within* a group about the group mean, and variability *between* the group means.

Why are we talking about variability? Aren't we testing hypotheses about means? Yes, we're testing hypotheses about population means; but as you've seen in previous chapters, your conclusions about population means are always based on looking at the variability of sample means. You have to determine if your sample mean is outside the usual range of variability of sample means from the population.

In analysis of variance, you'll look at how much your observed sample means vary. You'll compare this observed variability to the expected variability if the null hypothesis that all population means are the same is true. If the sample means vary more than you'd expect, you have reason to believe that this extra variability is because some of groups don't have the same population mean. (If you have two independent groups, you'll get the same results using ANOVA or the equal variance *t* test.) ■ ■ ■

Let's look a little more closely now at the two types of variability and how they are used to test the null hypothesis that the population values for average hours worked per week are the same for people in the five education categories. The game plan is as follows: You want to know whether your sample means vary more than you would expect if the null hypothesis is true. First, you'll see how much the observations in a group vary, and then you'll see how much the sample means vary. If the sample means vary more than you expect, you'll reject the null hypothesis.

Within-Groups Variability

The **within-groups estimate of variability**, as its name suggests, tells you how much the observations within a group vary. The sample variance of each group estimates within-groups variability. One of the assumptions of analysis of variance is that all groups come from populations with the same variance. That makes it possible for you to average the variances in each of the groups to come up with a single number, which is the within-groups variance. (You'll see later how this averaging is done. You can't just add up the sample variances and divide by the number of groups.)

You might wonder why you can't just put all of your observations together and compute the variance. The reason is that you don't know if all of the groups have the same population mean. If they don't, pooling all the values together will give you the wrong answer. For example, suppose that all people without a high school diploma work exactly 40 hours a week; all people with a high school diploma work exactly 43 hours a week; and all people with a college degree work exactly 45 hours. The variance in each of the groups is 0, since the values within a group don't vary at all. The correct estimate of the within-groups variance is also 0. If you compute the variance for all cases together, it wouldn't be close to 0. The observed variability would be the result of differences in the means of the three groups.

Between-Groups Variability

You have a sample mean for each of the groups in your study. If all of the groups have the same number of cases, you can find the standard deviation of the sample means. What would that tell you? If all the groups come from populations with the same mean and variance, the standard deviation of the sample means tells you how much sample means from the same population vary. The standard deviation of the sample means is an estimate of the standard error of the mean.

From the standard error of the mean, you can estimate the standard deviation of the observations. You do this by multiplying the standard error of the mean by the square root of the number of cases in a group.

Where did that come from? The standard error of the mean is the standard deviation of the observations divided by the square root of the sample size. So, using simple algebra, the standard deviation is the standard error of the mean multiplied by the square root of the sample size. Thus,

$$\text{standard error} = \frac{\text{standard deviation}}{\sqrt{\text{sample size}}}$$

and

$$\text{standard deviation} = \text{standard error} \times \sqrt{\text{sample size}}$$

If you square the estimate of the standard deviation, you have a quantity that's called the **between-groups estimate of variability**. It's called the between-groups estimate of variability because it's based on how much sample means vary *between* the groups.

Comparing the Two Estimates of Variability

You now have two estimates of how much the observations within a group vary: the within-groups estimate and the between-groups estimate. These two estimates differ in a very important way: the between-groups estimate of variance will be correct only if the null hypothesis is true. If the null hypothesis is false, the between-groups estimate of variance will be too large. The observed variability of the sample means will be the result of two factors: the variability of the observations within a group and the variability of the population means. The within-groups estimate of variability doesn't depend on the null hypothesis being true. It's always a good estimate.

Your decision about the null hypothesis will be based on comparing the between-groups and the within-groups estimates of variability. You'll see how much the number of hours worked varies for individuals in the same education group. This will give you the within-groups estimate of variability. Then you'll see how much the means of the five groups vary. Based on this, you'll calculate the between-groups estimate of variability. If the between-groups estimate is sufficiently larger than the within-groups estimate, you'll reject the null hypothesis that all of the means are equal in the population.

The Analysis-of-Variance Table

The estimates of variability that we've been talking about are usually displayed in what's called an **analysis-of-variance table**. Figure 15.3 is the analysis-of-variance table for the test of the null hypothesis that the population value for average hours worked per week is the same for people in five categories of education. By looking at this table, you'll be able to tell whether you have enough evidence to reject the null hypothesis.

Figure 15.3 Analysis-of-variance table

To obtain this output, select the variables hrs1 and degree in the One-Way ANOVA dialog box, as shown in Figure 15.5.

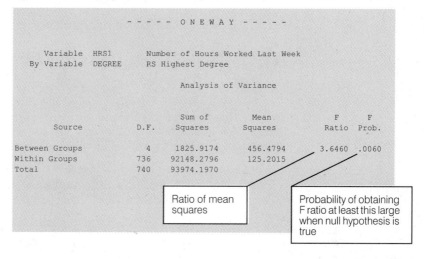

```
- - - - - O N E W A Y - - - - -


    Variable   HRS1      Number of Hours Worked Last Week
    By Variable DEGREE   RS Highest Degree


                              Analysis of Variance


                            Sum of        Mean            F      F
       Source        D.F.    Squares       Squares       Ratio  Prob.

Between Groups          4    1825.9174     456.4794      3.6460  .0060
Within Groups        736    92148.2796    125.2015
Total                740    93974.1970
```

Ratio of mean squares

Probability of obtaining F ratio at least this large when null hypothesis is true

The two estimates of variability are shown in the column labeled *Mean Squares*. Their ratio is in the column labeled *F Ratio*. If the null hypothesis is true, you expect the ratio of the between-groups mean square to the within-groups mean square to be close to 1, since they are both estimates of the population variance. Large values for the *F* ratio indicate that the sample means vary more than you would expect if the null hypothesis were true.

You can tell if your observed *F* ratio of 3.64 is large enough for you to reject the null hypothesis by looking at the observed significance level, which is labeled *F Prob*. You see that the probability of obtaining an *F* ratio of 3.65 or larger when the null hypothesis is true is 0.006. Only 6 times in 1000, when the null hypothesis is true, would you expect to see a ratio this large or larger. So you can reject the null hypothesis. It's unlikely that the number of hours worked per week is the same for the five groups in the population.

Now that you know the punch line, let's see where all the numbers are coming from.

Estimating Within-Groups Variability

You need three steps to compute the within-groups estimate of variability:

1. First, you must compute what's called the **within-groups sum of squares**. Take all of the standard deviations in Figure 15.1 and square them to obtain variances. Then multiply each variance by one less than the number of cases in the group. Finally, add up the values for all of the groups. The within-groups sum of squares is:

$$(8.72^2 \times 51) + (10.58^2 \times 386) + (11.66^2 \times 53) \qquad \textbf{Equation 15.1}$$
$$+ (12.89^2 \times 161) + (11.44^2 \times 85) = 92148.28$$

You see this number in the second row of Figure 15.3 in the column labeled *Sum of Squares*. (You have to use more decimal places for the standard deviation than shown above to get exactly the answer given.)

2. Next, you must compute the degrees of freedom. That's easy to do. For each group, you compute the number of cases minus 1, and then add up these numbers for all of the groups. In this example, the degrees of freedom are:

$$\text{degrees of freedom} = 51 + 386 + 53 + 161 + 85 = 736 \qquad \textbf{Equation 15.2}$$

This number is shown in the *Within Groups* row of Figure 15.3, in the column labeled *D.F.* (for degrees of freedom).

3. Finally, divide the sum of squares by its degrees of freedom, to get what's called a **mean square**. This is the estimate of the average variability in the groups. It's really nothing more than an average of the variances in each of the groups, adjusted for the fact that the number of observations in the groups differs. Your estimate of the variance for the number of hours worked, based on the variability of the observations within each of the groups, is 125.20.

Estimating Between-Groups Variability

You also need three steps to calculate the between-groups estimate of variability.

1. First, you compute the **between-groups sum of squares**. Subtract the overall mean (the mean of all of the observations) from each group mean. Then square each difference, and multiply the square by the number of observations in its group. Finally, add up all the results. For this example, the between-groups sum of squares is:

$$52 \times (43.69 - 46.29)^2$$
$$+ 387 \times (45.77 - 46.29)^2$$
$$+ 54 \times (45.87 - 46.29)^2$$
$$+ 162 \times (46.38 - 46.29)^2$$
$$+ 86 \times (50.27 - 46.29)^2 = 1825.92$$

Equation 15.3

2. Next, you must compute the degrees of freedom. The degrees of freedom for the between-groups sum of squares is just the number of groups minus 1. In this example, there are five education groups, so the degrees of freedom for the between-groups sum of squares is 4.

3. Finally, calculate the between-groups mean square by dividing the between-groups sum of squares by its degrees of freedom. The between-groups mean square is 456.48.

Calculating the F Ratio

You now have the two estimates of the variability in the population: the within-groups mean square and the between-groups mean square. The F ratio is simply the ratio of these two estimates. Take the between-groups mean square and divide it by the within-groups mean square:

$$F = \frac{\text{between-groups mean square}}{\text{within-groups mean square}} = \frac{456.48}{125.20} = 3.65$$

Equation 15.4

(Remember, the within-groups mean square is based on how much the observations within each of the groups vary. The between-groups mean square is based on how much the group means vary among themselves.) If the null hypothesis that the average hours worked per week is the same for the five groups is true, the two numbers should be close to each other. If you divide one by the other, the result should be close to 1.

As you see, the ratio of the two estimates is not 1. Does that mean you automatically reject the null hypothesis? No. You know that your sample ratio will not be exactly 1, even if the null hypothesis is true. You need to figure out how often you would expect to see a sample value of 3.65 or greater when the null hypothesis is true. That is, you need to determine whether your sample results are unlikely if the null hypothesis is true.

The observed significance level is calculated by comparing your observed *F* ratio to values of the *F* distribution. The observed significance level depends on both the observed *F* ratio and the degrees of freedom for the two mean squares.

What's the F *distribution?* Like the normal and *t* distributions, the **F distribution** is defined mathematically. It's used when you want to test hypotheses about population variances. The Central Limit Theorem doesn't work for variances. Their distributions are not normal. The ratio of two sample variances from normal populations has an *F* distribution. The *F* distribution is indexed by two values for the degrees of freedom, one for the numerator and one for the denominator. The degrees of freedom depend on the number of observations used to calculate the two variances. ■ ■ ■

In Figure 15.3, you see that the observed significance level for this example is 0.006. Since the value is small, you can reject the null hypothesis that the average hours worked per week in the population is the same for the five groups. The observed sample results are not likely to occur when the null hypothesis is true.

Multiple Comparison Procedures

A statistically significant F ratio tells you only that it appears unlikely that all population means are equal. It doesn't tell you which groups are different from each other. You can reject the null hypothesis that all population means are equal in a variety of situations. For example, it may be that the average hours worked differs for all of the five groups. Or it may be that only one or two of the groups differ from the rest. Usually when you've rejected the null hypothesis, you want to pinpoint exactly where the differences are. To do this, you must use multiple comparison procedures.

Why do you need yet another statistical technique? Why can't you just compare all possible pairs of means using t *tests?* The reason for not using many t tests is that when you make many comparisons involving the same means, the probability increases that one or more comparisons will turn out to be statistically significant, even when all the population means are equal. This is known as the **multiple comparison problem**.

For example, if you have 5 groups and compare all pairs of means, you're making 10 comparisons. When the null hypothesis is true, the probability that at least 1 of the 10 observed significance levels is less than 0.05 is about 0.29. With 10 means (45 comparisons), the probability of finding at least one significant difference is about 0.63. The more comparisons you make, the more likely it is that you'll find 1 or more pairs to be statistically different, even if all population means really are equal.

Multiple comparison procedures protect you from calling differences *significant* when they really aren't. This is accomplished by adjusting the observed significance level for the number of comparisons that you are making, since each comparison provides another opportunity to reject the null hypothesis. The more comparisons you make, the larger the difference between pairs of means must be for a multiple comparison procedure to call it statistically significant. That's why you should look only at differences between pairs of means that you are interested in. When you use a multiple comparison procedure, you can be more confident that you are finding true differences. ■ ■ ■

Many multiple comparison procedures are available. They differ in how they adjust the observed significance level. One of the simplest is the **Bonferroni procedure**. It adjusts the observed significance level by multiplying it by the number of comparisons being made. For example, if you are making five comparisons, the observed significance level for each comparison must be less than 0.05/5, or 0.01, for the difference to be significant at the 0.05 level. (For further discussion of multiple comparison techniques see Neter, Wasserman, & Kutner, 1985.)

Figure 15.4 Bonferroni multiple comparison test on hours worked

To obtain the Bonferroni test, select Post Hoc in the One-Way ANOVA dialog box. Then select Bonferroni, as shown in Figure 15.7.

```
- - - - - O N E W A Y - - - - -


        Variable   HRS1        Number of Hours Worked Last Week
     By Variable   DEGREE      RS Highest Degree

Multiple Range Tests:  Modified LSD (Bonferroni) test with significance
                       level .05

The difference between two means is significant if
  MEAN(J)-MEAN(I)  >= 7.9121 * RANGE * SQRT(1/N(I) + 1/N(J))
  with the following value(s) for RANGE: 3.98

  (*) Indicates significant differences which are shown in the lower triangle


                         L H J B G
                         e i u a r
                         s g n c a
                         s h i h d
                             o e u
                         t s r l a
                         h c   o t
                         a h c r e

     Mean       DEGREE

     43.6923    Less tha
     45.7726    High sch
     45.8704    Junior c
     46.3827    Bachelor
     50.2674    Graduate    * *
```

You can see in Figure 15.4 the results of running a Bonferroni multiple comparison test on the hours worked data. At the bottom of the output, all of the group means are ordered from smallest to largest in rows and in columns. Pairs of means that are different at the 0.05 level are marked with an asterisk in the lower half of the table. You see that there are two asterisks in Figure 15.4, and that they are in the *graduate degree* row. Looking at the column labels, you see that the asterisks are for the *less than high school* and *high school* groups. This means that there is a statistically significant difference in average hours worked between people with graduate degrees and those with a high school education and people with graduate degrees and those with less than a high school education.

? *How come the graduate degree group isn't different from the junior college group too?* Whether a difference between two groups is statistically significant depends on how big the difference is between the two groups and how many cases there are in each of the groups. (The same estimate of variance is used for all groups.) The average hours worked for junior college grads is very similar to the average hours worked for high school grads. However, there are only 54 people with junior college degrees. It's possible that you'll find in the pairwise table of differences that smaller differences between two groups may be significant, while larger differences between other groups are not. That's the result of differences in the sample sizes between the groups. ■ ■ ■

Differences are marked only in the lower half of the table. If the observed significance level isn't less than 0.05, no asterisk is printed; the space is left blank. The formula above the table indicates how large an observed difference must be for the comparison procedure to call it significant. If no pairs are found to be significantly different, the table is not printed at all. Instead a message alerts you.

Summary

How can you test the null hypothesis that several population means are equal?

- Analysis of variance is a statistical technique that is used to test hypotheses about two or more population means.
- To use analysis of variance, your groups should be random samples from normal populations with the same variance.
- The F ratio is the ratio of two estimates of the population variance: the between-groups and the within-groups mean squares.
- The analysis-of-variance F test does not pinpoint which means are significantly different from each other. That's why multiple comparison procedures, which protect you against calling too many differences significant, are used to identify groups that appear to be different from each other.

What's Next?

In this chapter, you learned how to test the null hypothesis that several population means are equal, when one variable is used to classify the cases into groups. That accounts for the name *one-way analysis of variance*. In Chapter 16, you will learn how to use analysis of variance techniques when cases are classified into groups based on more than one variable. You'll look at the relationship between average hours worked and highest degree for males and females.

How to Obtain a One-Way Analysis of Variance

The SPSS One-Way ANOVA procedure tests the null hypothesis that the population mean of a variable is the same in several groups of cases. (If there are only two groups, it is equivalent to the independent-samples t test.) In addition, the One-Way ANOVA procedure can display multiple-comparison statistics to evaluate the differences between all possible pairs of group means.

▶ To open the One-Way ANOVA dialog box (see Figure 15.5), from the menus choose:

Statistics
  Compare Means ▶
    One-Way ANOVA...

Figure 15.5 One-Way ANOVA dialog box

Select hrs1 and degree to obtain the output shown in Figure 15.3

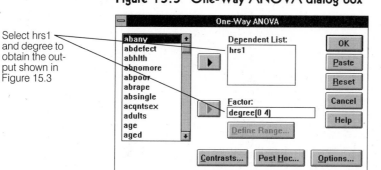

To obtain a one-way analysis of variance, you must indicate the variable(s) whose means you want to compare, and you must specify the groups to be compared. In the One-Way ANOVA dialog box:

▶ Select the variable whose mean you want to test and move it into the Dependent List. You can move more than one variable into the Dependent List to test all of them across the same set of groups.

▶ Select the variable whose values define the groups and move it into the Factor box. Click on Define Range and indicate the range of categories to test (see Figure 15.6 below).

▶ Click on OK.

For each test variable, SPSS calculates an F statistic and its observed significance level.

Define Range: Specifying the Subgroups

SPSS assumes that groups are identified by integer codes in the Factor variable. After moving a variable into the Factor box, click on Define Range to open the Define Range dialog box, as shown in Figure 15.6.

Figure 15.6 One-Way ANOVA Define Range dialog box

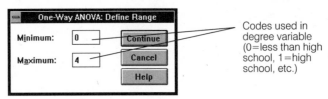

Codes used in degree variable (0=less than high school, 1=high school, etc.)

▶ Enter an integer for the lowest code that should be tested into the Minimum box in the Define Range dialog box, and another integer for the highest code that should be tested into the Maximum box.

Factor values outside the range specified here are ignored in the analysis. Empty categories—factor codes between the minimum and maximum values that do not correspond to any cases in your data file—are likewise ignored. Factor values that are not integers are truncated for the analysis.

Post Hoc Multiple Comparisons: Finding the Difference

If the overall *F* test indicates that subgroup means are significantly different, it is sometimes important to determine which categories of the factor variable are significantly different from which other categories.

To do so, click on Post Hoc. This opens the One-Way ANOVA Post Hoc Multiple Comparisons dialog box, as shown in Figure 15.7.

Figure 15.7 Post Hoc Multiple Comparisons dialog box

Select to obtain Bonferroni test, as shown in Figure 15.4

```
┌─ One-Way ANOVA: Post Hoc Multiple Comparisons ─┐
│ ┌─Tests─────────────────────────┐   ┌────────┐ │
│ │ ☐ Least-significant difference │   │Continue│ │
│ │ ☒ Bonferroni                   │   └────────┘ │
│ │ ☐ Duncan's multiple range test │   ┌────────┐ │
│ │ ☐ Student-Newman-Keuls         │   │ Cancel │ │
│ │ ☐ Tukey's honestly significant difference │  └────────┘ │
│ │ ☐ Tukey's b                    │   ┌────────┐ │
│ │ ☐ Scheffé                      │   │  Help  │ │
│ └───────────────────────────────┘   └────────┘ │
│ ┌─Sample Size Estimate──────────┐              │
│ │ ● Harmonic average of pairs    │              │
│ │ ○ Harmonic average of all groups│             │
│ └───────────────────────────────┘              │
└────────────────────────────────────────────────┘
```

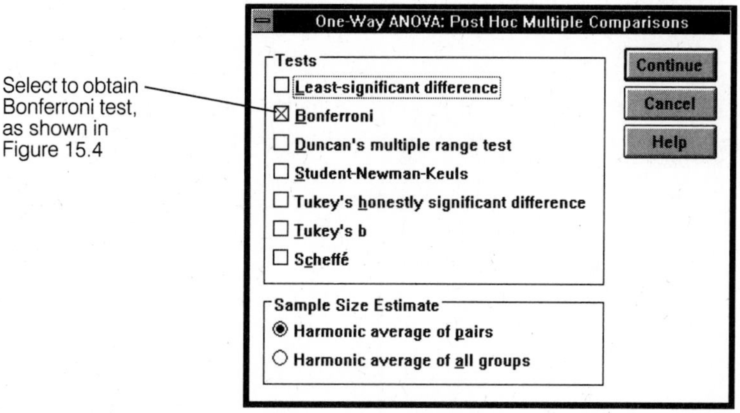

Tests. Two of the available tests are:

Least-significant difference. Equivalent to multiple t tests between all possible pairs of groups. It offers no protection against the problem of multiple comparisons.

Bonferroni. A modification of the least-significant difference test, modified to account for the number of differences being tested.

Sample Size Estimate. These alternatives concern analyses in which the subgroup sizes are not the same:

Harmonic average of pairs. A harmonic mean of group sizes is computed for each pair of groups being compared.

Harmonic average of all groups. A single harmonic mean of all the group sizes is used. With this alternative, SPSS computes homogeneous subsets, groups for which the means are not significantly different. You should not use this option unless all group sizes are very similar.

Options: Statistics, Labels, and Missing Data

In the One-Way ANOVA dialog box, click on Options. In the One-Way ANOVA Options dialog box (see Figure 15.8), you can request additional statistics as well as control the display of labels and the treatment of missing data.

Figure 15.8 One-Way ANOVA Options dialog box

Select to obtain descriptive statistics, as shown in Figure 15.1

Select to display value labels rather than integer codes in output

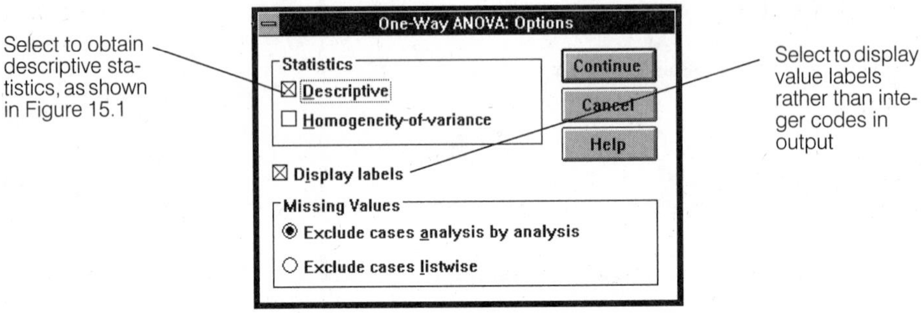

The additional statistics available are:

Descriptive. For each group, the number of cases, mean, standard deviation, standard error of the mean, minimum, maximum, and a 95% confidence interval for the population mean.

Homogeneity-of-variance. Calculates the Levene statistic, testing whether the variance of the dependent variable(s) is significantly different among the groups.

Display labels. Deselect to suppress the display of variable labels.

Missing Values. The missing value alternatives control the treatment of missing data for analyses using multiple dependent variables:

Exclude cases analysis by analysis. All cases that have valid data for the grouping variable and a test variable are used in the statistics for that dependent variable.

Exclude cases listwise. Uses only the cases that have valid data for the grouping variable and all specified dependent variables. This ensures that all of the tests are performed using the same cases.

Exercises

Statistical Concepts

1. A market researcher wants to see whether people in four regions of a city buy the same brand of dish detergent. He takes a random sample of people in the different areas and asks them which of 10 brands (coded from 1 to 10) they purchase most often. He enters the data into SPSS and runs the One-Way ANOVA procedure. The observed significance level for his F value is 0.00001. What can he conclude based on these results?

2. You wish to test the null hypothesis that, in the population, there is no difference in the average age of people who buy three models of a car. You run an analysis of variance and obtain the following output:

```
- - - - - O N E W A Y - - - - -


     Variable  AGE       Age of Respondent
   By Variable  MODEL     Model of Car

                          Analysis of Variance

                          Sum of        Mean          F      F
        Source     D.F.   Squares       Squares     Ratio  Prob.

Between Groups       2      46.6433      23.3216     1.0832  .3388
Within Groups     1164   25060.5461     21.5297
Total             1166   25107.1894
```

a. Is there sufficient evidence to reject the null hypothesis?

b. What conclusions can you draw from the table?

c. If you compute the average ages for the three groups, would you expect them to be similar or quite different?

3. Based on the following table, which groups are significantly different from each other using the Bonferroni test and a significance level of 0.05?

```
       Variable  STRENGTH
    By Variable  CONTENT

Multiple Range Tests:  Modified LSD (Bonferroni) test with significance
                       level .05

The difference between two means is significant if
   MEAN(J)-MEAN(I)   >= 1.8039 * RANGE * SQRT(1/N(I) + 1/N(J))
   with the following value(s) for RANGE: 4.14

   (*) Indicates significant differences which are shown in the lower triangle

                             G G G G
                             r r r r
                             p p p p

                             1 2 3 4
     Mean       CONTENT

    10.0000     Grp 1
    15.6667     Grp 2       *
    17.0000     Grp 3       *
    21.1667     Grp 4       * *
```

4. You are interested in comparing four methods of teaching. You randomly assign 20 students to each of the four methods and then administer a standardized test at the end of the study.

a. What null hypothesis are you interested in testing?

b. What statistical procedure might you use to test the hypothesis?

c. What assumptions are necessary for the statistical procedure you have selected?

Data Analysis

Use the *gss.sav* data file to answer the following questions:

1. In the General Social Survey people classified themselves as being very happy, pretty happy, or not too happy (variable *happy*). Consider the relationship between happiness and age.

a. Compute basic descriptive statistics for each of the three happiness groups.

b. Make boxplots of age for the three groups.

c. Does the assumption of equal variances in the groups appear reasonable? The assumption of normality?

d. Perform a one-way analysis of variance on these data. What can you conclude? Which groups are significantly different from one another using the Bonferroni test?

e. From the analysis-of-variance table, estimate the variance of the ages within each happiness group. What is your estimate of the standard deviation within the groups? How does this compare to the actual standard deviations of each group in the table of descriptive statistics?

f. What are the three sample means that you have observed in the table of descriptive statistics? Based on the three sample means, what is your estimate of the variance of the ages within each happiness group?

g. What is the value of the ratio of the two variances?

h. If the null hypothesis is true, how often would you expect to see a ratio of sample variances at least this large?

2. Run a one-way analysis of variance to test the null hypothesis that the average years of education (variable *educ*) are the same for men and women. Run an independent-samples *t* test to test the same hypothesis. Compare the results. (If you square the equal-variance *t* value you'll get the *F* value from the analysis of variance.)

3. You're interested in seeing whether there is a relationship between highest degree earned and number of hours of television viewed a day (variables *degree* and *tvhours*). Perform the appropriate analyses and summarize your results. Include appropriate descriptive statistics.

4. For the General Social Survey data, formulate four hypotheses that can be tested using analysis-of-variance procedures. (Do not use hypotheses from the chapters or exercises.) Explore two of these hypotheses and write a short paper summarizing your results.

5. Test whether Bush, Clinton, and Perot supporters (variable *pres92*) differ in average age and education. Summarize your findings.

Use the *salary.sav* data file to answer the following questions:

6. Use the Select Cases facility to restrict the analysis to clerical workers only (variable *jobcat* equals 1). Test the null hypothesis that the average current salary (variable *salnow*) is the same for the four gender/race groups (variable *sexrace*). Be sure to evaluate the assumptions needed for analysis of variance. If you reject the null hypothesis, indicate which groups are different from each other. Write a short paper summarizing your findings.

7. Repeat the analysis in question 6 but this time test the null hypothesis about the average years of education for clerical employees (variable *edlevel*) in the four gender/race groups. Summarize your findings.

Two-Way Analysis of Variance

16

How can you test hypotheses about population means when you have two factors?

- What is a factor?
- What kinds of hypotheses can be tested when you have two or more factors?
- What is an interaction?
- What assumptions are necessary for using an analysis of variance when you have two or more factors?
- What problems do you encounter if you have an unequal number of cases in the cells?

In Chapter 15, you used one-way analysis of variance (ANOVA) to test the null hypothesis that the average hours worked per week is the same for people in five categories of education. You classified the cases into groups based on their values for a single variable—highest degree earned. What if you are interested in the effects of more than one grouping or factor variable? For example, what if you want to know whether there are differences in the average hours worked per week for people with different degrees, and whether the differences are the same for males and females? Or, what if you are interested in the effects of both dosage and the type of drug in treating hypertension? In both of these examples, you must classify cases into groups based on two variables: degree and gender, and dosage and drug. In this chapter, you'll learn how to test hypotheses about the equality of population means when you classify your cases into groups based on two factors. The technique you'll use is an extension of one-way analysis of variance. Predictably, it's called **two-way analysis of variance**.

▶ This chapter uses the *gssft.sav* data file, which contains information only for people who work full time. For instructions on how to obtain the ANOVA output shown in the chapter, see "How to Obtain a Two-Way Analysis of Variance" on p. 317.

The Design

In Chapter 15, you found differences in the average hours worked for full-time employees with different educational backgrounds. In particular, you saw that people with graduate degrees fared poorly. On average, they worked a 50-hour work week. The conclusions you reached about average hours worked were based on the responses of males and females combined. However, the effects of gender were ignored. Cases were classified into groups based only on the values of the degree variable. Based on the results of the one-way analysis of variance, you could not say anything about differences between men and women in hours worked per week.

If you want to see whether there are differences in average hours worked by full-time employees based both on degree and gender, you must classify cases into groups based on their values for both variables. Since there are 5 values for the degree variable and 2 categories of the gender variable, you will have 10 cells, one for each possible combination of degree and gender. Based on the observed means and standard deviations in these 10 cells, you can statistically test whether, in the population, average hours worked is the same for people with different educational backgrounds; whether it is the same for males and for females; and whether the relationship between average hours worked and degree is the same for males and females.

Figure 16.1 Mean hours worked by degree and gender

To obtain this output, select the variables hrs1, degree, and sex in the Means dialog box. See Chapter 6 for more information.

```
              - - Description of Subpopulations - -

Summaries of     HRS1        Number of Hours Worked Last Week
By levels of     DEGREE      RS Highest Degree
                 SEX         Respondent's Sex


Variable         Value  Label              Mean    Std Dev    Cases

For Entire Population                      46.2888  11.2691     741

DEGREE             0   Less than HS        43.6923   8.7235      52
   SEX             1   Male                44.3611   7.5863      36
   SEX             2   Female              42.1875  10.9983      16

DEGREE             1   High school         45.7726  10.5769     387
   SEX             1   Male                47.6915  10.8984     201
   SEX             2   Female              43.6989   9.8330     186

DEGREE             2   Junior college      45.8704  11.6636      54
   SEX             1   Male                48.0000  11.0734      30
   SEX             2   Female              43.2083  12.0650      24

DEGREE             3   Bachelor            46.3827  12.8909     162
   SEX             1   Male                48.0476  12.1456      84
   SEX             2   Female              44.5897  13.4969      78

DEGREE             4   Graduate            50.2674  11.4382      86
   SEX             1   Male                53.2963  12.0481      54
   SEX             2   Female              45.1563   8.2231      32

   Total Cases = 747
Missing Cases = 6 or     .8 Pct
```

Examining the Data

As always, your first step should be to just look at the data. Make stem-and-leaf plots, histograms, or bar charts. Calculate summary statistics for the groups. See if you can get an idea of what's going on in your data. Figure 16.1 shows descriptive statistics for the 10 combinations of gender and degree.

You can obtain this bar chart using the Graphs menu, as described in "Bar Charts" on p. 538 in Appendix A.

In the Define Clustered Bar Chart Summaries for Groups of Cases dialog box, select the variables hrs1, degree, and sex.

Figure 16.2 Average number of hours worked by degree and gender

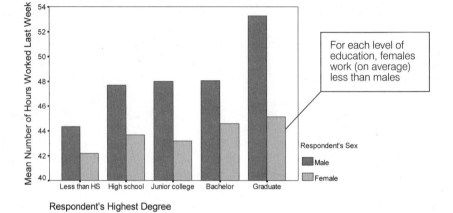

The means are plotted in Figure 16.2, which is a bar chart of the average number of hours worked. There are five clusters of bars, one for each degree category. Within each cluster, there are two bars, one for males and one for females. The height of the bar tells you the average hours worked for each group. The results are certainly interesting. For each level of education, on average, females in the sample work less than males. The largest difference between males and females is for those with graduate degrees. In the sample, men with graduate degrees work an average of eight hours more than women with graduate degrees.

Do you really believe that? There are several nonstatistical explanations that come to mind. First of all, the interviewers simply asked people how long they worked the previous week. That means that men didn't have to *actually* work longer than women, they only had to say they did.

Figure 16.3 Hours worked by degree and gender

You can obtain this boxplot using the Graphs menu, as described in "Boxplots" on p. 540 in Appendix A.

In the Define Clustered Boxplot Summaries for Groups of Cases dialog box, select the variables hrs1, degree, and sex.

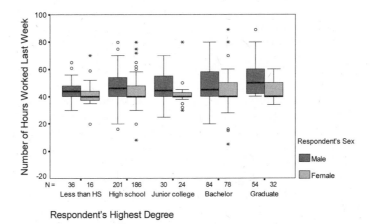

You can also examine differences between the 10 groups of cases by making a box-and-whiskers plot like that shown in Figure 16.3. This plot conveys much more information than the bar chart. It tells you about the distribution of values in each of the groups. You see that for each of the five degree categories, the median hours worked is higher for men than for women. The length of the boxes for the men is somewhat larger than for the women. However, if you look at the standard deviations for the groups, you don't see the same pattern. There are some outlying and extreme points on the plot. Since the groups are reasonably large and all of the extreme values are believable, we won't pursue them further.

Testing Hypotheses

In this example, there are three different questions about the population that need to be answered:

1. Are the average hours worked the same for the five degree categories?

2. Are the average hours worked the same for men and women?

3. Is the relationship between average hours worked and degree the same for men and for women?

Notice that the first two questions both involve only one of the factor variables. The first question asks about degree, ignoring the possible effect of gender. The second asks about the gender effect, ignoring degree status. Both of these questions are hypotheses about what are known as main effects.

> **?** *What's a main effect?* In analysis-of variance-terms, **main effects** are the effects of each of the individual factors, ignoring the other factors. For example, if you are studying the effects of marital status, gender, and degree on average hours worked using a three-way analysis of variance, the effect of each of the three variables, considered alone, is called a main effect. ■ ■ ■

The last question involves both of the factors simultaneously. It's called a test of the **interaction** between degree and gender. In statistics, the word interaction has a meaning similar to that in everyday language. When you talk about the interaction of a heavy lunch and a boring class on sleepiness, you usually mean that, considered together, the two factors have more (or less) of an effect than when they are considered individually. In statistics, when you talk about an interaction, you refer to an effect that is larger or smaller than would be predicted based on the main effects of the factors.

Interactions Between Factors: An Example

To learn more about the statistical meaning of interaction, consider the following example. You are interested in studying the effect of four different methods of teaching statistics to three types of students: high school students, undergraduate students, and graduate students. You have 12 independent groups of students, one for each combination of teaching method and student type. For each student, you have a score on the standardized statistics final. Figure 16.4 shows a line plot of the average scores for the 12 groups of students.

Figure 16.4 No interaction between factors

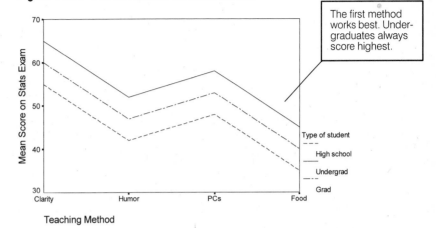

On the horizontal axis you see the four teaching methods. Each of the lines represents one of the student groups. What can you tell from this plot? For all four teaching methods, undergraduate students score highest, and high school students score lowest. For all three types of students, the first method appears to result in the highest average score; the fourth method in the lowest average score. Method three is a little more effective than method two.

It's particularly important to notice that the four methods seem to work in the same way for the three student groups. That is, the shape of the three line drawings is similar for high school students, undergraduate students, and graduate students. The distance between any pair of lines is the same for the entire plot. This means that there is no interaction between teaching method and type of student. When there is no interaction, it makes sense to talk about the main effects: the teaching methods main effect and the student type main effect. The first method is the best teaching method. Undergraduate students score highest on the standardized test. It's reasonable to reach each of these conclusions.

When there is no interaction, you can predict the average score for a student with the following equation:

predicted score = mean score + teaching method effect + student type effect

Equation 16.1

The equation tells you that the average predicted score depends only on teaching method and the type of student. That's because all four teaching methods work the same for the 3 types of students.

? *Where did that equation come from?* Assume that the average score for all participants is 50. Teaching method one raises the predicted score by 10 points. Teaching method two lowers it by 3, method three increases it by 3, and method four decreases the predicted score by 10 points. Similarly, being a high school student lowers the score by 5 points, being a graduate student leaves it unchanged, and being an undergraduate student adds 5 points to the score. Now, using the formula, you can compute the average scores for students in each of the 12 groups. For example, the predicted average score for undergraduates taught by method one is:

predicted score = mean score + method 1 effect + undergraduate effect

thus:

predicted score = $50 + 10 + 5 = 65$

Similarly, the average score for high school students taught by method two is $50 - 3 - 5 = 42$. To compute the average score for a group, you just look at the main effects. That is, you just consider the teaching method and the student type. The effects of the teaching methods are the same for all types of students. ■ ■ ■

Figure 16.5 is a plot that shows an interaction between the teaching methods and the student types.

Figure 16.5 Average scores with interaction effect

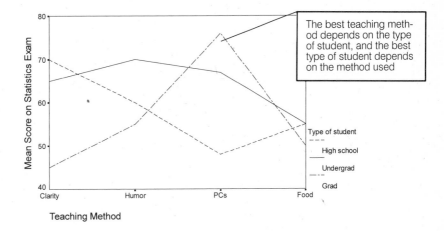

This plot is more difficult to interpret than the previous one. Note that, unlike the lines in Figure 16.4, the lines for groups cross one another. The difference between any pair of lines is not the same for the four teaching methods. The effect of the teaching methods is not the same for all three student groups. Method one performs best for high school students, method two performs best for undergraduates, while method three is the best for graduate students. In this situation, it doesn't make sense to talk about a best teaching method or a best student type. The best method depends on the type of student, and the best type of student depends on the teaching method used. You can no longer predict the average score for a group from just the effect of the method and the effect of the student type. You also need a term for the combination of each method and student type. That is, you need a student-type by teaching-method interaction term.

Necessary Assumptions

Now that you know what main effects and interactions mean, you're ready to test hypotheses about them using two-way analysis of variance. But first a word about the assumptions you have to make. To use two-way analysis of variance, you'll need to make assumptions similar to those required for one-way analysis of variance. The data for each cell must be an independent random sample from a normal population with a constant variance. (**Constant variance** is another way of saying that the population variance is the same for all cells.) You can check these assumptions the same way you do for one-way analysis of variance. You can check the normality assumption by examining normal probability plots for each of the cells. You can look at the spread of your observations in a box-and-whiskers plot to see if the variability is markedly different in the groups.

Analysis-of-Variance Table

The two-way analysis-of-variance table for testing hypotheses about the population values for average hours worked is shown in Figure 16.6. It's very similar to the one-way analysis-of-variance table you saw in Chapter 15. What has changed is the number of hypotheses that you are testing. In one-way analysis of variance, you tested a single hypothesis. Now you can test three hypotheses: one about the main effect of degree, one about the main effect of gender, and one about the degree-by-gender interaction.

Figure 16.6 Two-way analysis-of-variance table

To obtain this output, from the menus choose:

Statistics
  ANOVA Models ▶
    Simple Factorial...

In the Simple Factorial ANOVA dialog box, select the variables hrs1, degree, and sex, as shown in Figure 16.8.

```
                   * * *   A N A L Y S I S   O F   V A R I A N C E   * * *

                    HRS1      Number of Hours Worked Last Week     For each effect, F
              by    DEGREE    RS Highest Degree                    ratio should be
                    SEX       Respondent's Sex                     close to 1 if null hy-
                                                                   pothesis is true
                    UNIQUE sums of squares
                    All effects entered simultaneously


                                  Sum of                  Mean               Sig
      Source of Variation         Squares      DF         Square      F      of F

      Main Effects                3253.387     5          650.677     5.378  .000
        DEGREE                    1222.827     4          305.707     2.527  .040
        SEX                       2034.058     1          2034.058    16.813 .000

      2-Way Interactions           387.337     4           96.834      .800  .525
        DEGREE   SEX               387.337     4           96.834      .800  .525

      Explained                   5539.321     9          615.480     5.088  .000

      Residual                   88434.876   731          120.978

      Total                      93974.197   740          126.992


      747 cases were processed.
      6 cases (.8 pct) were missing.
```

In one-way analysis of variance, you will recall, you test whether the sample means vary too much to be from populations with the same mean (see Chapter 15). Basically the same thing is going on here. The major difference is that you now have three sets of means to consider: the 5 degree means, the 2 gender means and the 10 cell means.

1. First you see how much the observations within the ten cells vary. The *Residual Mean Square* in Figure 16.6 tells you that. (In one-way analysis of variance output, the same thing is called the *Within Cells Mean Square*.) This estimate of the population variance doesn't depend on the null hypothesis being true.

2. Then you see how much the sample means of the five degree groups vary. From the variability of these sample means you get the mean square for degree. Similarly, from the variability of the male and female means, you get the mean square for sex. From the variability of all 10 cell means, you get the mean square for the interaction. Instead of having just one between-groups mean square as you did in one-way analysis of variance, you now have three different between-groups mean squares: one for degree, one for gender, and one for the interaction. Remember that these estimates of the population variance depend on the appropriate null hypothesis being true. For example, the degree mean square will estimate the population variance only if the null hypothesis that all five degree means are equal is true.

3. The *F* ratios are computed by dividing each of the main effect and interaction mean squares by the residual mean square. If the null hypothesis for an effect is true, then the corresponding *F* ratio is expected to be 1. Of course, for samples, the *F* ratio won't be exactly 1. You look at the observed significance level for each observed *F* ratio to see if you can reject the corresponding null hypothesis.

Testing the Degree-by-Gender Interaction

The first test that you want to look at in Figure 16.6 is for the two-way interaction between degree and sex (the two factors). You test the interaction term first, since you've seen that it doesn't make sense to talk about main effects if there is a significant interaction between the factors. The null hypothesis for the interaction term is that the effect of type of degree on average hours worked is the same for males and females in the population.

In Figure 16.6, the observed significance level for the no-interaction hypothesis is 0.525, so you don't reject the null hypothesis that there is no interaction between the two variables. The effect of the type of degree on hours worked seems to be similar for males and females. The absence of interaction tells you that it's reasonable to believe that the difference in average hours worked between males and females is the same for all degree categories. You haven't shown otherwise.

Since you didn't find an interaction between degree and gender, it makes sense to test hypotheses about the main effects of degree and gender. You can ask whether the population means for the five degree groups are the same and whether the population means for the two gender groups are the same.

? *What would it mean if I were to find an interaction between degree and gender?* That would mean that the relationship between degree and hours worked was different for males and females. For example, it might be that males with graduate degrees work more than males with any other degrees, while the same is not true for females. If you find an interaction, then you can't comment on just the degree category or the gender category. Instead, you have to talk about males with graduate degrees or females with high school diplomas. You have to consider degree and gender together. ■ ■ ■

Testing the Main Effects

Now let's see whether there is a degree main effect. That is, are the population means the same for the five degree groups. In Figure 16.6, you see that the F statistic for the degree main effect is 2.53. The observed significance level is 0.04, so you can reject the null hypothesis. That's not surprising. That's what you concluded in Chapter 15.

? *How come I get different numbers for the degree sum of squares and mean square in the ANOVA table when I do a two-way analysis of variance and when I do a one-way analysis of variance?* If you don't have the same number of cases in each cell and have two or more factors, the computation of the ANOVA table can be quite complicated. That's because you can't neatly separate out the effects of each of the variables. You can get different values, depending on which of several methods you use. Stick with the default method in SPSS ANOVA. ■ ■ ■

To see whether you can reject the null hypothesis that the average hours worked is the same for males and females, look at the row labeled *SEX* in Figure 16.6. You see that the observed significance level for the sex main effect is very small, less than 0.0005. You can reject the null hypotheses that the average work week is the same for males and for females.

> *Why did I have to use a two-way analysis of variance for this problem? I could have computed a one-way analysis of variance for the degree groups and a two-sample* t *test for the gender groups?* The two-way analysis of variance lets you test the interaction between the two variables. You couldn't do that otherwise. As you've seen, testing for interaction is very important. If you find an interaction, it doesn't make much sense to talk about gender or degree differences alone. They must be considered together. ■ ■ ■

Putting It All Together

Look at Figure 16.7, which is a line plot of the 10 cell means. What you've concluded is that, in the population, the shape of the two lines is the same for males and females. Or, phrased more carefully, you've concluded that you don't have enough evidence to believe that there is a degree-by-gender interaction. You've also concluded that when both genders are considered together, the population means for average hours worked per week are not the same for the degree groups. Nor are they the same for males and females when all degrees are considered together.

Figure 16.7 Line plot of 10 cell means

You can obtain multiple line charts using the Graphs menu, as described in "Line and Area Charts" on p. 539 in Appendix A.

In the Define Multiple Line Summaries for Groups of Cases dialog box, select the variables hrs1, degree, and sex.

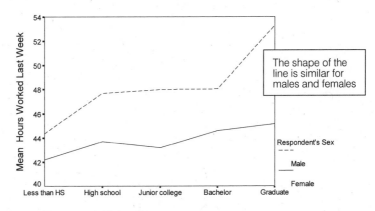

Extensions

In this example, you had two factor variables: gender and degree. Analysis of variance can be used to test hypotheses about any number of factors. For example, if your cases are classified by gender, degree, and marital status, you can test the equality of means for the two sexes, five degree categories, and five marital status categories. You can also test hypotheses about the interactions of pairs of factors (gender and degree, gender and marital status, degree and marital status) as well as the interaction of all three factors.

Summary

How can you test hypotheses about population means when you have two factors?

- You can use analysis of variance to test hypotheses about means when your cases are grouped on the basis of several variables or factors.

- With analysis of variance, you can test whether the population means are equal for all of the categories of a factor and whether there is an interaction between two factors.

- An interaction is present when the effect of one factor is not the same for all of the categories of the other factor.

- For analysis of variance, you must assume that you have independent samples from normal populations with the same variance.

- If you have different numbers of cases in the cells, several different methods can be used to calculate the analysis-of-variance table. There is no longer a unique solution.

What's Next?

You've learned to test a variety of hypotheses about population means. Now you'll turn your attention to testing hypotheses about data that are best summarized in a crosstabulation. You'll learn how to test whether the two variables that make up the rows and columns of a crosstabulation are independent.

How to Obtain a Two-Way Analysis of Variance

This section shows how to obtain a factorial analysis of variance using SPSS. The Simple Factorial ANOVA procedure can:

- Assess the independent effects of covariates on the dependent variable.
- Automatically include interactions among the factors in the model.
- Use different models to estimate the sums of squares.

▶ To open the Simple Factorial ANOVA dialog box (see Figure 16.8), from the menus choose:

Statistics
  ANOVA Models ▶
    Simple Factorial...

Figure 16.8 Simple Factorial ANOVA dialog box

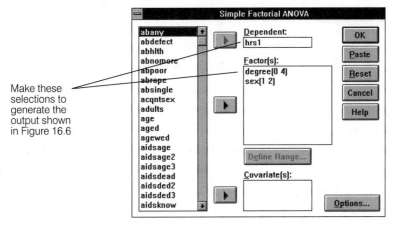

Make these selections to generate the output shown in Figure 16.6

To obtain a factorial analysis of variance, you must indicate the variable(s) whose means you want to compare, and you must specify variables that define the groups to be compared. In the Simple Factorial ANOVA dialog box:

▶ Select the variable whose mean you want to test and move it into the Dependent box. The dialog box allows you to test only one dependent variable at a time.

▶ Select the variable or variables whose values define the groups and move them into the Factor(s) list. Select each in turn in that list, click on Define Range, and indicate the range of categories to test (see Figure 16.9).

▶ Click on OK.

SPSS calculates an *F* statistic, and its probability, for the null hypothesis that the data are sampled from a population in which the mean values of the test variable are equal across the groups defined by the factors.

Define Range: Specifying the Subgroups

With a variable selected in the Factor box, click on Define Range to open the Define Range dialog box, as shown in Figure 16.9. (Select more than one variable before clicking on Define Range if you want to specify the same range for all of them.)

Figure 16.9 Simple Factorial ANOVA Define Range dialog box

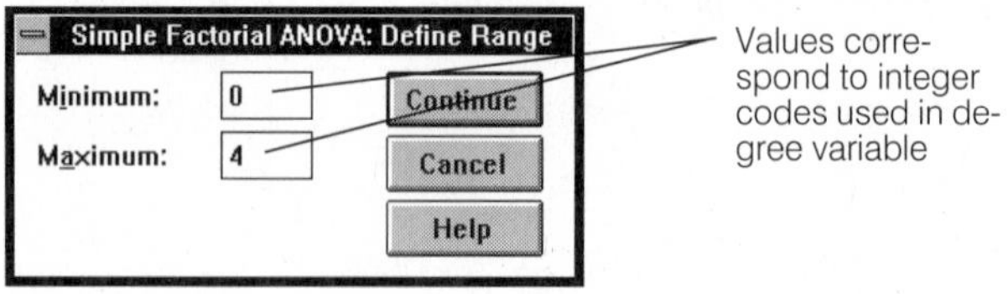

▶ SPSS assumes that groups are identified by integer codes, not less than zero, in the factor variable(s). Enter an integer for the lowest code of the selected factor(s) into the Minimum box and another integer for the highest code into the Maximum box.

Factor values outside the range specified here are ignored in the analysis. Empty categories—factor codes between the minimum and maximum values that do not correspond to any cases in your data file—are likewise ignored. Factor values that are not integers are truncated for the analysis.

Options: Analysis Method, Statistics, Interactions, and Labels

In the Simple Factorial ANOVA dialog box, click on Options. In the Simple Factorial ANOVA Options dialog box, as shown in Figure 16.10, you can control several different aspects of the analysis.

Figure 16.10 Simple Factorial ANOVA Options dialog box

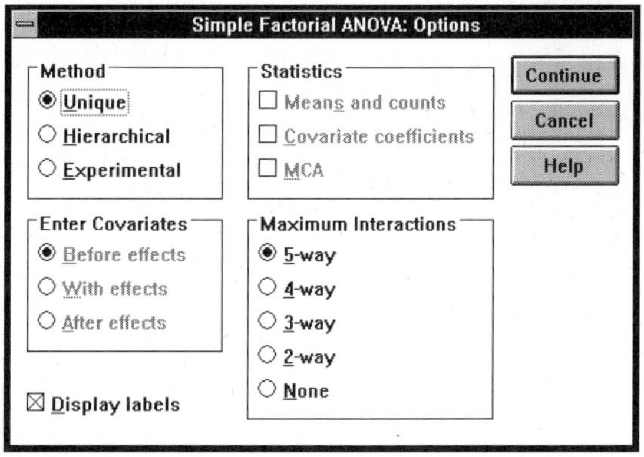

Method. The Method alternatives are:

Unique. The main effects of factors, interactions among factors, and the effects of covariates are assessed simultaneously.

Hierarchical. The main effects of factors and the effects of covariates are adjusted for factors and covariates that precede them in the Factor(s) list and the Covariate(s) list, respectively. Interactions among factors are adjusted for main effects, covariate effects, and lower-order interactions, without regard to the order of the Factor(s) and Covariate(s) lists.

Experimental. The main effects of factors and the effects of covariates are processed as specified by the Enter Covariates alternatives (below). Interactions among factors are adjusted for main effects, covariate effects, and lower-order interactions, as in the hierarchical method.

Enter Covariates. The Enter Covariates alternatives are available when either the Hierarchical method or the Experimental method is selected:

Before effects. Covariates are processed before main effects of factors.

With effects. Covariates and the main effects of factors are processed simultaneously.

After effects. Covariates are processed after main effects of factors.

Statistics. The Statistics options are:

Means and counts. The means of the dependent variable(s) and the count of cases in all of the groups defined by the factors. This is not available when the Unique method is selected.

Covariate coefficients. Unstandardized regression coefficients.

MCA. Multiple Classification Analysis, expressing effects as deviations from the grand mean. This is not available when the Unique method is selected.

Maximum Interactions. The Maximum Interactions alternatives let you specify whether interaction terms among the factors are included in the model. If you select 3-way, for example, interactions among all possible groups of 3 factors (including all possible pairs of factors) are assessed along with the main effects of factors and the effects of covariates.

Display labels. The Display labels check box lets you suppress the display of variable labels.

No alternatives are available for processing missing data, since only one dependent variable at a time is analyzed. Cases with missing data for any variable in the analysis are excluded from the calculations.

Exercises

Statistical Concepts

1. For each of the following situations, identify the statistical test that you would use to test the hypothesis of interest:

  a. You are interested in examining three temperatures and four combinations of ingredients to see if they all result in the same maximum height of a cake.

  b. You want to know if people in four regions of the country spend the same amount of money on fast food.

  c. You want to know if workers on an assembly line are more productive when they are offered an incentive. You measure the productivity of the same workers before and after the incentive program.

  d. You want to compare whether the average waiting time in the checkout line is the same for two chains of stores.

2. You are interested in observing changes in spending patterns for clothes during the year. For each person in the study, you obtain quarterly expenditures for clothing and then perform an analysis of variance with the respondent's gender as one factor and season of the year as the second factor. Do you see any problems with this analysis?

3. Based on the following plot of cell means of the average number of days of work missed during the year, do you think there is an interaction between gender and job classification?

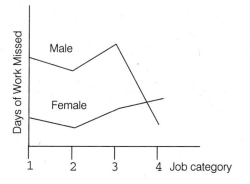

4. Complete the following two-way analysis-of-variance table:

```
* * *  A N A L Y S I S   O F   V A R I A N C E  * * *

        CHANGE    Annual Salary Increase
    by  JOBCAT    Employment Category
        SEX       Sex of Employee

        UNIQUE sums of squares
        All effects entered simultaneously
```

Source of Variation	Sum of Squares	DF	Mean Square	F	Sig of F
Main Effects	169710.656	7			.000
JOBCAT	153113.472	6			.000
SEX	4469.666	1			.085
Explained	169710.656	7			.000
Residual	135384.807	92			
Total	305095.463	99			

```
100 cases were processed.
0 cases (.0 pct) were missing.
```

5. You are studying the effects of store location and store hours on sales. You find that there is a significant interaction between location and hours. Is it reasonable to then test for the effect of location and the effect of store hours? Why or why not?

Data Analysis

Use the *gss.sav* data file to answer the following questions:

1. Use two-way analysis of variance to test the following hypotheses. Summarize your findings for each.

a. Average years of education (variable *educ*) are the same for people employed full time and people employed part time (codes 1 and 2 for variable *wrkstat*).

b. Average years of education are the same for males and females.

c. The relationship between education and work status (variable *wrkstat*) is the same for males and females.

2. You are interested in studying the voting behavior of males and females. Use Select Cases to restrict your analysis to respondents with codes 1 (voted) and 2 (did not vote) for *vote92*. Determine if there is a relationship between age and voting, and if it is the same for males and females. Summarize your findings. Explain why there is a significant gender main effect and what it means.

3. Repeat the analysis in question 2, but this time examine years of education instead of age.

4. Select two hypotheses of your choice that can be tested with two-way analysis of variance and test them. Write a paper summarizing your findings.

5. Consider the relationship between the age at which a person was first married (variable *agewed*), the happiness of their marriage (variable *hapmar*), and the person's gender. Use two-way analysis of variance to analyze the data. Indicate what hypothesis you are testing and what your conclusions are about each of them.

Use the *salary.sav* data file to answer the following questions:

6. You are interested in seeing whether current salaries (variable *salnow*) for clerical employees (variable *jobcat* equals 1) are related to gender and minority status (variables *sex* and *minority*).

    a. Run the appropriate analyses and interpret your results. Be sure to evaluate how well the data meet the required assumptions.

    b. Is there evidence of an interaction between gender and minority status? If there is, what does it mean?

7. Using the *salary.sav* data, select a hypothesis that can be tested using two-way analysis of variance and test it. Write a short explanation of your results.

Comparing Observed and Expected Counts

How can you test the null hypothesis that two variables are independent?

- What are observed and expected counts?
- How do you compute the chi-square statistic?
- What assumptions are needed for the chi-square test of independence?
- What is a one-sample chi-square test?
- Why is sample size important?

You know how to test a variety of hypotheses about population means. However, these tests are useful only when it makes sense to compute a mean for a variable. If you want to look at the relationship between preference among car colors and region of the country, or between type of treatment and remission of symptoms, you can't use a *t* test because it doesn't make sense to compare means. Rather, such variables are best summarized by a crosstabulation. In this chapter, you'll use the **chi-square test** to examine hypotheses about data that are best summarized by a crosstabulation.

▶ This chapter uses the *gss.sav* data file. The chi-square test output shown can be obtained using the SPSS Crosstabs procedure. (For more information on Crosstabs, see Chapter 8.)

Education and Anomia

The French sociologist Emile Durkheim introduced the concept of anomie to represent the feelings of alienation and rootlessness common in the modern world. The General Social Survey attempts to measure such feelings with a scale called *anomia*. One item on this scale asks respondents whether they agree or disagree with the following statement: "In spite of what some people say, the lot of the average man is getting worse, not better." Let's consider whether education is related to the likelihood of agreeing with this statement.

Figure 17.1 Crosstabulation of anomia5 and degree2

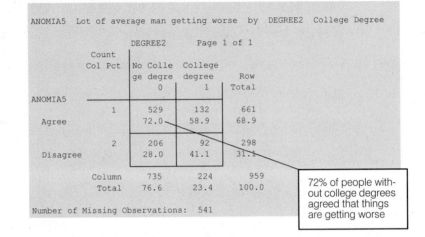

You can obtain a crosstabulation using the Crosstabs procedure, as discussed in Chapter 8.

Select anomia5 and degree2 in the Crosstabs dialog box.

Figure 17.1 is a crosstabulation of responses to the statement for those with and without college degrees. You see that 72% of respondents who have not completed college agree with the statement, while 58.9% of respondents with college degrees agree with this statement. Based on these results, do you think that, in the population, there is a difference between college graduates and non-college graduates in the perception of the lot of the average man? Certainly in this sample, college graduates are less pessimistic than nongraduates. But as usual, the sample results are not what you're interested in. You want to know what you can conclude about the population based on the observed sample results. You want to know whether you have enough evidence to reject the null hypothesis that, in the population, the same percentage of college graduates and nongraduates agree with the statement.

Observed and Expected Counts

The basic element of a crosstabulation table is the count of the number of cases in each cell of the table. The statistical procedure you'll use to test the null hypothesis is based on comparing the observed count in each of the cells to the expected count. The expected count is simply the number of cases you would expect to find in a cell if the null hypothesis is true. Here's how the expected counts are calculated.

Calculating Expected Counts

If the null hypothesis is true, you expect college graduates and non-graduates to answer the question in the same way. That is, you expect the *percentage* agreeing with the statement to be the same for the two groups of cases. You don't expect the same *number* of graduates and nongraduates to agree with the statement, since you don't have the same number of people in the two education categories.

From the row marginals in Figure 17.1, you see that in the sample, 68.9% of the respondents agreed with the statement and 31.1% disagreed. If the null hypothesis is true, these are the best estimates for the percentages you would expect for both graduates and nongraduates. To convert the percentages to the actual number of cases in each of the cells, multiply the expected percentages by the numbers of graduates and nongraduates. For example, the expected number of non-graduates agreeing with the statement is

$$68.93\% \times 735 = 506.6 \qquad \textbf{Equation 17.1}$$

Similarly, the expected number of nongraduates disagreeing with the statement is

$$31.07\% \times 735 = 228.4 \qquad \textbf{Equation 17.2}$$

For college graduates, the expected values are calculated in the same way, substituting the number of college graduates (224) for the number of nongraduates (735) in the above two equations.

? *Is there a simple way I can remember how to calculate expected values?* Sure. The following rule is equivalent to what you've just done: To calculate the expected number of cases in any cell of a crosstabulation, multiply the number of cases in the cell's row by the number of cases in the cell's column and divide by the total number of cases in the table. Try it. You'll see it always works. ■ ■ ■

Figure 17.2 Observed and expected counts

To obtain observed and expected counts, select Cells in the Crosstabs dialog box. See Chapter 8 for more information.

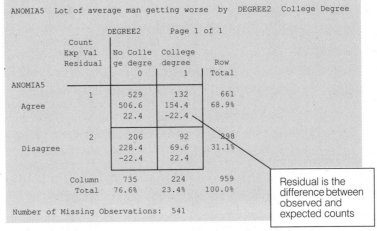

```
ANOMIA5  Lot of average man getting worse  by  DEGREE2  College Degree

                       DEGREE2        Page 1 of 1
                Count
                Exp Val  No Colle College
                Residual ge degre degree      Row
                             0         1     Total
   ANOMIA5
                  1        529       132       661
   Agree                 506.6     154.4     68.9%
                          22.4     -22.4

                  2        206        92       298
   Disagree              228.4      69.6     31.1%
                         -22.4      22.4

           Column         735       224       959
           Total        76.6%     23.4%    100.0%

   Number of Missing Observations:  541
```

Residual is the difference between observed and expected counts

You see in Figure 17.2 the observed and expected counts for all four cells. The last entry in a cell is the **residual**, the difference between the observed and expected counts. A positive residual means that you observed more cases in a cell than you would expect if the null hypothesis were true. A negative residual indicates that you observed fewer cases than you would expect if the null hypothesis were true.

The sum of the expected counts for any row or column is the same as the observed count for that row or column. For example, the expected counts for college graduates add up to the observed number of college graduates. Similarly, the expected counts for the number agreeing add up to the observed number of cases agreeing. Another way of saying this is that the residuals add up to 0 across any row and any column.

The Chi-Square Statistic

When you test the null hypothesis that two population means are equal, you compute the t statistic, and then, using the t distribution, calculate how unusual the observed value is if the null hypothesis is true. To test hypotheses about data that are counts, you compute what's called a chi-square statistic and compare its value to the chi-square distribution to see how unlikely the observed value is if the null hypothesis is true.

? *What assumptions are needed to use the chi-square test?* All of your observations must be independent. That implies that an individual can appear only once in a table. You can't let a person choose two favorite car colors and then make a table of color preference by gender. (Each person would appear twice in such a table.) It also means that the categories of a variable can't overlap. (For example, you can't use the age groups less than 30, 25–40, 35–90.) Also, most of the expected counts must be greater than 5, and none less than 1. ■ ■ ■

To compute the Pearson chi-square statistic, do the following:

1. For each cell, calculate the expected count by multiplying the number of cases in the cell's row by the number of cases in the cell's column and dividing the result by the total count.

2. Find the difference between the observed and expected counts.

3. Square the difference.

4. Divide the squared difference by the expected count for the cell.

5. Add up the results of the previous step for all of the cells.

In the current example, the value for the Pearson chi-square statistic is

$$\frac{(529 - 506.6)^2}{506.6} + \frac{(132 - 154.4)^2}{154.4} + \frac{(206 - 228.4)^2}{228.4} + \frac{(92 - 69.6)^2}{69.6} = 13.64$$

Equation 17.3

If the null hypothesis is true, the observed and expected values should be similar. Of course, even if the null hypothesis is true, the observed and expected values won't be identical, since the results you observe in a sample vary somewhat around the true population value. As before, you have to determine how often to expect a chi-square value at least as large as the one you've calculated, if the null hypothesis is true.

To determine whether a chi-square value of 13.64 is unusual, you compare it to the chi-square distribution. Like the *t* distribution, the chi-square distribution depends on the parameter called the degrees of freedom. The degrees of freedom for the chi-square statistic depend not on the number of cases in your sample, as they did for the *t* statistic, but on the number of rows and columns in your crosstabulation. The degrees of freedom for the chi-square statistic are (number of rows in the table − 1) × (number of columns in the table − 1)

Equation 17.4

For this example, there is one degree of freedom, since there are two rows and two columns.

> ❓ *What's the logic behind the calculation of the degrees of freedom?* For any row or column of a crosstabulation, the residuals sum to 0. That means that you can tell what the expected values must be for the last row and last column of a table without doing any calculations other than summing the expected values in the preceding rows or columns. The number of cells for which you have to calculate expected values is equal to the number of cells when you remove the last row and the last column from your table. The number of cells in a table when one row and one column are removed is the number of rows minus 1 multiplied by the number of columns minus 1, which is the formula for the degrees of freedom. ■ ■ ■

Figure 17.3 Pearson chi-square test for anomia by education

To obtain the Pearson chi-square test along with a crosstabulation, select Statistics in the Crosstabs dialog box.

See Chapter 8 for more information.

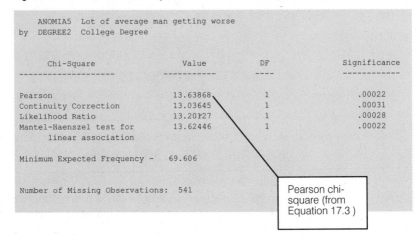

```
    ANOMIA5   Lot of average man getting worse
by  DEGREE2   College Degree


     Chi-Square                    Value        DF          Significance
----------------------           ---------      ----       -------------

Pearson                          13.63868         1            .00022
Continuity Correction            13.03645         1            .00031
Likelihood Ratio                 13.20127         1            .00028
Mantel-Haenszel test for         13.62446         1            .00022
     linear association

Minimum Expected Frequency -     69.606


Number of Missing Observations:   541
```

Pearson chi-square (from Equation 17.3)

In Figure 17.3, you see that the observed significance level for the Pearson chi-square value of 13.64 is 0.00022. This means that, if the null hypothesis is true, you expect to see a chi-square value at least as large as 13.64 only about twice out of 10,000 instances. Since the observed significance level is small, you can reject the null hypothesis that college graduates and those who did not graduate from college give the same responses to the question. It appears that college graduates are more optimistic about the lot of the common man than high school graduates.

? *What's all that other stuff in Figure 17.3 along with the Pearson chi-square?* The continuity-corrected chi-square is a modification of the Pearson chi-square for two-by-two tables. Most statisticians agree that the modification is unnecessary, so you can ignore it. The likelihood- ratio chi-square is a statistic very similar to the Pearson chi-square. For large sample sizes, the two statistics are close in value. The **Mantel-Haenszel test** is a measure of the linear association between the row and column variables. It's useful only if both the row and column variables are ordered from smallest to largest. Ignore it in other situations.

If you have a table with two rows and two columns in which at least one of the expected counts is less than 5, you'll also find something labeled Fisher's exact test on your output. The advantage of Fisher's exact test is that it is appropriate for 2×2 tables in which the expected value in one or more cells is small. The disadvantage is that it requires a very restrictive assumption about the data: that you know in advance the number of cases in the margins. There's controversy among statisticians about the appropriateness of Fisher's exact test when this assumption is not met. In general, Fisher's exact test is less likely to find true differences than it should. Statistically, a test like this is called **conservative**. ■ ■ ■

College Degrees and Perception of Life

In the previous example, you tested whether college graduates and those who are not college graduates respond in the same way to the question about the lot of the average man. The null hypothesis can be stated in several equivalent ways. You can say the null hypothesis is that the percentage agreeing with the statement is the same for the two categories of education. Another way of stating the null hypothesis is that educational status and response are independent.

Independence means that knowing the value of one of the variables for a case tells you nothing about the value of the other variable. For example, if marital status and happiness with life are independent, knowing a person's marital status gives you no information about how happy they are with life. College education and perception of the lot of man, on the other hand, don't seem to be independent. If you know that a person is a college graduate, you know that he or she is less likely to agree with the pessimistic statement about the lot of the average man than is a person who is not a college graduate.

A Larger Table

The chi-square test can be used to test the hypothesis of independence for a table with any number of rows and columns. The idea is the same as for the two-row and two-column table. As an example, let's look at the relationship between highest degree earned and whether life is perceived as exciting, routine, or dull.

Figure 17.4 is a crosstabulation of highest degree earned and the response to the perception of life question.

Figure 17.4 Crosstabulation of education and life

```
DEGREE   RS Highest Degree  by  LIFE   Is Life Exciting or Dull

                     LIFE                     Page 1 of 1
             Count
             Exp Val  Dull     Routine   Exciting
             Row Pct                              Row
             Residual   1        2         3      Total
   DEGREE
                0       24        96        66      186
   Less than HS         12.0      85.8      88.2    18.7%
                        12.9%     51.6%     35.5%
                        12.0      10.2     -22.2

                1       35        251       231     517
   High school          33.3      238.5     245.3   52.0%
                        6.8%      48.5%     44.7%
                        1.7       12.5     -14.3

                2       2         33        27      62
   Junior college       4.0       28.6      29.4    6.2%
                        3.2%      53.2%     43.5%
                       -2.0       4.4      -2.4

                3       2         58        97      157
   Bachelor             10.1      72.4      74.5    15.8%
                        1.3%      36.9%     61.8%
                       -8.1      -14.4      22.5

                4       1         21        51      73
   Graduate             4.7       33.7      34.6    7.3%
                        1.4%      28.8%     69.9%
                       -3.7      -12.7      16.4

          Column        64        459       472     995
          Total         6.4%      46.1%     47.4%   100.0%

Number of Missing Observations:  505
```

College graduates have large positive residuals in the Exciting column

From the row percentages, you see that almost 70% of people with graduate degrees find life exciting. (They probably don't read or write statistics books!) Only 36% of people with less than a high school diploma find life exciting. In fact, as education increases, so does the likelihood of finding life exciting. (Don't be alarmed by the large number of missing observations. Not all people in the General Social Survey were asked the question.)

To test the null hypothesis that highest degree and perception of life are independent, you compute a chi-square statistic for this table the same way you did for a 2×2 table. For example, if the null hypothesis is true, the expected number of people without high school diplomas who find life exciting is 88.2. (That can be calculated by multiplying the overall percentage of people who find life exciting, 47.4%, by the number of people without high school diplomas, 186.)

The Pearson chi-square value for the table is shown in Figure 17.5. You see that the observed significance level is less than 0.000005, which leads you to reject the null hypothesis that degree and perception of life are independent. By looking at the residuals in Figure 17.4, you see that college graduates have large positive residuals for the response *Exciting*. That means that the observed number of college graduates in those cells is larger than that predicted by the independence hypothesis. By examining the residuals in a crosstabulation, you can tell where the departures from independence are.

Figure 17.5 Pearson chi-square for crosstabulation of education and life

```
DEGREE  RS Highest Degree  by  LIFE  Is Life Exciting or Dull

Number of valid observations = 995


        Chi-Square              Value        DF        Significance
   --------------------      -----------    ----      ------------

   Pearson                    53.96180        8          .00000
   Likelihood Ratio           55.87366        8          .00000
   Mantel-Haenszel test for   47.63254        1          .00000
      linear association

   Minimum Expected Frequency -    3.988
   Cells with Expected Frequency < 5 -    2 OF    15 ( 13.3%)


   Number of Missing Observations:   505
```

Check these values to be sure your test is valid

After the chi-square statistics are printed, SPSS tells you what the smallest expected count is in any cell of the table. In this example, the *Minimum Expected Frequency* is 3.988. This is important because, if too many of the expected values in a table are less than 5, the observed significance level based on the chi-square distribution may not be correct. As a general rule, you should not use the chi-square test if more than 20% of the cells have expected values less than 5, or if the minimum expected frequency is less than 1.

What should I do if one of these conditions is not satisfied? If your table has more than two rows and two columns, you can see if it makes sense to combine some of the rows or columns. For example, if you have few people with graduate degrees, you can combine them into a single category with bachelor's degrees. Similarly, if necessary, you can combine the junior college graduates with the high school graduates, since their responses appear to be similar.

A One-Sample Chi-Square Test

So far, you've used the chi-square test to test for independence in a crosstabulation of two variables. You can also use the chi-square test to test null hypotheses about the distribution of values of a single variable. That is, you can see whether the distribution of observed counts in a frequency table is compatible with a set of expected counts. The expected counts are specified by the null hypothesis that you want to test. For example, you can test the hypothesis that people are equally likely to find life exciting, routine, or dull. Or you can test the null hypothesis that there are twice as many people without college degrees as there are with college degrees.

Figure 17.6 Chi-square test for life

You can obtain this output using the Chi-square Test procedure, as described in "Chi-Square Test" on p. 352 in Chapter 18. Select the variable life and All categories equal in the Chi-Square dialog box.

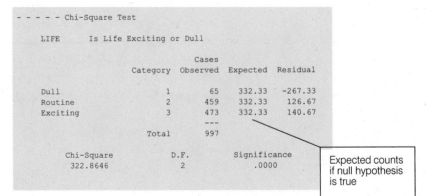

Look at Figure 17.6, which shows counts of the number of people who find life exciting, routine, and dull. Before you looked at the data, you might have thought that people were equally likely to find life exciting, routine, or dull. To test the null hypothesis that the three responses are equally likely in the population, you have to determine the expected counts for each of the categories. That's easy to do. For this hypothesis, the expected count for each category is just the total number of cases divided by 3.

You calculate the chi-square statistic the same way as before. Square each of the residuals (difference between observed and expected), divide by the expected count, and sum up for all of the cells. In Figure 17.6, you see that the chi-square value is a whopping 322.86. Its degrees of freedom are 2, one less than the number of categories in the table. Based on the observed significance level, you can handily reject the null hypothesis.

Let's try another test, this time specifying unequal numbers of expected counts for the categories. You want to test the null hypothesis that there are twice as many people in the population without college degrees as there are people with college degrees. That means you expect two-thirds of the people not to have college degrees and one-third to have college degrees.

Figure 17.7 Chi-square test for degree

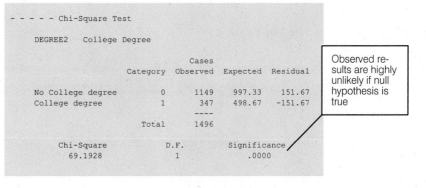

```
- - - - - Chi-Square Test

    DEGREE2    College Degree

                              Cases
                   Category  Observed  Expected  Residual

    No College degree     0     1149    997.33    151.67
    College degree        1      347    498.67   -151.67
                                 ----
                    Total        1496

         Chi-Square            D.F.        Significance
          69.1928               1              .0000
```

Observed results are highly unlikely if null hypothesis is true

The results of this test are shown in Figure 17.7. You see that the expected count for people without a degree is twice as large as it is for people with a college degree. From the residuals, you see that the two-to-one-ratio hypothesis predicts more college graduates than you observe. In the sample, the ratio is slightly larger than three to one. Again the chi-square statistic is large, so you reject the null hypothesis that in the population, non-college graduates are twice as common as college graduates.

Power Concerns

You know that your ability to reject the null hypothesis when it's false, the **power** of a test, depends not only on the size of the discrepancy from the null hypothesis, but also on the sample size. The same is true, of course, for chi-square tests. The value of the chi-square statistic depends on the number of observations in the sample. For example, if you leave the table percentages unchanged but multiply the number of cases in each cell by 10, the chi-square value will be multiplied by 10 as well. This means that if you have small sample sizes, you may not be able to reject the null hypothesis even when it's false. Similarly, for large sample sizes, you will find yourself rejecting the null hypothesis even when the departures from independence are quite small.

When one or both of the variables in your crosstabulation is measured on an ordinal scale (for example, good/better/best), the chi-square test is not as powerful as some other statistics for detecting departures from independence. These other statistics make use of the additional information available for ordinal variables to measure both the strength and the direction of the relationship between two variables. If examination of the residuals in such a table leads you to suspect that there are departures from independence, you should use one of the measures described in Chapter 19.

Summary

How can you test the null hypothesis that two variables are independent?

- In a crosstabulation, the observed count is the number of cases in a particular cell.

- An expected count is the number of cases predicted if the two variables are independent.

- The chi-square statistic is based on a comparison of observed and expected counts.

- To use the chi-square test, your observations must be independent, and most of the expected values must be at least 5.

- A one-sample chi-square test is used to test whether a sample comes from a population with specified probabilities for the occurrence of each value.

- If your sample size is small, you won't be able to detect departures from independence when they are present.

What's Next?

Many of the statistical tests you've used so far to test hypotheses about population means require that the distribution of values in the population is normal or that the sample size is large enough to compensate for non-normality. In Chapter 18, you'll learn about statistical tests that require fewer assumptions about the distribution of the data.

Exercises

Statistical Concepts

1. Consider the following table:

```
SATJOB   Job or Housework  by  AGE Age of Respondent

                    AGE
            Count
                    18-29     30-45     46-59    60 & over
                                                                Row
                                                                Total
    SATJOB  ─────────────────────────────────────────────────
                1     75        234       123       59          491
        Very satisfied                                          43.0

                2     119       215       98        40          472
        Mod satisfied                                           41.3

                3     33        58        29        7           127
        A little dissati                                        11.1

                4     14        21        13        5           53
        Very dissatisfie                                        4.6

            Column   241       528       263       111          1143
            Total    21.1      46.2      23.0      9.7          100.0

    Number of Missing Observations:  357
```

a. Calculate the number of cases you would expect in each cell if the two variables are independent.

b. For each cell, calculate the difference between the observed and the expected number of cases.

c. Calculate the chi-square statistic for the table.

d. What are the degrees of freedom for the table?

e. What null hypothesis are you testing with the chi-square statistic you computed?

2. The observed significance level for a chi-square value of 7.83753 with 3 degrees of freedom is 0.0495.

a. What conclusion would you draw about the relationship between the two variables based on the observed significance level?

b. How often would you expect to see a chi-square value at least as large as the one you observed if the two variables are independent?

c. If you reject the null hypothesis that the two variables are independent, can you conclude that one of the variables causes the other?

3. You are studying the relationship between productivity and length of employment. Both variables are coded into three categories. You compute a chi-square test of independence and find the observed significance level to be 0.35. A personnel consultant does a similar study using the same criteria and categories. He calculates a chi-square test of independence and finds an observed significance level of 0.002. You examine his results and notice that the percentage of cases in each cell of the table is almost identical to the percentages that you observed. You conclude that he doesn't know how to calculate a chi-square value. Give another explanation for why his chi-square could differ from yours.

4. Which pairs of variables do you think are independent, and which are dependent?

a. Zodiac sign and number of hamburgers consumed per week

b. Severity of a disease and prognosis

c. Shoe size and glove size

d. Color of car and highest degree earned

e. Husband's highest degree and wife's highest degree

Data Analysis

Use the *gss.sav* data file to answer the following questions:

1. Test the null hypothesis that men and women are equally likely to believe that there is a life after this one (variable *postlife*). What can you conclude?

a. Which variable in the table is the dependent variable?

b. If the null hypothesis is true, what's your best guess for the percentage of people who believe in life after death? Who don't believe in life after death?

c. Calculate the expected values for the four cells. Compare them to those you get from SPSS. If you know the expected value for one cell, can you calculate the expected values for the other cells? How and why?

2. Test whether belief in life after death and highest degree earned (variable *degree*) are independent. What do you conclude?

3. See if the relationship between belief in life after death and highest degree earned is the same for males and for females. What can you conclude?

4. Test the null hypothesis that men and women were equally likely to vote for Perot, Bush, and Clinton (variable *pres92*). (You'll have to exclude people whose response was Other. You can do this by making the code 4 (Other) a missing value, or by selecting cases for which *pres92* does not equal 4.) Summarize your findings.

5. Use the Crosstabs procedure to look for other differences among supporters of the three presidential candidates.

6. The variable *jobinc* measures how important a high income is to a person. Examine the variables in the *gss.sav* file that might be related to *jobinc*. Write a short paper detailing your findings. Don't restrict your analyses to variables for which crosstabulation is appropriate. Use all of the techniques you've learned so far.

7. What variables are related to a person's taste in music? Select one of the music types (variables *opera*, *classicl*, or *country*) and see if you can identify variables which are associated with people who like it.

8. Look at the relationship between zodiac sign (*zodiac*) and a person's perception of life (variable *life*). What problems do you see with using the chi-square statistic for the *zodiac* by *life* crosstabulation? Fix the problem and rerun the table. What can you conclude?

9. Test the null hypothesis that all zodiac signs are equally likely. What do you conclude?

Use the *salary.sav* data file to answer the following questions:

10. Test the hypothesis that highest degree earned (variable *degree*) and gender/race group (variable *sexrace*) are independent. (Variable *degree* was computed in the exercises to Chapter 8.) Summarize your conclusions. Based on the residuals, which cells contain fewer than the expected number of cases and which cells contain more than the expected number of cases?

11. Test the null hypothesis that job classification (variable *jobcat*) and gender/race group are independent.

a. What problem do you see with the chi-square test for the *jobcat* by *sexrace* table?

b. What can you do to the table so the chi-square test is appropriate?

c. Based on the new table, what can you conclude about the null hypothesis?

Use the *renal.sav* data file to answer the following question:

12. In Chapter 14, you used the independent-samples *t* test to identify differences between cardiac surgery patients who developed renal failure (variable *type* equals 1) and those who did not (variable *type* equals 0). Now use the Crosstabs procedure to look for differences between the two groups. Identify the variables for which a chi-square test is appropriate. Summarize your findings.

Nonparametric Tests

What are nonparametric tests, and when are they useful?

- When do you use the sign test?
- What is the Wilcoxon signed-rank test, and what is its advantage over the sign test?
- What is a nonparametric alternative to the independent-samples *t* test?
- When do you use the Kruskal-Wallis test?
- Why would you use the runs test?

Most of the statistical procedures you have used so far require fairly detailed assumptions about the populations from which the samples are selected. For example, to use analysis of variance, you have to assume that each group is an independent random sample from a normal population, and that the group variances are equal. You know that many of the procedures work reasonably well even when the assumptions are not completely met.

However, when you analyze data, especially from small samples, you'll encounter situations in which there are serious departures from the necessary assumptions. In such situations, you need procedures that require less stringent assumptions about the data. Collectively, these procedures are called distribution-free or **nonparametric tests**. The disadvantage of these tests is that they are less likely to find a true difference when it exists than the tests based on the assumption of normality.

▶ This chapter uses the *gss.sav*, *electric.sav*, and *runs.sav* data files. For information about how to obtain the nonparametric test output shown in this chapter, see "How to Obtain Nonparametric Tests" on p. 352.

Nonparametric Tests for Paired Data

In Chapter 13, you used the paired *t* test to test the null hypothesis that the average difference between a pair of measurements is 0 in the population. You tested whether the average β–endorphin levels are the same before and after a marathon run. To use the paired *t* test you had to assume that the distribution of average differences is approximately normal. For large sample sizes and for all samples from a normal population, that's usually not a problem. However, if your sample size is small and the distribution of values is far from normal, or if you have outliers in your data, you should consider using a nonparametric replacement for the paired *t* test. We'll consider two nonparametric alternatives to the paired t test: the sign test and the Wilcoxon test. Of these two, the Wilcoxon test is more powerful, but it has slightly more stringent requirements.

Sign Test

The null hypothesis for the **sign test** is that the median difference between the two members of a pair is 0. You don't have to make any assumptions about the shapes of the distributions from which the data are obtained. The only requirement is that the different pairs of observations are selected independently and the values can be ordered from smallest to largest. That's because the test is based on seeing which of a pair of values is larger.

You'll use data from the General Social Survey to test the hypothesis that the median difference is 0 between years of mother's and father's education. For each person who answered the question, you have two paired values—mother's education in years and father's education in years.

Computing the sign test is easy. You count the number of cases in each of three categories: mother's and father's educational levels are the same (these are called **tied cases**), mother's education exceeds father's education, and father's education exceeds mother's education. If the null hypothesis is true, you would expect to see similar numbers of cases in the last two categories. That is, the number of cases in which mother's education exceeds father's education should be roughly the same as the number of cases in which father's education exceeds mother's education.

Figure 18.1 Sign test comparing mother's and father's education

```
- - - - - Sign Test

    MAEDUC     Highest Year of School Completed, Mother
with PAEDUC    Highest Year of School Completed, Father


        Cases

         335   - Diffs (PAEDUC LT MAEDUC)              Z =        .2330
         328   + Diffs (PAEDUC GT MAEDUC)
         381     Ties                          2-Tailed P =        .8157
        ----
        1044     Total
```

Father's education is less than mother's for 335 cases and greater than mother's for 328 cases

To obtain this sign test, use the gss.sav data file.

In the Two-Related-Samples dialog box, make selections for the sign test, as shown in Figure 18.14.

In Figure 18.1, you see that of the 1044 respondents who provided information about parental educational levels, 381 had parents with equal years of education. Mother's education exceeded father's education for 335 cases, while the reverse was true for 328 cases. The number of times mother's education exceeds father's education is roughly equal to the number of times the reverse is true, so even without a formal statistical test, it appears that there's little reason to doubt that the median difference is 0. In fact, if you look at the two-tailed probability value, you see that over 80% of the time, you would expect to see a sample difference at least as large as the one you observed when the null hypothesis is true.

McNemar's Test

The sign test is often used to test hypotheses about pairs of dichotomous variables. (A **dichotomous variable** has only two values, typically coded 0 and 1.) In this situation the sign test is often called **McNemar's test**. As an example of McNemar's test, let's repeat the previous analysis looking not at the actual years of education, but at whether a person is a college graduate.

The possible values for the mother-father pairs are 0-0 if neither is a college graduate, 1-1 if both are college graduates, 1-0 if the mother is a graduate and the father is not, and 0-1 if the mother is not a graduate and the father is. If you run the sign test on this dichotomous data, you'll be testing the null hypothesis that women and men college graduates are equally likely to marry non-college graduates. If the null hypothesis is true, you expect roughly half of the non-tied cases to have a positive difference between the two variables, and roughly half to have a negative difference.

> *Why don't you use the usual chi-square test for a crosstabulation?* The chi-square tests a different hypothesis from the one we're interested in here. It tests whether mother's and father's education are independent. We're interested only in couples that are not tied on education. We want to know whether they are evenly split between the two cells. ■ ■ ■

Figure 18.2 is the output from the sign test on the dichotomous variables. You see that most of the mother-father pairs are tied for education (both college graduates or both nongraduates). These cases don't tell you anything about the hypothesis you're testing, so they are not included in the analysis.

Figure 18.2 Sign test on dichotomous variables

```
- - - - - Sign Test

    MACOLLEG  mother a college grad
with PACOLLEG  father a college grad


      Cases

        38   - Diffs (PACOLLEG LT MACOLLEG)              Z =      6.4440
       120   + Diffs (PACOLLEG GT MACOLLEG)
       969     Ties                            2-Tailed P =       .0000
      ----
      1127     Total
```

If the null hypothesis is true, the 158 non-tied cases should be split about evenly between positives (father's education greater than mother's) and negatives (father's education less than mother's). In Figure 18.2, you see that the preponderance of non-tied cases are positive. The two-tailed observed significance level is less than 0.00005, so you can reject the null hypothesis that female and male college graduates are equally likely to marry non-college graduates. Men are more likely to choose a less educated spouse than are women.

McNemar's test is often used in before-after designs. For example, a voter indicates a preference for one of two candidates. Then he or she watches a campaign speech or some other propaganda, after which the voter is again asked for a preference. What the campaign staff wants to know is whether the intervention is effective. If people who change their opinion are equally likely to switch to both candidates, the intervention is ineffective. If the switch is predominantly to the candidate footing the bill, the intervention is effective.

I tried running a procedure called McNemar in the nonparametric menu and I get different results than when I do the sign test. Why? If you did it right, you didn't really get different results, just different statistics. Both procedures give exactly the same observed significance level. If you square the Z-value output by the sign test, you'll get the chi-square value shown in McNemar.

Wilcoxon Test

When you calculate the sign test, all you look at is which of the two numbers for a pair is larger. You ignore the magnitude of the difference. For example, a mother-father pair with 13 and 12 years of education is treated the same way as a pair with 20 and 4 years of education. You ignore the fact that for the first pair, the education difference is 1 year, while for the second pair, it is 16 years. The sign test ignores a lot of useful information about the data.

The **Wilcoxon matched-pairs signed-rank test** uses the information about the size of the difference between the two members of a pair. That's why it's more likely to detect true differences when they exist. However, the Wilcoxon test requires that the differences be a sample from a symmetric distribution. That's a less stringent assumption than requiring normality, since there are many other distributions besides the normal distribution that are symmetric. Figure 18.3 is a histogram of the differences between mother's and father's education. You see that the symmetry assumption is not unreasonable.

Figure 18.3 Difference between mother's and father's education

You can obtain histograms using the Graphs menu, as described in Appendix A.

In the Histograms dialog box, select the variable educdiff.

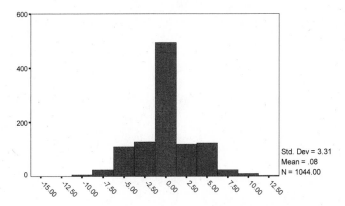

Std. Dev = 3.31
Mean = .08
N = 1044.00

Difference Between Mother's and Father's Years of Education

To calculate the Wilcoxon test, first you find the difference between the two values for each pair. Next, for all cases in which the difference is not 0, you rank the differences from smallest to largest, ignoring the sign of the differences. That is, the smallest difference in absolute value is assigned a rank of 1, the second smallest difference is assigned a rank of 2 and so on. In the case of ties (equal differences) you assign the average rank to the tied cases.

? *You do what to the tied cases?* Consider the following eight differences: 0, 2, –3, 3, –3, 4, 7, and –10. They are arranged from smallest to largest, ignoring the sign. You ignore all 0 differences. Then you assign a rank of 1 to the smallest number, which is 2. To get the ranks for the next three cases, which are tied in value, you give them the next available ranks. In this case they are 2, 3, and 4. Then you find the average of the ranks you've given to the tied cases—the average of 2, 3, and 4, which is 3—and use that as the rank for all of them. The ranks for the seven differences are then 1, 3, 3, 3, 5, 6, and 7. ■ ■ ■

Once you have the ranks, you calculate the average of the ranks separately for the positive and negative differences. If the null hypothesis is true, you expect the mean rank to be similar for the two groups. Since you replace the observed differences with ranks, the effect of unusual couples with very large differences in education is less severe than if you were to calculate a *t* test using the observed data values.

Figure 18.4 Wilcoxon test for mother's and father's education

To obtain this sign test, use the gss.sav data file.

In the Two-Related-Samples dialog box, make selections for the Wilcoxon test, as shown in Figure 18.14.

```
- - - - - Wilcoxon Matched-Pairs Signed-Ranks Test

      MAEDUC      Highest Year of School Completed, Mother
with PAEDUC      Highest Year of School Completed, Father


    Mean Rank     Cases

       341.59        335   - Ranks  (PAEDUC LT MAEDUC)
       322.20        328   + Ranks  (PAEDUC GT MAEDUC)
                     381     Ties   (PAEDUC EQ MAEDUC)
                    ----
                    1044     Total

       Z =    -.8869              2-Tailed P =  .3752
```

In Figure 18.4, you see that the mean rank for cases in which mother's education is greater than father's is 341.59, while for the cases for which father's education is greater, the mean rank is somewhat less, 322.20. From the two-tailed significance level, you see that the difference in mean ranks is not large enough for you to reject the null hypothesis that the population mean difference between mother's and father's education is 0. So even based on this more powerful test you're unable to reject the null hypothesis.

? *If nonparametric tests require so few assumptions about the data, why not just use them all of the time?* The disadvantage to nonparametric tests is that they are usually not as good at finding differences when there are differences in the population. Another way of saying this is that nonparametric tests are not as powerful as tests that assume an underlying normal distribution, the so-called **parametric tests**. That's because nonparametric tests ignore some of the available information. For example, you've just seen that data values are replaced by ranks in the Wilcoxon test.

In general, if the assumptions of a parametric test are plausible, you should use the more powerful parametric test. You've seen that many of these tests can handle reasonable violations of the assumptions. That is, they are **robust**. (That's a compliment for a statistical procedure!) Nonparametric procedures are most useful for small samples when there are serious departures from the required assumptions. They are also useful when outliers are present, since the outlying cases won't influence the results as much as they would if you used a test based on an easily influenced statistic like the mean. ■ ■ ■

Mann-Whitney Test

The **Mann-Whitney test** is the most commonly used alternative to the independent-samples *t* test. If you want to use this test to test the null hypothesis that the population means are the same for the two groups, the shape of the distributions must be the same in both groups. This implies that the population variances for the two groups must be the same. It doesn't matter what the shape is, but it has to be the same in the two groups. If you just want to test whether one population has larger values than the other, you don't have to worry about the shapes of the distributions being the same. Strictly speaking, the variables should come from continuous distributions so there are no ties. However, the test performs reasonably well when there are ties.

To see how the Mann-Whitney test is used, let's consider a sample of data from the Western Electric Study (Paul et al., 1963), which monitored 2017 men for 20 years to track the incidence of coronary heart disease. Let's see whether there was a difference in cigarette smoking at the beginning of the study between those who were alive ten years later and those who were not. Figure 18.5 shows the distributions of number of cigarettes smoked for the two groups. They certainly don't appear to be normal. The assumption that the shape of the distribution is the same in the two groups is also questionable. However, you can still use the Mann-Whitney test to test whether one population has larger values than the other.

Figure 18.5 Number of cigarettes per day in 1958

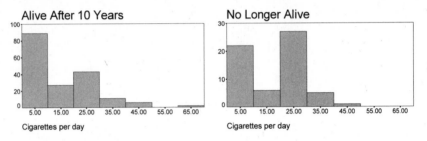

The actual computation of the Mann Whitney test is simple. You rank the combined data values for the two groups. Then you find the average rank in each group.

Figure 18.6 Mann-Whitney test for survival by cigarette consumption

To obtain this output, use the electric.sav data file.

In the Two-Independent-Samples dialog box, select the variables cgt58 and vital10, as shown in Figure 18.12.

```
- - - - - Mann-Whitney U - Wilcoxon Rank Sum W Test

    CGT58     No of Cigarettes per Day in 1958
  by VITAL10   Status at 10 Years


    Mean Rank    Cases

      114.51       178   VITAL10 = 0  Alive
      136.02        61   VITAL10 = 1  Dead
                   ---
                   239   Total

                                  Corrected for ties
        U            W            Z      2-Tailed P
     4452.0       8297.0      -2.2070      .0273
```

> Alive participants had smaller ranks for cigarette smoking

In Figure 18.6, you see that the average rank for those who are alive is 114.5, while for those who are dead, it is 136. Since the rank of 1 is assigned to the smallest value, those who are alive had smaller ranks in cigarette smoking than those who did not fare as well. The observed two-tailed significance level is 0.027, leading you to conclude that the number of cigarettes smoked is smaller for those who are alive after 10 years than for those who are dead.

Kruskal-Wallis Test

The **Kruskal-Wallis test** is a nonparametric alternative to one-way analysis of variance. It is computed exactly like the Mann-Whitney test, except that there are more groups. If you want to test the null hypothesis that all population means are equal, the data must be independent samples from populations with the same shape. Again, this is a less stringent assumption than having to assume that the data are from normal populations. The assumption of equal variances, however, remains. If you just want to test whether values from one population are larger than values from another, you don't need the assumption that the shapes are the same.

In the previous example, you found a relationship between the number of cigarettes smoked and mortality. Now consider the relationship between cigarettes smoked and education. Figure 18.7 shows the average ranks for the number of cigarettes smoked for three groups of people: grammar school education only, high school. only, and some college. You see that the mean ranks are similar for the three groups. The observed significance level is large (0.78), so you don't reject the null hypothesis that the distributions are the same for the three groups. (You should use the *Corrected for ties* output, which adjusts the statistics for the presence of ties.)

Figure 18.7 Kruskal-Wallis test for cigarette consumption by education

To obtain this output, use the electric.sav data file.

In the Several-Independent-Samples dialog box, select the variables cgt58 and educcat, as shown in Figure 18.13.

```
- - - - - Kruskal-Wallis 1-Way Anova

     CGT58      No of Cigarettes per Day in 1958
  by EDUCCAT    Highest Level of Schooling


    Mean Rank    Cases

       101.44        32    EDUCCAT = 1    Grammar School
       108.57       112    EDUCCAT = 2    High School
       103.89        67    EDUCCAT = 3    College


                    ---

                    211    Total

                                          Corrected for ties
  Chi-Square      D.F.  Significance    Chi-Square      D.F.  Significance
       .4568         2         .7958         .5051         2         .7768
```

What should I do if I'm not sure if I should be using a nonparametric test or a parametric test? When in doubt, do them both! If you reach the same conclusions based on both types of tests, there's nothing to worry about. If the results from the nonparametric test are not significant while those from the parametric test are, try to figure out why. Do you have one or two data values that are much smaller or larger than the rest? If so, they may be affecting the mean and having a large impact on your conclusions. Examine them carefully to make sure they're OK. If the problem is with the non-normal distribution of data values, see if you can transform the data to better conform with the parametric assumptions. If your transformation is successful, you can use one of the more powerful parametric procedures for your analysis.

Runs Test

Whenever your data values occur in a sequence, you should check to see whether adjacent values are more likely to be similar than nonadjacent values. The nonparametric procedure known as the **Wald-Wolfowitz runs test** tests the null hypothesis that a sequence of values is random.

For example, suppose you are monitoring items coming off a production line to see if they are defective or not. You observe the following sequence, where N indicates that the item is not defective and D indicates that it is:

N N N D N N N N D D D D N N D D D D D N

You want to know whether the sequence is random. The Wald-Wolfowitz test is based on sequences of like observations, called runs. In the sequence above there are seven runs:

NNNN D NNNN DDDD NN DDDDD N

If the sequence is not random, you will have too few or too many runs, compared to chance. If like values tend to occur together, you will have too few runs. If defective items are more likely to be followed by non-defective items, you will see too many runs.

? *Can I use the runs test only for dichotomous variables?* The runs test requires the values to be dichotomous. However, you can easily convert a nondichotomous variable into one with two values. For example, if you sequentially administer a test to students and are concerned that they're sharing information, you can dichotomize the actual score into pass/fail or above the mean/below the mean. Then use the runs test for the variable with two values. ▪ ▪ ▪

Figure 18.8 Runs test for production line defects

To obtain this runs test, use the runs.sav data file.

In the Runs Test dialog box, make the selections shown in Figure 18.11.

```
- - - - - Runs Test

    WIDGETS    Status


        Runs:    7                Test value =  .48 (Mean)

        Cases:  11    LT Mean
                10    GE Mean          Z = -1.7847
                --
                21    Total       2-Tailed P =   .0743
```

Figure 18.8 contains the output from the runs test for the above example. Defective items are coded as 1; nondefective items are coded as 0. The observed number of runs is 7. The two-tailed significance level is 0.07, so you don't have quite enough evidence to reject the null hypothesis that the observations are independent. You should increase your sample size and study the problem further.

Summary

What are nonparametric tests, and when are they useful?

- The advantage of nonparametric tests is that they require fewer assumptions than other tests.
- The disadvantage is that they are less powerful than other tests, meaning they are not as good at finding differences when they exist in the population.
- The sign test is a less powerful alternative to the paired *t* test.
- The Wilcoxon matched-pairs signed-rank test is used to test the same null hypothesis as the sign test. It is usually more powerful than the sign test.
- The Mann-Whitney test is used to test the hypothesis that two independent groups come from populations with the same distribution. It is an alternative to the independent-samples *t* test.
- The Kruskal-Wallis test is a nonparametric alternative to one-way analysis of variance.
- The runs test is a test of randomness. It tests whether adjacent observations in a series are independent.

How to Obtain Nonparametric Tests

This section shows how to obtain nonparametric tests from SPSS. The Nonparametric Tests submenu of the Statistics menu offers several different procedures for tests that make limited assumptions about your data.

Chi-Square Test

The chi-square test tests the distribution of a categorical variable against the hypothesis that each category has a specified proportion of cases in the population. To open the Chi-Square Test dialog box (see Figure 18.9), from the menus choose:

Statistics
  Nonparametric Tests ▶
    Chi-Square...

Figure 18.9 Chi-Square Test dialog box

Open the gss.sav data file and select the variable life (not shown here) and All categories equal to obtain the test shown in Figure 17.6

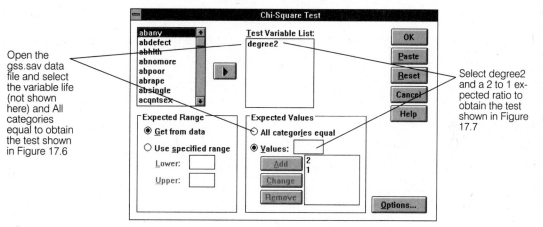

Select degree2 and a 2 to 1 expected ratio to obtain the test shown in Figure 17.7

▶ Select one or more categorical variables and move them into the Test Variable List. Then specify the assumptions you want to test.

▶ Select one of the alternatives for Expected Range. The expected range must be a sequence of consecutive integers. (If it isn't, use the Automatic Recode procedure in the Transform menu first.) Get from data does not impose an assumption about values that are expected to occur. Use specified range tells SPSS to assume that the test variables have values in the range between the values you specify as lower and upper.

▶ Select one of the alternatives for Expected Values. All categories equal tests the hypothesis that the values of the test variables are equally distributed across the categories in the expected range. Values lets you enter a list of values that are proportional to your expectations. For each category in the expected range, type in a value and click on Add to add it to the bottom of the list. If you click on a value in the list, you can remove it or change it to a newly specified value by clicking on the appropriate button.

You must enter one expected value for each category in the expected range. The values must appear in the list in order: the first expected value in the list corresponds to the first (lowest) category in the expected range, and so on.

The expected values must all be positive, but their scale doesn't matter. If you expect twice as many cases in the first of two categories, you can enter the expected values as 2 and 1, or as 66 and 33, or as any pair of numbers in that proportion.

▶ Click on Options for optional descriptive statistics or to control the treatment of missing values.

Binomial Test

The binomial test compares the distribution of one or more dichotomous variables to the binomial distribution with a specified probability of being in the first group. To open the Binomial Test dialog box (see Figure 18.10), from the menus choose:

Statistics
  Nonparametric Tests ▶
    Binomial...

Figure 18.10 Binomial Test dialog box

Open the simul.sav data file and select binom10 and binom40 to obtain the output shown in Figure 10.5 and Figure 10.6

Type .50 for test proportion

▶ Select one or more variables and move them into the Test Variable List.

If they are dichotomous (if they have precisely two categories), use the Get from data alternative in the Define Dichotomy group. Otherwise, select Cut point and enter a value. Data values less than the cut point form the first group, while data values equal to or greater than the cut point form the second group.

▶ Specify the test proportion (the proportion that should be in the first group if the null hypothesis is true) and click on OK.

▶ Click on Options for optional descriptive statistics or to control the treatment of missing values.

Runs Test

The runs test compares the order in which values occur to a random sequence. Runs are sequences of consecutive values that are either all less than a cut point, or all equal to or greater than the cut point. An unusually low or high number of runs indicates a pattern in the data. The test is useful only when the cases in your data file are arranged in a meaningful (nonrandom) order.

▶ To open the Runs Test dialog box (see Figure 18.11), from the menus choose:

Statistics
  Nonparametric Tests ▶
    Runs...

Figure 18.11 Runs Test dialog box

Open the runs.sav data file and select widgets and mean to obtain the output shown in Figure 18.8

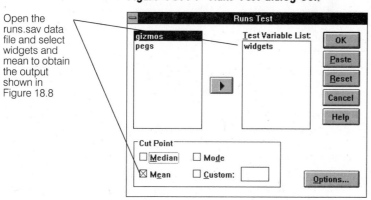

▶ Select one or more numeric variables and move them into the Test Variable List.

▶ Choose a cut point for defining runs and click on OK. You can use the median, mode, or mean of the data, or you can specify a value.

(Remember, cases equal to the cut point are classified into the greater than group.)

Click on Options for optional descriptive statistics or to control the treatment of missing values.

Two-Independent-Samples Tests

The two-independent-samples tests compare the distribution of one or more numeric variables between two groups. To open the Two-Independent-Samples Tests dialog box (see Figure 18.12), from the menus choose:

Statistics
  Nonparametric Tests ▶
    2 Independent Samples...

Figure 18.12 Two-Independent-Samples Tests dialog box

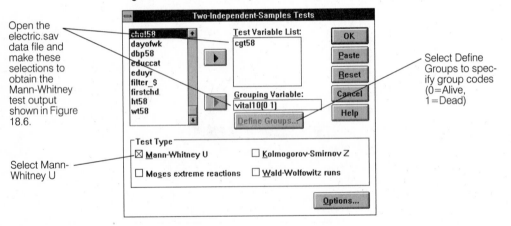

Open the electric.sav data file and make these selections to obtain the Mann-Whitney test output shown in Figure 18.6.

Select Define Groups to specify group codes (0=Alive, 1=Dead)

Select Mann-Whitney U

▶ Select one or more numeric variables and move them into the Test Variable List.

▶ Select a numeric grouping variable with a code corresponding to each of the two groups and move it into the Grouping Variable box. Click on Define Groups and indicate the group codes.

▶ Select one or more of the tests in the Test Type group and click on OK.

Click on Options for optional descriptive statistics or to control the treatment of missing values.

Test Type. The available tests are:

Mann-Whitney U. Based on ranking the observations in the two groups.

Moses extreme reactions. Tests whether the range (excluding the lowest 5% and the highest 5%) of an ordinal variable is the same in the two groups.

Kolmogorov-Smirnov Z. Based on the maximum differences between the observed cumulative distributions in the two groups.

Wald-Wolfowitz runs. Based on the number of runs within each group when the cases are placed in rank order.

Define Groups (2 Independent Samples)

The Define Groups dialog box for the two-independent-samples tests asks you to enter an integer for group 1 and an integer for group 2. Cases with other values of the grouping variable are ignored.

Several-Independent-Samples Tests

The several-independent-samples tests compare the distribution of one or more numeric variables between several groups. To open the Tests for Several Independent Samples dialog box (see Figure 18.13), from the menus choose:

Statistics
 Nonparametric Tests ▶
  K Independent Samples...

Figure 18.13 Tests for Several Independent Samples dialog box

Open the electric.sav data file and make the selections shown to obtain the Kruskal-Wallis output shown in Figure 18.7

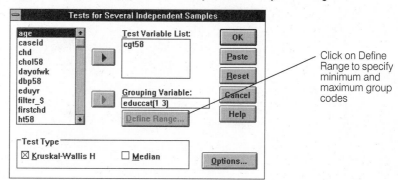

Click on Define Range to specify minimum and maximum group codes

▶ Select one or more numeric variables, measured at the ordinal level, and move them into the Test Variable List.

▶ Select a numeric grouping variable with a code corresponding to each of the several groups and move it into the Grouping Variable box. Click on Define Range and indicate the range of group codes.

▶ Select one or both of the tests in the Test Type group and click on OK.

Click on Options for optional descriptive statistics or to control the treatment of missing values.

Test Type. The available tests are:

Kruskal-Wallis H. Tests whether the distribution of ordinal variables is the same in all groups by comparing the sum of ranks in the groups.

Median. Tests whether the groups are sampled from a population in which the median of the test variable is the same.

Define Range (K Independent Samples)

The Define Range dialog box for the several-independent-samples tests asks you to enter an integer for the minimum value of the grouping variable and another integer for its maximum value. Non-integer values of the grouping variable encountered in the data are truncated to integers, and cases with truncated values outside the range specified here are ignored.

Two-Related-Samples Tests

The two-related-samples tests compare the distribution across one or more pairs of numeric variables. (A case in the data file must include the values for both related samples, in two different variables.) To open the Two-Related-Samples Tests dialog box (see Figure 18.14), from the menus choose:

Statistics
  Nonparametric Tests ▶
    2 Related Samples...

Figure 18.14 Two-Related-Samples Tests dialog box

Open the gss.sav data file and select maeduc and paeduc to obtain the output shown in Figure 18.1 and Figure 18.4. On the Macintosh, you must hold down ⌘ as you select the second variable in a pair.

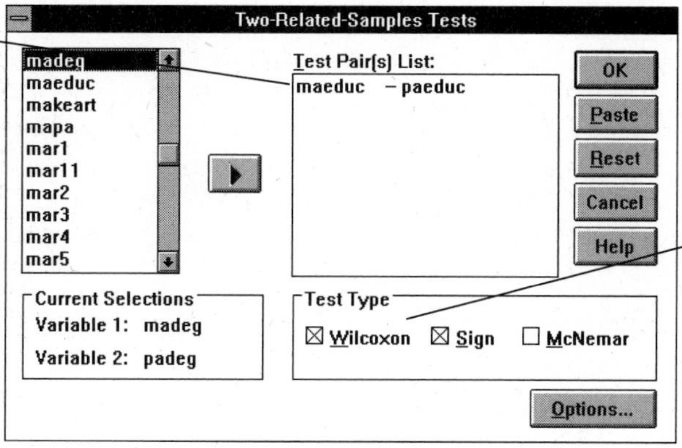

Select desired test(s)

▶ Click on each of the two variables you want to compare. Make sure that their names appear in the Current Selections box. Then move them into the Test Pair(s) List.

▶ Select any other pairs of variables in the same way.

▶ If you click on a variable by mistake but have not yet moved the pair into the Test Pair(s) List, simply click it again to remove it from the Current Selections box. If you add an incorrect pair to the Test Pair(s) List, select it in that list and move it back out.

▶ Select one or more of the tests in the Test Type group and click on OK.

▶ Click on Options for optional descriptive statistics or to control the treatment of missing values.

Test Type. The available tests are:

Wilcoxon. Based on the ranks of the absolute values of the difference between the two variables, compared between cases in which that difference is positive and cases in which it is negative.

Sign. Based on a comparison of positive and negative differences between the two variables, using either the binomial distribution or (for more than 25 cases) a normal approximation.

McNemar. Tests whether the two possible combinations of unlike values for the variables are equally likely. Requires that the test variables be dichotomous, with the same two categories for each pair.

Options: Descriptive Statistics and Missing Values

In any of the Nonparametric Tests dialog boxes, open the Options dialog box (see Figure 18.15) by clicking on Options.

Figure 18.15 Chi-Square Test Options dialog box

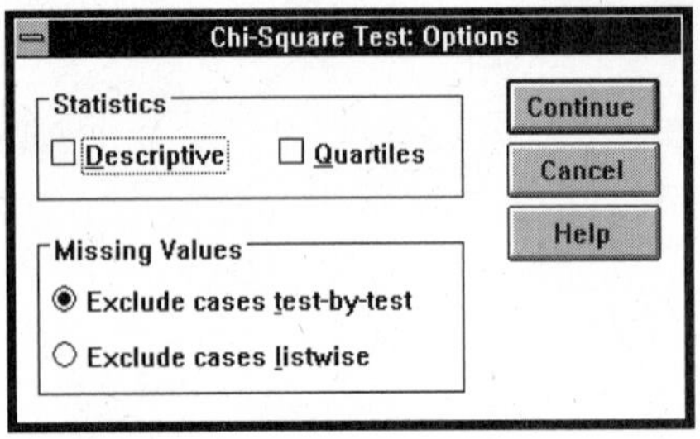

Statistics. The Statistics options allow you to display statistics for the test variables:

Descriptive. These statistics include the mean, minimum, maximum, standard deviation, and the number of nonmissing cases.

Quartiles. Displays the 25th, 50th, and 75th percentiles.

Missing Values. The Missing Values alternatives control the exclusion of cases with missing data, when more than one set of variables is tested. These alternatives are not available for the tests of several related samples.

Exclude cases test-by-test. Calculates each test on the basis of all cases that have valid data for the variables used in that test.

Exclude cases listwise. Calculates all tests on the basis of the cases that have valid data for all the variables used in any test. This ensures that all of the tests are performed using the same cases.

Exercises

Statistical Concepts

1. Indicate which nonparametric test you would use in each of the following situations:

    a. You are interested in comparing the satisfaction rankings given by male and female purchasers of a new product.

    b. You are interested in comparing the family incomes of purchasers of four different types of products.

    c. You are interested in whether product rating differs before and after use.

2. State a hypothesis that can be tested by each of the following procedures:

    a. Sign test

    b. Wilcoxon signed-rank test

    c. McNemar's test

    d. Kruskal-Wallis test

3. For each of the following situations, indicate which statistical test(s) you would use:

    a. You want to know if patients lose weight during radiation therapy, so you conduct a study in which you weigh each patient before and after radiation therapy.

    b. You want to know if women marry men who earn more than they do, so you select 100 working couples and obtain salaries for both spouses.

    c. You want to know whether men and women are equally likely to like opera.

    d. You want to know whether Eskimos, Alaskans, and Canadians have the same average heart rate.

    e. You want to know if there is a difference in high-school GPA for students who complete college and those who enroll but do not complete it.

    f. You want to know if four treatments for curing acne are equally effective. Each of 50 adolescents receives one of the treatments for four months and is then classified as improved, same, or worsened.

g. You want to know whether men and women in four regions of the country have the same average cholesterol levels.

h. You want to know if the average IQ of schizophrenics is 100.

Data Analysis

Use the *gss.sav* data file to answer the following questions:

1. Use a nonparametric test to see if the median difference in years of education between husbands and wives is 0 (variables *husbeduc* and *wifeduc*). What do you conclude? Compare your results to those from a paired-samples *t* test. If the assumptions are met for the paired *t* test, which test should you use?

2. Restrict your analysis to full-time workers (variable *wrkstat* equals 1). Use a nonparametric test to see if there is a difference in hours worked for males and females (variable *hrs1*). What do you conclude?

3. Restrict your analysis to husbands and wives, both of whom are employed full time. Perform a nonparametric test to see if husbands and wives work the same number of hours a week (variables *husbhr* and *wifehr*). What factors are you controlling for in this analysis that you weren't in question 2? What can you conclude?

4. The variables *husbft* and *wifeft* tell you whether a husband and wife are employed full time. Use the sign test to test whether husbands and wives are equally likely to be employed full time. What do you conclude?

5. Use the McNemar test to test the same hypothesis as in question 4. What is the relationship between the two tests? Square the *Z* value from the sign test. What does this correspond to in McNemar's test?

6. Compute a nonparametric test to see whether the distribution of hours of television watched per day (variable *tvhours*) is the same for people in the five degree categories (variable *degree*). What do you conclude? How do your conclusions compare to those from a one-way analysis of variance?

7. Select four hypotheses based on the *gss.sav* data that you can test using nonparametric procedures. Perform the appropriate analyses. Check the requisite assumptions.

Use the *salary.sav* data file to answer the following questions:

8. Use a nonparametric test to see if there is a relationship between gender (variable *sex*) and beginning salary (variable *salbeg*) for clerical employees (*jobcat* equals 1). Compare your findings to those you obtain from a parametric test of the same hypothesis. Summarize the results.

9. Repeat the analysis in question 8 for years on the job (variable *time*). What can you conclude about possible differences in time on the job between males and females? Perform a parametric test of the same hypothesis. Which test do you think is more appropriate in this situation? Why?

10. Use a nonparametric test to see whether current salaries (variable *salnow*) for clerical employees differ for the four gender/race groups (variable *sexrace*). Compare your results from those from a parametric analysis. Summarize your conclusions.

11. Select a hypothesis of interest that can be tested with a nonparametric procedure. Test the hypothesis and write a brief summary of your results.

Use the *schools.sav* data file to answer the following question:

12. Using nonparametric tests, rerun some of the analyses you performed on the *schools.sav* data in previous chapters. For example, use the sign test and the Wilcoxon signed-rank test to look at changes in school scores between 1993 and 1994. Do any of your conclusions change?

Measuring Association

How can you measure the strength of the relationship between two categorical variables?

- What are measures of association, and why are they useful?
- Is there a single best measure of association?
- Why is the chi-square statistic not a good measure of association?
- What is proportional reduction in error?
- When a measure of association equals 0, does that always mean the two variables are unrelated?
- For variables measured on an ordinal scale, how can the additional information about order be incorporated into a measure of association?
- How do you measure the agreement between two raters?

One of the most frequently asked questions in studies is, Are these two variables related? Is education related to voting behavior? Is marital status related to happiness? Is ability to close a sale related to the experience of the salesperson? You usually want to know more than just *whether* the two variables are related. You also want to know the strength and nature of the relationship. If job satisfaction is related to perceiving life as exciting, does increased job satisfaction increase or decrease the likelihood of perceiving life as exciting? And how strongly related are the two variables?

Many different statistical techniques are used to study the relationships among variables. In Chapter 20 through Chapter 24, you'll learn about regression models, which are used to predict the values of a dependent variable from a set of independent variables. Regression analysis is used when your dependent variable has many possible values and is measured on an interval or ratio scale. In this chapter, you'll look at techniques that are useful for measuring the strength and nature of relationships between two categorical variables. Categorical variables have a limited number of possible values, and their joint distribution can be examined with a crosstabulation.

▶ Unless otherwise indicated, this chapter uses the *gss.sav* data file. For instructions on how to obtain crosstabulations and associated statistics, see Chapter 8.

The Strength of a Relationship

In Chapter 17, you looked at the relationship between education and a person's perception of life. Using the chi-square test of independence, you rejected the null hypothesis that the two variables are independent. The next questions that come to mind are, In what way are the variables related, and how strongly? As you can see in Figure 19.1 on p. 367, the observed significance level for the Pearson chi-square statistic is very small, less than 0.000005. Does that mean that the relationship is very strong?

Unfortunately, the actual value of the chi-square statistic and its associated observed significance level provide little information about the strength and type of association between two variables. All you can conclude from the observed significance level is that two variables are not independent. Nothing more.

You know that the value of the chi-square statistic depends on the sample size, the number of rows and columns in the table, and the extent of the departure from independence. If you multiply all cell frequencies in Figure 19.1 by 10, you also increase the value of the chi-square by a factor of 10. The Pearson chi-square value becomes 539.61. Are the two variables more strongly related just because the cell frequencies have been multiplied by 10? Of course not. The relationship has stayed the same; it's simply the sample size that has increased.

Since the value of the chi-square statistic depends on the sample size, you can't compare chi-square values for the same table from studies with different sample sizes. Another drawback to the chi-square statistic is that many different types of relationships between two variables result in the same chi-square value. The chi-square value doesn't tell you anything about how two variables are related.

Figure 19.1 Highest degree received and perception of life

To obtain this crosstabulation, select the variables life and degree in the Crosstabs dialog box.

In the Crosstabs Statistics dialog box, select Chi-square, Contingency coefficient, and Phi and Cramér's V.

In the Crosstabs Cells dialog box, select Column.

See Chapter 8 for a description of the Crosstabs procedure.

```
LIFE   Is Life Exciting or Dull  by  DEGREE  RS Highest Degree

                     DEGREE                                   Page 1 of 1
              Count
              Col Pct  Less     High     Junior   Bachelor Graduate
                       than HS  School   college                        Row
                          0        1        2        3        4       Total
LIFE
                1        24       35        2        2        1         64
        Dull           12.9      6.8      3.2      1.3      1.4        6.4

                2        96      251       33       58       21        459
        Routine        51.6     48.5     53.2     36.9     28.8       46.1

                3        66      231       27       97       51        472
        Exciting       35.5     44.7     43.5     61.8     69.9       47.4

            Column      186      517       62      157       73        995
            Total      18.7     52.0      6.2     15.8      7.3      100.0

     Chi-Square                    Value          DF          Significance
    --------------------          ----------      ----        ------------

Pearson                          53.96180          8              .00000
Likelihood Ratio                 55.87366          8              .00000
Mantel-Haenszel test for         47.63254          1              .00000
    linear association

Minimum Expected Frequency -      3.988
Cells with Expected Frequency < 5 -     2 OF    15 ( 13.3%)


                                                              Approximate
     Statistic                    Value    ASE1    Val/ASE0  Significance
    --------------------          -------- ------- --------  ------------

Phi                              .23288                        .00000 *1
Cramer's V                       .16467                        .00000 *1
Contingency Coefficient          .22681                        .00000 *1


*1 Pearson chi-square probability

Number of Missing Observations:  505
```

Measures of Association

To quantify the strength and nature of the relationship between two variables in a crosstabulation, you must compute what are called **measures of association.** A measure of association is just a number whose magnitude tells you how strongly two variables are related. In general, measures of association range in absolute value from 0 to 1. If the two variables are measured on an ordinal scale, a positive sign tells you that the values of the two variables increase together, while a negative sign tells you that as the values of one variable increase, the values of the other variable decrease. The larger the absolute value of the measure, the stronger the relationship between the two variables.

There are many different measures of association, since there are many different ways to define "association." The measures differ in how they can be interpreted and in how they define perfect and intermediate levels of association. They also differ in the level of measurement required for the variables. For example, if two variables are measured on an ordinal scale, it makes sense to talk about their values increasing or decreasing together. Such a statement is meaningless for variables measured on a nominal scale.

Measures of Association for Nominal Variables

When you have two variables measured on a nominal scale, you're limited in what you can say about their relationship. It doesn't make sense to say that marital status increases as religious affiliation increases, or that automobile color decreases with increasing state of residence. If the categories of the variables don't have a meaningful order, it doesn't make sense to say that their values increase together or that the values of one variable increase as the values of the other variable decrease. In this situation, you can't talk about the direction of the association—all you can do is measure its strength.

Two types of measures of association are useful for nominal variables: measures based on the chi-square statistic and measures of proportional reduction in error (called PRE measures). These measures can also be used for variables whose values are ordered, but they make no use of this ordering.

Measures Based on Chi-Square

You know why the chi-square statistic itself is not a good measure of association. However, since it's so often used in tests of independence, it serves as the basis for several commonly used measures of association. These measures modify the chi-square statistic so that it isn't influenced by sample size and it falls in the range from 0 to 1, with 0 corresponding to no association and 1 to perfect association. Without such adjustments, you can't compare chi-square values from tables with different sample sizes and different dimensions.

The Phi Coefficient

The phi coefficient is one of the simplest modifications of the chi-square statistic. To calculate a phi coefficient, just divide the chi-square value by the sample size and then take the square root. For Figure 19.1,

$$\phi = \sqrt{\frac{\chi^2}{N}} = \sqrt{\frac{53.96}{995}} = 0.23 \qquad \textbf{Equation 19.1}$$

The maximum value of phi depends on the size of the table. If a table has more than two rows or two columns, the phi coefficient can be greater than 1, which is an undesirable feature.

The Coefficient of Contingency

Unlike the phi coefficient, the coefficient of contingency is always less than 1. To calculate it for the data in Figure 19.1, use the following formula:

$$C = \sqrt{\frac{\chi^2}{\chi^2 + N}} = \sqrt{\frac{53.96}{53.96 + 995}} = 0.23 \qquad \textbf{Equation 19.2}$$

Although the value of C is always between 0 and 1, it can never get as high as 1, even for a table showing what seems to be a perfect relationship. The largest value it can have depends on the number of rows and columns in the table. For example, if you have a 4×4 table, the largest possible value of C is 0.87.

Cramér's V

Cramér's V is a chi-square-based measure of association that *can* attain the value of 1 for tables of any dimension. You calculate it for Figure 19.1 using the formula:

$$V = \sqrt{\frac{\chi^2}{N(k-1)}} = \sqrt{\frac{53.96}{995(2)}} = 0.16 \qquad \text{Equation 19.3}$$

where k is the smaller of the number of rows and columns. If the number of rows or columns is 2, Cramér's V is identical in value to phi.

Interpreting the Measures

Although the three measures of association calculated for the table in Figure 19.1 aren't equal, they're of the same magnitude. On a scale of 0 to 1, none of the numbers is particularly large. The observed significance level for the chi-square statistic on which they are based is very small, not because there is a strong association between the two variables, but because the sample size is large.

The "not particularly large" interpretation of the chi-square-based measures isn't very satisfying. You'd like to have a more concrete interpretation—that is, some way of putting into words what it means for two variables to have a Cramér's V of 0.16. Unfortunately, there is none. Chi-square-based measures are difficult to interpret. Although they can be used to compare the strength of association in different tables, the strength of association being compared isn't easily related to an intuitive concept of association.

Proportional Reduction in Error

Proportional reduction in error (PRE) measures, unlike chi-square-based measures, have a clear interpretation. They look at how much better you can predict the values of a dependent variable when you know the values of an independent variable. PRE measures compare the errors in two different situations: one where you don't use the independent variable for prediction and one where you do.

Consider the example shown in Figure 19.1 again. You'll try to predict whether life is seen as dull, routine, or exciting (the dependent variable), using information about the highest degree earned (the independent variable).

- In the first situation, you predict how a person feels about life, knowing only that 6.4% of the sample find life dull, 46.1% find it routine, and 47.4% find it exciting.
- In the second situation, you have an additional piece of information available—the highest degree a person has earned.

If the two variables are related, knowing a person's highest degree may improve your ability to predict correctly how the person feels about life. For example, if all people with graduate degrees find life exciting, all people with junior college or bachelor's degrees find life routine, and all people with high school diplomas or less find life dull, by knowing a person's highest degree, you can predict perfectly whether they find life exciting, routine, or dull. There is a perfect relationship between the variables. If you know a person's highest degree, you know how they perceive life. (Note, however, that knowing a person's view of life doesn't let you predict perfectly their highest degree.) Most of the time, though, a relationship is less than perfect.

Let's consider how you can compute the error rates in these two situations and calculate lambda, a commonly used PRE measure.

Calculating Lambda

If you have no information about a person's education, what would you predict for the person's perception of life? If you're interested in making as few errors as possible, you should predict the life perception category that occurs most often in the sample. More people said they find life exciting than any other response, so that's your best guess when you don't know anything about a person.

Now count the number of cases in Figure 19.1 that you'd misclassify if you predicted *Exciting* for everyone. Your prediction would be wrong for the 64 people who said life is dull and the 459 people who said life is routine. The total number of misclassified people is the sum of these two numbers, 523. This is the error for the first situation, when you only know how often the different values of the dependent variable occur in the sample.

Let's take a look at the second situation. The rule is straightforward: for each category of the *independent* variable, predict the category of the *dependent* variable that occurs most frequently. If you know that someone has less than a high school degree, predict *Routine*, because that's the most frequent choice of people who don't have a high school diploma. Using this rule, you'd incorrectly classify 90 people without a high school diploma: 66 who found life exciting and 24 who found life dull.

Applying the same rule, predict *Routine* for people with a high school diploma. You are wrong for the 266 people with high school diplomas who find life dull or exciting. For people with junior college degrees, also predict *Routine*. You're wrong for 29 of these people. For people with bachelor's degrees and graduate degrees, predict *Exciting*. You incorrectly classify 82 such people.

Now compare the errors. In the first situation, you incorrectly classified 523 people. In the second situation, you incorrectly classified 467 (90+266+29+82) people. The **lambda statistic** tells you the proportion by which you reduce your error in predicting the dependent variable when you use the independent variable. That's why it's called a proportional reduction in error measure. Lambda (λ) is calculated as

$$\lambda = \frac{\text{Misclassified in situation 1} - \text{Misclassified in situation 2}}{\text{Misclassified in situation 1}}$$

Equation 19.4

For Figure 19.1,

$$\lambda = \frac{523 - 467}{523} = \frac{56}{523} = 0.1071$$

Equation 19.5

By knowing the highest degree a person has earned, you reduced your error by almost 11%.

The largest value that lambda can be is 1. Figure 19.2 shows a table in which lambda is 1. For each category of the independent variable, there is one cell with all of the cases. If you guess that value for all cases, you make no errors. The introduction of the independent variable lets you predict perfectly, and it results in a 100% reduction in error rate.

Figure 19.2 Crosstabulation in which lambda equals 1

To obtain lambda along with the crosstabulation, select Lambda in the Crosstabs Statistics dialog box.

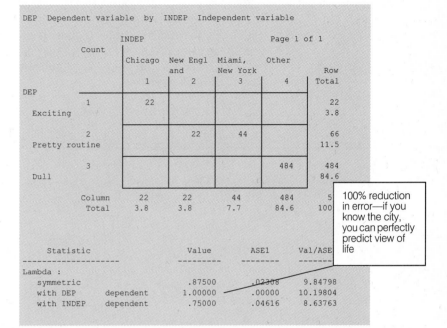

A value of 0 for lambda means that the independent variable is of no help in predicting the dependent variable. When two variables are statistically independent, lambda is 0; but a lambda of 0 does not necessarily imply statistical independence. As with all measures of association, lambda measures association in a very specific way—reduction in error when values of one variable are used to predict values of the other. If this particular type of association is absent, lambda is 0. Even when lambda is 0, other measures of association may find association of a different kind. No measure of association is sensitive to every type of association imaginable.

Two Different Lambdas

Lambda is not a symmetric measure. Its value depends on which variable you predict from which. Suppose that instead of predicting the view of life category from highest degree, you tried to predict the reverse—a person's highest degree based on how exciting the person found life to be. You'd get a different value for lambda. You'd get a value of 0. That's because high school diploma is the best prediction if you have no information about how life is perceived. It is also the best prediction for all categories of how life is perceived. Look back at Figure 19.1. In all three view-of-life categories, the largest number of respondents has a high school diploma. Knowing how a person perceives life doesn't help you in predicting their highest degree.

Both of these values for lambda are shown in Figure 19.3. The first is in the line labeled *with LIFE dependent*, and the second is in the line labeled *with DEGREE dependent*.

Figure 19.3 Different versions of lambda

To obtain lambda along with the crosstabulation, select Lambda in the Crosstabs Statistics dialog box.

```
LIFE   Is Life Exciting or Dull  by  DEGREE  RS Highest Degree

                                                             Approximate
       Statistic                 Value     ASE1    Val/ASE0  Significance
    -------------------          -------   ------  --------  ------------

Lambda :
    symmetric                    .05594    .02571   2.11532
    with LIFE       dependent    .10707    .04794   2.11532
    with DEGREE     dependent    .00000    .00000
Goodman & Kruskal Tau :
    with LIFE       dependent    .02918    .00899             .00000 *2
    with DEGREE     dependent    .01240    .00346             .00000 *2


*2 Based on chi-square approximation
```

Knowing highest degree helps you predict view of life, but knowing view of life doesn't help you predict highest degree

How can I test a hypothesis that a measure of association is 0 in the population? This doesn't involve anything new. You just have to calculate the probability that you'd obtain a value at least as large (in absolute value) as the one you observed if the value is 0 in the population. SPSS prints the approximate significance levels for some of the measures of association we've discussed in this chapter.

In Figure 19.3, the ratio of the coefficient to its standard error is in the column labeled *Val/ASE0*. The column labeled *Approximate Significance* is left blank because it's difficult to estimate the observed significance level exactly, especially for small samples. You reject the null hypothesis when the absolute value of the ratio of the coefficient to its standard error is large. The standard error of the lambdas is in the column labeled *ASE1*. This tells you how much the value of lambda varies from sample to sample. (The ASE0 value is based on the assumption that the population coefficient is 0. ASE1 doesn't make that assumption.)

Symmetric Lambda

In the previous example, you considered view of life as the dependent variable and highest degree as the independent variable. But this need not be the case. It's certainly possible that a person's perception of life influences educational attainment. If you have no reason to consider one of the variables dependent and the other independent, you can compute a **symmetric lambda** coefficient. You predict the first variable from the second and then the second variable from the first.

For example, if highest degree is predicted without knowledge of the life perception category, you misclassify 478 people. Knowing how a person perceives life, you still misclassify 478 people. When you calculated lambda with view of life as the dependent variable, you found that using highest degree decreased the number misclassified from 523 to 467.

Symmetric lambda is the sum of the two misclassification differences, divided by the total number misclassified without additional information. In other words, you just add up the numerators for the two lambdas, then add up the denominators, and then divide:

$$\text{Symmetric } \lambda = \frac{(478 - 478) + (523 - 467)}{478 + 523} = 0.0559 \qquad \textbf{Equation 19.6}$$

This number is the symmetric lambda in Figure 19.3.

? *Is it really possible for variables to be related and still have a lambda of 0? That doesn't sound right.* Actually, this can happen easily. For example, consider Figure 19.4. The two variables are clearly related. Chicagoans are unlikely to be unsatisfied, while Los Angelenos are unlikely to be satisfied. However, *Indifferent* is the response that occurs most often in each city. You predict that value whether or not you know the city. Since knowing the independent variable doesn't help prediction at all, lambda equals 0. Remember: a measure of association is sensitive only to a particular kind of association. ■ ■ ■

Figure 19.4 Variables related but lambda equals 0

```
DEP  Satisfaction  by  INDEP  City

                       INDEP                       Page 1 of 1
             Count
             Col Pct  Chicago   New York   LA
                                                      Row
                        1.00      2.00     3.00      Total
DEP
              1.00       19        10        1         30
           Satisfied    47.5      25.0      2.5       25.0

              2.00       20        20       20         60
           Indifferent  50.0      50.0     50.0       50.0

              3.00        1        10       19         30
           Unsatisfied   2.5      25.0     47.5       25.0

             Column      40        40       40        120
             Total      33.3      33.3     33.3      100.0
```

The best guess for the dependent variable is always Indifferent, regardless of the city

```
                                                     Approximate
        Statistic              Value    ASE1   Val/ASE0  Significance
    -------------------        ------   ------  ------   ------------
Lambda :
   symmetric                  .12857   .02684  4.32762
   with DEP    dependent      .00000   .00000
   with INDEP  dependent      .22500   .04921  4.32762
```

Measures of Association for Ordinal Variables

Lambda can be used as a measure of association for variables measured on any scale. All it requires is that the variables have a limited number of distinct values. You can't compute a lambda for salary and age unless you recode the variables to have a smaller number of values. Both of the variables you looked at in the previous example, highest degree and perception of life, are ordinal variables. However, you didn't use the order information in computing lambda. You can interchange the order of the rows and columns in any way you want (for example, you can put *Exciting* before *Routine,* or *Dull* before *Exciting*) and not change the value of lambda.

There are measures of association that make use of the additional information available for ordinal variables. They tell you not only about the strength of the association but also about the direction. If the degree of excitement with life increases as the years of education increase, you can say that the two variables have a **positive relationship**. If, on the other hand, the values of one variable increase while those of the other decrease, you can say the variables have a **negative relationship**. You can't make statements like these about nominal variables, since there's no order to the categories of the variables. Values can't increase or decrease unless they have an order.

Concordant and Discordant Pairs

Many ordinal measures of association are based on comparing pairs of cases. For example, look at Table 19.1, which contains a listing of the values of *life* (the view of life variable) and *degree* (the education variable) for three cases.

Table 19.1 Values of variables life and degree

	life	degree
Case 1	1	2
Case 2	2	3
Case 3	3	2

Consider the pair of cases, case 1 and case 2. Both case 2 values are larger than the corresponding values for case 1. That is, the value for *life* is larger for case 2 than for case 1, and the value for *degree* is larger for case 2 than for case 1. Such a pair of cases is called **concordant**. A pair of cases is concordant if the value of each variable is larger (or each is smaller) for one case than for the other case.

A pair of cases is **discordant** if the value of one variable for a case is larger than the value for the other case but the direction is reversed for the second variable. For example, case 2 and case 3 are a discordant pair, since the value of *life* is larger for case 3 than for case 2, but the value of *degree* is larger for case 2 than for case 3.

When two cases have identical values on one or both variables, they are said to be **tied**.

There are five possible outcomes when you compare two cases. They can be concordant, discordant, tied on the first variable, tied on the second variable, or tied on both variables. When data are arranged in a crosstabulation, it's easy to compute the number of concordant, discordant, and tied pairs just by looking at the table and adding up cell frequencies.

If most of the pairs are concordant, the association between the two variables is said to be positive. As values of one variable increase (or decrease), so do the values of the other variable. If most of the pairs are discordant, the association is negative. As values of one variable increase, those of the other variable tend to decrease. If concordant and discordant pairs are equally likely, there is no association.

Measures Based on Concordant and Discordant Pairs

The ordinal measures of association that we'll consider are all based on the difference between the number of concordant pairs (P) and the number of discordant pairs (Q), calculated for all *distinct* pairs of observations. Since we want our measures of association to fall within a known range for all tables, we must standardize the difference, P–Q, so that it falls between –1 and 1, where –1 indicates a perfect negative relationship, +1 indicates a perfect positive relationship, and 0 indicates no relationship. The various measures differ in the way they attempt to standardize P–Q.

Goodman and Kruskal's Gamma

One way of standardizing the difference between the number of concordant and discordant pairs is to use **Goodman and Kruskal's gamma**. You calculate the difference between the number of concordant and discordant pairs (P–Q) and then divide this difference by the sum of the number of concordant and discordant pairs (P+Q).

In Figure 19.5, you see that the value of gamma for the *life* by *degree* crosstabulation is 0.309.

Figure 19.5 Goodman and Kruskal's gamma

To obtain gamma along with the crosstabulation, select Gamma in the Crosstabs Statistics dialog box.

```
LIFE  Is Life Exciting or Dull  by  DEGREE  RS Highest Degree


        Statistic                    Value       ASE1       Val/ASE0
    --------------------             ---------   ---------   --------

Gamma                                 .30927      .04381      6.78138
```

What does this mean? A positive gamma tells you that there are more "like" (concordant) pairs of cases than "unlike" pairs. There is a positive relationship between highest degree and view of life. As level of education increases, so does excitement with life. A negative gamma would mean that as level of education increases, excitement with life decreases.

The absolute value of gamma has a proportional reduction in error interpretation. That is, you use two different rules to make a prediction and see how much you reduce the error by using one rule rather than the other. You are trying to predict whether a pair of cases is concordant or discordant. In the first situation, you classify pairs as like or unlike based on the flip of a coin. In the second situation, you base your decision rule on whether there are more concordant or discordant pairs. If most of the pairs are concordant, you predict "like" for all pairs. If most of the pairs are discordant, you predict "unlike." The absolute value of gamma is the proportional reduction in error when the second rule is used instead of the first.

For example, if only slightly more than half of the pairs of cases are concordant, guessing randomly and classifying all cases as "like" leads to a similar number of misclassified cases—approximately one half. The value of gamma is close to 0. If all of the pairs are concordant, guessing "like" will result in the correct classification of all pairs. Guessing randomly will classify only half of the pairs correctly. In this situation, the value of gamma is 1.

If two variables are independent, the value of gamma is 0. However, a gamma of 0, like a lambda of 0, does not necessarily mean independence. (If the table is a 2×2 table, however, a gamma of 0 *does* mean that the variables are independent.)

Kendall's Tau-b

Gamma ignores all pairs of cases that involve ties. A measure that attempts to normalize P–Q by considering ties on each variable in a pair separately (but not ties on both variables) is **tau-b**. It's computed as

$$\tau_b = \frac{P - Q}{\sqrt{(P + Q + T_X) \times (P + Q + T_Y)}}$$

Equation 19.7

where T_X is the number of ties involving only the first variable and T_Y is the number of ties involving only the second variable. Tau-b can have the value of +1 and –1 only for tables that have the same number of rows and columns.

Figure 19.6 Kendall's tau-b, tau-c, and Somers' d

To obtain these
statistics, select
Kendall's tau-b,
Kendall's tau-c,
and Somers' d in
the Crosstabs
Statistics
dialog box.

```
LIFE  Is Life Exciting or Dull  by  DEGREE  RS Highest Degree


                                                              Approximate
     Statistic                    Value      ASE1    Val/ASE0 Significance
--------------------             --------   --------  -------- ------------

Kendall's Tau-b                   .18833     .02735   6.78138
Kendall's Tau-c                   .17156     .02530   6.78138
Somers' D :
   symmetric                      .18766     .02726   6.78138
   with LIFE      dependent       .17306     .02520   6.78138
   with DEGREE    dependent       .20496     .02986   6.78138
```

In Figure 19.6, the value of tau-*b* is 0.188. Since the denominator is complicated, there's no simple explanation in terms of proportional reduction of error. However, tau-*b* is a commonly used measure of association.

Kendall's Tau-c

A measure that can attain, or nearly attain, the values of +1 and –1 for a table of any size is **tau-c**. It's computed as

$$\tau_c = \frac{2m\,(P-Q)}{N^2\,(m-1)}$$

Equation 19.8

where *m* is the smaller of the number of rows and columns. For this example, tau-*c* is 0.172. Unfortunately, there is no simple proportional reduction of error interpretation of tau-*c* either.

Somers' d

Gamma, tau-*b*, and tau-*c* are all symmetric measures. It doesn't matter which variable is considered dependent. The value of the statistic is the same. Somers proposed an extension of gamma when one of the variables is considered dependent. It differs from gamma only in that the denominator is the sum of all pairs of cases that are not tied on the independent variable. (In gamma, *all* cases involving ties are excluded from the denominator.) When perception of life is considered the dependent variable, Somers' *d*, in Figure 19.6, is 0.173.

![?] *How can I decide what measure of association to use?* No single measure of association is best for all situations. To choose the best one for a particular situation, you must consider the type of data and the way you want to define association. If a certain measure has a low value for a table, this doesn't necessarily mean that the two variables are unrelated. It can also mean that they're not related in the way that the measure can detect. But you shouldn't calculate a lot of measures and then report only the largest. Select the appropriate measures in advance. If you look at enough different measures, you increase your chance of finding significant associations in the sample that do not exist in the population. ■ ■ ■

Correlation-Based Measures

When your variables are measured on a scale in which order is meaningful, you can calculate correlation coefficients that measure the strength of the linear association between two variables. Two variables are linearly related if in a scatterplot the points cluster around a straight line. If all of the points fall exactly on a line with a positive slope, the correlation coefficient is 1. If they fall exactly on a line with a negative slope, the correlation coefficient is –1. The absolute value of the correlation coefficient tells you how tightly the points cluster around the line. (A correlation coefficient of 0 doesn't necessarily mean that the two variables are not related. They may be related in a nonlinear way. This is discussed in more detail in Chapter 20.)

Two commonly encountered correlation coefficients are the Pearson correlation coefficient and the Spearman correlation coefficient. Both of these coefficients range in value from –1 to +1. The Pearson correlation coefficient is calculated using the actual data values. The Spearman correlation coefficient, a nonparametric alternative to the Pearson correlation coefficient, replaces the actual data values with ranks.

Figure 19.7 Pearson and Spearman correlation coefficients

To obtain these coefficients, select Correlations in the Crosstabs Statistics dialog box.

```
LIFE  Is life exciting or dull  by  DEGREE  RS Highest Degree


                                                              Approximate
      Statistic                    Value      ASE1    Val/ASE0  Significance
--------------------              ---------  --------  --------  ------------
Pearson's R                        .21891    .02836   7.06963    .00000 *4
Spearman Correlation               .20783    .03026   6.69547    .00000 *4


*4 VAL/ASE0 is a t-value based on a normal approximation, as is the significance
```

In Figure 19.7, you see that the Pearson correlation coefficient for the perception of life and degree data is 0.22, while the Spearman correlation coefficient is 0.21. Since the two variables in the crosstabulation have a small number of values, the correlation coefficients are not particularly informative measures. (The assumptions for testing the null hypothesis that the Pearson correlation coefficient is 0 are discussed in Chapter 21.)

Measuring Agreement

If you ask two people to rate the same object or person on a scale with a small number of distinct values, you often want to know how closely the two raters agree. For example, you might ask two physicians to rate the severity of illness in 40 patients using the same four-point scale. Or you might ask two instructors to grade the exams of 40 students, using a five-point scale. What you want to know is how closely their ratings agree. None of the measures of association we've considered so far provide an index of agreement between the two raters. That's what Cohen's kappa coefficient does.

To see how Cohen's kappa is interpreted and calculated let's look at data from a study by Davis and Ragsdale (1983) in which they asked married couples to rate the likelihood that they would purchase various items. Each person rated how likely they were to purchase the item and how likely they thought their spouse was to purchase the item. The item you're looking at is a combination washer/dryer unit. You're interested in the relationship between the husbands' answers and their wives' predictions of their answers

Figure 19.8 Cohen's kappa

To obtain this crosstabulation, use the buying.sav data file.

In the Crosstabs dialog box, select the variables wifepred and husbsays.

In the Crosstabs Statistics dialog box, select Kappa.

```
                              HUSBSAYS                    Page 1 of 1
                    Count
                    Tot Pct   Buy      Indiffer  Not buy
                                       ent
                                1 |      2 |       3 |    Row
      WIFEPRED      ─────────────                        Total
                       1        23        6        13      42
        Buy                   23.0       6.0      13.0    42.0

                       2         8       13         9      30
        Indifferent            8.0      13.0      9.0    30.0

                       3        12        6        10      28
        Not buy               12.0       6.0     10.0    28.0

                    Column     43        25        32     100
                    Total    43.0      25.0      32.0   100.0
```

If husbands and wives agreed perfectly, all cases would be on the diagonal

```
                                                              Approximate
      Statistic                Value       ASE1    Val/ASE0   Significance
      -----------------        ---------   -------- --------  ------------

      Kappa                     .17532      .07501   2.47100
```

Figure 19.8 is a crosstabulation of the data. The rows are the wives' predictions of their husbands' responses, and the columns are the husbands' responses. If the husbands and wives agreed perfectly, all of the cases would be on the diagonal of the table. As you can see, that's not the case here.

A simple measure of agreement that comes to mind is the percentage of the time that husbands and wives agree. You see that 46% of the cases fall on the diagonal. The problem with using this as a measure of agreement is that it doesn't take into account how much agreement there should be by chance. That is, even if there is no relationship between husbands' and wives' responses, sometimes they will agree by chance.

Cohen's kappa corrects the observed percent agreement for chance. It also normalizes the resulting value so that the coefficient always ranges from –1 to +1. A value of 1 indicates perfect agreement, while a value of –1 indicates perfect disagreement. A value of 0 indicates that the similarity between the two raters is the same as you would expect by chance. In Figure 19.8 you see that kappa is 0.17, indicating that there is some agreement, but it is not very strong.

Summary

How can you measure the strength of the relationship between two categorical variables?

- Measures of association are used to measure the strength of the relationship between two categorical variables.
- Measures of association differ in the way they define association.
- You should select a measure of association based on the characteristics of the data and how you want to define association.
- The chi-square statistic is not a good measure of association. Its value doesn't tell you anything about the strength of the relationship between two variables.
- Measures of proportional reduction in error (PRE) compare the error you make when you predict values of one variable based on values of another with the error when you predict them without information about the other variable.
- Two variables may be related and yet have a value of zero for a particular measure of association.
- Cohen's kappa measures agreement between two raters.
- Special measures of association are available for ordinal variables. They are based on counting the number of concordant pairs (as one variable increases, so does the other) and the number of discordant pairs (as one variable increases, the other decreases).

What's Next?

In this chapter, you computed coefficients that measure the strength of the association between two variables in a crosstabulation. In the remainder of this book, you'll learn how to measure the strength of the linear relationship between a dependent variable and a set of independent variables. You'll build a linear regression model to predict the value of the dependent variable from the independent variables.

Exercises

Statistical Concepts

1. The following table shows the relationship between depth of hypnosis and success in treatment of migraine headaches (Cedercreutz, 1978). Calculate the appropriate lambda statistic. How can you interpret this value?

```
HIPONOSI  Depth of Hyponosis  by  MIGRAINE  Success in Treatment

                     MIGRAINE                   Page 1 of 1
             Count
                     Cured    Better   No Change
                                                     Row
                        1  |     2  |      3  |    Total
   HIPONOSI     ─────────────────────────────────
                1      13         5                    18
      Deep                                           18.0

                2      10        26         17         53
      Medium                                         53.0

                3                 1         28         29
      Light                                          29.0

             Column     23        32         45       100
             Total    23.0      32.0       45.0     100.0
```

2. Discuss the difference you would see in the gamma statistic if you coded job satisfaction from low to high and condition of health from good to poor, as compared to the value you would get if both job satisfaction and condition of health are coded in the same direction.

Data Analysis

Use the *gss.sav* data file to answer the following questions:

1. Consider the relationship between how happy a person is in general (*happy*) and the happiness of their marriage (*hapmar*).

   a. Compute the chi-square statistic.

   b. Do the two variables appear to be independent? Explain.

c. What does the value of the chi-square statistic tell you about the strength of the relationship between the two variables?

d. What would happen to the value of the chi-square statistic if you tripled the number of cases in each cell of the crosstabulation?

e. Do you think the chi-square test is appropriate for this table? Or are there too many cells with small expected values? Is the smallest expected value *too* small?

2. Compute phi, Cramér's *V*, and the contingency coefficient for the table in question 1. What can you say about the strength of the association between the two variables based on the values of the coefficients?

3. Compute the lambda coefficients for the table in question 1.

a. If you want to predict general happiness without any other information, what would you predict? How many people would you incorrectly classify using this rule?

b. For someone whose marriage is very happy, what would you predict for general happiness? How many people do you misclassify using this rule?

c. What would you predict for general happiness for someone whose marriage is pretty happy? How many people do you misclassify using this rule?

d. What would you predict for general happiness for someone whose marriage is not too happy? How many people do you misclassify using this rule?

e. Based on your answers for questions 3a–d, compute the lambda statistic for predicting a person's general happiness from the happiness of their marriage.

4. Repeat question 3 but this time predict happiness with marriage from general happiness.

5. Is it obvious whether general happiness or happiness with marriage is the dependent variable? Compute symmetric lambda based on the results you obtained from questions 3 and 4. Do your answers agree with those from SPSS? If not, assume SPSS is correct and find your mistakes.

6. What does the gamma statistic tell you? How would you interpret gamma if it was negative?

7. For full-time employees only (variable *wrkstat* equals 1) make a crosstabulation of *satjob* and *income4*, income in quartiles. For each cell, obtain the appropriate percentages, observed and expected cell counts, and residuals. Also obtain the chi-square statistic, gamma, and lambda.

a. Can you conclude that income and job satisfaction are independent? Why or why not?

b. What percentage of people earning $60,000 or more are very satisfied with their jobs? What percentage of people earning less than $25,000 are very satisfied with their jobs?

c. Look at the value for gamma. Why is it negative? Wouldn't you expect it to be positive?

d. Which variable in the table would you consider to be the dependent variable? What is the value of lambda when you try to predict the dependent variable from the independent variable?

e. Based on the gamma statistic, is it reasonable to conclude that the association between *happy* and *hapmar* is stronger than the association between *satjob* and *income4*? What can you conclude based on lambda?

8. Now look at the relationship between job satisfaction and income separately for men and women.

a. Does it make sense to compare the two chi-square values? Why or why not?

b. Can you conclude that for men, job satisfaction and income are independent? How about for women?

c. Compare the strength of the association between the two variables for men and for women. What can you conclude?

Linear Regression and Correlation

How can you choose the line that best summarizes the linear relationship between two variables?

- What is the least-squares line?
- What does the slope tell you? The intercept?
- How can you tell how well a line fits the data?
- How do you calculate predicted values and residuals?

How much can sales be expected to increase if the advertising budget is doubled? How much does the cholesterol level rise as fat intake increases? What would you expect the selling price of a company to be based on its net revenues? To answer questions like these for variables measured on at least an ordinal scale, you must determine if there is a relationship between the two variables, and if so, you must describe that relationship.

In Chapter 9, you saw that plotting the values of two variables is an essential first step in examining the nature of their relationship. From a plot, you can tell whether there is some type of pattern between the values of the two variables or whether the points appear to be randomly scattered. If you see a pattern, you can try to summarize the overall relationship by fitting a mathematical model to the data. For example, if the points on the plot cluster around a straight line, you can summarize the relationship by finding the equation for the line. Similarly, if some type of curve appears to fit the data points, you can determine the equation for the curve.

In this and the remaining chapters in Part 4, you will learn about linear regression models. You will begin with fitting the simplest of mathematical models, a straight line.

▶ This chapter uses the *cntry15.sav* data file. For instructions on how to obtain the linear regression output shown in this chapter, see "How to Obtain a Linear Regression" on p. 407.

Life Expectancy and Birthrate

Figure 20.1 is a scatterplot of 1992 life expectancy for females and birthrate per 1000 population for 15 countries. Two of the points, Mongolia and France, are identified by country name. Mongolia has a birthrate of 34 births per 1000 and a life expectancy for females of 68 years. France has a birthrate of 13 and a life expectancy for females of 82 years. Looking at the plot, you see that the points are not randomly scattered over the grid. Instead, there appears to be a pattern. Countries with high birthrates have lower life expectancies than countries with low birthrates. Another way of saying this is that as birthrate increases, life expectancy decreases.

Figure 20.1   Life expectancy and birthrate

You can create scatterplots using the Graphs menu, as discussed in Chapter 9. Select the variables lifeexpf and birthrat in the Simple Scatterplot dialog box.

If you had to describe the pattern of points in Figure 20.1, you might say that they cluster around a straight line; that is, the relationship between the two variables is linear. Since life expectancy decreases as birthrate increases, you can also characterize the relationship as "negative." (If life expectancy increased with increasing birthrate, the relationship would be termed "positive.") Of course, the observed points don't fall exactly on a straight line. If they did, the plot would look like Figure 20.2.

Figure 20.2 Perfect linear relationships

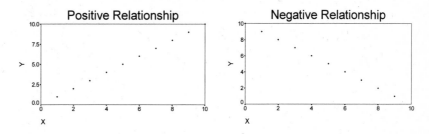

Why aren't we using all of the countries that we plotted in Chapter 9? Simplicity. Sometimes it's easier to understand what's going on when you have a small number of data points that you can easily manipulate. As an exercise, you can rerun all of the analyses in this chapter on the larger (corrected) data file. You'll also use the larger data file in Chapter 23 to build a multiple regression model to predict life expectancy for females from several independent variables. ▨ ▨ ▨

Remember to correct the value for Bhutan as discussed in Chapter 9.

Choosing the "Best" Line

If all of the points fall exactly on a straight line, you don't have to worry about determining which line summarizes the data points best. All you have to do is connect the observed points and you have the line that best fits the data. When the points don't fall exactly on a straight line, choosing a line is more complicated.

You can see in Figure 20.3 that there are many different lines that can be drawn through the observed data values for life expectancy for females and birthrate.

Figure 20.3   Three possible lines

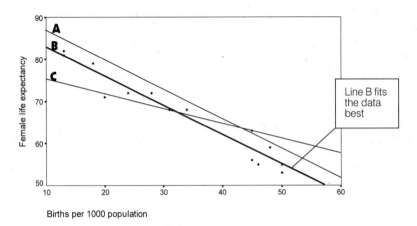

Common sense tells you that some of the lines in Figure 20.3 summarize the data better than others. For example, line A has many more points below it than above it. It doesn't really pass closely through the majority of the data points. Line C has similar numbers of points above and below it, but the distance from the points to the line is unnecessarily large. Line B fits the data best. It passes close to most of the observed data points.

The Least-Squares Line

Line B is not just any line that appears to summarize the data values well. Line B is unique. It is the **least-squares regression line**, which means that, of all possible lines that can be drawn on the plot, line B has the smallest sum of squared vertical distances between the points and the line. To understand what this means, look at Figure 20.4, which shows the observed data points and line B, the least-squares regression line.

Figure 20.4   Least-squares regression line

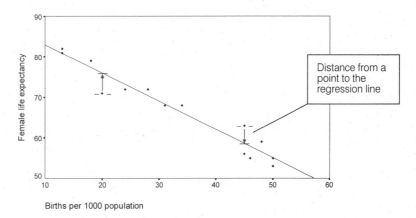

You can add a regression line to a scatterplot after you create it. See "Scatterplot Options" on p. 169 in Chapter 9.

For each of the data points, you can calculate the distance between the point and the regression line by drawing a vertical line from the point to the regression line. (That's the dotted line for some of the points in Figure 20.4.) If you calculate the vertical distances between each of the points and the line, square each of them, and then add them up for all of the points, you have the **sum of squared distances** between the points and the regression line. (You use squared distances, since you don't want positive and negative differences between the points and the line to cancel out.) The least-squares regression line is the line that has the smallest sum of squared vertical distances between the points and the line. Any other line you draw through the points will have a larger sum of squared distances.

The Equation for a Straight Line

Before you learn how to calculate the least-squares regression line, let's consider the equation for a straight line. If y is the variable plotted on the vertical axis and x is the variable plotted on the horizontal axis, the equation for a straight line is

$$y = a + bx \qquad \qquad \textbf{Equation 20.1}$$

The value a is called the **intercept**. It is the predicted value for y when x is 0. The value b is called the **slope**. It is the change in y when x changes by one unit. *Y* is often called the dependent variable since you can try to predict its values based on the values of *x*, the independent variable. In this example, the dependent variable is life expectancy for females. You want to predict its values based on birthrate, the independent variable.

Consider the line

life expectancy $= 90 - (0.70 \times \text{birthrate})$ **Equation 20.2**

Figure 20.5 is a plot of the line. The slope is –0.70. This tells you that for an increase of 1 in birthrate, there is a decrease in life expectancy of 0.70 years. For the birthrate variable, an increase of 1 means an increase of 1 live birth per 1000 population per year. For example, a country with a birthrate of 10 is predicted to have a life expectancy of 83 years. A country with a birthrate of 11 is predicted to have a life expectancy of 82.3 years. The difference between 83 and 82.3 is –0.70 years, which is the value for the slope.

Figure 20.5   Regression line

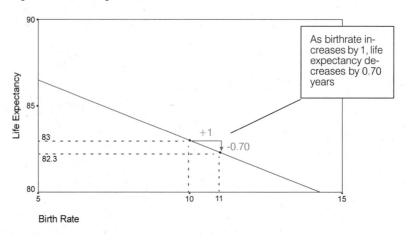

If the value for the slope is positive, you know that as the values of one variable increase, so do the values of the other variable. If the slope is negative, you know that as the values of one variable increase, the values of the other variable decrease. If the slope is large, the line is steep, indicating that a small change in the independent variable results in a large change in the dependent variable. If the slope is small, there is a more gradual increase or decrease. If the slope is 0, the changes in *x*

have no effect on *y*. In this case, the least-squares regression line is horizontal, as shown in Figure 20.6.

Figure 20.6   No linear relationship (slope=0)

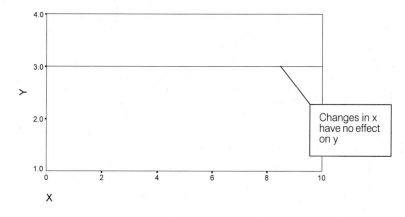

The value of the intercept is 90. That's the point where the line hits the vertical axis, that is, where *x*=0.

Why does the line hit the vertical axis at about 86 in Figure 20.5, not at 90? The reason is that the vertical axis is not drawn at the point where the birthrate is 0. In Figure 20.5, the scale starts at 5 births per 1000 population. The predicted life expectancy for 5 births is 86.5 years. That's the point at which the line crosses the vertical axis. Look at Figure 20.7. The horizontal axis starts at a birthrate of 0, so the intercept is 90, as you would expect.

Figure 20.7   Regression line with horizontal axis starting at 0

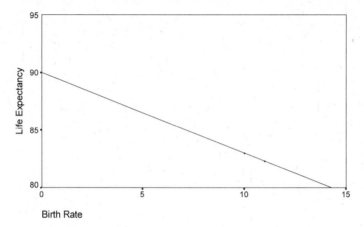

You can change the scale of the x or y axis in a scatterplot after you create it. Move the chart into a chart window and then double-click on the axis to open a dialog box with options for that axis.

You should be careful in interpreting the intercept. Unless a value of 0 makes sense for the independent variable, the intercept may not have any substantive meaning. In this example, the intercept, 90, is the value for life expectancy when the birthrate is 0. Since there aren't any countries with birthrates of 0, the life expectancy for a hypothetical non-reproducing nation is meaningless.

Will I get the same answer for the slope and the intercept if I switch which variable is the dependent variable and which is the independent variable? No, you'll get different answers. The slope and the intercept are not symmetric measures—it matters which variable is the dependent variable and which is the independent variable. ■ ■ ■

Calculating the Least-Squares Line

It's easy to calculate the slope and the intercept when all of the points fall exactly on a straight line. It's somewhat more complicated to calculate them for a least-squares regression line when the points don't fall exactly on the line. It's easiest to let SPSS do the calculations for you. Look at the output shown in Figure 20.8.

Figure 20.8   Linear regression of life expectancy and birthrate

To obtain this regression output, from the menus choose:

Statistics
  Regression ▶
    Linear...

Select the variables lifeexpf and birthrat, as shown in Figure 20.15.

```
             * * * *   M U L T I P L E   R E G R E S S I O N   * * * *

Listwise Deletion of Missing Data

Equation Number 1    Dependent Variable..   LIFEEXPF   Female life expectancy 19

Block Number  1.  Method:  Enter      BIRTHRAT


Variable(s) Entered on Step Number
   1..    BIRTHRAT  Births per 1000 population, 1992


Multiple R           .96835
R Square             .93770
Adjusted R Square    .93290
Standard Error      2.53697

Analysis of Variance
                    DF      Sum of Squares      Mean Square
Regression           1          1259.26263      1259.26263
Residual            13            83.67070         6.43621

F =     195.65289      Signif F =  .0000


----------------- Variables in the Equation -------------------

Variable            B          SE B         Beta        T   Sig T

BIRTHRAT          -.697318     .049853    -.968347   -13.988  .0000
(Constant)       89.985172    1.764574                50.995  .0000


End Block Number   1   All requested variables entered.
```

Slope

Intercept

The slope and the intercept values from the least-squares regression are shown in the column labeled *B*. The regression equation is

$$\text{predicted life expectancy} = 89.99 - (0.697 \times \text{birthrate})$$ **Equation 20.3**

(You'll learn the meaning of the other numbers in Chapter 21.)

? *How would I calculate the least-squares slope and intercept on a desert island without SPSS?*

You can calculate the slope using

$$b = \sum_{i=1}^{N} \frac{\left(x_i - \bar{x}\right)\left(y_i - \bar{y}\right)}{(N-1)\,s_x^2}$$

For each case, subtract the mean of the independent variable, $\bar{x}$, from the case's value for the independent variable, x_i. Then subtract the mean of the dependent variable, $\bar{y}$, from the case's value for the dependent variable, y_i. Multiply these two differences for each case and then sum them for all of the cases. For the last step, divide this sum by the product of the number of cases minus 1 ($N–1$) and the variance of the independent variable (s_x^2). Since the least-squares regression line passes through the point $(\bar{x}, \bar{y})$, you can calculate the intercept as

$$a = \bar{y} - b\bar{x}$$

Calculating Predicted Values and Residuals

You can use the least-squares regression line to predict the life expectancy for any country whose birthrate you know. For example, the 1992 birthrate for Spain is 11 births per 1000 population. You predict the life expectancy of females, based on the regression equation, to be

life expectancy $= 89.99 - (0.697 \times 11) = 82.32$ years   **Equation 20.4**

(You'll get the same predicted value if you find the point on the least-squares line in the plot that corresponds to a birthrate of 11, and read off the corresponding value for life expectancy.) The actual life expectancy for Spanish women in 1992 is 82 years, so you see that your prediction is excellent. The difference between the observed and predicted value is only –0.32 years.

You see in Figure 20.9 the birthrates and observed and predicted female life expectancies for the 15 countries included in the regression. The last column contains the **residual**, which is the difference between the observed and predicted value of the dependent variable. You see that the smallest residual in absolute value is 0.08 for the Netherlands.

The largest in absolute value is –5.04 for Thailand. A positive residual means that the observed value is greater than the predicted value, while a negative residual means that the observed value is smaller than the predicted value.

The residual for a case is nothing more than the vertical distance from the point to the line. The sign tells you whether the observed point is above or below the least-squares regression line. Another way of saying that the least-squares line has the smallest sum of squared vertical distances from the points to the line is to say that the least-squares line has the smallest sum of squared residuals. As you'll see in Chapter 22 and Chapter 24, the analysis of residuals plays an important role in regression analysis.

Figure 20.9   Observed and predicted values, plus residuals

To save predicted values and residuals along with the regression, see "Linear Regression Save: Creating New Variables" on p. 411.

To list cases as shown here, from the menus choose:

Statistics
  Summarize ▸
    List Cases...

COUNTRY	BIRTHRAT	LIFEEXPF	PREDICT	RESIDUAL
Somalia	46	55	57.90856	-2.90856
Tanzania	50	55	55.11929	-.11929
Zambia	48	59	56.51393	2.48607
Zaire	45	56	58.60588	-2.60588
Algeria	31	68	68.36833	-.36833
Namibia	45	63	58.60588	4.39412
Burkina Faso	50	53	55.11929	-2.11929
Cuba	18	79	77.43346	1.56654
Equador	28	72	70.46028	1.53972
North Korea	24	72	73.24955	-1.24955
Mongolia	34	68	66.27637	1.72363
Thailand	20	71	76.03882	-5.03882
Turkey	28	72	70.46028	1.53972
France	13	82	80.92004	1.07996
Netherlands	13	81	80.92004	.07996

Number of cases read: 15   Number of cases listed: 15

Determining How Well the Line Fits

The least-squares regression line is the line that fits the data best in the sense of having the smallest sum of squared residuals. However, this does not necessarily mean that it fits the data *well*. Before you use the regression line for making predictions or describing the relationship between the two variables, you must determine how well the line fits the data. If the line fits poorly, any conclusions based on it will be unreliable.

> ❓ *Can't I tell how well the line fits by looking at how big the slope is?* No. The value of the slope depends not only on how closely two variables are related but also on the units in which they are measured. If you're predicting income in dollars from years of education, the slope will (hopefully) be large. If you're predicting college GPA from SAT scores, the slope will be small, not necessarily because the relationship between the two variables is weak, but because college GPA's range somewhere from 1 to 5, while SAT scores range from 200 to 800. You'll have to multiply SAT scores (which are measured in hundreds) by a small slope to end up with predicted changes in GPA values. ■ ■ ■

The Correlation Coefficient

To describe how well the model fits the data you want an *absolute* measure that doesn't depend on the units of measurement and is easily interpretable. The statistic most frequently used for this purpose is the **Pearson correlation coefficient (*r*)**. It ranges in value from –1 to +1. If all of the points fall exactly on a line with a positive slope, the correlation coefficient has a value of +1. If all of the points fall exactly on a line with negative slope, the correlation coefficient is –1. The absolute value of the correlation coefficient tells you how closely the points cluster around a straight line. Both large positive values (near +1) and large negative values (near –1) indicate a strong linear relationship between the two variables—the points are close to the line.

> ❓ *If two variables have a large correlation coefficient, does that mean that one of them causes the other?* Not at all. You can't assume that because two variables are correlated, one of them causes the other. If you find a large correlation coefficient between the ounces of coffee consumed in a day and salary, you can't conclude that drinking more coffee will increase your salary. In certain regions of the world, there is a reasonably large correlation coefficient between the number of storks in an area and the birthrate. No doubt you are aware of the causal link there. ■ ■ ■

Unlike the slope and the intercept, the correlation coefficient is a symmetric measure. That means you get the same value regardless of which of the two variables is the dependent variable. That makes sense, since life expectancy is linearly related to birthrate as strongly as birthrate is to life expectancy.

You can calculate the correlation coefficient from the slope using the formula

$$r = b \times \left(\frac{s_x}{s_y} \right)$$

Equation 20.5

where s_x and s_y are the standard deviations of the independent and dependent variables. You see from the formula that if the dependent and independent variables are standardized to have standard deviations of 1, the correlation coefficient and the slope are equal.

Look at Figure 20.10, which shows two pairs of variables that have the same least-squares values for the slope and the intercept. They differ in how well the straight-line model fits the data. In Plot A, the data points cluster fairly tightly about the line, while in Plot B, the data points are more widely scattered about the line.

Figure 20.10 Two plots with the same slope and intercept

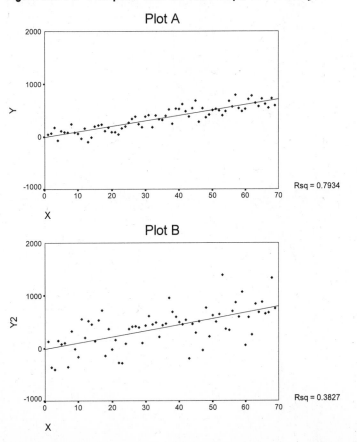

The correlation coefficient for Plot A is about 0.9, while for Plot B it is about 0.6. Since the correlation coefficient for the first plot is larger in absolute value than that for the second, you can tell without looking at the plot that the points cluster more tightly about the line in Plot A than in Plot B.

If there is no *linear* relationship between the two variables, the correlation coefficient is close to 0. A correlation coefficient of 0 does not mean that there isn't any type of relationship between two variables. It is possible for two variables to have a correlation coefficient close to 0 and yet be strongly related in a nonlinear way.

Figure 20.11 Strong nonlinear relationship

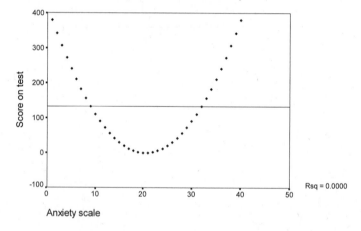

Figure 20.11 is a plot of two variables that have a correlation coefficient of 0 but have a strong *nonlinear* relationship. Test scores are strongly related to anxiety levels, but not linearly. You should always plot the values of the two variables before you compute a regression line or a Pearson correlation coefficient. Plotting allows you to detect nonlinear relationships for which the regression line and correlation coefficient are not good summaries.

? *What if I just want to look at correlation coefficients between pairs of variables? Do I have to run the SPSS Regression procedure?* No. There's a special procedure called Correlations, which allows you to calculate correlation coefficients between two or more pairs of variables. You can calculate Pearson correlation coefficients or either of two nonparametric alternatives, called Spearman's and Kendall's correlation coefficients. In Chapter 21, you'll see the circumstances under which you might want to calculate nonparametric correlation coefficients. ■ ■ ■

Explaining Variability

In Figure 20.4 you see that for the life expectancy and birthrate example, the data points cluster fairly tightly around the straight line. The absolute value of the correlation coefficient between life expectancy and birthrate is 0.97. That's the value labeled *Multiple R* in Figure 20.12. The actual correlation coefficient between the two variables is –0.97, since the slope of the regression line is negative. It's unusual to find such a large correlation coefficient between two variables.

Figure 20.12 Linear regression of female life expectancy and birthrate

To obtain this analysis, select the variables lifeexpf and birthrat in the Linear Regression dialog box. (This is the same analysis shown in Figure 20.8.)

```
             * * * *   M U L T I P L E   R E G R E S S I O N   * * * *


Listwise Deletion of Missing Data

Equation Number 1     Dependent Variable..    LIFEEXPF    Female life expectancy 19

Block Number  1.  Method: Enter        BIRTHRAT


Variable(s) Entered on Step Number
   1..     BIRTHRAT  Births per 1000 population, 1992         Absolute value
                                                             of correlation
                                                             coefficient

Multiple R          .96835
R Square            .93770                                    Proportion of
Adjusted R Square   .93290                                    variation that is
Standard Error     2.53697                                    "explained" by
                                                             model
Analysis of Variance
                    DF     Sum of Squares      Mean Square
Regression           1        1259.26263       1259.26263
Residual            13          83.67070          6.43621

F =     195.65289      Signif F =  .0000


------------------ Variables in the Equation ------------------

Variable            B         SE B       Beta         T   Sig T

BIRTHRAT       -.697318     .049853   -.968347   -13.988   .0000
(Constant)    89.985172    1.764574               50.995   .0000


End Block Number   1   All requested variables entered.
```

If you square the value of the correlation coefficient, you obtain another useful statistic. The square of the correlation coefficient tells you what proportion of the variability of the dependent variable is "explained" by the regression model. In this example, close to 94% of the variability in observed female life expectancies is explained by birthrate.

What does that mean? You know that all countries do not have the same life expectancy. There is substantial variability. One of the explanations for the observed variability is differences in the degree of development of the countries. Birthrate is one indicator of this. If there is a perfect relationship between life expectancy and birthrate, you can attribute all of the observed differences in life expectancy to differences in birthrate. In other words, birthrate would explain all of the observed variability in life expectancy. In this situation, the correlation coefficient and its square are both 1. When all of the data points don't fall exactly on the regression line, you can calculate how much of the observed variability in female life expectancy can be attributed to differences in birthrates.

How do you do that? If you square the residuals for all of the cases and add them up, you have a measure of how much variability in life expectancy is *not* explained by birthrates. In this example, the sum of the squared residuals is 83.67. (This is the *Sum of Squares* for *Residual* in Figure 20.12.) You obtain the total variability of the dependent variable by calculating its variance and multiplying by the number of cases minus 1. That gives you 1,342.93. (This is the sum of the *Regression* and *Residual Sum of Squares* in Figure 20.12.) To calculate the proportion of variability that is *not* explained by the regression, divide 83.67 by 1,342.93. This gives you 0.0623. The proportion of variability explained by the regression is 1 minus the proportion not explained, or 0.9377.

A quick way of arriving at the proportion of explained variability is to square the correlation coefficient between the dependent and independent variable. From the value of R^2 (labeled *R Square* in Figure 20.12), you can see that almost 94% of the variability in life expectancies can be explained by differences in birthrates. The remaining 6% is not explained.

The entry in Figure 20.12 labeled *Adjusted R Square* is an estimate of how well your model would fit another data set from the same population. Since the slope and the intercept are based on the values in your data set, the model fits your data somewhat better than it would another sample of cases. The value of adjusted R^2 is always smaller than the value of R^2. In this example, the value of adjusted R^2 is 0.933, slightly less than the R^2 value of 0.938.

Some Warnings

- *Don't use the linear regression equation to make predictions when values of the independent variable are outside of the observed range.* For example, in this data set, the smallest observed birthrate is 13 for France and the Netherlands. The largest is 50 for Burkina Faso and Tanzania. Although a straight line appears to be a reasonable summary for countries with birthrates between 13 and 50, you have no reason to expect that the same relationship will hold for birthrates much smaller or much larger than those observed. It's certainly possible that life expectancy will decline in a nonlinear fashion for birthrates larger than 50. That's why you should restrict your predictions to countries that have birthrates in the same range as your data. Otherwise, it's possible for your predictions to be way off target.

- *Don't calculate a regression equation unless the relationship between the two variables appears to be linear over the entire observed range of the independent variable.* For example, look at Figure 20.13, a hypothetical plot of birthrates and life expectancies for 20 countries. Note that the countries fall into two distinct clusters. Within each cluster, there is no linear relationship between the two variables. However, if you combine the data and calculate a regression line (shown), you may erroneously conclude that there is a linear relationship. The "relationship" is due solely to the fact that the clusters have different average values for the two variables.

Figure 20.13 Not a linear relationship

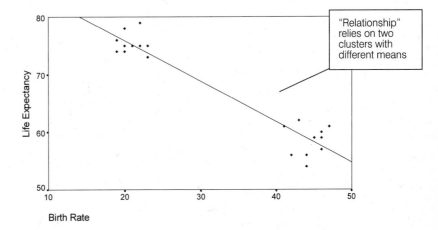

- *Beware of a relationship that depends heavily on a single point.* Consider Figure 20.14. Without the circled point, there is no linear relationship between the two variables. If the indicated point is included in the analysis, the least-squares regression line no longer has a slope of 0. The entire observed relationship is due to a single influential point. In Chapter 22, you'll learn how to identify such influential points.

Figure 20.14 Two related variables

See Chapter 7 for information on how to identify outliers.

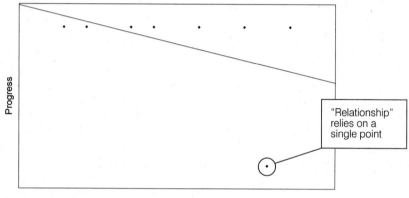

Summary

> How can you choose the line that best summarizes the linear relationship between two variables?
>
> - The equation for a straight line is $y=a+bx$. The intercept a is the value of y when x is 0. The slope b tells you how much y increases or decreases for a one-unit change in x.
>
> - The least-squares line has, of all possible lines, the smallest sum of squared vertical distances from the point to the line.
>
> - The absolute value of the Pearson correlation coefficient between two variables tells you how closely the points cluster around a straight line.
>
> - You calculate the predicted value by substituting the observed value of the independent variable into the least-squares regression equation. A residual is the difference between the observed and predicted values.

What's Next?

In this chapter, you simply fit a regression line to a set of data. You did not test any hypotheses about the population from which the sample is selected. In Chapter 21 and Chapter 22, you'll see what assumptions are needed to test hypotheses about the population regression line based on the observed sample. You'll also see how to use residuals from the regression to look for violations of these assumptions.

How to Obtain a Linear Regression

This section describes the basics of obtaining a linear regression analysis using the SPSS Linear Regression procedure. Optional statistics and plots available with Regression are also discussed, including saving the residuals used for diagnostics.

This section focuses on bivariate linear regression, as discussed in this chapter and in Chapter 21 and Chapter 22. Options specific to obtaining a multiple linear regression are discussed in Chapter 23.

▶ To open the Linear Regression dialog box (see Figure 20.15), from the menus choose:

Statistics
  Regression ▶
    Linear...

Figure 20.15 Linear Regression dialog box

Select lifeexpf and birthrat to obtain the linear regression discussed in this chapter and in Chapter 21 and Chapter 22

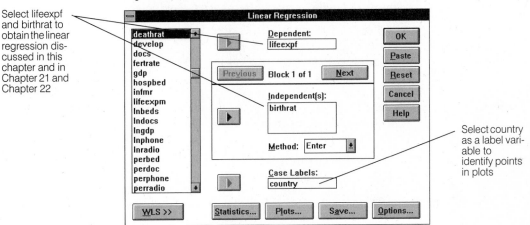

Select country as a label variable to identify points in plots

> ▶ Select the dependent variable and move it into the Dependent box.

> ▶ Select the independent variable and move it into the Independent(s) list and click on OK.

This performs a basic regression analysis and displays an analysis-of-variance table for the regression, along with the constant, the regression coefficient, and the other statistics for the regression equation. You can also obtain a multiple linear regression by selecting more than one variable for the Independent(s) list. (Multiple linear regression is discussed in Chapter 23.)

Statistics: Further Information on the Model

In the Linear Regression dialog box, click on Statistics to open the Linear Regression Statistics dialog box, as shown in Figure 20.16.

Figure 20.16 Linear Regression Statistics dialog box

Select to save confidence intervals, as discussed in Chapter 21

Descriptive statistics are discussed in Chapter 23

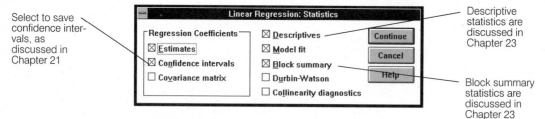

Block summary statistics are discussed in Chapter 23

Regression Coefficients. The Regression Coefficients options are:

Estimates. For each independent variable in the model, unstandardized and standardized coefficients, standard error, t value, and the two-tailed significance level for the t value. For independent variables not in the model, the standardized coefficient if it were in the model, t value, significance of t, partial correlation with the dependent variable controlling for independent variables in the equation, and minimum tolerance. These statistics are displayed by default. Deselect this option to suppress them.

Confidence intervals. For each unstandardized regression coefficient, a 95% confidence interval.

Covariance matrix. For multiple regression models (with two or more independent variables), a square matrix with covariances of the unstandardized regression coefficients below the main diagonal, correlations above the diagonal, and variances on the diagonal.

Additional available statistics include:

Descriptives. Means and standard deviations for all selected variables and a correlation matrix.

Model fit. The R statistic, R^2, adjusted R^2, and the standard error of the estimate, plus an ANOVA table. These statistics are displayed by default. Deselect this option to suppress them.

Block summary. For multiple regression using a stepwise method or multiple blocks (see Chapter 23), summary statistics for each step or block.

Durbin-Watson. Summary statistics for standardized and unstandardized residuals and predicted values, plus the Durbin-Watson statistic measuring serial correlation among the residuals.

Collinearity diagnostics. For multiple regression (see Chapter 23), several statistics and tests for collinearity among the independent variables.

Residual Plots: Basic Residual Analysis

In the Linear Regression dialog box, click on Plots to display the Linear Regression Plots dialog box, as shown in Figure 20.17.

Figure 20.17 Linear Regression Plots dialog box

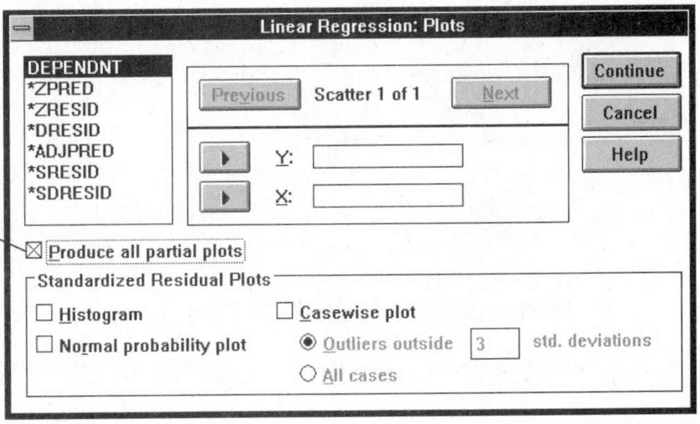

Select to obtain partial residual plots for multiple regression models, as discussed in Chapter 24

You can request scatterplots with any combination of the dependent variable and any of the residuals listed (these are described in detail below).

▶ To obtain a scatterplot of any two of these, select one of them and move it into the Y (vertical axis) box, then select the other and move it into the X (horizontal axis) box.

For additional plots, click on Next and select another pair. To review or modify previously specified plots, click on Previous until you reach the plot of interest. You can then select the Y or X variable, move it out of its box, and (if you want) move another variable into its place.

▶ To plot predicted values or residuals against an independent variable, use the Save dialog box to create a new variable containing the predicted values or residuals. (See "Linear Regression Save: Creating New Variables" on p. 411.) Then choose Scatter from the Graphs menu and specify the scatterplot.

Available variables for these plots include:

*ZPRED. The standardized predicted values of the dependent variable.

*ZRESID. The standardized residuals.

*DRESID. Deleted residuals, the residuals for a case when it is excluded from the regression computations.

*ADJPRED. Adjusted predicted values, the predicted value for a case when it is excluded from the regression computations.

*SRESID. Studentized residuals.

*SDRESID. Studentized deleted residuals.

Produce all partial plots. These are diagnostic plots used in multiple regression analysis. They will be discussed in Chapter 24. A plot is displayed for each independent variable in the equation, provided that there are at least two independent variables.

Standardized Residual Plots. The available plots are:

Histogram. A histogram of the standardized residuals, to help you check whether they are normally distributed.

Normal probability plot. A P-P plot of the distribution of standardized residuals against a standard normal distribution.

Casewise plot. This is a character plot, which appears in the output window rather than the Chart Carousel. It plots the standardized residual against case sequence number for each specified case. Choose an alternative for the cases to plot: either Outliers outside n std. deviations or All cases. If you choose Outliers, you can specify a cutoff for the minimum absolute value of the residual for a case to be plotted.

Linear Regression Save: Creating New Variables

In the Linear Regression dialog box, click on Save to display the Linear Regression Save New Variables dialog box, as shown in Figure 20.18. Each of the options in this dialog box creates a new variable in your working data file. (This is similar to saving standard scores using the Descriptives procedure, as discussed in "Standard Scores" on p. 79 in Chapter 5.) These variables are used primarily for diagnostics, as discussed in Chapter 22 and Chapter 24.

Figure 20.18 Linear Regression: Save New Variables

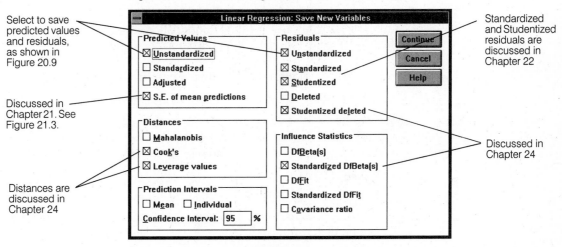

For each option you select, one or more variables will be added to the working data file in the Data Editor. To help you keep track, the names of the newly created variables are displayed in the output window along with the regression output, as shown in Figure 20.19.

Figure 20.19 Newly created variables listed in output window

```
From Equation   1:  10 new variables have been created.

    Name          Contents
    ----          --------

    PRE_1         Predicted Value
    SRE_1         Studentized Residual
    COO_1         Cook's Distance
    LEV_1         Leverage
    SDB0_1        Sdfbeta for Intercept
    SDB1_1        Sdfbeta for LNBEDS
    SDB2_1        Sdfbeta for LNDOCS
    SDB3_1        Sdfbeta for LNGDP
    SDB4_1        Sdfbeta for LNRADIO
    SDB5_1        Sdfbeta for URBAN
```

Check list to see which Sdfbeta corresponds to which independent variable (the order may vary). Sdfbetas are discussed in Chapter 24.

Summary statistics are calculated and displayed for any new variables requested from the Predicted Values, Distances, and Residuals groups.

Predicted Values. The Predicted Values group includes:

Unstandardized. The value predicted by the regression model for the dependent variable.

Standardized. The predicted value for the dependent variable standardized to have a mean of 1 and a standard deviation of 1.

Adjusted. The predicted value for a case if that case is excluded from the calculation of the regression coefficients.

S. E. of mean predictions. An estimate of the standard error of the mean predicted value.

Distances. Options include:

Mahalanobis. A measure of the distance of a case from the average values of all the independent variables.

Cook's. A measure of how much the residuals of all cases would change if the current case were omitted from the calculations.

Leverage values. A measure of how greatly the current case influences the fit of the regression model.

Prediction Intervals. The Prediction Intervals group includes:

Mean. Two new variables containing lower and upper bounds for the prediction interval of the mean value of the dependent variable, for all cases with the given values of the independent variable(s).

Individual. Two new variables containing lower and upper bounds for the prediction interval for the dependent variable for a case with the given values of the independent variables.

Below these options you can specify the level for the confidence interval by entering a percentage value greater than 0 and less than 100.

Residuals. The Residuals group includes:

Unstandardized. The value of the dependent variable minus its predicted value.

Standardized. The residual divided by an estimate of its standard error.

Studentized. The residual divided by an estimate of its standard error that varies from case to case, depending on the distance of the case's values of the independent variable(s) from the mean values.

Deleted. The residual if the current case were excluded from the calculation of the regression coefficients.

Studentized deleted. The deleted residual divided by an estimate of its standard error.

Influence Statistics. Finally, the Influence Statistics group includes:

DfBeta(s). A new variable for each term in the regression model, including the constant, containing the change in the coefficient for that term if the current case were omitted from the calculations. DfBetas are discussed in Chapter 24.

Standardized DfBeta(s). A new variable for each term in the regression model, including the constant, containing the DfBeta value divided by an estimate of its standard error. Standardized DfBetas are discussed in Chapter 24.

DfFit. The change in the predicted value of the dependent variable if the current case is omitted from the calculations.

Standardized DfFit. The DfFit value divided by an estimate of its standard error.

Covariance ratio. The determinant of the covariance matrix with the current case excluded from the calculations, divided by the determinant of that matrix with the current case included.

Linear Regression Options

In the Linear Regression dialog box, click on Options to request regression through the origin or to control the treatment of missing data (see Figure 20.20).

Figure 20.20 Linear Regression Options dialog box

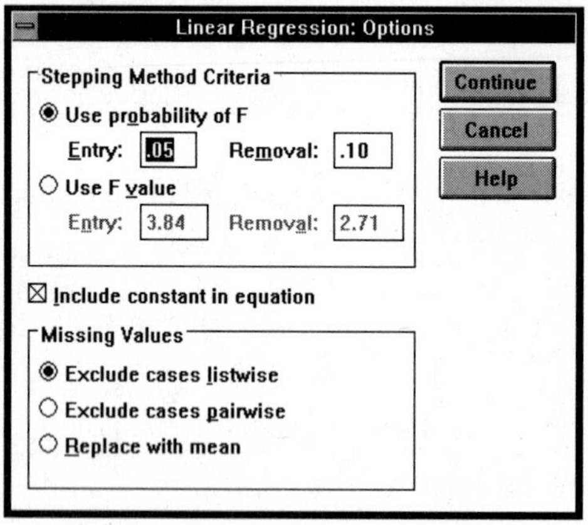

Available options include:

Stepping Method Criteria. These criteria do not apply to bivariate regression. They are described in Chapter 23.

Include constant in equation. Leave this option checked for an ordinary regression equation. Deselect it if you want to constrain the constant term to equal 0. (This leads to regression through the origin, a specialized topic not discussed in this book.)

Missing Values. The available treatments of missing data control the way SPSS obtains the correlation matrix from which the regression statistics are calculated:

Exclude cases listwise. Computes each correlation coefficient using only the cases that have valid data for all variables in the matrix, so that the coefficients in the matrix are all based on the same cases.

Exclude cases pairwise. Computes each correlation coefficient using all of the cases with valid data for the variables involved. In some circumstances, a matrix of such coefficients can be inconsistent (an inconsistent correlation matrix is one that could not possibly be calculated from a single set of cases).

Replace with mean. Missing values for a variable are replaced with the variable's mean value before the correlation matrix is computed.

Exercises

Statistical Concepts

1. Plot the following two points:

Point 1:   Age of home = 20, appraised value = $40,000

Point 2:   Age of home = 30, appraised value = $50,000

a. Write the equation of the straight line that passes through them.

b. What is the value for the intercept?

c. What is the value for the slope?

d. If the line you've drawn predicts appraised value exactly, what would be the appraised value for a 25-year-old home?

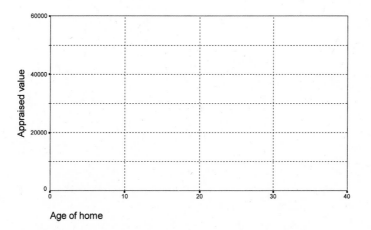

2. A mail-order house is interested in studying the relationship between income and type of product purchased. They take a random sample of orders and then call people to determine family income. They then calculate the correlation coefficient between income and product code. The value is 0.76. Based on this study, what can you conclude about the relationship between income and type of product purchased? Explain.

3. Here are the equations for two regression lines:

Profit = –1000 + 0.25 (Sales)

Profit = 2000 + 2.0 (Advertising Budget)

Can you tell from the regression lines if the correlation coefficient is larger for profit and sales or for advertising budget and sales? Why or why not?

4. You are a production manager interested in the relationship between defect rate and volume at one of your plants. You've taken a random sample of 160 shifts and recorded the percentage of defective items and the volume. Here is the plot of the two variables and the regression statistics:

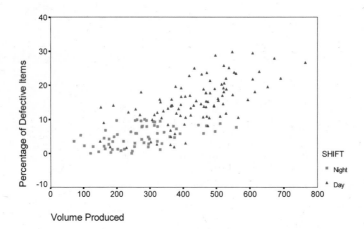

Volume Produced

```
Multiple R              .74041
R Square                .54821
Adjusted R Square       .54535
Standard Error          4.92336

Analysis of Variance
                    DF        Sum of Squares      Mean Square
Regression           1              4647.12423      4647.12423
Residual           158              3829.83867        24.23949

F =      191.71712       Signif F =  .0000


------------------ Variables in the Equation ------------------

Variable            B          SE B       Beta         T   Sig T

VOLUME          .027031     .001952    .740410     13.846  .0000
(Constant)   -97.073120    7.818726             -12.415  .0000
```

a. Is there a relationship between defect rate and volume? If so, is it positive or negative?

b. Which variable is the independent variable and which is the dependent variable?

c. Write out the regression equation and sketch it on the plot.

d. What percentage of the variability in the defect rate can be explained by differences in volume?

e. What defect rate would you predict for a shift with a volume of 4000 units?

f. What defect rate would you predict for a shift with a volume of 9000 units?

g. Would you expect all shifts that produced 4000 items to have the same defect rate?

h. What would you estimate the standard deviation of the distribution of the defect rate to be for a volume of 4000 units?

i. If a particular shift produced 4000 items and had a defect rate of 10%, based on the regression model what would be the residual for the shift?

5. Plot the following points and sketch the least-squares line:

Number of ads	Sales revenues
10	20,000
18	28,000
24	35,000
32	44,000
35	48,000
37	50,000
42	55,000

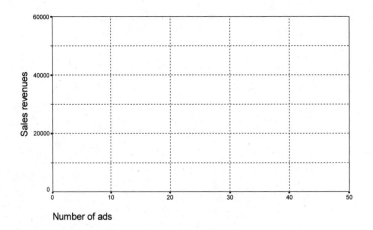

6. For which of the following situations would you consider using linear regression?

a. To predict car model preference from age.

b. To predict car mileage from its weight in pounds.

c. To compare sales performance for three regional offices.

d. To examine the relationship between profitability and growth rate.

e. To examine the relationship between type of product and customer satisfaction.

Data Analysis

Use the *gss.sav* data file to answer the following questions:

1. Using the Graphs menu, make a scatterplot of husband's education against wife's education (variables *husbeduc* and *wifeduc*). Edit the chart to draw the regression line and print R^2.

   a. Does there appear to be a linear relationship between the two variables?

   b. Would you characterize the relationship as positive or negative?

   c. From the plot, estimate the slope and the intercept. (It's easier to estimate the intercept if you edit the x axis to start at 0.)

   d. What's the value for the correlation coefficient?

   e. Describe the points that are far from the regression line.

2. From the Regression procedure obtain the least-squares estimates for the slope and the intercept.

   a. Write the regression equation to predict a husband's education from his wife's education. What proportion of the variability in husbands' education can be "explained" by wives' education?

   b. What is the predicted value for husband's education if a wife's education is 13 years?

   c. If the observed value for a husband's years of education is 14 and his wife's 13 years, what's the residual?

   d. Write the regression equation to predict husband's education, if husbands' and wives' years of education are always the same.

   e. Write the regression education to predict husband's education if there is no linear relationship between husbands' and wives' education.

3. Run the Regression procedure to obtain the least-squares line that predicts wife's education from husband's education.

   a. Write the regression equation. Is it the same as that for predicting husband's education from wife's education?

   b. What proportion of the variability in wives' education can be explained by husbands' education? Compare this to the proportion of variability in husbands' education that can be explained by wives' education.

4. Run the Descriptives procedure to standardize the values of *husbeduc* and *wifeduc*.

   a. Write the linear regression equation to predict *zhusbedu* from *zwifeduc*. (Instead of displaying 0 for the intercept, SPSS displays a very small number. For example, SPSS might display 15E–19, which means 15 times 10^{-19}. The correct value to use in your equation is 0.)

   b. What's the relationship between the slope and the multiple R?

   c. Write the linear regression equation to predict *zwifeduc* from *zhusbedu*. How does that compare to the equation that predicts *zhubedu* from *zwifeduc*?

   d. Summarize what you learned about the relationship of the slope and correlation coefficient when both the dependent and independent variables are in standardized form.

5. Now let's look at the relationship between husband's education and wife's education separately for couples in which the wife is employed full time (variable *wifeft* equals 1) and in which the wife is not employed full time (*wifeft* equals 0).

   a. Use the Graphs menu to make the appropriate scatterplot using *wifeft* as the Set Markers by variable.

   b. Edit the chart so that separate regression lines are drawn for the two types of couples. Print separate R^2 values as well.

   c. Does there seem to be a linear relationship between husband's and wife's education for both groups of couples? What is the correlation coefficient between husband's and wife's education for couples in which the wife is employed full time? For couples in which the wife is not employed full time?

6. Select full-time workers only (variable *wrkstat* equals 1). Use the Graphs menu to obtain a plot of hours worked last week (*hrs1*) with education (*educ*). Set the markers by the value of *sex*. Edit the chart to draw regression lines and display R^2 for the subgroups (males and females) and for all cases combined. What can you conclude from the plot?

7. Use the Bivariate Correlations procedure to find all pairs of correlation coefficients between mother's education, father's education, respondent's education, and spouse's education (variables *maeduc, paeduc, educ,* and *speduc*).

   a. What is the correlation coefficient between a person's years of education and their spouse's years of education? Why isn't this the same correlation coefficient as that between husband's and wife's education?

   b. What proportion of the variability in father's education can be explained by mother's education?

   c. Discuss the statement "Father's education is a much more powerful predictor of the educational attainment of children than is mother's education."

Use the *salary.sav* data file to answer the following questions:

8. Use the Graphs menu to make a scatterplot of current salary on the *y*-axis against beginning salary (variables *salnow* and *salbeg*). Identify the points based on gender.

  a. Edit the chart to include the regression line and R^2 for the entire sample. Does the relationship appear to be linear? What proportion of variability in current salaries is "explained" by beginning salary? From the plot estimate the equation for the regression line to predict current salary from beginning salary.

  b. Edit the chart to show separate regression lines for males and females. Does the relationship between current salary and beginning salary appear to be different for males and females?

9. Use the Regression procedure to estimate the least-squares regression line to predict current salary from beginning salary. Write the equation. For a person with a beginning salary of $12,000, what would you predict for the current salary? If the actual current salary is $14,000, what is the residual?

10. Rerun the analysis in question 9 to predict beginning salary from current salary. Do you get the same results? Why not?

11. Use the Descriptives procedure to standardize current salary and beginning salary. Rerun the regression model in question 9 using the standardized variables. What's the relationship between the slope and the correlation coefficient?

12. Use the Bivariate Correlations procedure to calculate Pearson correlation coefficients between beginning salary, current salary, job seniority, work experience, and age (variables *salbeg, salnow, time, work,* and *age*). Which pair of variables is most strongly linearly related?

Use the *country.sav* data file to answer the following questions:

13. Plot female life expectancy against birthrate (variables *lifeexpf* and *birthrat*) for all countries in the data file. Edit the plot to include the regression line and R^2. What proportion of the variability in female life expectancy is "explained" by birthrate? How does this value compare to that from the data file with 15 countries used in this chapter?

14. What is the linear regression equation to predict female life expectancy from birthrate when all of the cases are used? Did the coefficients change much? Based on the regression model predict female life expectancy for a country with a birthrate of 20 per 1000 population.

15. Plot male life expectancy (variable *lifeexpm*) against female life expectancy. Edit the chart to draw the regression line and give R^2. Using point selection mode, identify any unusual countries.

  a. From the plot, estimate the intercept and slope of the regression equation. Compare them to the intercept and slope from the Regression procedure.

b. If male and female life expectancy were the same, write the regression equation to predict male life expectancy from female life expectancy.

c. If male life expectancy was exactly 75% of female life expectancy, write the corresponding regression equation.

d. What proportion of the variability in male life expectancy is "explained" by female life expectancy?

e. What's the correlation coefficient between male life expectancy and female life expectancy? Is the relationship positive or negative?

f. Based on the regression equation, what's the male life expectancy for a country with a female life expectancy of 60? For a country with a female life expectancy of 40? For a country with a female life expectancy of 35? What reservations do you have about predicting male life expectancy when female life expectancy is 35?

16. Plot female life expectancy against the number of phones per 100 people (variable *phone*).

a. Is the relationship between the two variables linear? Calculate the correlation coefficient between the two variables. Is it a reasonable summary of the relationship? Explain.

b. Plot female life expectancy against the natural log of the number of phones (variable *lnphone*). How would you characterize the relationship? Edit the chart to include the regression line and R^2. What proportion of the observed variability in female life expectancy is "explained" by the log of the number of phones?

c. Run the Regression procedure to estimate the slope and intercept of the regression line that predicts female life expectancy from the log of the number of phones.

Use the *schools.sav* data file to answer the following questions:

17. Plot ACT scores in 1993 (variable *act93*) and the percentage of students taking the ACT in 1993 (variable *pctact93*), using variable *medloinc* (whether a school is above or below the median in percentage of low income students) to set the markers. Edit the chart to include separate regression lines and R^2 for the two groups. Summarize your findings.

18. Look at the relationship between ACT scores (variable *act93*), percentage of low income students (*loinc93*), percentage of limited English proficiency students (*lep93*), and graduation rates (*grad93*). Describe the relationships you see. Based on the plots, which variable do you think is the best predictor of ACT scores?

Testing Regression Hypotheses

How can you test hypotheses about the population regression line based on the results you obtain in a sample?

- What is the population regression line?
- What assumptions do you have to make about the data to test hypotheses about the population regression line?
- How do you test the null hypothesis that the slope or the correlation coefficient is 0 in the population?
- What is the difference between the confidence interval for the mean prediction and the prediction interval for an individual case?

In Chapter 20, you summarized the relationship between two variables by fitting a regression line to the sample data. Often, however, you want to do more than that. You want to draw conclusions about the relationship of the two variables in the *population* from which the sample was selected. For example, you want to draw conclusions about the relationship between female life expectancy and birthrate not only for the 15 countries in your sample, but for all nations. In this chapter you'll learn how to test hypotheses about the population regression line.

The Population Regression Line

Whenever you test a hypothesis, you draw a conclusion about one or more populations based on results you've observed in a sample. For example, in previous chapters you tested a variety of hypotheses about population means based on sample results. You test regression hypotheses in the same way. You draw conclusions about the relationship of two variables in the population based on results you observed in a sample. If you observed the entire population, your regression line would be the "true" or population regression line. However, since you have only a sample from the population, you don't know the true slope and intercept. Instead, you estimate their values based on sample results.

▶ This chapter continues the linear regression analysis discussed in Chapter 20. For instructions on how to obtain the output shown, see "How to Obtain a Linear Regression" on p. 407 in that chapter.

Assumptions Needed for Testing Hypotheses

When you fit a regression line only to summarize the observed relationship between two variables, you must keep two questions in mind:

- Are the variables measured on at least an ordinal scale? It makes no sense to calculate a regression line between variables such as color preference and state of residence. If there is no meaningful order to the values of the variables, the slope and intercept are meaningless statistics.

- Does the relationship between the two variables appear to be linear? You shouldn't use a straight line regression if the data points fall on a curve. (Transforming a nonlinear relationship to a linear one is discussed in Chapter 22.)

If you want to test hypotheses about the population regression line, your data must satisfy additional assumptions. If these assumptions are met, the distributions of all possible sample values of the slope and intercept are normal. You can then easily determine whether observed values of the slope and intercept are "unusual."

- *All of the observations must be independent.* Inclusion of one case in your sample must not influence the inclusion of another case. If you obtain several pairs of values from the same case, you are violating the assumption of independence. For example, when studying the relationship between systolic blood pressure and age, if you measure the same person's blood pressure at three different ages, the observations are not independent.

- *For each value of the independent variable, the distribution of the values of the dependent variable must be normal.* You know that all countries with a birthrate of 13 don't have the same life expectancy. Instead, there is a distribution of life expectancies for each value of birthrate. This distribution must be normal.

- *The variance of the distribution of the dependent variable must be the same for all values of the independent variable.* The variance of the distribution of female life expectancy must be the same for all birthrates.

- *The relationship between the dependent and the independent variable must be linear in the population.* In other words, the means of the distributions of the dependent variable must fall on a straight line.

Figure 21.1 Linear regression assumptions

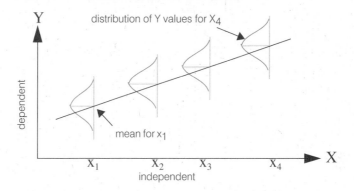

Figure 21.1 illustrates these assumptions. You see that for each value of the independent variable (x) there is a normal distribution of values of the dependent variable (y). The variances of all of the distributions are the same. The means of all of the distributions fall on the population regression line. In the next chapter, you'll learn how examine your data to see if they violate any of the required assumptions. You'll also see what you can do if the required assumptions are not met.

Testing Hypotheses

To see how to test hypotheses about the population regression line, consider again the life expectancy and birthrate data. Figure 21.2 contains the slope and intercept values calculated in the previous chapter. The slope and intercept values define the least-squares regression line that passes through your data points. These values can also be thought of in another way: they are your best guess or estimate of the unknown population values for the slope and the intercept. Based on these estimates, you can test hypotheses about the population values for the slope and intercept.

Figure 21.2 Linear regression of life expectancy and birthrate

This is the same
analysis described
in Chapter 20.
Select the variables
lifeexpf and birthrat
in the Linear
Regression dialog
box, as shown in
Figure 20.15.

In the Linear
Regression
Statistics dialog box,
select Confidence
intervals, as shown
in Figure 20.16.

In the Linear
Regression Save
New Variables
dialog box, select
S.E. of mean
predictions, as
shown in Figure
20.18.

```
* * * *   M U L T I P L E   R E G R E S S I O N   * * * *

Listwise Deletion of Missing Data

Equation Number 1    Dependent Variable..   LIFEEXPF   Female life expectancy 19

Block Number  1.  Method:  Enter       BIRTHRAT


Variable(s) Entered on Step Number
  1..    BIRTHRAT  Births per 1000 population, 1992


Multiple R              .96835
R Square                .93770
Adjusted R Square       .93290
Standard Error         2.53697

Analysis of Variance
                      DF      Sum of Squares      Mean Square
Regression             1          1259.26263      1259.26263
Residual              13            83.67070         6.43621

F =       195.65289       Signif F =  .0000


--------------------- Variables in the Equation ----------------------

Variable              B         SE B       95% Confdnce Intrvl B       Beta

BIRTHRAT          -.697318     .049853     -.805018     -.589618   -.968347
(Constant)       89.985172    1.764574    86.173042    93.797303


----------- in ------------

Variable          T   Sig T

BIRTHRAT      -13.988   .0000
(Constant)     50.995   .0000
```

The values that you obtained for the slope and intercept are based on one sample from the population. If you take a different sample from the same population, you will get different values for the slope and intercept. The distributions of all possible values of the slope and intercept are normal if the regression assumptions are met. The standard deviations of these distributions are called the standard error of the slope and the standard error of the intercept. They are estimated from the data. In Figure 21.2, the standard errors of the slope and intercept are shown in the column labeled *SE B*. (The estimate of the variance of the dependent variable for each value of the independent variable is the entry labeled *Standard Error* in Figure 21.2.)

Testing that the Slope Is Zero

When you calculate a linear regression, you want to test whether there is a linear relationship between the two variables in the population. This is equivalent to testing the null hypothesis that the population slope is 0. You must calculate the probability of obtaining a sample slope at least as large in absolute value as the one you observed, if the null hypothesis is true. As always, you reject the null hypothesis if this probability, the observed significance level, is small.

In this example, the sample slope is –0.70 and its standard error is 0.05, so the value for the t statistic is –0.70/0.05, which is –14. (You use the t distribution, since the distribution of the sample slopes is normal and the standard error is not known but is estimated from the sample.) The sample slope is 14 standard error units below the hypothesized value of 0. Since this is a most unlikely event (the observed significance level is less than 0.00005), you can reject the null hypothesis. There appears to be a linear relationship between 1992 female life expectancy and birthrate.

Does this mean that the straight line is the correct model for these data? Not necessarily. All it says is that a straight line is better than a model that does not include the independent variable. For example, if your data points fall on a curve but you fit a straight line to them, you may well reject the null hypothesis that the slope is 0. The values of the two variables may increase or decrease together, though not in a completely linear fashion. Always plot your data values to see if a straight line model is appropriate.

The test that the slope is 0 is the same as the test that the population correlation coefficient is 0. So, if you reject the null hypothesis that the slope is 0, you can also reject the null hypothesis that the population correlation coefficient is 0. This isn't surprising, since as you saw in Chapter 20, the correlation coefficient is the slope when both the independent and dependent variables are standardized to have a mean of 0 and a standard deviation of 1.

> *If one of the variables doesn't have a normal distribution for each value of the other variable, can I still test hypotheses about the population correlation coefficient?* In this situation, you may want to consider a nonparametric alternative to the Pearson correlation coefficient. For example, you can compute Spearman's correlation coefficient. It's the Pearson correlation coefficient when the data values for each variable are replaced by ranks. It measures the linear relationship between the two sets of ranks. You don't need the assumption of normality to use it. ■ ■ ■

You can also test the null hypothesis that the population value of the intercept is 0 using the same procedure as outlined for the slope. This test is of limited interest, however, since it simply tells you whether the regression line passes through the origin, which is the point where the values of both variables are 0. To find out whether there is a linear relationship between two variables, you test that the slope is 0.

Confidence Intervals for the Slope and Intercept

The sample values for the slope and intercept are your best guesses for the population values. However, as is always the case when you're estimating population values from a sample, it's most unlikely that the sample values are exactly on target. You can get an idea of a range of possible population values by calculating confidence intervals for the population slope and the intercept. All values that fall within these intervals are plausible population values. In Figure 21.2, you see that the 95% confidence interval for the population slope ranges from –0.805 to –0.590.

> *Where does that come from?* The 95% confidence interval for the slope is calculated just like the 95% confidence interval for the mean. Instead of the mean and the standard error of the mean, you substitute the slope and the standard error of the slope. For example, the lower limit of the 95% confidence interval for the slope is $-0.697 - 2.16 \times 0.05$. (2.16 is the t value with 13 degrees of freedom, which has 2.5% of the area to the right of it, and 0.05 is the standard error of the slope.) Similarly, the upper limit is $-0.697 + 2.16 \times 0.05$. ■ ■ ■

Notice that the 95% confidence interval does not include the value 0. The 95% confidence interval will include 0 only if the observed significance level for the test that the slope is 0 is greater than 0.05. You can't reject the null hypothesis that the population slope is any of the values within the confidence interval. (Recall that the same relationship was true for testing hypotheses about means.)

Predicting Life Expectancy

In Chapter 20, you used the regression equation to predict values for life expectancy based on birthrates. To predict female life expectancy, use the equation

predicted life expectancy $= 89.99 - 0.697 \times$ birthrate   **Equation 21.1**

For a country with a birthrate of 30 per 1000 population,

predicted life expectancy $= 89.99 - 0.697 \times 30 = 69.08$ years

Equation 21.2

Do you have absolute confidence in this prediction? Of course not. First of all, you know that if you take another sample of countries, you would get slightly different estimates of the slope and intercept. You also know that all countries with birthrates of 30 don't have the same life expectancy. All kinds of values are possible. To make your prediction more useful, you must estimate the variability associated with it. If you know that for a birthrate of 30, the range of plausible values for life expectancy is from 40 to 100, you know that your prediction is pretty useless. On the other hand, if the range of values is from 65 to 73, your estimate is more useful.

Predicting Means and Individual Observations

Before you can estimate the variability of your predicted value, you must decide which of two types of predictions you are interested in making. Do you want to predict the average life expectancy for females for *all* countries with a birthrate of 30? Or do you want to predict the life expectancy for a particular country such as Morocco, which has a birthrate of 30? In both cases, the predicted value is the same; what differs is the variability.

In previous chapters, you saw that means vary less than individual observations. So, you shouldn't be surprised that you can predict the average life expectancy for all countries with the same birthrate with less variability than you can predict the life expectancy for an individual country. When you predict the mean, you just worry about how much the predicted mean differs from the population mean for that birthrate. When you predict an individual case, you also have to worry about how much the individual case differs from the predicted mean for that birthrate.

Consider the unlikely situation when your sample and population regression lines are identical. For each birthrate, you can predict the mean life expectancy values perfectly, but you still can't predict values for individual countries perfectly. That's because the values for individual countries don't fall exactly on the regression line—only the average values for countries with the same birthrate do.

Whether you are predicting the value for the mean or for an individual case, the variability of the prediction also depends on the values of the independent variable. Predictions are most stable for values of the independent variable close to the sample mean. That's because the regression line always passes through the point corresponding to the mean of the dependent variable and the mean of the independent variable. Different samples from the same population don't change the predicted value as much for points close to the mean as they do for points farther away. As the distance from the mean increases, so does the variability associated with the prediction. For the 15 countries in your sample, the average birthrate is 32.87. So, you would expect the variability of the predicted value to be smallest for birthrates close to 33.

Standard Error of the Predicted Mean

Figure 21.3 is a plot of the standard error of the predicted mean life expectancy for different values of birthrate.

Figure 21.3 Plot of standard error of predicted mean

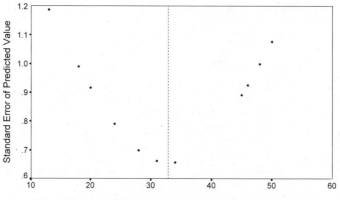

Births per 1000 population, 1992

You can obtain scatterplots using the Graphs menu, as described in Chapter 9. Select the variables birthrat and sep_1 in the Simple Scatterplot dialog box.

The variable sep_1 is created by the Regression procedure. See "Linear Regression Save: Creating New Variables" on p. 411 in Chapter 20.

The vertical line at 32.9 is the average birthrate for all cases. You see that the standard error is smallest at the mean. The farther birthrates are from the sample mean, the larger the standard error of the predicted means.

? *How do you compute the standard error of the predicted mean?*
You can calculate the standard error of the predicted mean female life expectancy for all countries with a birthrate of 30 (denoted as X_0) using the following formula:

$$S_{\hat{Y}} = S\sqrt{\frac{1}{N} + \frac{\left(X_0 - \bar{X}\right)^2}{(N-1)\,S_X^2}} = 2.54\sqrt{\frac{1}{15} + \frac{(30 - 32.87)^2}{14\,(13.60)^2}} = 0.67$$

In the formula, S is the standard error of the estimate, N is the number of cases in the sample, $\bar{X}$ is the mean and S_X^2 is the variance of the independent variable. The standard error of the estimate is your best guess for the standard deviation of the dependent variable for any value of the independent variable. It's simply the standard deviation of the residuals, using the number of cases minus 2 in the denominator instead of the number of cases minus 1. You can find it in Figure 21.2. ■ ■ ■

Confidence Intervals for the Predicted Means

Once you have the standard error of the predicted mean value, you can calculate a confidence interval for the population mean for any value of the independent variable.

In Figure 21.4, you see a plot of the data, the regression line and the 95% confidence interval for the mean predictions. As you expect, the confidence interval is narrowest for values close to 32.9, the sample mean. It grows wider as the distance from the average birthrate increases.

Figure 21.4 Data, regression line, and 95% confidence intervals

To obtain this scatterplot, select the variables lifeexpf and birthrat in the Simple Scatterplot dialog box.

To display the regression line and mean confidence intervals, see Figure 9.21.

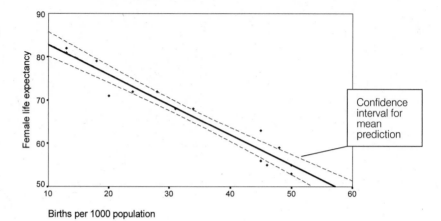

Consider a birthrate of 30. The predicted value for the average female life expectancy for countries with a birthrate of 30 is 69.08 years. The standard error of the mean prediction is 0.67. The 95% confidence interval for the mean prediction is from 67.62 years to 70.51 years. You calculate the 95% confidence interval for the mean prediction the same way you've calculated other confidence intervals. The lower limit is $67.62 - 2.16 \times 0.67$; the upper limit is $67.62 + 2.16 \times 0.67$. (2.16 is the t value with 13 degrees of freedom, which has 2.5% of the area to the right of it.)

Although you don't know if this particular confidence interval includes the population value for the average female life expectancy in 1992 for countries with a birthrate of 30, you do know that 95 times out of 100, the 95% confidence interval will include the true population mean.

Prediction Intervals for Individual Cases

Now consider what's involved in predicting the female life expectancy for Morocco, a country with a birthrate of 30. Your predicted value is the same as before: 69.08 years. What changes is the standard error of the prediction. The standard error of the individual prediction is

$$S_{ind} = \sqrt{S^2 + S_{\hat{Y}}^2} = \sqrt{2.54^2 + 0.67^2} = 2.63$$

Equation 21.3

where S is the standard error of the estimate and $S_{\hat{Y}}$ is the standard error of the mean prediction.

The standard error of the individual prediction depends both on how much the mean prediction varies and how much the values of the dependent variable vary for a particular value of the independent variable. When you predict an individual observation, you have two sources of error: the regression line differs from the actual population line and an individual observation differs from the mean. The standard error of the mean prediction takes care of the first source of variability, and the standard error of the estimate takes care of the second. (For large sample sizes, the standard error of an individual prediction will be equal to the standard error of the estimate. That's why it's called the standard error of the estimate.)

For an individual prediction, you can calculate an interval closely akin to a confidence interval. It's called a **prediction interval.** This is a range of values that you expect to include the actual value for a particular case. (Confidence intervals are for population values like the mean, slope or intercept, not for values of individual cases.) A 95% prediction interval is calculated similarly to a 95% confidence interval for the mean prediction. The standard error of the individual prediction is used in place of the standard error of the mean prediction.

The 95% prediction interval for Morocco is from 63.40 years to 74.73 years. The true female life expectancy for Morocco is 67 years, so the true value falls within the prediction interval. As you would expect, the 95% prediction interval for Morocco is wider than the 95% confidence interval for the predicted mean value for all countries with a birthrate of 30 (67.62 years to 70.51 years).

That's because the standard error of the individual prediction is always larger than the standard error of the mean prediction.

Figure 21.5 Prediction intervals and confidence intervals

To display the regression line and confidence intervals, see Figure 9.21.

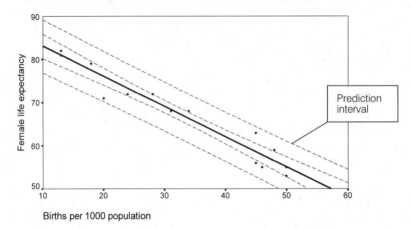

Births per 1000 population

Figure 21.5 illustrates much of what we've been talking about in this chapter. You see the 15 data points and the least-squares regression line. The two bands closest to the regression line show the 95% confidence intervals for the predicted mean. The distance between the two bands is narrowest at 32.87, the mean birthrate for all cases. You see that quite a few of the data points don't fall within these bands. That's because the interval is for predicting mean values, not values for individual cases. The prediction intervals, shown by the two outermost bands, are much wider than the confidence intervals. In this example, all of the observed data points fall within the prediction intervals, though that need not be the case.

Summary

How can you test hypotheses about the population regression line based on the results you obtain in a sample?

- The population regression line is the line that describes the relationship between the dependent variable and the independent variable in the population.
- To draw conclusions about the population regression line, you must assume that for each value of the independent variable, the distribution of values of the dependent variable is normal with the same variance. The means of these distributions must all fall on the population regression line.
- The confidence interval for the mean prediction provides you with a range of values that you expect will include the population mean value. The prediction interval for an individual case provides you with a range of values that you expect will contain the observed value for a particular case.

What's Next?

In this chapter, you learned about the assumptions necessary for testing hypotheses about a population regression line. You also learned how to test hypotheses and compute confidence intervals for commonly used regression statistics and predicted values. In Chapter 22, you'll see how to examine your data to see if they violate these assumptions.

How to Obtain a Bivariate Correlation

This section shows how to obtain Pearson correlation coefficients and two different nonparametric correlation coefficients from SPSS using the Bivariate Correlations procedure. The Pearson correlation coefficient is appropriate for variables measured at the interval level, while the Kendall and Spearman coefficients assume only an ordinal level of measurement.

In addition, the Correlations command can:

- Display full or condensed information about statistical significance.
- Display univariate statistics, cross-product deviations, and covariances.
- Compute one- or two-tailed observed significance levels.

▶ To open the Bivariate Correlations dialog box (see Figure 21.6), from the menus choose:

Statistics
　Correlate ▶
　　Bivariate...

Figure 21.6　Bivariate Correlations dialog box

Select life and degree to obtain the Pearson and Spearman coefficients shown in Figure 19.8

Select coefficients desired

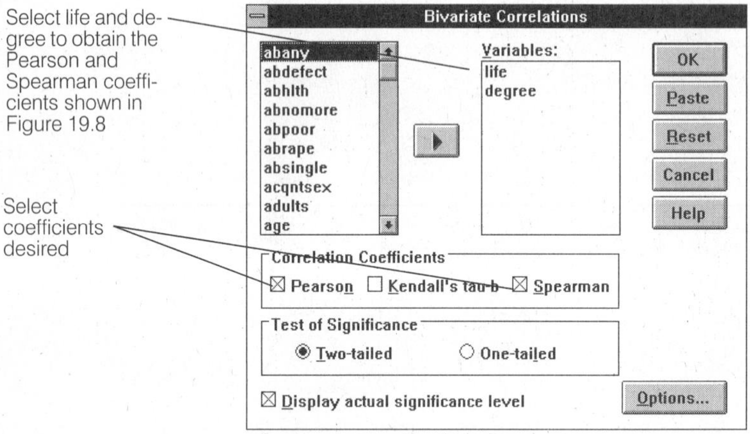

▶ In the Correlations dialog box, select two or more numeric variables and move them into the Variable(s) list.

This produces a matrix of correlation coefficients for all pairs of the selected variables.

Correlation Coefficients. At least one type of correlation must be selected. You can choose one or more of the following:

Pearson. Describes the strength of the linear association between variables measured at the interval level.

Kendall's tau-b. Describes the strength of the association between variables measured at the ordinal level.

Spearman. A rank-order correlation coefficient which also measures association at the ordinal level. This is simply the Pearson correlation when the data values are replaced by ranks.

Test of Significance. Select one of the alternatives to obtain two-tailed or one-tailed tests of statistical significance.

Display actual significance level. Normally, SPSS calculates and displays the observed significance level. If you deselect the Display actual significance level option, significance levels are not displayed, but correlations significant at the 0.05 level are marked with an asterisk, and those significant at the 0.01 level with two asterisks.

Options: Additional Statistics and Missing Data

In the Correlations dialog box, click on Options to obtain additional statistics or to control the treatment of missing data (see Figure 21.7).

Figure 21.7 Bivariate Correlations Options dialog box

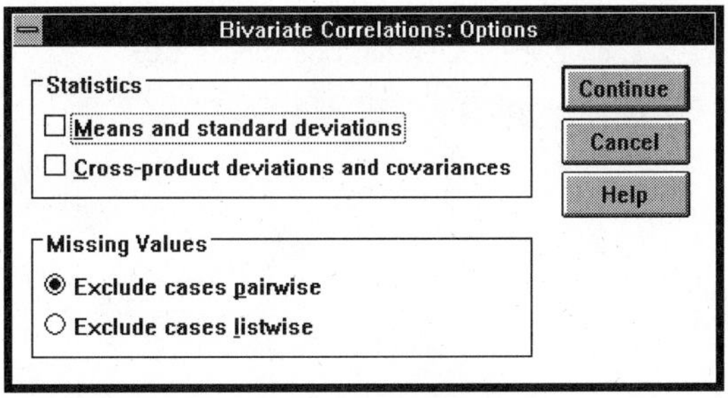

Statistics. The optional statistics are:

> **Means and standard deviations.** Displayed for the variables in the correlation matrix.
>
> **Cross-product deviations and covariances.** Displayed for each pair of variables.

Missing Values. The available treatments of missing data are:

> **Exclude cases pairwise.** This computes each correlation coefficient using all of the cases with valid data for the two variables involved.
>
> **Exclude cases listwise.** This computes each correlation coefficient using only the cases that have valid data for all variables in the matrix, so that the coefficients in the matrix are all based on the same cases.

How to Obtain a Partial Correlation

This section shows how to obtain partial correlation coefficients among a group of variables from SPSS, while controlling for one or more additional variables. SPSS first calculates a matrix of zero-order Pearson correlation coefficients among all variables, including the control variables. It then uses these zero-order coefficients to compute the matrix of partial correlation coefficients among variables in the Variables list, controlling for all of the specified control variables.

▶ To open the Partial Correlations dialog box (see Figure 21.8), from the menus choose:

Statistics
  Correlate ▶
    Partial...

Figure 21.8 Partial Correlations dialog box

Select the variables shown to obtain the partial correlations output shown in Figure 23.6.

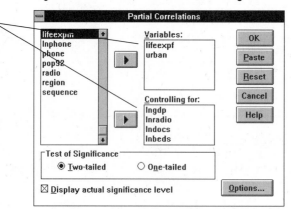

▶ Select two or more numeric variables and move them into the Variables list.

▶ Move one or more numeric control variables into the Controlling for list.

SPSS calculates and displays the observed significance level. If you deselect the Display actual significance level option, significance levels are not displayed, but correlations significant at the 0.05 level are marked with one asterisk, and those significant at the 0.01 level with two asterisks.

Test of Significance. Select one of the alternatives to obtain two-tailed or one-tailed tests of statistical significance.

Options: Additional Statistics and Missing Data

In the Partial Correlations dialog box, click on the Options button to obtain additional statistics or to control the treatment of missing data (see Figure 21.9).

Figure 21.9 Partial Correlations Options dialog box

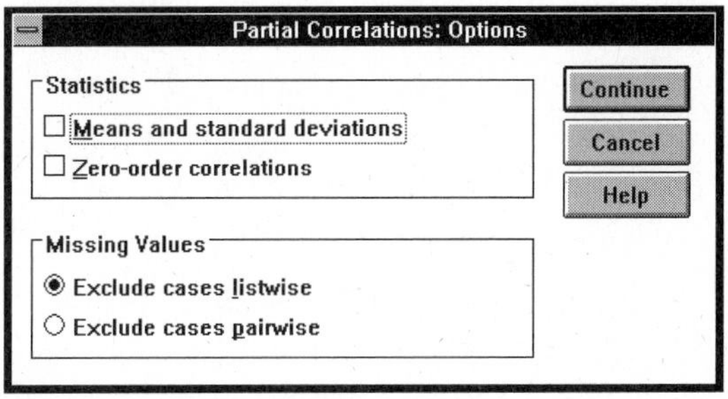

Statistics. You can choose from the following options:

Means and standard deviations. Displays statistics for the variables in both lists.

Zero-order correlation matrix. This is the matrix from which partial correlations are computed.

Missing Values. The available treatments of missing data are:

Exclude cases listwise. This computes each correlation coefficient using only the cases that have valid data for all variables in both variable lists, so that all partial correlation coefficients in the matrix are based on the same set of cases.

Exclude cases pairwise. This computes each zero-order correlation using all of the cases with valid data for the two variables involved. This uses as much of the data as possible, but means that the partial correlation coefficients may not be based on the same set of cases.

Exercises

Statistical Concepts

1. As a personnel manager, you're interested in studying the relationship between salary and years on the job for sales associates. You're also interested in whether males and females are similarly reimbursed. You have obtained salary and experience data from a sample of 1000 associates.

   a. Explain how you would go about analyzing the data.

   b. If the years of experience were less than 5 for all your associates, what difficulties do you see with drawing conclusions about salaries for employees with more than 5 years of experience?

2. You are reading an article that presents the following equation for the relationship of weekly dollars spent for restaurant meals and total family income:

   restaurant dollars = 2.1 + 0.12 (weekly income)

   The observed significance level for the slope is reported as 0.03.

   a. From the value of the slope, can you tell how well the model fits the data?

   b. Interpret the observed significance level reported for the equation.

   c. If the value of the slope in the regression model is tripled, does that mean that the model fits the data better? Does it mean that the observed significance level will necessarily be smaller?

   d. Is it possible to reject the null hypothesis that the slope is 0 and not reject the null hypothesis that there is no linear relationship between the two variables?

3. You obtain the following regression statistics for the relationship between defect rate and volume at one of your plants. You have a random sample of results from 160 shifts at the plant.

```
Multiple R              .74041
R Square                .54821
Adjusted R Square       .54535
Standard Error         4.92336

Analysis of Variance
                    DF      Sum of Squares      Mean Square
Regression           1         4647.12423       4647.12423
Residual           158         3829.83867         24.23949

F =    191.71712       Signif F =  .0000


------------------ Variables in the Equation ------------------

Variable            B         SE B      Beta        T    Sig T

VOLUME          .027031     .001952   .740410    13.846  .0000
(Constant)   -97.073120    7.818726            -12.415  .0000
```

a. What are the null and alternative hypotheses?

b. What is the population of interest? What is the sample?

c. On the basis of the output, what can you conclude about the null hypothesis?

d. Can you reject the null hypothesis that the slope is 0?

e. Can you reject the null hypothesis that there is no linear relationship between the dependent and independent variables?

f. Can you reject the null hypothesis that the population correlation coefficient is 0?

g. What would you predict the defect rate to be on a day when the volume is 4200 units? What would you predict the average defect rate to be for all days with production volumes of 4200? What problems do you see with this prediction?

h. In what way do the two estimates in question 3g differ?

4. Here are two equations for predicting sales volume:

Predicted sales = 120 + 6 (Advertising Budget)

Predicted sales = 50 + 20 (Sales Force)

Which of the two equations is the better predictor of sales? Explain your answer.

5. A marketing analyst writes his own regression analysis program. The program produces the following regression line and 95% confidence interval for the mean prediction. Do you think the new program is producing correct results? Why or why not?

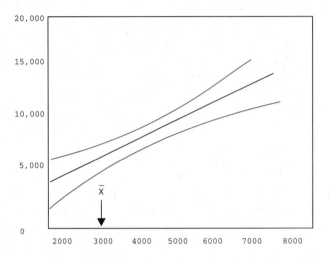

6. Fill in the missing entries in the following output :

```
------------------ Variables in the Equation ------------------

Variable                B        SE B       Beta      T   Sig T

X                  1.700000   .822600    .766420          .1307
(Constant)                    2.728250            1.576  .2131
```

Would you reject the null hypothesis that there is no linear relationship between X and the dependent variable? On what do you base your decision?

Data Analysis

Use the *gss.sav* data file to answer the following questions:

1. Run a regression equation to predict father's education from mother's education (variables *paeduc* and *maeduc*). Include 95% confidence intervals for the slope and intercept. Save the standard error of the mean prediction.

   a. Write the linear regression equation to predict father's education from mother's education.

   b. Based on the results of the linear regression, can you reject the null hypothesis that there is no linear relationship between father's and mother's education?

c. What proportion of the variability in mother's education is explained by father's education?

d. How can you tell from the slope if the correlation coefficient between the two variables is positive or negative?

e. What can you conclude about the population correlation coefficient based on what you know about the slope? Can you reject the null hypothesis that the population correlation coefficient is 0?

f. Based on the 95% confidence interval for the slope, can you reject the null hypothesis that the population value for the slope is 1? Explain.

2. Based on the regression equation developed in question 1, answer the following:

a. What do you predict for father's education for a person who has a mother with 12 years of education?

b. What do you predict for average father's education for all people who have a mother with 12 years of education?

c. Using the Graphs menu, plot the standard error of the mean prediction (*sep_1*) against the independent variable. For what value of the independent variable is the standard error of the mean prediction smallest? Why?

d. Using the Graphs menu, plot father's education against mother's education. Edit the chart so that it shows the points, the regression line, and the 95% confidence interval for the mean prediction. Explain what the confidence interval for the mean prediction tells you.

e. Most of the data points do not fall within the 95% confidence interval for the mean prediction. Why is that?

f. Edit the chart to remove the 95% confidence intervals for the mean prediction. Instead, plot the 95% prediction interval. What is a 95% prediction interval? Why is it so much wider than the 95% confidence interval? Explain why most of your data points fall within this interval.

3. Develop a regression model to predict hours worked (variable *hrs1*) for full-time employees (*wrkstat* equals 1) based on their years of education (variable *educ*).

a. Write the regression equation.

b. Test the null hypothesis that the slope is 0.

c. Determine the proportion of the variability in the dependent variable that is explained by the independent variable.

d. Graph your results. Include 95% confidence intervals for the mean prediction.

4. Is there a linear relationship between the age at which a woman first marries (variable *agewed*) and her mother's educational attainment (variable *maeduc*)? Analyze this question and summarize your findings.

5. Develop a regression equation that predicts the number of hours of television viewing (variable *tvhours*) from some other characteristic, such as education, income in dollars, and so forth. Summarize your findings. Be sure to make appropriate plots.

Use the *salary.sav* data file to answer the following questions:

6. Estimate the regression model that predicts current salary (variable *salnow*) from beginning salary (variable *salbeg*). Save the standard error of the predicted mean.

   a. Can you reject the null hypothesis that there is no linear relationship between the two variables?

   b. Based on the 95% confidence interval for the slope, can you reject the null hypothesis that the population value for the slope is 2? Explain.

7. Estimate the standard deviation of current salary for each value of beginning salary.

8. Plot the standard error of the predicted mean against the values of beginning salary. At what point is the standard error the smallest? Why?

9. Using the Graphs menu, plot the points, the regression line, and the 95% confidence interval for the mean prediction. Compare this to a plot with the 95% prediction intervals for an individual observation. Explain why the 95% prediction intervals are wider than the 95% confidence intervals for the mean.

Use the *country.sav* data file to answer the following questions:

10. Estimate the regression equation that predicts male life expectancy (variable *lifeexpm*) from female life expectancy (variable *lifeexpf*). Obtain 95% confidence intervals for the slope and the intercept. Save the standard error of the mean prediction.

   a. Can you reject the null hypothesis that there is no linear relationship between female life expectancy and male life expectancy?

   b. What is the 95% confidence interval for the population slope? Based on it, can you reject the null hypothesis that the population value for the slope is 0?

   c. What is the correlation coefficient between female life expectancy and male life expectancy? Is it positive or negative?

   d. When female life expectancy increases by one year, how much does male life expectancy increase?

11. Plot the standard error of the mean prediction against the values of female life expectancy. For what value of female life expectancy is the standard error of the mean prediction smallest? What does the value correspond to? What can you conclude from the plot?

12. Plot male life expectancy against female life expectancy. Include the regression line and the 95% confidence interval for the mean prediction.

    a. Explain why it doesn't bother you that many of the observed data points are not within the confidence interval. Why is the 95% confidence interval for the mean prediction so narrow?

    b. What average value for male life expectancy would you predict for all countries with a female life expectancy of 65?

    c. What male life expectancy would you predict for Botswana, a country with a female life expectancy of 65?

    d. Do you think your prediction for Botswana or for all countries with an observed female life expectancy of 65 is closer to the truth?

    e. Edit the chart to include the 95% prediction intervals. Explain why these are wider than the corresponding 95% confidence intervals for the mean prediction.

13. Repeat question 10 using two variables of your choice from the *country.sav* file.

Analyzing Residuals

How can you tell if the assumptions necessary for hypothesis testing in regression are violated?

- How can you use residuals to check the assumptions of independence, linearity, normality, and constant variance?
- What can you do if one or more of the assumptions are violated?
- What are influential points, and why are they important?

When you begin studying the relationship between two variables, you usually don't know whether your data violate the assumptions needed for regression analysis. You don't know whether there is a linear relationship between the two variables, much less whether the distribution of the dependent variable is normal and has the same variance for all values of the independent variable. An important part of regression analysis is checking whether the required assumptions of linearity, normality, constant variance, and independence of observations are met.

When you are fitting models to data, residuals play a very important role. By examining the distribution of the residuals and their relationships to other variables, you can detect departures from the regression assumptions. In this chapter, you'll examine the residuals from the linear regression model you developed in Chapter 20.

▶ This chapter primarily analyzes the residuals from the linear regression described in Chapter 20, which uses the *cntry15.sav* data file. To obtain the output shown, you must first run the analysis described in that chapter and save residuals as described in "Linear Regression Save: Creating New Variables" on p. 411.

Residuals

As you saw in Chapter 20, a residual is what's left over after the model is fit. It's the difference between the observed value of the dependent variable and the value predicted by the regression line. If the assumptions required for a regression analysis are met, the residuals should have the following characteristics:

- They should be approximately normally distributed.
- Their variance should be the same for all values of the independent variable.
- They should show no pattern when plotted against the predicted values.
- Successive residuals should be approximately independent.

Figure 22.1 Residuals from linear regression

To create these variables, run the regression described in Chapter 20 and save new variables, as shown in Figure 20.18.

To obtain the casewise listing shown at the right, from the menus choose:

Statistics
  Summarize ▶
    List Cases...

COUNTRY	BIRTHRAT	LIFEEXPF	PRE_1	RES_1	ZRE_1	SRE_1
Somalia	46	55	57.90856	-2.90856	-1.14647	-1.23146
Tanzania	50	55	55.11929	-.11929	-.04702	-.05193
Zambia	48	59	56.51393	2.48607	.97994	1.06610
Zaire	45	56	58.60588	-2.60588	-1.02716	-1.09715
Algeria	31	68	68.36833	-.36833	-.14518	-.15039
Namibia	45	63	58.60588	4.39412	1.73204	1.85005
Burkina Faso	50	53	55.11929	-2.11929	-.83536	-.92252
Cuba	18	79	77.43346	1.56654	.61749	.67055
Equador	28	72	70.46028	1.53972	.60691	.63132
North Korea	24	72	73.24955	-1.24955	-.49254	-.51832
Mongolia	34	68	66.27637	1.72363	.67940	.70344
Thailand	20	71	76.03882	-5.03882	-1.98616	-2.13011
Turkey	28	72	70.46028	1.53972	.60691	.63132
France	13	82	80.92004	1.07996	.42569	.48171
Netherlands	13	81	80.92004	.07996	.03152	.03566

Predicted values

Standardized residuals

Studentized residuals

In this chapter, you'll learn how to check your residuals to see if they violate any of the criteria just mentioned. But first, you'll learn about several types of residuals that you can use when searching for problems. These residuals are all modifications of the usual residual. Their advantage is that they make it easier for you to spot problems.

Standardized Residuals

Figure 22.1 contains observed and predicted female life expectancies, as well as residuals, for the countries you used to develop your regression model. You see that Equador has an observed female life expectancy of 72 years, while the regression model predicts 70.46. The residual for Ecuador is therefore +1.54 years. Since the residual is positive, it means that the observed life expectancy for Ecuador is larger than that predicted by your model. A negative residual for Ecuador would tell you that the observed life expectancy was smaller than the predicted value.

Without looking at the residuals for the other cases, can you tell if Equador's residual is large or small compared with the other countries? The answer is no. You really can't judge the relative size of a residual by looking at its value alone (just like you can't tell whether you did brilliantly or poorly on a test without knowing how the rest of the class did).

It's easier to determine the relative magnitudes of residuals if you standardize them so that they have a mean of 0 and a standard deviation of 1. (Remember from Chapter 5 that a standard score—Z score—tells you how many standard deviations above or below the mean an observation falls.) To calculate the standardized residual, you divide the observed residual by the estimated standard deviation of the residuals. (This is the entry labeled *Standard Error* in Figure 20.8. For this example, it's 2.54.) There's no need to subtract the mean, since the mean of the residuals is 0 when an intercept term is in the model. Standardized residuals have a standard deviation of slightly less than 1, since the standard error of the estimate is a little larger than the sample standard deviation of the residuals.

If the distribution of residuals is approximately normal, you know that about 95% of the standardized residuals should be between –2 and +2. Ninety-nine percent of the standardized residuals should be between –2.58 and +2.58. Cases with standardized residuals outside this range are unusual. If there are many cases with standardized residuals larger than 2, that may indicate that the model fits the data poorly. Of course, even if the model fits well, you expect to see about 5% of the cases with standardized residuals greater than 2 in absolute value.

For Equador, the standardized residual is 1.54/2.54, which is 0.61. That's a little more than one half of a standard deviation above the mean. It's not at all unusual. In Figure 22.1, you see that only Thailand has a standardized residual that is close to 2 in absolute value.

Studentized Residuals

When you compute a standardized residual, all of the observed residuals are divided by the same number. However, in Chapter 20, you saw that the variability of the predicted value is not constant for all points but depends on the value of the independent variable. Cases with values of the independent variable close to the sample mean have smaller variability for the predicted value than cases with values far removed from the mean. The **Studentized residual** takes into account the differences in variability from point to point. You calculate it by dividing the observed residual by an estimate of the standard deviation of the residual at that point. The Studentized residual makes it easier to see violations of the regression assumptions, so it's preferred to the standardized residuals.

If the regression assumptions are met, you can use the t distribution, with the degrees of freedom equal to the number of cases minus the number of coefficients (including the intercept), to calculate the probability of observing a Studentized residual at least as large in absolute value as the one observed. For example, the probability of observing a Studentized residual as large in absolute value as that for Thailand (–2.13) is approximately 0.053. So, the residual for Thailand is somewhat unusual, but not extreme enough to cause real concern.

When you single out the largest residuals in a sample to see if they are unlikely, you should multiply the probabilities from the t distribution by the number of residuals in your sample. This adjusts for the fact that you are looking at many residuals. It prevents you from calling too many residuals unlikely. If the corrected probability is less than 0.05, you can be confident that the residual is unlikely. If you multiply the observed probability for Thailand by 15, Thailand's residual is not at all unusual.

How can I get these probabilities from SPSS? First, you have to save the Studentized residuals from the regression. You do this by selecting Studentized residuals in the Linear Regression Save New Variables dialog box. They are automatically assigned a name such as *sre_1*. Then you use the Compute dialog box to compute a new variable that contains the probability for each case (see "Example: Cumulative Distribution Function" on p. 553 in Appendix B for an example of how to compute a cumulative distribution function.). The formula is:

$$2*(1-cdf.t(abs(sre\_1),13))$$

This will give you the desired probabilities using a t distribution with 13 degrees of freedom. To use the formula for another data set, you must replace the number 13 with the appropriate degrees of freedom. Use the degrees of freedom for the Residual Mean Square in the ANOVA table. ▪ ▪ ▪

See "Linear Regression Save: Creating New Variables" on p. 411 for information on how to save residuals.

See Appendix B for instructions on computing the CDF function.

Checking for Normality

If the regression assumptions are met, the distribution of the ordinary residuals and the standardized residuals should be approximately normal. For samples larger than 30 cases or so, the distribution of Studentized residuals should be normal as well. (For smaller samples, the distribution of the Studentized residuals should be a *t* distribution, which has more observations in the tails than the normal distribution.)

The first step for assessing normality is to make a stem-and-leaf plot or a histogram of the residuals. (The distributions of the residuals and standardized residuals will look the same, since you're dividing all of the residuals by a constant to get standardized residuals.) From these displays, you can judge the shape of the distribution of the residuals as well as identify outlying values. Figure 22.2 is a stem-and-leaf plot of the standardized residuals.

Figure 22.2   Stem-and-leaf plot of standardized residuals

You can obtain stem-and-leaf plots using the Explore procedure, described in Chapter 7. Select the variable zre_1 in the Explore dialog box.

```
ZRE_1         Standardized Residual

Frequency     Stem &  Leaf

     3.00        -1 .  019
     4.00        -0 .  0148
     7.00         0 .  0466669
     1.00         1 .  7

 Stem width:   1.00000
 Each leaf:        1 case(s)
```

Nothing about the stem-and-leaf plot suggests that the data couldn't be a sample from a normal population. There are no extreme outlying values, and the distribution has a single peak that is more or less in the middle. When you have a small number of cases, it can be difficult to judge if the sample comes from a normal population. Small samples from a normal population don't necessarily look "normal." However, if the distribution is very asymmetrical, or if you have many outliers, the normality assumption is suspect.

Figure 22.3   Q-Q plot of standardized residuals

*You can obtain
normal probability
plots using the
Explore procedure.
(See Chapter 7.) In
the Explore Plots
dialog box, select
Normality plots with
tests.*

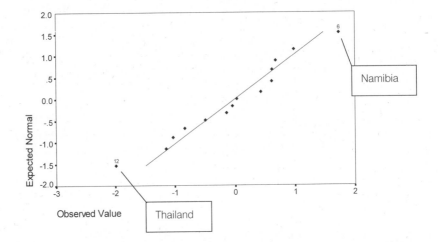

As you recall from Chapter 13, you can use special plots and statistical
tests to see if a sample comes from a normal population. Figure 22.3 is
a Q-Q plot of the standardized residuals. If the data are a sample from
a normal distribution, you expect the points to fall more or less on a
straight line. You see that the two largest residuals in absolute value
(Thailand and Namibia) are stragglers from the line. This means that
they're somewhat larger in absolute value than you would expect.

Figure 22.4   Detrended Q-Q plot of residuals

*You can obtain
detrended normal
probability plots
using the Explore
procedure. (See
Chapter 7.)*

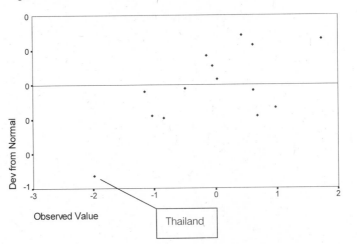

Figure 22.4 is a detrended normality plot. For each of the points in the Q-Q plot, it shows the distance from the observed point to the line. If your data are a sample from a normal population, the points in the detrended normal plot should fall randomly in a band around 0. Again, you see that the residual for Thailand sticks out.

If you look at the results of the statistical tests of normality in Figure 22.5, you see that there's not enough evidence to reject the assumption of normality. However, when the sample is small, the tests are not very powerful. That is, you often won't reject the hypothesis of normality even when it is incorrect. If your sample size is large, the tests of normality may lead you to reject the normality assumption based on small departures that won't affect the regression analysis. As long as the normality assumption is not badly violated, the results of regression analysis will not be seriously affected.

Figure 22.5   Tests of normality of residuals

You can obtain normality tests using the Explore procedure. (See Chapter 7.)

	Statistic	df	Significance
Shapiro-Wilks	.9707	15	.8306
K-S (Lilliefors)	.1071	15	> .2000

? *What should I do if there are large departures from normality?*
Several different regression problems can produce non-normal residuals. It's possible that the population distribution of the dependent variable is not normal. But it's also possible that the residuals appear to be non-normal because the regression model doesn't fit the data, or because the variance of the dependent variable is not constant over the values of the independent variable. Make sure that you have fixed any other known problems in your regression before you worry about the lack of normality of the residuals.

Once you've ruled out other problems as the cause for non-normality of the residuals, you can try to transform the values of the dependent variable. For example, if the distribution of residuals is not symmetric but has a tail toward larger values, you can try taking the log of the dependent variable, provided all of the values are positive. If the tail is toward smaller values, you can try squaring the values of the dependent variable. ■ ■ ■

Checking for Constant Variance

To check whether the variance of the dependent variable is the same for all values of the independent variable, you can plot the Studentized residuals against the predicted values. If the variance is constant, you won't see any pattern in the data points. That's the case in Figure 22.6. The residuals appear to be randomly scattered around a horizontal line through 0.

Figure 22.6   Studentized residuals versus predicted values

You can obtain scatterplots using the Graphs menu, described in Chapter 9. Select the variables sre_1 and pre_1 in the Scatterplot dialog box.

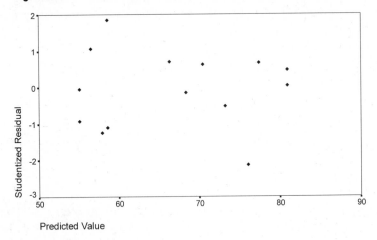

In Figure 22.7, you see a funnel shape. The variability of the residuals is increasing with increasing predicted values. That means the variance of the residuals is smaller for small values of the predicted dependent variable than for larger values.

Figure 22.7 Variance increasing with predicted values of the dependent variable

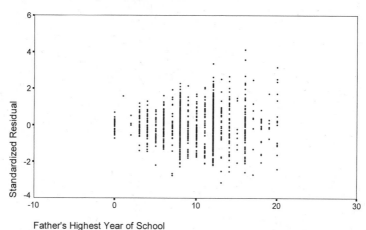

Father's Highest Year of School

That's not unusual, since the variability of the dependent variable often increases with the value of the independent variable. For example, if you are looking at the relationship between salary and years of education, you would expect to see more variability in MBA salaries than in those of high school graduates.

What should I do if the variance of the dependent variable appears not to be constant? If the variance of the dependent variable isn't constant, you can try transforming the values of the dependent variable and then going back and rerunning the regression using the transformed variable in place of the original variable. If the variance of the dependent variable increases linearly with values of the independent variable, and all values of the dependent variable are positive, try taking the square root of the dependent variable. If the standard deviation increases linearly with increasing values of the independent variable, try taking logs of the dependent variable. ∎ ∎ ∎

Checking Linearity

The first step of any regression analysis is plotting the dependent variable against the independent variable. You should fit a linear regression model only if the points cluster around a straight line. You can also evaluate the linearity assumption by plotting the Studentized residuals against the predicted values. If the relationship between the dependent variable and the independent variable is not linear, you will see a curve in the plot.

Figure 22.8 Female life expectancy and phones per 100

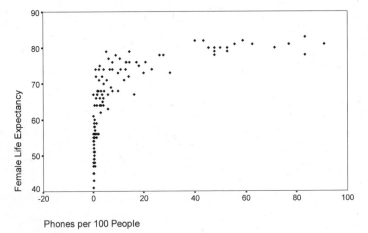

Figure 22.8 is a plot of female life expectancy against the number of phones per 100 people (from the larger data file of statistics on different countries in the world). The relationship between the two variables is not linear. If you run a linear regression with these two variables and then plot the Studentized residuals against the predicted values, you will see a strong nonlinear relationship between the residuals and the predicted values (see Figure 22.9).

Figure 22.9 Studentized residuals versus predicted values

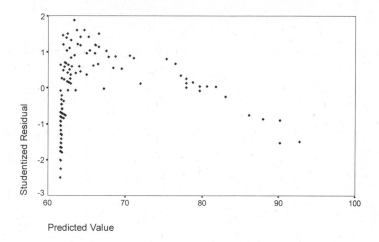

When the relationship between two variables isn't linear, you can sometimes transform the variables to make the relationship linear. For example, if you take the natural log of the number of phones per 100 people, you get the plot shown in Figure 22.10. The relationship between female life expectancy and the natural log of the number of phones per 100 people is now more or less linear.

Figure 22.10 Female life expectancy and natural log of phones per 100

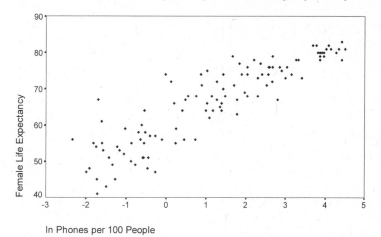

? *How do I decide what transformation to use?* Sometimes you might know the mathematical formula that relates two variables. In this case, you can use mathematics to figure out what transformation you need. This situation happens more often in the physical or biological sciences than in the social sciences. For example, if the equation that relates the dependent variable and the independent variable is

$$Y = AX^B$$

you can take the natural log of both sides of the equation and obtain the equation

$$\log(Y) = \log(A) + B \times \log(X)$$

There is now a linear relationship between the log of the dependent variable (Y) and the log of the independent variable (X). (Remember that $y = a + bx$ is the equation for a straight line.) If the relationship isn't known, you can choose a transformation by looking at the plot of the data. Often, a relationship appears to be nearly linear for part of the data but is curved for the rest. The log transformation is useful for "straightening out" a relationship when the values of the dependent variable increase more quickly than a linear model predicts. The square transformation may be helpful when the data points fall on a downward curve with the values of the dependent variable decreasing more quickly than a linear model predicts. ■ ■ ■

When you try to make a relationship linear, you can transform either the independent variable, the dependent variable, or both. If you transform only the independent variable, the distribution of the dependent variable doesn't change. If it was normally distributed with a constant variance for each value of the independent variable, it remains that way. However, if you transform the dependent variable, you change its distribution. For example, if you take logs of the dependent variable, the log of the dependent variable—not the original dependent variable—must be normally distributed with a constant variance. In other words, the regression assumptions must hold for the transformed variables you actually use in the regression equation.

Isn't transforming the data more or less cheating, or at least distorting the true picture? No. All that transforming a variable does is change the scale on which it's measured. Instead of saying that there is a linear relationship between work experience and salary, for example, you say that there is a linear relationship between work experience and the log of salary. It's much easier to build models for relationships that are linear than for those that are not. That's why transforming variables is often a convenient strategy. ■ ■ ■

Checking Independence

Another assumption needed for regression hypothesis testing is that all of the observations are independent. This means that the value of one observation is in no way related to the value of another observation. Nonindependence can be a serious problem when the data are gathered in a sequence. For example, if you're looking at the length of time required to perform a new surgery and if surgeons become more proficient as the number of operations they do increases, earlier patients may have longer surgical times than later patients. In such a situation, successive patients will be more similar than you would expect if the observations are independent.

You can check the independence assumption by plotting the Studentized residuals against the sequence variable. (Strictly speaking, the residuals are not independent, since they sum to 0. However, if there are many more points than coefficients, this dependency can be ignored.)

Figure 22.11 Studentized residuals versus order of observations

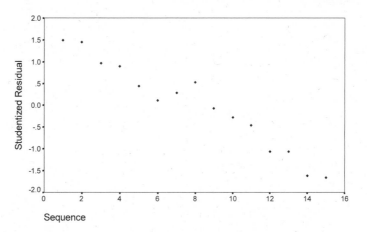

Figure 22.11 is a plot of Studentized residuals against the order in which the observations are taken for the hypothetical study of the length of surgery. You see that the value of the residual is related to the order in which the data are obtained. Early observations have large positive residuals, while later ones have large negative residuals. This is a pattern you might see if you're performing surgery and getting more proficient as you do more operations.

You can use the **Durbin-Watson test** to see if adjacent observations are correlated. This statistic ranges in value from 0 to 4. If there is no correlation between successive residuals, the Durbin-Watson statistic should be close to 2. Values close to 0 indicate that successive residuals are positively correlated, while values close to 4 indicate strong negative correlation. The value of the Durbin-Watson statistic for the plot in Figure 22.11 is 0.13, suggesting that adjacent residuals are positively correlated. To test whether the observed Durbin-Watson statistic is significantly different from 2, you need special tables that are available in books about time series analysis. As a rule of thumb, if your observed value is between 1.5 and 2.5, you need not worry.

A Final Comment on Assumptions

You should always examine your data for violations of the regression assumptions because significance levels, confidence intervals, and other regression tests are sensitive to certain types of violations. These tests cannot be interpreted in the usual fashion if there are serious departures from the regression assumptions. If you carefully examine the residuals, you'll have an idea of whether problems exist. If you observe problems you can try to remedy them using transformations.

Looking for Influential Points

It's possible for one or more cases to have a large impact on your regression model, especially if the sample size is small. That is, the slope or intercept values change a lot when certain cases are excluded from the computation of the coefficients. This is undesirable since you want a regression model that doesn't depend heavily on the values for a small number of points. You want all points to contribute more or less equally to the model.

For example, look at Figure 22.12, which is the life expectancy and birthrate data with an additional point in the lower left corner. You know that the slope of the regression line without the point is -0.697.

With the point the slope is – 0.470, almost a 32% change. You can have SPSS calculate the change in slope when each point is eliminated in turn from the calculation of the regression statistics.

Figure 22.12 Life expectancy and birthrate with outlier

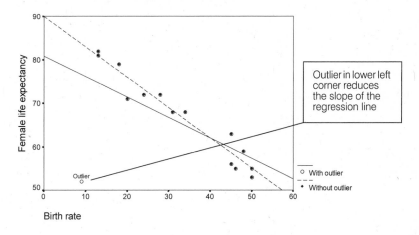

In Figure 22.13, you see the actual change in the slope associated with the removal of each case from the analysis in the column labeled *DFB1_1*. There's only one point for which the change is not close to 0. That's the outlying point added to the data. An easier way to look for points that have a large impact on the slope is to plot the change in slope against an arbitrary case sequence number, as shown in Figure 22.14. By clicking on the outlying point, you can immediately see what country it belongs to.

To figure out whether a change in slope is large, you have to compare the change to the actual value for the slope. For example, a change of 0.2 is large for a slope of 0.6 but small for a slope of 200. To avoid having to compare the change in slope to the slope, you can look at the standardized change in slope shown in Figure 22.13. You should be suspicious of standardized changes in absolute value larger than $2/\sqrt{N}$, where N is the number of cases in the sample. You can see that the standardized change observed for the outlier (5) is much larger than $2/\sqrt{16} = 1/2$.

Figure 22.13 Change in slope

COUNTRY	DFB1_1	SDB1_1
Somalia	-.02289	-.15873
Tanzania	-.01708	-.11749
Zambia	.00434	.02972
Zaire	-.01847	-.12772
Algeria	-.00022	-.00149
Namibia	.01630	.11247
Burkina Faso	-.03151	-.21882
Cuba	-.03204	-.22602
Equador	-.00496	-.03438
North Korea	-.00618	-.04248
Mongolia	.00279	.01925
Thailand	.00192	.01318
Turkey	-.00496	-.03438
France	-.05131	-.36513
Netherlands	-.04422	-.31153
Outlier	.22713	5.00376

Change in slope

Standardized change in slope

Figure 22.14 Sequence plot of change in slope

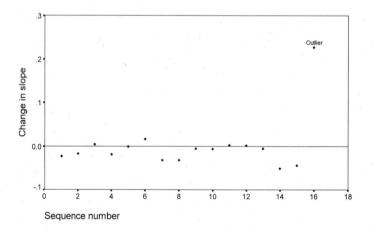

? *What should I do if I find a point that influences the results a lot?* First of all, make sure that it's not the result of errors in data collection or entry. If there are errors, correct them. If the data values are correct, try to determine if the case is unusual in ways other than altering your regression line. For example, if you are looking at the relationship between life expectancy and birthrate and find a country with very high values for both variables, look for an explanation. It may be that the predominant religious affiliation or some other characteristic of the country is different from the rest. In that case, you may want to develop separate regression models for countries with and without the characteristic in question. If you can't identify anything unusual about the point, you are stuck with it. You may want to present the results of your analyses with and without the point. What you shouldn't do is arbitrarily discard points that don't fit the model in some way. ▪ ▪ ▪

Studentized Deleted Residuals

To see the impact of a case on the computation of the slope, you calculated the regression with and without the case. The same idea can be extended to other regression statistics. For example, you can calculate what's called the **Studentized deleted residual**, also known as the **jackknifed residual**. The Studentized deleted residual is the Studentized residual for a case when the case is excluded from the computation of the regression statistics. When there are departures from the regression assumptions, you can see them easier using Studentized deleted residuals than you can using Studentized residuals. You won't go wrong if you always use the Studentized deleted residuals for analyzing residuals. (If the regression assumptions are met and you have roughly equal numbers of observations at each value of the independent variable, standardized, Studentized, and Studentized deleted residuals will show the same patterns on residual plots.)

Summary

> *How can you tell if the assumptions necessary for hypothesis testing in regression are violated?*
>
> - You can look for violations of the regression assumptions by examining the residuals. If the assumptions are correct, the distribution of the residuals should be approximately normal with constant variance.
> - You can transform your data values to better conform to the necessary regression assumptions.
> - It's important to identify influential points, since you don't want your regression results to depend too heavily on any single point.

What's Next?

In this chapter, you saw how to use residuals and related statistics to check the assumptions needed for the linear regression model. In Chapter 23, you'll learn how to build a regression model that contains more than one independent variable.

Statistical Concepts

1. What violations of assumptions, if any, are suggested by the following plots?

a.

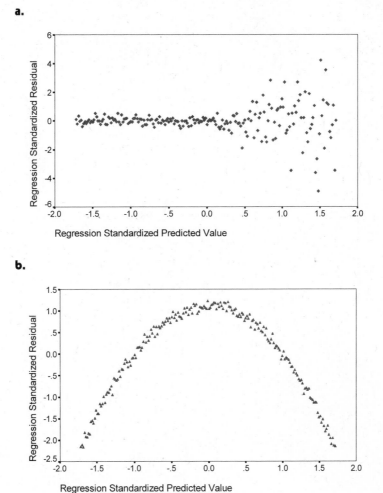

b.

c.

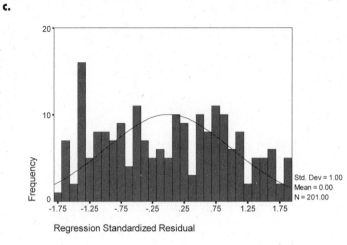

Regression Standardized Residual

2. What can you learn from the following?

a. A histogram of the residuals

b. A sequence plot of the residuals

c. A plot of the independent variable and the dependent variable

d. A plot of the residuals against the independent variable

3. You are the decision maker for a major savings and loan. You must estimate what percentage of your CD deposits are likely to be cashed prematurely during the year. You've computed a regression equation that predicts the percentage of premature CD withdrawals from banks based on unemployment rates for the area. You obtain the following regression statistics:

```
Multiple R              .88776
R Square                .78812
Adjusted R Square       .77697
Standard Error         1.05985

Analysis of Variance
                    DF      Sum of Squares      Mean Square
Regression          1            79.38843          79.38843
Residual           19            21.34256           1.12329

F =    70.67476       Signif F =  .0000


------------------ Variables in the Equation ------------------

Variable            B         SE B       Beta        T   Sig T

UNEMPLOY      1.117019     .132870    .887763    8.407   .0000
(Constant)   -2.245943     .757228              -2.966   .0079
```

a. Based on the above statistics, what can you conclude about the relationship between unemployment and premature CD withdrawal?

b. Can you tell if the relationship is linear, based on the above statistics?

c. Consider the following plot of the residuals against unemployment rate:

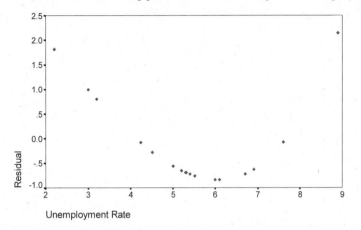

What do you think about the adequacy of the linear model now?

d. Based on the plot of the residuals, sketch the plot of CD withdrawal and unemployment rates.

e. Why do you think the correlation coefficient between the two variables is large?

Data Analysis

Use the *gss.sav* data file to answer the following questions:

1. Build a linear regression model to predict a person's education (variable *educ*) from the father's (variable *paeduc*). Save the Studentized residual, the predicted value, and the change in the coefficients (*dfbeta*).

a. Plot the two variables and draw the regression line.

b. Write the regression equation.

c. Test the null hypothesis that there is no linear relationship between the two variables.

d. What proportion of the variability in a person's education is "explained" by their father's education?

2. For the model you developed in question 1, examine the assumptions you need for linear regression.

    a. Make a histogram and Q-Q plot of the Studentized residual. What do these suggest about the violation of the normality assumption?

    b. Use the Explore procedure to make a stem-and-leaf plot of the Studentized residual and to list the five largest and five smallest values for the Studentized residual. Describe the values for education and father's education for the cases that are outliers.

    c. Make a scatterplot of the Studentized residual against the predicted education. What should you look for in this plot? What assumption are you checking? Do you suspect that the assumption is not met?

    d. Plot the change in slope associated with removing a point against case ID. From the plot, what is the largest change in slope that would occur if you eliminated a point? Use point selection mode to identify the cases with large values for the change in slope. What are their values for the dependent and independent variables?

3. Develop a regression equation to predict husband's education (variable *husbeduc*) from wife's education (variable *wifeduc*). Using the steps outlined in question 2, check the regression assumptions. Summarize your conclusions about how well the data conform to the assumptions necessary for linear regression.

4. Select two variables of your choice from the *gss.sav* file, develop a linear regression model, and test the necessary assumptions. Write a short summary of your results.

Use the *salary.sav* data file to answer the following questions:

5. Develop a regression equation to predict current salary (variable *salnow*) from beginning salary (variable *salbeg*). Save the predicted values, Studentized residuals, and changes in the coefficients.

    a. Make a histogram and a Q-Q plot of the Studentized residuals. Does their distribution appear to be approximately normal? If not, in what way is the distribution not normal?

    b. Plot the Studentized residuals against the predicted values. What kind of pattern are you looking for in this plot? Do you see anything that suggests possible problems? Explain.

    c. Plot the changes in the value of the slope against case ID number. Are there any employees who have a big impact on the estimate of the regression coefficient?

6. Using the Compute facility, create new variables that are the natural log of current salary and of beginning salary. Plot the natural log of current salary against the natural log of beginning salary. How does this plot differ from the one you made of the original values?

7. Repeat question 5 using the transformed values of the salaries. Do you think the regression assumptions are better met for the transformed variables?

Use the *country.sav* data file to answer the following questions:

8. Develop a regression equation to predict female life expectancy (variable *lifeexpf*) from birthrate (variable *birthrat*) for all countries in the data file. Save the predicted values, Studentized residuals, and changes in the values of the slope and the intercept.

   a. Make stem-and-leaf plots or histograms of the Studentized residuals. Make a Q-Q plot as well. Do you think the residuals are normally distributed? If not, how does their distribution differ from a normal distribution?

   b. Plot the Studentized residuals against predicted female life expectancies. What are you looking for in this plot? Is the variability of the residuals pretty much constant over the entire range of values of predicted female life expectancy?

   c. Plot the change in slope against ID number. Identify any points that have a large effect on the value of the slope. Which country will change the slope most if it is excluded from the regression computations? What are its values for female life expectancy and birthrate?

9. Repeat question 8, predicting male life expectancy (variable *lifeexpm*) from female life expectancy.

10. Predict female life expectancy from the number of phones per 100 people (variable *phone*). Save the Studentized residuals and predicted values. Make a stem-and-leaf plot of the Studentized residuals. Test the null hypothesis that the residuals come from a normal population. Plot the residuals against the predicted values. Do you think the data satisfy the regression assumptions?

11. Repeat question 8 using the natural log of the number of phones (variable *lnphones*) instead of the actual number of phones. Examine all of the diagnostic plots. What do you conclude now about violations of the regression assumptions?

Use the *buying.sav* data file to answer the following questions:

12. Build a regression model to predict a husband's buying score (variable *hsumbuy*) from his wife's buying score (*wsumbuy*). Check the regression assumptions. Summarize your results.

13. Build a regression model to predict wife's buying score from her husband's prediction of her score (*hpredsum*). Do you think you have a useful model? Explain.

Use the *schools.sav* data file to answer the following questions:

14. Build a linear regression model to predict ACT scores. Use the variable you think is the best predictor as the independent variable. Check all of the necessary assumptions. Write a short report explaining your regression results.

15. Build a linear regression model to predict graduation rates. Again, select the independent variable that you think is the best predictor. Check the regression assumptions.

16. Calculate the correlation coefficients between *act93, loinc93, grad93,* and *pctact93*. Which variables have the largest correlation coefficient in absolute value? For which pairs of variables is the correlation coefficient a good summary measure of their relationship?

Building Multiple Regression Models

How do you build a regression model with more than one independent variable?

- What are partial regression coefficients?
- How can you test the null hypothesis that all of the population partial regression coefficients are 0?
- What can you tell from the partial regression coefficient about the relationship between the dependent variable and an independent variable?
- What are variable selection methods and why are they useful?

In Chapter 20 through Chapter 22, you used linear regression analysis to examine the relationship between a dependent variable and an independent variable. In most real life situations, however, predicting the values of a dependent variable requires more than a single independent variable. If you want to predict how long a patient stays in the hospital after surgery, you need to consider a myriad of possible predictors: the patient's age, severity of illness as measured by numerous laboratory and physical findings, as well as type of surgery. To predict salary, you must consider a variety of characteristics of the employee and the job: work experience, education, seniority, and type of position. In this chapter, you will learn how to build a linear regression model that has more than one independent variable. The technique you'll use is called **multiple linear regression analysis**.

▶ This chapter uses the *country.sav* data file described in Chapter 9. To duplicate the results shown, you must correct the value for Bhutan in the data file, as described in that chapter. For instructions on how to obtain the multiple regression analysis shown, see "How to Obtain a Multiple Linear Regression" on p. 496.

Predicting Life Expectancy

In the previous chapters, you predicted female life expectancy from birthrate for a sample of 15 countries. You found that for your sample, birthrate is an excellent predictor, since it explains almost 94% of the observed variability in female life expectancy. Birthrate predicts life expectancy well because both variables are strongly related to a country's economic development and prosperity. In this chapter, you'll try to predict female life expectancy from a combination of variables that measure specific economic and health care delivery characteristics of a country.

Table 23.1 describes the independent variables you have available. For most of the 122 countries, the data are for 1992.

Table 23.1 Predictors of life expectancy

Variable Name	Description
urban	Percentage of the population living in urban areas
docs	Number of doctors per 10,000 people
beds	Number of hospital beds per 10,000 people
gdp	Per capita gross domestic product in dollars
radios	Radios per 100 people

The Model

You can write the multiple linear regression equation that predicts female life expectancy from all of the variables in Table 23.1 as

Predicted life expectancy =   **Equation 23.1**
constant + B_1urban + B_2docs + B_3beds + B_4gdp + B_5radios

Instead of just an intercept and slope, the multiple linear regression equation contains a constant (analogous to the intercept) and five coefficients (B_1 through B_5)—one for each of the five independent variables. These coefficients are called **partial regression coefficients**. If your data are a sample from a population about which you want to draw conclusions, then the sample partial regression coefficients are estimates of the unknown population coefficients. (The population partial regression coefficients are usually designated with the Greek letter β.)

You can again use the method of least squares to estimate the values of the coefficients. That is, you select the coefficients that result in the smallest sum of squared differences between the observed and predicted values of the dependent variable. Any other coefficients have a larger sum of squared residuals.

> *Can I include a nominal variable like type of government or region of the world in a regression model?* Yes, but not without some effort. If you have a variable that has only two possible values—for example, democracy/not democracy or developed/not developed—you can code the two responses using 0 and 1. Then you can treat the variable like any other variable in the regression model. The partial regression coefficient for the variable tells you how much the predicted value for the dependent variable changes when the code is 1. For example, a coefficient of 0.5 for democracy tells you that life expectancy increases by half of a year for democracies compared to nondemocracies. If you have a nominal variable with more than two categories, you have to create a new set of variables to represent the categories. How that's done is beyond the scope of this book. ■ ■ ■

Assumptions for Multiple Regression

To test hypotheses about the population regression line when you have a single independent variable, your data must be a random sample from a population in which the following assumptions are met:

- The observations are independent.
- The relationship between the two variables is linear.
- For each value of the independent variable, there is a normal distribution of values of the dependent variable.
- The distributions have the same variance.

You need only a slight modification of these assumptions for multiple regression. You must assume that the relationship between the dependent and the independent variables is linear and that for each *combination* of values of the independent variables, the distribution of the dependent variable is normal with a constant variance.

Examining the Variables

Before you estimate the coefficients, you must make sure that the independent variables are linearly related to the dependent variable. If they're not, you may have to transform the data as described in the previous chapter. For example, you may have to take logs or square roots of one or both of a pair of variables to make the relationship linear.

Figure 23.1 is a scatterplot matrix of the independent variables and the dependent variable. You're particularly interested in looking at the last row of the matrix. It shows you the relationships between female life expectancy and the other independent variables.

Figure 23.1 Scatterplot matrix

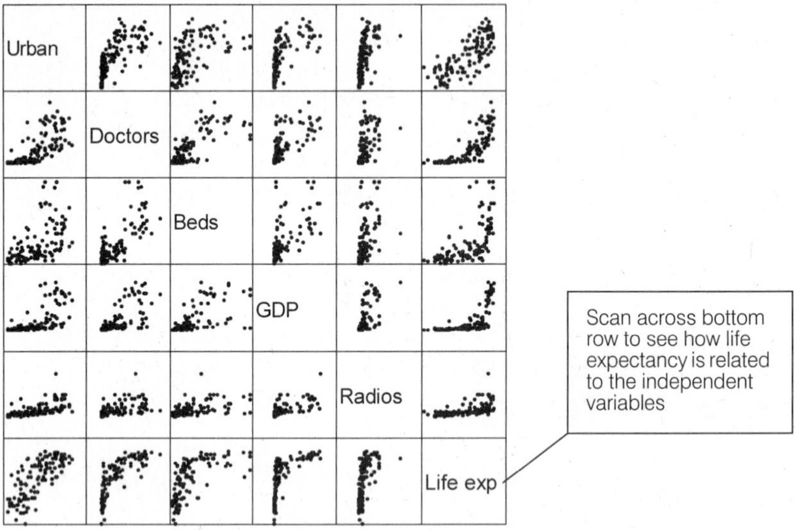

To obtain this matrix, in the Scatterplot Matrix dialog box, select the variables urban, docs, hospbed, gdp, radio, and lifeexpf.

See Chapter 9 for instructions on how to obtain matrix scatterplots.

Scan across bottom row to see how life expectancy is related to the independent variables

The relationship between female life expectancy and the percentage of the population living in urban areas appears to be more or less linear. The other four independent variables appear to be related to female life expectancy, but the relationship is not linear. Before you can use these variables in the multiple linear regression equation, you have to transform the data so that the relationships are more or less linear. Let's see what happens when you take the natural log of the values of the four independent variables.

Figure 23.2 Scatterplot matrix after transformations

To obtain this matrix, in the Scatterplot Matrix dialog box, select the variables urban, lndocs, lnbeds, lngdp, lnradio, and lifeexpf.

See Chapter 9 for instructions on how to obtain matrix scatterplots.

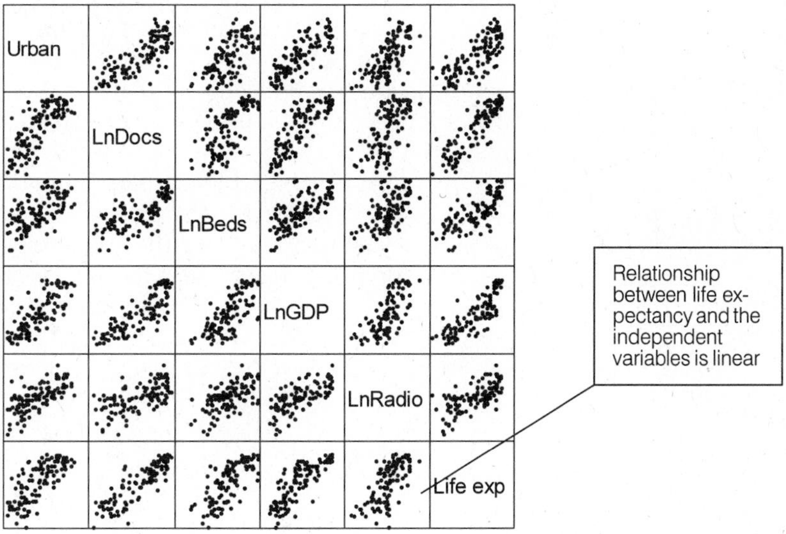

Relationship between life expectancy and the independent variables is linear

Figure 23.2 is the scatterplot matrix after you've changed the scale on which doctors, hospital beds, per capita gross domestic product and radios are measured. The transformations were successful. All of the independent variables have a linear relationship with female life expectancy. Now it makes sense to compute the multiple linear regression equation using the values of the transformed variables in place of the original variables. (For simplicity, in the rest of the chapter we'll usually refer to the variables using their original names. So, instead of always saying the log of the number of doctors, we'll say the doctors variable, which means the transformed variable representing the log of the number of doctors per 10,000 population.)

What happens if some of the cases have missing values for the dependent variable or the independent variables? By default, SPSS excludes all cases that have missing values for any of the variables in the regression from the computation of the regression statistics. This is known as **listwise deletion**. (You'll find this term in some of the procedure dialog boxes.) The alternative to listwise deletion is called **pairwise deletion**. If you request pairwise deletion, each correlation coefficient between two variables is calculated using all cases that have values for the two variables. (Calculating the correlation matrix between all pairs of variables is the first step of the regression computations.) For example, if a case only has values for variables A and B, those values are used when calculating the correlation coefficient between variables A and B. The case contributes nothing to the calculation of the other coefficients. This sounds like a good idea, but it's not. If you use pairwise deletion when you have many cases with missing values, you can end up with correlation coefficients that are based on entirely different groups of cases. That's why you should usually stick to listwise deletion of missing values.

Looking at How Well the Model Fits

Figure 23.3 shows the results of the multiple linear regression analysis.

Figure 23.3 Multiple regression output

To obtain this regression, from the menus choose:

*Statistics
  Regression ▶
  Linear...*

Select the variables shown in Figure 23.13.

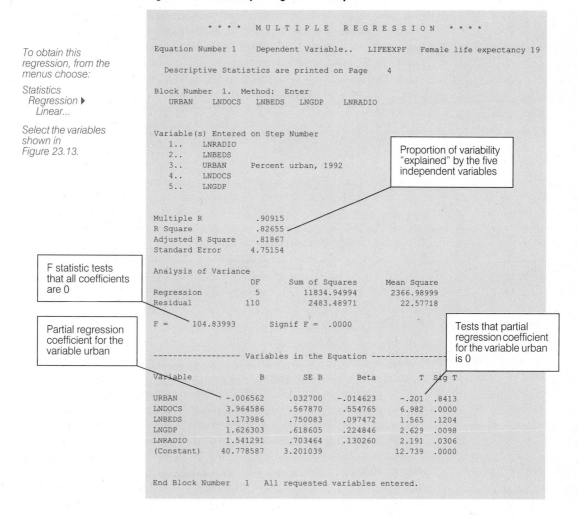

```
        * * * *   M U L T I P L E   R E G R E S S I O N   * * * *

Equation Number 1    Dependent Variable..   LIFEEXPF   Female life expectancy 19

    Descriptive Statistics are printed on Page    4

Block Number  1.  Method:  Enter
    URBAN    LNDOCS    LNBEDS    LNGDP    LNRADIO


Variable(s) Entered on Step Number
    1..    LNRADIO
    2..    LNBEDS
    3..    URBAN      Percent urban, 1992
    4..    LNDOCS
    5..    LNGDP



Multiple R              .90915
R Square               .82655
Adjusted R Square      .81867
Standard Error        4.75154

Analysis of Variance
                    DF       Sum of Squares      Mean Square
Regression           5          11834.94994      2366.98999
Residual           110           2483.48971        22.57718

F =     104.83993      Signif F =  .0000


------------------ Variables in the Equation ------------------

Variable          B        SE B       Beta        T   Sig T

URBAN       -.006562     .032700    -.014623    -.201  .8413
LNDOCS      3.964586     .567870     .554765    6.982  .0000
LNBEDS      1.173986     .750083     .097472    1.565  .1204
LNGDP       1.626303     .618605     .224846    2.629  .0098
LNRADIO     1.541291     .703464     .130260    2.191  .0306
(Constant)  40.778587   3.201039              12.739  .0000


End Block Number   1   All requested variables entered.
```

- Proportion of variability "explained" by the five independent variables
- F statistic tests that all coefficients are 0
- Partial regression coefficient for the variable urban
- Tests that partial regression coefficient for the variable urban is 0

One of the first things you want to look at is how well the model fits. The entry labeled *R square* in Figure 23.3 tells you that 82.7% of the observed variability in life expectancy is "explained" by the five independent variables. That's quite a lot, though not as good as when birthrate is used alone. The *Multiple R* is the correlation coefficient between the observed value of the dependent variable and the predicted value based on the regression model. A value of 1 tells you that the dependent variable can be perfectly predicted from the independent variables. A value close to 0 tells you that the independent variables are not linearly related to the dependent variable. The observed value of 0.91 is quite large, indicating that the linear regression model predicts well.

The analysis-of-variance table in Figure 23.3 is used to test several equivalent null hypotheses: that there is no linear relationship in the population between the dependent variable and the independent variables, that all of the population partial regression coefficients are 0, and that the population value for multiple R^2 is 0.

The test of the null hypothesis is based on the ratio of the regression mean square to the residual mean square. In Figure 23.3, the ratio of the two mean squares, labeled F, is 104.84. Since the observed significance level is less than 0.00005, you can reject the null hypothesis that there is no linear relationship between female life expectancy and the five independent variables. At least one of the population regression coefficients is not 0. (This test is sometimes known as the **overall regression F test**.)

Where does an analysis-of-variance table come from in regression analysis? The analysis-of-variance table is similar to the one you calculated in Chapter 15. The total observed variability in the dependent variable is subdivided into two components: that explained by the linear regression (labeled *Regression)* and that not explained by the linear regression (labeled *Residual)*. ■ ■ ■

If there is no linear relationship between the dependent variable and the independent variables, then both the regression mean square and the residual mean square (the variance of the residuals) are estimates of the variance of the dependent variable for each combination of values of the independent variables. If there is a linear relationship, the estimate based on the regression mean square will be too large. How much it is too large depends on the magnitude of the regression coefficients.

You can calculate multiple R^2 from the sums of squares in the analysis-of-variance table. First, add up the *Regression* and *Residual* sums of squares. That's the total sum of squares. Then divide the regression sum of squares by the total sum of squares. This gives you 0.827, which is R^2, the proportion of the variability in the dependent variable explained by the linear regression.

Examining the Coefficients

The coefficients for the independent variables are listed in the column labeled *B* in Figure 23.3. Using these coefficients, you can write the estimated regression equation as

$$\hat{Y} = 40.78 - 0.007 \times \text{urban} + 3.96 \times \text{lndocs}$$
$$+ 1.17 \times \text{lnbeds} + 1.63 \times \text{lngdp} + 1.54 \times \text{lnradio}$$

Equation 23.2

where $\hat{Y}$ is the predicted female life expectancy. In the multiple regression equation, the partial regression coefficient for a variable tells you how much the value of the dependent variable changes when the value of that independent variable increases by 1 and the values of the other independent variables do not change. A positive coefficient means that the predicted value of the dependent variable increases when the value of the independent variable increases. A negative coefficient means that the predicted value of the dependent variable decreases when the value of the independent variable increases.

The coefficient for the doctors variables tells you that predicted female life expectancy increases by 3.96 years for a change of 1 in the value of the doctors variable. Since the doctors variable is measured on a natural log scale, the change refers to an increase of 1 on the log scale. So, instead of telling you how much life expectancy increases when the number of doctors per 10,000 increases by 1, it's telling you how much life expectancy increases when the *logarithm* of the number of doctors per 10,000 increases by 1. (For example, if the number of doctors increases from 2.72 to 7.39 per 10,000 that's a change of 1 on a log scale, since the natural log of 2.72 is 1, and the natural log of 7.39 is 2.)

You test the null hypothesis that the population partial regression coefficient for a variable is 0 using the *t* statistic and its observed significance level. As in the case of bivariate regression (regression with a single independent variable), you calculate the *t* statistic by dividing the estimated coefficient by its standard error. You can calculate confidence intervals for the population partial regression coefficients the same way as you did for the slope and intercept.

From Figure 23.3, you can reject the null hypothesis that the coefficients for doctors, radios, and per capita GDP are 0. You can't reject the null hypothesis that the coefficients for urbanization and hospital beds are 0. (If you request 95% confidence intervals for these two coefficients, you'll see that they include the value 0.) You'll learn later in this chapter that this finding doesn't mean that urbanization and hospital beds are not good predictors of female life expectancy when considered alone or in combination with other variables. They just don't contribute significantly to the model being considered.

All of the variables except urbanization have positive coefficients, which means that life expectancy increases with increasing values of the variables. That makes sense. You expect that more doctors, more hospital beds, more radios and larger per capita GDP's would be associated with longer life expectancies. All of these variables are indicators of the prosperity of a country. Doctors and hospital beds, unlike radios, might even contribute directly to the health of the population. Urbanization has a small negative coefficient, which is unexpected since life expectancy generally increases with urbanization. Since you can't reject the hypothesis that its coefficient is 0 in the population, the fact that the sign is wrong isn't of much concern. You'll look at this variable more closely later.

Interpreting the Partial Regression Coefficients

When there is only one independent variable in a regression model, the interpretation of its regression coefficient is straightforward. If you reject the null hypothesis that the population value for the coefficient is 0, you can conclude that it's quite likely that there is a linear component to the relationship between the dependent variable and the independent variable. In multiple linear regression, the interpretation is considerably more complicated, because any conclusion about a particular independent variable depends on the relationship of that variable both to the dependent variable and to the other independent variables in the model.

For example, in Figure 23.3, the partial regression coefficients for urbanization and hospital beds are not statistically different from 0. Can you conclude that these two variables are not linearly related to female life expectancy? Not necessarily. Look at Figure 23.4, which is a matrix of Pearson correlation coefficients for all of the variables in the model. For each pair of variables, you see the observed correlation coefficient and underneath it the one-tailed observed significance level (the probability of observing a correlation coefficient at least that large and of the same sign when the population correlation coefficient is 0).

You obtain these correlation coefficients as part of the same regression analysis shown in Figure 23.3.

Figure 23.4 Correlation matrix

Correlation, 1-tailed Sig:

	LIFEEXPF	URBAN	LNDOCS	LNBEDS	LNGDP	LNRADIO
LIFEEXPF	1.000	.750	.880	.730	.836	.693
	.	.000	.000	.000	.000	.000
URBAN	.750	1.000	.794	.619	.789	.668
	.000	.	.000	.000	.000	.000
LNDOCS	.880	.794	1.000	.711	.824	.633
	.000	.000	.	.000	.000	.000
LNBEDS	.730	.619	.711	1.000	.741	.616
	.000	.000	.000	.	.000	.000
LNGDP	.836	.789	.824	.741	1.000	.716
	.000	.000	.000	.000	.	.000
LNRADIO	.693	.668	.633	.616	.716	1.000
	.000	.000	.000	.000	.000	.

The correlation coefficient between female life expectancy and urbanization is 0.750. Based on the observed significance level, you can reject the null hypothesis that there is no linear relationship between the two variables. Similarly, you see that the correlation coefficient between female life expectancy and hospital beds is 0.730. Again, you can reject the null hypothesis that there is no linear relationship between the two variables. So what's going on? The variables are individually related to life expectancy, but in the multiple regression equation, their coefficients are not significantly different from 0.

The explanation is actually quite simple. Look at Figure 23.4 again. You see that the independent variables are highly correlated with each other. The correlation coefficient between doctors and urbanization is 0.794. The correlation coefficient between hospital beds and doctors is 0.711. That means that if you have a regression model that includes doctors as an independent variable, urbanization and hospital beds don't contribute much unique information. Much of the information they convey is already being supplied by the other independent variables.

? *Why bother looking at scatterplots when I can compute a whole matrix of correlation coefficients so easily?* Correlation matrices are useful for looking at the strength of the linear relationship between pairs of variables. However, don't use them as a substitute for scatterplot matrices which show you what the relationship between two variables *really* looks like. From a correlation coefficient, you can't tell if a straight line is a good summary of the data or if it's just better than no line. You also can't tell if there are unusual points in your data or if there are distinct clusters of points that make it look like there is a relationship between the variables when there really isn't one.

You should also be careful when looking at a whole matrix of observed significance levels for correlation coefficients. If you have a lot of coefficients, you expect some of them to be statistically significant even if the variables are not linearly related. Out of 100 coefficients, you expect 5 to be significant by chance alone. A simple correction for the fact that you're examining many coefficients is to multiply the observed significance level by the number of coefficients you're looking at. ■ ■ ■

Figure 23.5   Coefficients with doctors removed from the model

To obtain this output, repeat the analysis shown in Figure 23.3 without including Indocs as one of the independent variables.

```
------------------ Variables in the Equation ------------------

Variable            B          SE B        Beta         T   Sig T

URBAN            .085451     .035789     .190417     2.388   .0186
LNBEDS          2.503557     .867608     .207862     2.886   .0047
LNGDP           3.234851     .686545     .447238     4.712   .0000
LNRADIO         1.389525     .840849     .117434     1.653   .1013
(Constant)     26.859972    2.994941                 8.968   .0000

End Block Number   1   All requested variables entered.
```

Changing the Model

Consider what happens to the multiple regression equation when you remove the doctors variable from the model. Figure 23.5 shows the coefficients for the model with only four independent variables. You see that when the doctor variable is removed, the coefficients of the other variables change. The coefficient for the hospital beds variable is more than twice as large as before and is now significantly different from 0. The coefficient for urbanization changes from –0.007 to +0.085. It's also significantly different from 0. The coefficient for radios is no longer significantly different from 0.

When the independent variables are correlated with each other, the coefficient for a particular variable depends on the other variables included in the model. That's why you must be very careful about the conclusions you draw about individual variables based on a multiple regression model. You would be wrong if you conclude based on Figure 23.3 that urbanization and hospital beds are not linearly related to life expectancy. They certainly are!

Partial Correlation Coefficients

When you want to measure the strength of the linear relationship between the dependent variable and an independent variable, while "controlling" or keeping constant, the effects of other independent variables, you can compute what's called the partial correlation coefficient. The **partial correlation coefficient** is the correlation between two variables when the linear effects of other variables are removed. For example, you can estimate the correlation between female life expectancy and urbanization, controlling for hospital beds, doctors, GDP and radios. This is done by calculating a linear regression model which predicts each of the two variables from the other independent variables. For example, both urbanization and female life expectancy are separately predicted from beds, GDP, radios, and doctors. The partial correlation coefficient is then the Pearson correlation coefficient between the two sets of residuals.

In SPSS, you can use the Partial Correlation procedure to calculate partial correlation coefficients for any pair of variables, controlling for the linear effects of other variables. For example, Figure 23.6 shows the partial correlation coefficient between urbanization and life expectancy when the linear effects of GDP, radios, doctors, and hospital beds are eliminated.

Figure 23.6 Partial correlation between urbanization and life expectancy

To obtain these
coefficients, from
the menus choose:

Statistics
  Correlate ▶
    Partial...

Select the variables
shown in Figure
21.8.

```
- - - P A R T I A L   C O R R E L A T I O N   C O E F F I C I E N T S - - -

Controlling for..    LNGDP     LNRADIO   LNDOCS    LNBEDS

           LIFEEXPF        URBAN

LIFEEXPF     1.0000        -.0191
            (      0)      (   110)
             P= .           P= .841

URBAN        -.0191         1.0000
            (   110)       (      0)
             P= .841        P= .

(Coefficient / (D.F.) / 2-tailed Significance)

" . " is printed if a coefficient cannot be computed
```

The partial correlation coefficient is –0.019. Since the observed significance level is large, you can't reject the null hypothesis that the population value for the partial correlation coefficient is 0. If you look at the observed significance level (0.841), you'll see that it's exactly the same as the observed significance level for the partial regression coefficient for urbanization when the other four independent variables are in the model. That's not a coincidence. The two tests are equivalent. That is, when you test whether a partial regression coefficient is 0, you're also testing whether the partial correlation coefficient between the dependent variable and the independent variable, controlling for the effects of the other independent variables in the model, is 0.

Tolerance and Multicollinearity

The strength of the linear relationships among the independent variables is measured by a statistic called the tolerance. For each independent variable, the tolerance is the proportion of variability of that variable that is *not* explained by its linear relationships with the other independent variables in the model. Since tolerance is a proportion, its values range from 0 to 1. A value close to 1 indicates that an independent variable has little of its variability explained by the other independent variables. A value close to 0 indicates that a variable is almost a linear combination of the other independent variables. Such data are called **multicollinear**.

How can I tell if multicollinearity is a problem for my data? Look at the tolerances for each of the independent variables in the model. (These are printed if you select Collinearity diagnostics in the Linear Regression Statistics dialog box.) If any of the tolerances are small—say, less than 0.1—multicollinearity may be a problem. If your variables are multicollinear, you may find that although you can reject the null hypothesis that all the population coefficients are 0 based on the overall F statistic, none of the individual coefficients in the model is significantly different from 0 based on the t statistic. Or you may encounter coefficients with the wrong sign.

For example, you might find that the coefficients for doctors and hospital beds are negative, when you know they should be positively related to life expectancy. In such a situation, you should identify the variables that are almost linear combinations of each other and remove some of them from the model. If the independent variables are very highly related, you may not even be able to estimate a regression model that contains all of them. In this event, SPSS will issue a warning and omit the offending variables from the model.

Beta Coefficients

A common mistake in regression analysis is equating the magnitude of the partial regression coefficients to the relative importance of the variables. For example, in Figure 23.5 the coefficient for urbanization is quite small compared to that for radios. What does that tell you? Not much. The magnitude of the partial regression coefficient depends, among other things, on the units in which the variable is measured. In this example, urbanization is measured as a percentage, while radios are expressed as the natural log of the number of radios per 100 people. Consider what happens if you express urbanization not as a percentage, but as a proportion—for example, the value 50% is changed to 0.50. The coefficients are shown in Figure 23.7. As you can see, the coefficient for urbanization is 100 times as large as that in Figure 23.5. The coefficients for the other independent variables are the same.

Figure 23.7 Coefficients with urbanization divided by 100

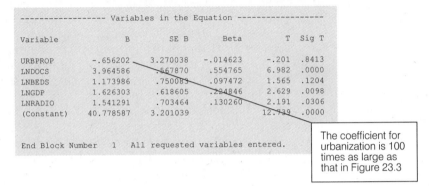

```
------------------ Variables in the Equation ------------------

Variable            B        SE B      Beta        T   Sig T

URBPROP        -.656202   3.270038   -.014623    -.201   .8413
LNDOCS         3.964586    .567870    .554765    6.982   .0000
LNBEDS         1.173986    .750083    .097472    1.565   .1204
LNGDP          1.626303    .618605    .224846    2.629   .0098
LNRADIO        1.541291    .703464    .130260    2.191   .0306
(Constant)    40.778587   3.201039              12.739   .0000


End Block Number    1    All requested variables entered.
```

> The coefficient for urbanization is 100 times as large as that in Figure 23.3

One way to make partial regression coefficients somewhat more comparable is to calculate what are called *beta weights*. These are the partial regression coefficients when all independent variables are expressed in standardized (Z score) form. In the output, these coefficients are in the column labeled *Beta*. You can see by comparing Figure 23.3 with Figure 23.7 that dividing the urbanization variable by 100 does not affect the Beta coefficient. However, the values of the beta coefficients still depend on the other independent variables in your model, so they don't reflect in any absolute sense the importance of the individual independent variables.

Building a Regression Model

The five variables you used to predict life expectancy were selected from among a large number of variables that describe a country. No doubt, additional information about the countries could be useful in building a model to predict life expectancy. It's also possible that some of the selected variables are not particularly good predictors. This is the usual situation in model building.

Your goal is to build a simple model that predicts well. If you can predict life expectancy well using two variables instead of five, the simpler model is better. If you include irrelevant variables in a model, you increase the standard errors of the coefficients without improving prediction. If you exclude variables that are important predictors, your model is biased. That is, it doesn't represent the true underlying model.

The following sections describe techniques that are used for identifying a subset of independent variables that results in a "good" regression model. None of the methods results in a model that is "best" in any absolute sense. However, these methods may help you identify a group of variables that predicts the dependent variable reasonably well.

Methods for Selecting Variables

You can build many different models from the same set of independent variables. For example, if you have 5 independent variables, you can build 32 different models: 1 model with only the constant, 5 models with only one independent variable, 10 models with 2 independent variables, 10 models with 3 independent variables, 5 models with 4 independent variables, and 1 model with all 5 independent variables. As the number of independent variables increases, so does the number of possible models.

Although for a small number of independent variables it is possible for you to evaluate all possible models, several methods that do not require as much computation are commonly used. These methods sequentially add or remove variables from a model. The decision to enter or remove a variables is based on how much it changes multiple R^2. Whenever you add an independent variable to a regression model, R^2 increases or remains the same. It never decreases when a variable is added. Similarly, when you remove a variable from a regression model, R^2 decreases or remains the same.

- **Forward selection.** Forward selection starts with a model that contains only the constant term. At each step, you add the variable that results in the largest increase in multiple R^2, provided that the change in R^2 is large enough for you to reject the null hypothesis that the true change is 0, using a preset significance level. (The default criterion is an observed significance level of 0.05 or less. If you increase the significance level, you make it easier for variables to enter the model.) You stop entering variables into the model when there are no more variables that result in a significant increase in R^2.

- **Backward elimination.** In backward elimination, you start with a regression model that contains all of the independent variables. At each step, you remove the variable that changes R^2 least, provided that the change is small enough so that you can't reject the null hypothesis that the true change is 0, using a preset significance level. (The default criterion is an observed significance level of 0.1 or larger.) You stop removing variables when removal of any variable in the model results in a significant change in R^2.

- **Stepwise variable selection.** The most commonly used method for model building is stepwise variable selection. It resembles forward selection except that after you enter a variable into the model, you remove any variables already in the model that are no longer significant predictors. This means that variables whose importance diminishes as additional predictors are added are removed. Stepwise variable selection is a combination of forward selection and backward elimination. You have two criteria: one for entering a variable and one for removing a variable. You select the first two variables for entry the same way as in forward selection. Then you examine the variables in the model to see if either of them meet the removal criteria. If so, you remove it from the model. At each step, you enter a new variable using the same rules as in forward selection; then you examine the variables already in the model for removal, using the same rules as in backward elimination. You stop when no more variables meet the entry criterion. (The significance level for entering a variable should be smaller than the significance level for removing a variable. Otherwise, if the computer didn't stop you, you might end up entering and removing the same variable over and over.)

Whenever you use one of the variable selection methods to build a model, the observed significance levels for the coefficients are not really correct, since you're looking at many variables and choosing the one with the smallest significance level for entry or the one with the largest significance level for removal. Unfortunately, the true significance level is difficult to compute, since it depends not only on the number of cases and variables but also on the correlations of the independent variables. So, although we'll be referring to observed significance levels for the coefficients as variables are entered and removed from the model, in a strict statistical sense they are not really correct.

Why do you look at the statistical significance of the change in multiple R^2 instead of looking at the observed significance levels for the regression coefficients? In multiple linear regression, there are many statistics that are equivalent. Choosing the variable that results in the largest increase in R^2 is the same as choosing the variable that has the smallest observed significance level for the test of its partial regression coefficient. It's also the same as choosing the variable with the largest absolute value for the t statistic, the variable with the largest absolute value for its partial correlation coefficient, and the variable that results in the smallest residual sum of squares.

Forward Selection

Consider first an example of forward selection. You'll enter a variable into the model only if it results in a change in R^2 that is significantly different from 0 at the 5% significance level. Testing that the change in R^2 is 0 when a variable enters is the same as testing that the partial regression coefficient for the variable is 0, so you can use the observed significance levels for the partial regression coefficients.

Figure 23.8   Forward selection

To obtain this regression, repeat the analysis shown in Figure 23.3. For Selection Method, select Forward.

```
Equation Number 1    Dependent Variable..  LIFEEXPF   Female life expectancy 19

Block Number  1.  Method:  Forward       Criterion   PIN  .0500
   LNBEDS    LNDOCS   LNGDP    LNRADIO   URBAN


Variable(s) Entered on Step Number
   1..    LNDOCS


Multiple R           .88010
R Square             .77458
Adjusted R Square    .77260
Standard Error      5.32097

Analysis of Variance
                   DF        Sum of Squares       Mean Square
Regression          1           11090.78504       11090.78504
Residual          114            3227.65462          28.31276

F =      391.72391      Signif F =  .0000


------------------ Variables in the Equation -------------------

Variable              B         SE B         Beta        T   Sig T

LNDOCS         6.289581      .317784      .880103   19.792   .0000
(Constant)    57.232317      .687618                83.233   .0000


------------- Variables not in the Equation -------------

Variable      Beta In  Partial  Min Toler        T   Sig T

LNBEDS        .210583  .312093    .495122    3.492   .0007
LNGDP         .344631  .411646    .321610    4.802   .0000
LNRADIO       .226199  .368715    .598951    4.217   .0001
URBAN         .140373  .179845    .370013    1.943   .0544
```

The doctors variable enters first

GDP has the largest t value; it enters next

In Figure 23.8, you see that the doctors variable enters at the first step. Its partial regression coefficient has the smallest observed significance level of any of the independent variables, and the observed significance level meets the entry criterion of being less than or equal to 0.05. With the doctors variable in the regression equation, you can explain 77.46% of the variability in the observed female life expectancies.

Look now the output labeled *Variables not in the Equation*. For each variable, you see what would happen if it entered the model next. If the hospital beds variable enters at the second step, its beta coefficient will be 0.21. The partial correlation coefficient (labeled *Partial*) for hospital beds is 0.31. That's the correlation coefficient between hospital beds and female life expectancy, controlling for doctors, the independent variable already in the model. The partial correlation coefficient displayed here controls for all of the independent variables already in the model. If the partial correlation coefficient is large in absolute value, the variable has unique information to contribute to the equation.

The column labeled *Min Toler* is the smallest tolerance for any independent variable in the model, if the variable enters next. SPSS will not enter a variable into the model if it results in a very small tolerance for any independent variable. The reason for this is that very small tolerances may cause computational problems.

In the last two columns of Figure 23.8, you see, for each independent variable not in the model, the t statistic for its partial regression coefficient and its observed significance level, if the variable enters next. To get the largest change in R^2, you must enter the variable with the smallest observed significance level or, equivalently, the largest t statistic. The GDP variable has the largest t value, and its observed significance level is less than 0.05, so it enters next.

Figure 23.9 Forward selection with GDP variable added

This output continues the forward selection analysis begun in Figure 23.8.

```
Equation Number 1     Dependent Variable..   LIFEEXPF   Female life expectancy 19


Variable(s) Entered on Step Number
    2..    LNGDP


Multiple R              .90154
R Square                .81278
Adjusted R Square       .80946
Standard Error         4.87065

Analysis of Variance
                       DF      Sum of Squares      Mean Square
Regression              2         11637.71816       5818.85908
Residual              113          2680.72149         23.72320

F =      245.28138       Signif F =  .0000


------------------ Variables in the Equation ------------------

Variable                B          SE B        Beta        T   Sig T

LNDOCS            4.261047      .512935     .596249     8.307  .0000
LNGDP             2.492701      .519146     .344631     4.802  .0000
(Constant)       42.137784     3.206078                13.143  .0000


------------ Variables not in the Equation ------------

Variable      Beta In  Partial  Min Toler       T  Sig T

LNBEDS        .120309  .180044   .272354     1.937  .0553
LNRADIO       .142349  .228348   .258691     2.482  .0145
URBAN         .016501  .021326   .266974      .226  .8218
```

There are now two variables in the model

Radio enters next

In Figure 23.9, you see the statistics when the GDP variable is entered into the model. The *t* value for its coefficient is 4.802, the value you saw in Figure 23.8. When GDP is added to the model, the multiple R^2 increases from 0.775 to 0.813. The change in R^2 is significantly different from 0, since the observed significance level for the coefficient of the variable is less than 0.05.

Looking at the statistics for the variables not in the model, you see that the radio variable has the largest t statistic for its coefficient. The observed significance level of 0.0145 is less than the entry criterion of 0.05, so the radio variable enters next.

Figure 23.10 Forward selection with radio variable added

This output continues the forward selection analysis begun in Figure 23.8.

```
Equation Number 1     Dependent Variable..   LIFEEXPF   Female life expectancy 19


Variable(s) Entered on Step Number
   3..    LNRADIO


Multiple R              .90694
R Square               .82254
Adjusted R Square      .81779
Standard Error        4.76309

Analysis of Variance
                     DF      Sum of Squares       Mean Square
Regression            3         11777.49796       3925.83265
Residual            112          2540.94169         22.68698


F =     173.04343       Signif F =  .0000


------------------ Variables in the Equation ------------------

Variable               B         SE B        Beta         T   Sig T

LNDOCS          4.122571     .504700     .576872      8.168   .0000
LNGDP           1.871222     .566064     .258708      3.306   .0013
LNRADIO         1.684329     .678568     .142349      2.482   .0145
(Constant)     41.696793    3.140306                 13.278   .0000


------------- Variables not in the Equation -------------

Variable      Beta In  Partial  Min Toler        T   Sig T

LNBEDS         .098325  .149173    .235419    1.589   .1148
URBAN         -.022410 -.029057    .237862    -.306   .7600


End Block Number   1   PIN =    .050 Limits reached.
```

Forward selection stops because the observed significance for the remaining variables is larger than 0.05

You see the results when the radio variable is added to the model in Figure 23.10. Note how little R^2 has changed with the entry of the radio variable. It has gone from 0.813 to 0.823. Although the magnitude of the change is small, you can reject the null hypothesis that the change is 0, based on the observed significance level for the test that the partial regression coefficient is 0. That's why the variable is added.

From the statistics for the variables not in the model, you see that there are two independent variables—urbanization and hospital beds—which can be considered for inclusion in the model. The observed significance level for both of the coefficients is larger than the entry criterion of 0.05, so neither variable is entered and forward selection stops.

Compare the five-independent-variables model shown in Figure 23.3 with the three-independent-variables model shown in Figure 23.10. You see that there is a very small difference in the R^2 between the two models. If you look at the adjusted R^2, which takes into account the fact that adding variables to a model always increases R^2 or leaves it unchanged without necessarily improving the fit of the model in the population, you also see that the two additional variables are of little use in the regression model. The standard errors of the coefficients in the three-variable model are smaller than the standard errors of the same coefficients in the five-variable model. That's because the five-variable model includes poor predictors. They increase the variability of the regression coefficients without improving prediction.

Backward Elimination

In forward selection, you start with a model that has no independent variables and sequentially add variables to the model. In backward elimination, you start with a model that contains all of the independent variables and at each step you eliminate the variable that causes the smallest change in R^2. By default, SPSS removes a variable from the model if the observed significance level for its coefficient is greater than 0.10.

In this example, backward elimination starts with the complete five-variable model shown in Figure 23.3. You see that the largest observed significance level (0.84) is for the urban coefficient. Since it is greater than the removal criterion of 0.10, urbanization is the first variable removed from the model. The results are shown in Figure 23.11.

Figure 23.11 Backward elimination

To obtain this regression, repeat the analysis shown in Figure 23.3. For Selection Method, select Backward.

```
Equation Number 1     Dependent Variable..   LIFEEXPF   Female life expectancy 19

Block Number  2.  Method:  Backward      Criterion   POUT  .1000
    LNBEDS    LNDOCS    LNGDP     LNRADIO   URBAN


Variable(s) Removed on Step Number
    6..    URBAN ── Percent urban, 1992


Multiple R              .90911
R Square                .82649                 ┌─────────────────────┐
Adjusted R Square       .82024                 │ Urban is removed    │
Standard Error         4.73096                 │ from the model      │
                                               └─────────────────────┘
Analysis of Variance
                     DF      Sum of Squares       Mean Square
Regression            4         11834.04079       2958.51020
Residual            111          2484.39887         22.38197

F =      132.18273      Signif F =  .0000


------------------ Variables in the Equation ------------------


Variable            B          SE B         Beta        T   Sig T

LNBEDS         1.184264      .745090      .098325     1.589   .1148
LNDOCS         3.918658      .517453      .548339     7.573   .0000
LNGDP          1.590253      .589381      .219862     2.698   .0081
LNRADIO        1.509890      .682868      .127606     2.211   .0291
(Constant)    40.856552     3.163607                 12.915   .0000


------------ Variables not in the Equation ------------

Variable    Beta In  Partial  Min Toler       T   Sig T

URBAN       -.014623 -.019130    .215565     -.201   .8413
```

There are four independent variables in the model and one not in the model. At this point, the *t* value for the hospital beds variable is the smallest. Its observed significance level of 0.11 is larger than the removal criterion of 0.10, so you remove hospital beds. The observed significance level for all of the coefficients is larger than 0.10, so variable removal stops. The forward selection and backward elimination techniques have resulted in the same model. That's not always the case.

Stepwise Selection

The results of building the model using stepwise regression are shown in summary form in Figure 23.12. When you select Block summary in the Linear Regression Statistics dialog box, the coefficients and other statistics are printed only for the final model. At step 1, the doctors variable is entered and has a beta coefficient of 0.88. The model has an R^2 of 0.775 and an F statistic of 391.7 for the test that all coefficients are 0. The observed significance level for the F statistic is less than 0.0005. At step 2, the GDP variable enters the model; at step 3, the radio variable. You'll recognize that the final model is exactly the same as the one you obtained from forward selection and backward elimination.

Figure 23.12 Stepwise selection

To obtain this regression, repeat the analysis shown in Figure 23.3. For Selection Method, select Stepwise. In the Linear Regression Statistics dialog box, select Block summary.

```
Equation Number 1     Dependent Variable..   LIFEEXPF   Female life expectancy 19

Block Number  1.  Method: Stepwise      Criteria   PIN  .0500   POUT  .1000
    LNBEDS    LNDOCS    LNGDP     LNRADIO   URBAN

Step   MultR    Rsq     F(Eqn)   SigF        Variable  BetaIn
   1   .8801   .7746   391.724   .000   In:  LNDOCS    .8801
   2   .9015   .8128   245.281   .000   In:  LNGDP     .3446
   3   .9069   .8225   173.043   .000   In:  LNRADIO   .1423
```

In this example, the models from forward selection and stepwise selection are the same. That's because when you added variables to the model, the coefficients for the variables already in the model stayed significant. Stepwise selection will differ from forward selection only if, at some step, a variable already in the model becomes "unimportant" when another variable is added.

? *What should I do if the methods result in different models?* You should examine the different models and choose among them based on how easy they are to interpret, how easily the values for the independent variables can be obtained, and how well the regression assumptions are met. If you have a large data file, you can split it into two parts (80% for estimating the coefficients and 20% for testing is a good split), estimate the coefficients from one part, and use those coefficients to predict values for the other part. You can see which model works best on the test part of the sample. ■ ■ ■

Summary

How do you build a regression model with more than one independent variable?

- A multiple linear regression model is used to predict values of a dependent variable from a set of independent variables.

- The coefficient for an independent variable in a multiple regression equation is called a partial regression coefficient. Its magnitude and observed significance level depends on the other independent variables in the model.

- The overall regression F test is used to test the null hypothesis that all of the population regression coefficients are 0.

- Forward entry, backward elimination, and stepwise variable selection help you select a regression model that contains only independent variables that meet certain criteria.

What's Next?

In this chapter, you learned how to interpret the results of a multiple regression model. You also developed a multiple regression model using different techniques for variable selection. Although the assumptions needed for testing hypotheses were outlined, you did not examine your data for violations of the requisite assumptions. In Chapter 24, you'll see how to use residuals and other diagnostic information to check for violations of the multiple regression assumptions.

How to Obtain a Multiple Linear Regression

This section provides information about obtaining a multiple linear regression analysis (a regression with more than one independent variable), using the SPSS Linear Regression procedure. For a basic overview of the Linear Regression procedure, see Chapter 20.

▶ To open the Linear Regression dialog box (see Figure 23.13), from the menus choose:

Statistics
  Regression ▶
    Linear...

Figure 23.13 Linear Regression dialog box

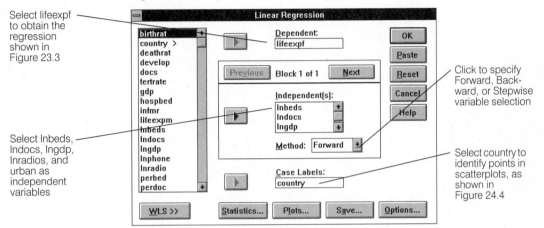

Select lifeexpf to obtain the regression shown in Figure 23.3

Select lnbeds, lndocs, lngdp, lnradios, and urban as independent variables

Click to specify Forward, Backward, or Stepwise variable selection

Select country to identify points in scatterplots, as shown in Figure 24.4

▶ Select the dependent variable and move it into the Dependent box.

▶ Move two or more independent variables into the Independent(s) list and click on OK.

The list holds more variables than are visible; use the scroll bar to see all of them. To remove a variable from the Independent(s) list, click on the same button that you used to add it to the list.

You can specify more than one list, or "block," of variables, using the Next and Previous buttons to display the different lists. You can specify up to nine blocks.

Method. SPSS offers a great deal of control over the way in which variables are entered into, and removed from, the regression equation. The Method alternatives available for a block of variables are:

Enter. All variables in the block are entered into the equation as a group.

Stepwise. Selection of variables within the block proceeds by steps. At each step, variables already in the equation are evaluated according to the selection criteria for removal; then variables not in the equation are evaluated for entry. This process repeats until no variable in the block is eligible for entry or removal.

Remove. All variables in the block that are already in the equation are removed as a group. (If no variables have yet been entered, SPSS first enters all the variables that are included in any block and then proceeds according to specifications.)

Backward. All variables in the block that are in the equation are evaluated according to the selection criteria for removal. Those eligible are removed one at a time until no more are eligible. (If no variables have yet been entered, SPSS first enters all the variables that are included in any block and then proceeds according to specifications.)

Forward. All variables in the block that are not in the equation are evaluated according to the selection criteria for entry. Those eligible are entered one at a time until no more are eligible.

If you specify more than one list (or "block") of independent variables using the Next and Previous buttons, each block of variables has its own method associated with it. SPSS processes each block of independent variables in order, starting with Block 1. Within each block, SPSS selects variables for entry into the equation or removal from the equation according to the procedure specified by that block's Method alternative.

Options: Variable Selection Criteria

The stepwise, backward, and forward methods must choose variables one at a time for entry into the equation or removal from it. They do this according to statistical criteria that you can specify in the Linear Regression Options dialog box. In the Linear Regression dialog box, click on Options to open the Linear Regression Options dialog box, as shown in Figure 23.14.

Figure 23.14 Linear Regression Options dialog box

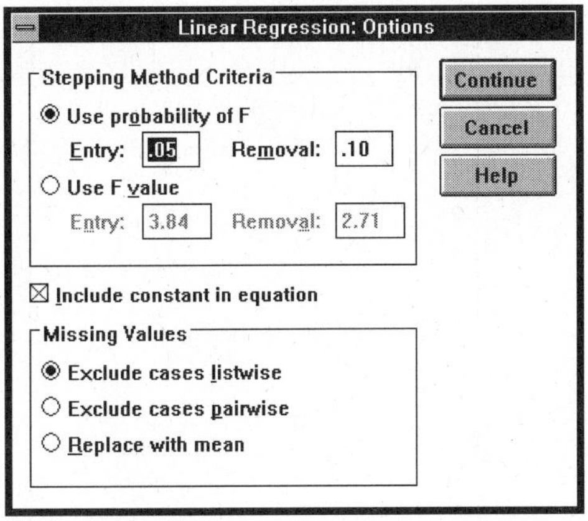

Stepping Method Criteria. In addition to the options discussed in Chapter 20, you can choose between two alternatives in the Stepping Method Criteria group. Both are based on the F statistic for the statistical significance of the change in R^2 when the variable in question enters or is removed from the equation. (The observed significance levels of the F statistic are the same as those for the t test for the coefficients. Similarly, if you square the t value, you get the F value described.) They are:

Use probability of F. The variable with the lowest probability of F is entered first provided that this probability is lower than the Entry value specified in this dialog box; or the variable with the highest probability of F is removed first provided that this probability is higher than the Removal value specified in this dialog box. You can change the Entry and Removal probabilities. Both values must be greater than 0 and less than or equal to 1, and the Entry value must be less than the Removal value.

Use F value. The variable with the highest F statistic is entered first provided that this value is greater than the Entry value specified in this dialog box; or the variable with the lowest F statistic is removed first provided that this value is less than the Removal value specified in this dialog box. You can change the Entry and Removal values. Both values must be greater than 0, and the Entry value must be greater than the Removal value.

The combination of blocks of independent variables with the variable selection methods can be confusing. Usually you can do what you want by moving all of your independent variables into a single block and choosing a suitable Method alternative. The enter and stepwise methods are sufficient for most purposes. Use multiple blocks of variables only when you need to control exactly the way in which your equation is built regardless of the statistical criteria for variable selection.

Exercises

Statistical Concepts

1. The following output is from a regression used to predict the percentage of defective items from the percentage of machines in operation, the percentage of employees present, and the volume produced:

```
Equation Number 1    Dependent Variable..   PCTDEF   Percentage of Defective Ite

Block Number  1.  Method:  Enter      PCTMACH  PCTSTAFF  VOLUME


Variable(s) Entered on Step Number
   1..    VOLUME     Volume Produced
   2..    PCTMACH    Percentage of Machines in Operation
   3..    PCTSTAFF   Percentage of Empoyees Present


Multiple R           .83867
R Square             .70338
Adjusted R Square    .69767
Standard Error      4.01478

Analysis of Variance
                    DF      Sum of Squares      Mean Square
Regression           3         5962.48436       1987.49479
Residual           156         2514.47853         16.11845


F =    123.30556     Signif F =  .0000



------------------ Variables in the Equation ------------------

Variable            B         SE B       Beta        T   Sig T

PCTMACH        -.118892     .035424    -.158154    -3.356  .0010
PCTSTAFF       -.238432     .031424    -.377168    -7.588  .0000
VOLUME          .027412     .002648     .518595    10.350  .0000
(Constant)    30.923252    4.056634                 7.623  .0000
```

a. From the output above, write the multiple linear regression equation that predicts the percentage of defective items from the percentage of machines in operation, the percentage of employees present, and the volume produced.

b. What does the negative sign for two of the coefficients tell you?

c. Can you reject the null hypothesis that in the population all coefficients are 0? On what do you base your conclusion?

d. What percentage of the variability in the percentage of defective items is explained by the three independent variables?

e. From the coefficients, can you determine which variable is the single best predictor of the defective percentage?

f. If you built the model using forward or backward elimination, do you think the model would change? Why or why not?

2. For the regression in question 1, indicate what steps you would take to test whether the assumptions necessary for the linear regression are violated.

3. For the regression in question 1, what would you predict the defective rate to be when 90% of the machines are in operation, 90% of the staff is present, and 4000 items are produced?

4. Is the following regression output possible if a variable is added at each step and none are removed from the equation?

Step	Multiple R	R square
1	0.5821	0.3388
2	0.6164	0.3799
3	0.6025	0.3630
4	0.6399	0.4095

Data Analysis

Use the *gss.sav* data file to answer the following questions:

1. Run a linear regression model to predict a person's education (*educ*) from their father's education (*paeduc*) and the number of hours of television watched per day (*tvhours*). Save the Studentized residuals, the unstandardized predicted values, and the changes in the regression coefficients when a case is removed from the analysis.

a. Write the equation.

b. Can you reject the null hypothesis that all the population values for the regression coefficients are 0? On what do you base your conclusion?

c. Can you reject the null hypothesis that the population value for the proportion of variability in the dependent variable explained by the independent variables is 0? On what do you base your conclusion? What proportion of the sample variability in education is explained by the two independent variables?

d. Can you reject the null hypothesis that there is no linear relationship between a person's education and their father's education and the number of hours of television they watch a day? On what do you base your conclusion?

e. Can you reject the null hypothesis that the population value for the partial regression coefficient for father's education is 0? On what do you base your conclusion?

f. Can you reject the null hypothesis that the population value for the partial regression coefficient for television hours is 0? On what do you base your conclusion?

g. How many years of education would you predict for a person whose father has 14 years of education and who watches 3 hours of television a day?

h. Does the predicted value for education increase or decrease as television watching increases? As father's education increases?

i. How much does the predicted value for education change for a 1-year increase in father's education? For a 1-hour increase in hours of television watched?

2. Test the required regression assumptions for the regression in question 1.

a. Obtain a histogram and Q-Q plot of the Studentized residuals. Is the distribution of residuals approximately normal?

b. Plot the Studentized residuals against the predicted values and against the values of each independent variable. Do you see any patterns that concern you?

c. Plot the change in the coefficient for father's education when each case is removed from the computation of the coefficients. Identify the ID's of the cases that cause the largest changes in the coefficient. Go to the Data Editor and list their values for the dependent variable and both independent variables.

d. Repeat question 2c for the change in the coefficient for hours of television watched.

e. Give your assessment of how well the assumptions required for the regression model are met.

3. Use stepwise linear regression to obtain a model to predict years of education from the following independent variables: father's education (variable *paeduc*), spouse's education (*speduc*), hours of television watched per day (*tvhours*), age (*age*), income in dollars (*rincomdol*), and hours worked (*hrs1*). Use the default criteria for variable entry and removal.

a. By including the variable *speduc,* you are restricting your analysis to what kind of people?

b. What is the first independent variable to enter the model? How is it selected?

c. What proportion of the variability in the dependent variable is explained by the independent variable? Can you reject the null hypothesis that the population value for the regression coefficient is 0?

d. Based on the model, what do you predict for years of education for a 50-year-old person whose father has 12 years of education, whose spouse has 14 years of education, who watches 3 hours of television a day, has an income of $30,000, worked 42 hours last week, and is male?

e. What variable enters the model at the second step? What is the change in R^2 when the variable enters? Write the regression equation and obtain the predicted years of education for the person described in question 3d. How has your prediction changed?

f. What variable enters at the third step? How much does R^2 change? Write the regression equation and obtain the predicted years of education for the person described in question 3d.

g. What is the last variable to enter the model? How much does R^2 change when it is entered? What is the predicted value for years of education for the person described in question 3d? How much has the predicted value for the person changed from question 3d to question 3g?

h. Why does variable selection stop?

i. What is the partial correlation between education and father's education, "controlling" for spouse's education and respondent's income in dollars?

j. Based on the size of the partial regression coefficients, is it reasonable to conclude that a person's income is least strongly related to education? Why or why not?

k. Consider the spouse's education variable. How has its coefficient changed at each step of model building? Why has this happened?

4. Look for violations of the regression assumptions for the model you built in question 3. Use the steps outlined in question 2 as a guide. Summarize your findings.

5. Use the Partial Correlations procedure to calculate the following partial correlation coefficients:

a. The partial correlation between *educ* and *paeduc,* controlling for *tvhours.*

b. The partial correlation between *educ* and *speduc,* controlling for *paeduc* and *rincome.*

    c. The partial correlation between *educ* and *paeduc,* controlling for *maeduc* and *rincome.*

    d. The partial correlation coefficient between *educ* and *speduc,* controlling for *tvhours, rincome, age,* and *hrs1.*

    e. Interpret each of the coefficients and indicate what type of relationship the coefficients are measuring.

6. Develop a regression model to predict education for all adults, not just those who are married. That means you can't use any variables that are available only for married people (such as spouse's education). Check the regression assumptions and summarize your findings.

7. Develop a regression equation to predict hours worked last week for full-time employees only (variable *wrkstat* equals 1). Summarize your findings. Be sure to check for violations of the regression assumptions. If the assumptions appear to be violated, try taking the square root of the number of hours worked as the dependent variable. Rerun the model and check the diagnostics again. Do you see any improvement?

Use the *salary.sav* data file to answer the following questions:

8. Use the Regression procedure to obtain a multiple linear regression model that predicts the natural log of the beginning salary (variable *salbeg*) from age, gender, minority status, education level, and work experience (variables *age, sex, minority, edlevel,* and *work*).Write the multiple linear regression model. Remember, you're now predicting the natural log of the beginning salary, not the actual salary.

    a. Can you reject the null hypothesis that there is no linear relationship between the dependent variable and the independent variables?

    b. What proportion of the variability in transformed beginning salary is explained by the independent variables?

    c. For which variables can you reject the null hypothesis that the population values for the partial regression coefficients are 0?

    d. What does the negative sign for the *sex* and *minority* variables tell you?

    e. What can you tell from the size of the partial regression coefficients about the individual independent variables as predictors of beginning salary?

9. Rerun the equation without the age variable. Do the partial regression coefficients for the other variables change when age is removed from the model? Why? Obtain the correlation coefficients between all pairs of variables in question 8. Which variable is most strongly linearly related to the log of beginning salary?

10. For the variables described in question 8, use stepwise variable selection to develop a multiple linear regression model. Save the Studentized residuals, the predicted values, and the changes in the coefficients.

a. Which variable enters the model first? Why? What proportion of the variability in the dependent variable is explained by this single variable?

b. How is the second variable to enter the model selected? Which variable enters? What proportion of the variability in the dependent variable is "explained" by the two independent variables?

c. What is the last variable to enter the model? Why does variable selection end? What proportion of the variability in the dependent variable is explained by all the independent variables in the model?

d. Look at the partial correlation coefficient between age and the log of the beginning salary. What does it tell you? Use the Partial Correlations procedure to calculate the same coefficient.

11. For the model in question 10, look for violations of the assumptions needed for multiple linear regression.

a. Make a histogram and Q-Q plot of the Studentized residuals. Is the distribution approximately normal? Do you see any outliers? If so, identify them in the Data Editor and look at their values for the dependent variable and the independent variables.

b. Make a plot of the Studentized residuals against the predicted values. What should you look for in this plot? Do you see any problems? Explain.

c. Plot the Studentized residuals against the values of each independent variable. Do these plots look all right?

d. Look at the impact of individual points on the estimates of each partial regression coefficient. Identify points that cause large changes in the coefficients.

Use the *country.sav* data file to answer the following questions:

12. Build a multiple linear regression model that predicts male life expectancy (variable *lifeexpm*) from percentage urban (variable *urban*), the natural log of doctors per 10,000 people (*lndocs*), the natural log of hospital beds per 10,000 people (*lnbeds*), the natural log of GDP (*lngdp*), and the natural log of radios per 100 people (*lnradio*).

a. Write the regression equation.

b. Can you reject the null hypothesis that there is no linear relationship between the dependent variable and the independent variables?

c. What proportion of the variability in male life expectancy is "explained" by the independent variables? Can you reject the null hypothesis that the population value for R^2 is 0?

d. For which variables can you reject the null hypothesis that their partial regression coefficients are 0?

e. Compare this model to the one developed in this chapter for predicting female life expectancy. Are the coefficients similar in value for the two models?

13. Using the Bivariate Correlations procedure obtain the correlation matrix for the dependent and independent variables. Which variables appear to be most highly correlated with male life expectancy? For which variables can you reject the null hypothesis that the population value for the correlation coefficient is 0?

14. Using stepwise variable selection, build a model to predict male life expectancy from the independent variables listed in question 12. Save the Studentized residuals, the predicted values, and the changes in the coefficients.

a. What is the first variable to enter the regression model? How was it selected?

b. Why does the natural log of radios variable not enter the model?

c. Write the final regression model. Compare it to the model for female life expectancy. Are they basically similar?

d. What proportion of the variability in male life expectancy is "explained" by the natural log of doctors and the natural log of GDP?

e. Use the Partial Correlations procedure to estimate the partial correlation coefficient between the natural log of radios and male life expectancy, "controlling" for the natural log of hospital beds and the natural log of GDP. Where does this appear on the regression output? What does it mean?

15. Examine the regression assumptions for the model developed in question 14.

a. Obtain histograms and Q-Q plots of the Studentized residuals. Identify any outlying points. What countries do they represent? Are they the same countries that were unusual in the regression of female life expectancy?

b. Plot the Studentized residuals against the predicted values and against the values of each independent variable. Do you see any suspicious patterns?

c. Plot the changes in each of the regression coefficients against the sequence number. Which countries cause the largest changes in the coefficients?

16. Using the same variables as in question 12, use backward elimination to build the regression model. Does the model change?

Multiple Regression Diagnostics

How can you check for violations of the multiple linear regression assumptions, and how can you identify cases that are influencing the regression results more than the other cases are?

- What can you learn by plotting residuals against the predicted values and the values of the independent variables?
- What is leverage and why is it important?
- Why is Cook's distance useful?
- What can you tell from a partial regression plot?

In Chapter 23, you built a multiple regression model to predict female life expectancy from per capita measures of the GDP and numbers of doctors and radios. In this chapter, you'll use residuals and other diagnostics to check for violations of the regression assumptions and to identify data points that are in some way unusual. All of the diagnostic techniques described in Chapter 22 are also useful for a multiple regression model. This chapter emphasizes techniques that are not described in Chapter 22.

▶ This chapter analyzes the residuals and other diagnostics for the multiple regression model described in Chapter 23. To duplicate the results shown, rerun the regression with only the three independent variables in the final model (the variables *lndocs*, *lngdp*, and *lnradios*). In the Linear Regression Save New Variables dialog box, save Studentized deleted residuals, predicted values, leverages, Cook's distance, and the standardized changes in the regression coefficients (SdfBetas), as shown in Figure 20.18 in Chapter 20. In the Linear Regression Plots dialog box, request all partial regression plots, as shown in Figure 20.17.

507

Examining Normality

You'll use Studentized deleted residuals to look for violations of the regression assumptions because they make it easier to spot unusual points. The Studentized deleted residual for a case is the Studentized residual when the case is excluded from the regression computations. If the regression assumptions are met, their distribution is a Student's t with $N-p-2$ degrees of freedom, where N is the number of cases and p is the number of independent variables in the model. Since your sample size is much larger than 30, the distribution of the Studentized deleted residuals should be approximately normal. (We'll refer to Studentized deleted residuals as simply residuals throughout the rest of this chapter.)

Figure 24.1   Plot of Studentized deleted residuals

You can obtain stem-and-leaf plots using the Explore procedure, as discussed in Chapter 7. Select the variable sdr_1 in the Explore dialog box.

```
 Frequency     Stem &  Leaf

     1.00 Extremes     (-3.4)
     2.00        -2 *  02
     5.00        -1 .  57899
    12.00        -1 *  000012233444
    15.00        -0 .  555555666778889
    22.00        -0 *  0000000011111122334444
    28.00         0 *  0000000011111111122233334444
    18.00         0 .  555555556677888899
    11.00         1 *  00011122234
     5.00         1 .  55669
     2.00 Extremes     (2.7), (3.3)

 Stem width:    1.00000
 Each leaf:        1 case(s)
```

Look first at the stem-and-leaf plot of the residuals in Figure 24.1. The shape of the distribution looks pretty good. It's symmetric and has a single peak. The three outlying values are identified in Figure 24.2, the boxplot of the residuals. (They're discussed in detail later.)

Figure 24.2 Boxplot of residuals

You can obtain boxplots using the Explore procedure, as discussed in Chapter 7. Select the sdr_1 variable in the Explore dialog box.

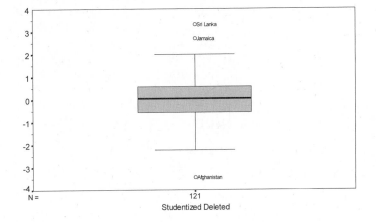

In the boxplot, you see that the distribution is fairly symmetric, since the median is in the middle of the plot. The middle half of the residuals are between –0.57 and +0.57, the values for the first and third quartiles. The corresponding quartiles for the normal distribution are –0.68 and +0.68, so the sample results match quite well. The whiskers extend to +2 and –2, which is what you expect for a sample from a normal population.

Figure 24.3 Q-Q plot of residuals

You can obtain normal probability plots using the Explore procedure, as discussed in Chapter 7. Select the variable sdr_1 in the Explore dialog box.

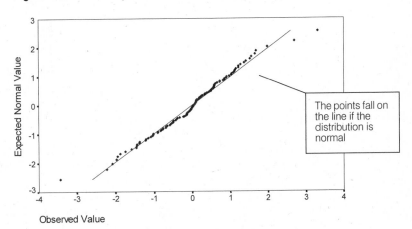

Figure 24.3 is the Q-Q plot of the residuals. If the residuals are from a normal population, they should fall close to the straight line. That's the case, except for the three outlying points. As you learned in Chapter 22, many different types of problems, such as unequal variances or violations of the linearity assumption, can cause the distribution of residuals to appear non-normal. That's why you should correct any other problems in your model before worrying about normality.

Scatterplots of Residuals

Figure 24.4 is a scatterplot of predicted and observed values of female life expectancy. Except for the cluster of points in the upper right corner, you see that the points are reasonably evenly distributed above and below the line. That's good, since clusters of points above or below the line indicate that you're consistently overpredicting or underpredicting for certain values of observed female life expectancy. That's an indication that a linear model might not be a good choice.

Figure 24.4 Scatterplot of predicted and observed values

You can obtain scatterplots using the Graphs menu, as discussed in Chapter 9. Select the variables pre_1 and lifeexpf in the Simple Scatterplot dialog box.

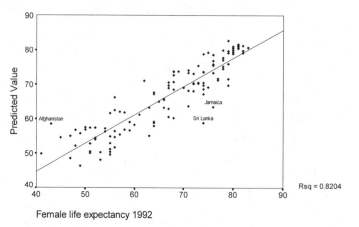

For each observed value of female life expectancy, you see a range of predicted values. If the assumption of equal variances is met, the range should be pretty much the same for all observed female life expectancies. For large observed values of female life expectancy, you see that the range of the predicted values is much narrower than elsewhere in the plot. That's probably because there is a natural limit on life expectancy that most of the highly developed nations have reached. There's just not much observed variability in life expectancy for the highly developed nations. Their residuals are small and bunched together. That's an undesirable situation for the regression model, since it requires the variance of the residuals to be constant over the entire range of predicted values.

Note that the R^2 for the regression line of the predicted and observed life expectancies is the same as the multiple R^2 from the final stepwise model in Chapter 23. That's always the case. Multiple R is the correlation between the observed and predicted values of the dependent variable.

? *I distinctly remember that the multiple R^2 for the final model in Chapter 23 was 0.8225, not 0.8204; what gives?* When you estimated the stepwise regression model, only cases that had non-missing values for all of the possible variables were included in the regression computations. That means that a country with missing values for any variable, regardless of whether it appears in the final model, is excluded from the computations. In this chapter, you estimated a model that includes only three independent variables. All cases with valid values for the three variables are included in the computations. It doesn't matter if they have missing values for other variables not in the model. This causes a slight change in the regression coefficients and in the multiple R^2 from Chapter 23. The multiple R^2 is really 0.8204.

When you have cases with missing values, you should rerun the regression after you select a model. That way, you include all cases that have values for the variables in the model. ■ ■ ■

In Figure 24.5, the residuals are plotted against the predicted values of female life expectancy. It's easier to see problems in this plot than in the previous one. You see that most of the residuals fall in a horizontal band around 0. Again, you see that the residuals for predicted values above 75 have somewhat less spread than the residuals for the smaller predicted values.

Sri Lanka, Jamaica, and Afghanistan stand out in Figure 24.5, since they have large absolute values for the residuals. The observed female life expectancy for Afghanistan (43 years) is low compared to the predicted value of 58.5 years. The residual of –3.4 has a probability of 0.0008, although if you multiply it by 121 to correct for picking out the largest residual from 121, the corrected probability of 0.10 is no longer particularly unusual. There are reasons why Afghanistan may be an outlier from the regression. It's been devastated by a long and fierce war, so it may be different in important ways from the other countries in the data base. While it may appear to have some of the trappings of economic development, such as doctors, hospital beds, and radios, the war has probably had a large effect on the health of the population. Since the regression model doesn't include a variable for recent war, it's not that troublesome that Afghanistan's life expectancy is poorly predicted. It may make sense to eliminate Afghanistan from the model altogether and to restrict the model to countries that have not recently experienced unusual natural or man-made calamities.

Jamaica and Sri Lanka both have large positive residuals, meaning that their observed life expectancies are greater than those predicted by the model. The uncorrected probability of a residual in absolute value as large as that for Jamaica (2.7) is 0.008, for Sri Lanka (3.3) it is 0.001. If you correct for looking at many residuals, these two residuals are not unusually large.

Figure 24.5   Residuals versus predicted values

Select the variables sdr_1 and pre_1 in the Simple Scatterplot dialog box.

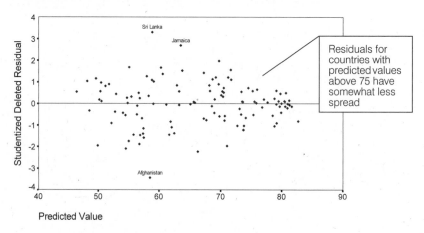

You can go to the Data Editor and examine the values of the independent variables for the three countries with the largest residuals in absolute value. You'll see that the individual values for GDP, doctors, and radios are not unusual. If they were, you would see them as outliers on stem-and-leaf plots or boxplots. What you really want to know, though, is whether these countries have unusual *combinations* of values. For example, does a country have a very high GDP and a very low number of radios? From the Data Editor, you can't easily tell if the observed combinations of values of the independent variable are unusual. However, there are diagnostic statistics in regression that make it easy for you to spot such cases.

? *I plotted the residuals against the observed values of the dependent variable, and they're not randomly distributed. What should I do?* Nothing. You don't expect to see a random distribution of points in this plot. The least-squares line for this plot will always have a slope of $1 - R^2$. ▪ ▪ ▪

Leverage

You can use a statistic called the leverage to identify cases with unusual combinations of values of the independent variables. **Leverage** measures how far the values for a case are from the means of all of the independent variables. Leverage values computed by SPSS range in value from 0 to close to 1. Cases with high leverage values may have a large impact on the estimates of the regression coefficients. A rule of thumb is to look at cases with leverage values greater than $2p/N$ (0.0496 in this case—see the reference line in Figure 24.6), where p is the number of independent variables in the model and N is the number of cases. (For a small number of independent variables, this rule of thumb singles out too many points.)

Figure 24.6 Leverage for points in the regression

To obtain this scatterplot, select the variables lev_1 and sequence in the Simple Scatterplot dialog box.

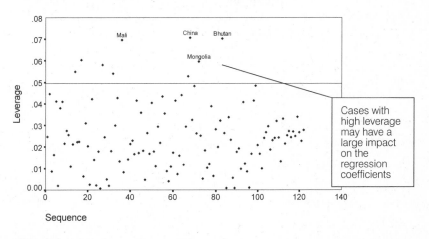

If you click on the points with the highest leverages in Figure 24.6, you'll see that they represent Mali, China, and Bhutan. Mali and Bhutan have the two smallest values for radios per 100 people. (Mali has 1.9 radios per 100 people, Bhutan has 1.6, and the United States has 200 radios per 100 people!) Mali and Bhutan are also "below average" for the other two independent variables. China has an unusual combination of values. It's above average on the number of doctors and below average on GDP and radios.

> *What should I do if I find points with large leverages?* If you find points that have large leverage values, look at the data values to make sure that the data file doesn't contain errors for these cases. That's one possible explanation for high leverage. If the values are correct, try to think of possible explanations for why the point is unusual. Often, you can learn a lot about a problem by scrutinizing cases with unusual values.

Problems with data collection may introduce unusual points. For example, it's possible that the statistics for the numbers of doctors, hospital beds, radios, etc., may not be equally accurate for all countries in the data base. A good question to ask is, Where did these numbers come from? Are they official government statistics, or were they obtained in a uniform manner from a reputable large-scale survey? That may explain some unusual findings.

Changes in the Coefficients

In Chapter 22, you identified points that change the value of the slope and the intercept. You calculated the slope with and without each case and saw how much the value changed. You can do the same thing in a multiple regression model. But now you have to look at the effect of removing a case on the values of each of the coefficients, including the constant.

Figure 24.7 Standardized changes in the doctor coefficient

To obtain this scatterplot, select the variables sdb*_1* and sequence in the Simple Scatterplot dialog box.

*There will be three sdb*_1 variables, one for each of the independent variables in the model. To find out which corresponds to the doctor coefficient, check the output window after you run the model. (See Figure 20.19 in Chapter 20.)

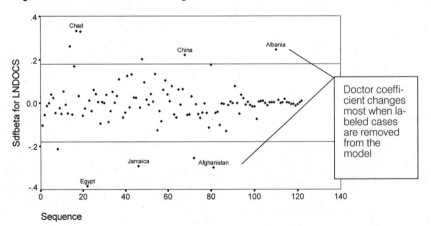

Look at Figure 24.7, which is a plot of the standardized changes in the doctor coefficient when each case is eliminated from the computations. Ideally, the points should fall in a horizontal band around 0. You see that there are several points which stick out from the rest. (A rule of thumb is to look at cases with absolute values greater than $2/\sqrt{N}$.) Egypt causes the largest standardized change in the doctor coefficient when it is eliminated from the analysis. Egypt has one doctor for every 616 people. The observed female life expectancy for Egypt, however, is not as large as you would predict based on all those doctors. If you remove Egypt from the model, the doctor coefficient changes from 4.19 to 4.38. (You have to compute DfBeta, the actual change in the coefficient, to know how much the coefficient changes.) When you have a large number of cases, it's unlikely that removal of a single case will change the actual value of a coefficient very much.

Cook's Distance

You can also compute Cook's distance (named after a statistician— nothing to do with kitchens or food!), which measures the change in all of the regression coefficients when a case is eliminated from the analysis. Cook's distance for a case depends on both the Studentized residual and the leverage values.

Figure 24.8 Cook's distances

To obtain this scatterplot, select the variables coo_1 and sequence in the Simple Scatterplot dialog box.

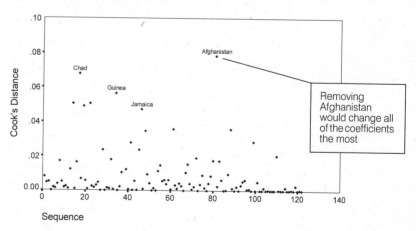

Figure 24.8 is a plot of Cook's distances for all of the cases in the regression. The largest Cook's distance is for Afghanistan, meaning that its removal would change all of the coefficients the most. That's not surprising, since Afghanistan has the largest residual. You've already seen that the life expectancy for Afghanistan is poorly predicted by the model. You can calculate probabilities for Cook's distances using the F distribution with $p+1$ and $N-p-1$ degrees of freedom, where p is the number of independent variables in the model and N is the number of cases. Cook's distances greater than 1 usually deserve scrutiny.

? *Why are you plotting the values of the diagnostic statistics against an arbitrary sequence number instead of getting stem-and-leaf plots of them?* If you plot the diagnostics using a scatterplot, you can readily identify the points. There's no easy way to do that in a histogram or a stem-and-leaf plot. However, you can identify outliers on boxplots or from lists of outliers in the Explore procedure. ■ ■ ■

Plots Against Independent Variables

If the regression model is correct, when you plot the residuals against the values of the independent variables in the model, you should not see a pattern. If you do, the relationship between the dependent and the independent variable may not be linear.

Figure 24.9 Residual versus transformed doctors variable

To obtain this scatterplot, select the variables sdr_1 and Indocs in the Simple Scatterplot dialog box.

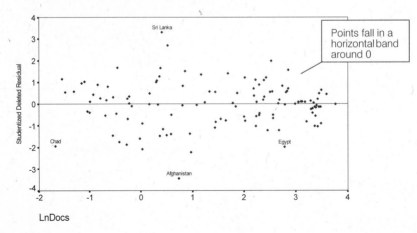

For example, Figure 24.9 is a scatterplot of the residual against the transformed doctors variable. You don't see a pattern—the points fall in a horizontal band around 0. If you didn't take logs of the doctors variable so that it would be linearly related to female life expectancy but instead used the original variable in the model, you would get the scatterplot shown in Figure 24.10. You see that the residuals are no longer randomly distributed in a horizontal band around 0. Instead, there is a definite pattern. That tells you there's something wrong.

Figure 24.10 Using untransformed doctor variable

To duplicate this plot, you need to repeat the stepwise regression described at the beginning of this chapter, substituting the untransformed variable docs for lndocs. Save the residuals again and plot the resulting variable sdr_2 in a scatterplot against the variable docs, as shown.

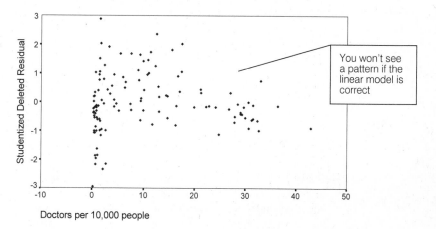

You can also plot the residuals against values of independent variables that are not in the model. If you see a relationship between the residuals and the values of the independent variable, you should consider including the variable in the model.

Figure 24.11 Residual versus ln of phones variable

To obtain this scatterplot, select the variables sdr_1 and lnphone in the Simple Scatterplot dialog box.

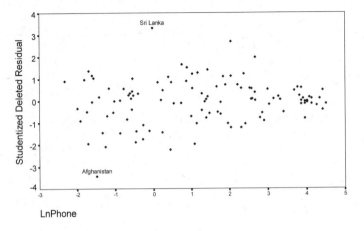

For example, Figure 24.11 is a plot of the residual against the natural log of the number of phones. You see that the points are scattered around a horizontal line through 0, indicating that it's probably unnecessary to include phones in the model. In contrast, look at Figure 24.12, which is a plot of the residuals against the death rate. Here you see that there is a relationship between the two variables. However, you probably don't want to include death rate in the model, since it's really just a somewhat different way of measuring life expectancy.

Figure 24.12 Residuals against death rate

To obtain this scatterplot, select the variables sdr_1 and deathrat in the Simple Scatterplot dialog box.

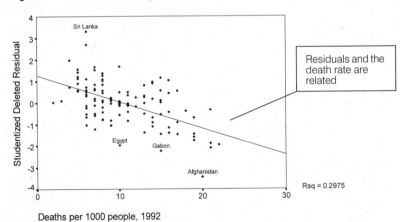

Partial Regression Plot

Another plot that helps you assess the adequacy of the regression model is the partial regression plot. Figure 24.13 is the partial regression plot for the doctors variable. It's a plot of two residuals. On the vertical axis, you plot the residuals from predicting female life expectancy from all of the independent variables except the doctors variable. On the horizontal axis, you plot the residuals from predicting the doctors variable from all of the other independent variables. By calculating the residuals, you remove the linear effects of the other independent variables from both the dependent variable and the independent variable.

If the assumption of linearity is met, as it appears to be in this example, the partial regression plot is linear. If it isn't, you may need to transform your independent variable or include additional terms, such as squares of the independent variable in the model.

Figure 24.13 Partial regression plot for lndocs

To obtain this scatterplot, select the variables lifeexpf and lndocs in the Simple Scatterplot dialog box.

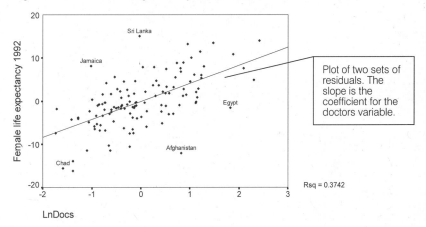

The slope of the regression line for the two residuals in Figure 24.13 is 4.19, the coefficient for the doctors variable in the multiple regression. The correlation coefficient between the two variables is the partial correlation coefficient—the correlation between the two variables when the other independent variables are held constant. From the square root of the R^2 value, you see that the partial correlation between female life expectancy and the doctors variable is 0.61.

The outliers on a partial regression plot are points that are influential in determining the coefficient of the independent variable. For example, you see that Afghanistan, Jamaica, and Sri Lanka are outliers on this plot as well.

> **?** *My partial regression plot is unreadable. There are labels everywhere.* By default SPSS prints case labels for all of the points on the partial regression plot. Move the chart into a chart window and turn the labels off (see "Identifying Unusual Points" on p. 162 in Chapter 9).   ■ ■ ■

Why Bother?

You've learned a lot of different ways you can examine the results of a regression analysis. It's important that you do so. Identify outliers and see if you can think of reasons why the model doesn't fit them. If possible, modify the model to include additional predictors that may improve the fit. If the independent variables aren't linearly related to the dependent variable, try to transform the variables. If you encounter points that are having a large influence on individual coefficients, worry about them. You want to have a regression model that doesn't depend heavily on one or two points. If you are careful in building the regression model, you'll have a useful summary of the relationship between a dependent variable and a set of independent variables.

Summary

How can you check for violations of the multiple linear regression assumptions, and how can you identify cases that are influencing the regression results more than the other cases are?

- By plotting residuals against the independent variables, you can see if there are additional variables that should be included in the model and if the variables that are in the model are linearly related to the dependent variable.

- Leverage is a measure of how much a case influences the regression.

- Cook's distance tells you how much the coefficients change when a case is removed from the model.

- A partial regression plot is a plot of two residuals. It's useful for assessing departures from the regression assumptions.

Exercises

Statistical Concepts

1. What regression assumptions can you test with each of the following displays?

   a. Histogram of residuals

   b. Plot of residuals against predicted values

   c. Plot of residuals against the independent variables

   d. Partial regression plot

   e. Plot of the residuals in the sequence the observations are taken

2. The following is a stem-and-leaf plot of Studentized residuals when salary is predicted from five independent variables:

```
Frequency    Stem &  Leaf

    1.00      -2 *  &
    4.00      -1 .  6&
   36.00      -1 *  000001122344
  102.00      -0 .  555555666666677777888888889999999
  137.00      -0 *  0000000000000001111111111222222233333444444
   99.00       0 *  00000011111122222222333333333344444
   48.00       0 .  5555667778888899
   27.00       1 *  0001122334
    6.00       1 .  56&
   10.00 Extremes    (2.0), (2.1), (2.2), (2.7), (3.0), (3.1), (3.4), (4.2)
    4.00 Extremes    (4.2), (4.9), (6.5), (9.1)


Stem width:    1.00000
Each leaf:        3 case(s)
```

Below is the same plot when the natural log of salary is the dependent variable:

```
Frequency    Stem &  Leaf

    1.00 Extremes    (-2.6)
    4.00      -2 *  3&
   12.00      -1 .  5667&
   44.00      -1 *  000011122233444
   89.00      -0 .  555556666667777788888888999999
  101.00      -0 *  0000011122222223333333333334444444
   94.00       0 *  0000000111111122222223334444444
   60.00       0 .  55566666777788888899
   42.00       1 *  0001122223344
   13.00       1 .  5677
    5.00       2 *  0&
    9.00 Extremes    (2.6), (2.7), (3.4), (3.5), (3.7), (3.8), (4.5), (4.7)

Stem width:    1.00000
Each leaf:        3 case(s)



& denotes fractional leaves.
```

Based on the distribution of residuals, which model do you prefer?

3. The following is the partial regression plot for years of education when the natural log of salary is predicted from age, work experience, education, gender, and minority status.

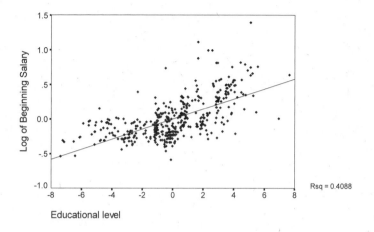

a. What is the partial correlation coefficient between log of salary and years of education?

b. Do you see any problems with the plot?

c. How can you try to remedy the problem?

Data Analysis

Use the *gss.sav* data file to answer the following questions:

1. Consider the regression model you developed in the exercises to Chapter 23 to predict a person's education from their spouse's education, father's education, income in dollars, and number of hours of television watched. Run the model again and produce all partial residual plots. Save the Studentized residuals, predicted values, leverages, Cook's distance, and standardized changes in the regression coefficients when cases are excluded from the model.

a. Check the normality assumption.

b. Plot Studentized residuals against predicted values, the values of the independent variables in the model, and mother's education. Do you see any disturbing patterns?

c. Plot the leverages against case ID numbers. Identify any points that have large leverage values.

d. Plot the standardized changes in the partial regression coefficients when cases are excluded from the analysis. Do you see any problems?

e. Plot Cook's distance. Do you see any points that have a large effect on the coefficients?

f. Look at each of the partial regression plots. Edit them to show the regression line and R^2. Do you see any problems with these plots?

2. Develop a multiple linear regression equation to predict husband's education from wife's education and other independent variables you have available. Check all of the regression assumptions. Look for influential points. Write a short paper summarizing your conclusions.

3. Build a multiple linear regression equation using any of the variables in the *gss.sav* file that interest you. Check all of the assumptions. Write a short summary of your model.

Use the *salary.sav* data file to answer the following questions:

4. Rerun the final equation you developed in the exercises to Chapter 23. (Predict the natural log of beginning salary from gender, education level, work experience, and minority status (variables *sex, edlevel, work,* and *minority*).) Save the leverages, Studentized residuals, standardized changes in the regression coefficients, and Cook's distance. Obtain all of the partial regression plots.

a. Plot the leverages against the ID variable. Are there any points that stand out from the rest?

b. Are there any unusual Cook's distances?

c. Look at each partial regression plot. Edit them to include the regression line and R^2. For the work experience variable, use the Partial Correlations procedure to show the relationship between R^2 for the partial regression plot and the partial regression coefficient.

d. Does the partial regression plot for education level look linear? What does it suggest?

5. Compute a new variable that is equal to the education level squared. Rerun the model in question 4, including education level and education level squared. Save the partial regression plots. Look at the partial regression plot for education level and education level squared. Does the plot appear more linear? How much has multiple R^2 increased with the inclusion of education level squared? Do you think this model is better than the model without education level squared? Explain.

6. What does the coefficient for the gender and minority status variables tell you? What reasons besides discrimination can explain the observed findings?

Use the *country.sav* data file to answer the following questions:

7. Build a multiple linear regression model to predict birthrate (variable *birthrat*) from the same variables that were used to predict female life expectancy in Chapter 23.

a. What percentage of the variability in birthrate can be "explained" by the other independent variables? Can you reject the null hypothesis that there is no linear relationship between the dependent variable and the independent variables?

b. Use either backward elimination or stepwise variable selection to build a model that contains fewer variables. Why are the partial regression coefficients for the variables negative? Are the same variables useful for predicting female life expectancy useful for predicting birthrate?

8. Check the regression assumptions for the model you developed in question 7b.

a. Make a stem-and-leaf plot of the Studentized residuals. Check for normality. Does the distribution appear more or less normal?

b. Plot the Studentized residuals against the predicted values and against the values of the independent variables. Do you see anything suspicious?

c. Obtain plots of leverage and Cook's distance against the sequence number. Identify the countries that have unusual values for the two statistics. Are they the same countries that were unusual when you predicted female life expectancy?

d. Plot the standardized changes in the regression coefficients against the sequence number. Do you see anything unusual?

e. Examine the partial regression plots for each of the independent variables. Edit them to include the regression line and R^2. Do you see departures from linearity in any of the plots? Use the Partial Correlations procedure to calculate the partial correlation coefficients that correspond to the values for R^2 displayed on the partial regression plots.

9. Develop a multiple linear regression model of your choice using the variables in the data file. Write a short paper explaining your model and showing the results of checking for departures from the regression assumptions.

Use the *schools.sav* data file to answer the following questions:

10. Build a multiple linear regression equation to predict 1993 ACT scores (variable *act93*). Be sure to check all of the assumptions and to identify points with a big effect on the partial regression coefficients. Write a short report outlining your final model, how you arrived at it, and what it means.

11. Repeat question 10 to predict 1993 graduation rates (variable *grad93*).

Obtaining Charts in SPSS

Charts are extremely important in statistical analysis and are used throughout this book. Leaving discussions of how to interpret charts to the relevant chapters, this appendix focuses on how to obtain high-resolution charts using SPSS.

Regardless of the chart type, the basic steps for creating and modifying a chart are similar. This appendix begins by demonstrating these steps, using clustered bar charts as typical examples. Specific instructions on how to obtain some of the different charts discussed in this book are then provided.

Scatterplots are not covered in this appendix, since they are discussed in detail in Chapter 9. In addition, a number of the charts available in SPSS are not used in this book and are not discussed here. The online Help system describes in detail all of the charts available in SPSS.

Overview

Roughly speaking, the steps in working with charts are these:

▶ **Create a chart.** You create charts using the Graphs menu. Many statistics procedures also create charts to accompany their statistical output.

▶ **Look at the chart.** Newly created charts appear in the Chart Carousel window.

▶ **Modify the chart.** To modify a chart, click on the Edit button in the Chart Carousel. This moves the chart from the Chart Carousel into a chart window of its own, where you can modify it.

▶ **Save the chart.** Use the File menu to save a chart onto your disk. You can then reopen the chart to modify or print it, or use it as a template or model for the formatting of other charts.

▶ **Print the chart.** Use the File menu to print charts.

Creating Clustered Bar Charts

Regardless of the chart type, the basic steps for creating a chart are similar. What can be confusing is knowing exactly which options to select and understanding the relationship between chart structure and data structure.

Creating a Chart Comparing Groups of Cases

Chapter 6 shows a clustered bar chart summarizing years of education within different job satisfaction categories for both men and women. To create this chart, follow these steps:

▶ Open the *gssft.sav* data file.

▶ From the menus choose:

Graphs
　Bar...

This opens the Bar Charts dialog box, as shown in Figure A.1.

Figure A.1　Bar Charts dialog box

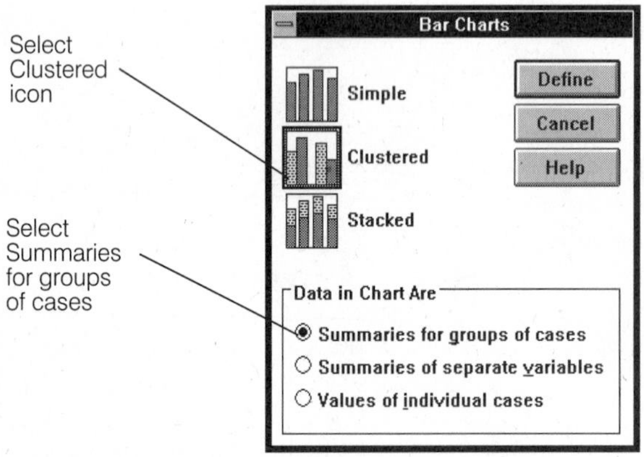

Select Clustered icon

Select Summaries for groups of cases

▶ Click on the Clustered bar chart icon.

▶ Click on Summaries for groups of cases if it is not selected already.

▶ Click on Define.

This opens the Define Clustered Bar Summaries for Groups of Cases dialog box, as shown in Figure A.2.

Figure A.2   Define Clustered Bar Summaries for Groups of Cases dialog box

Select Other summary function and select educ

Select satjob and sex

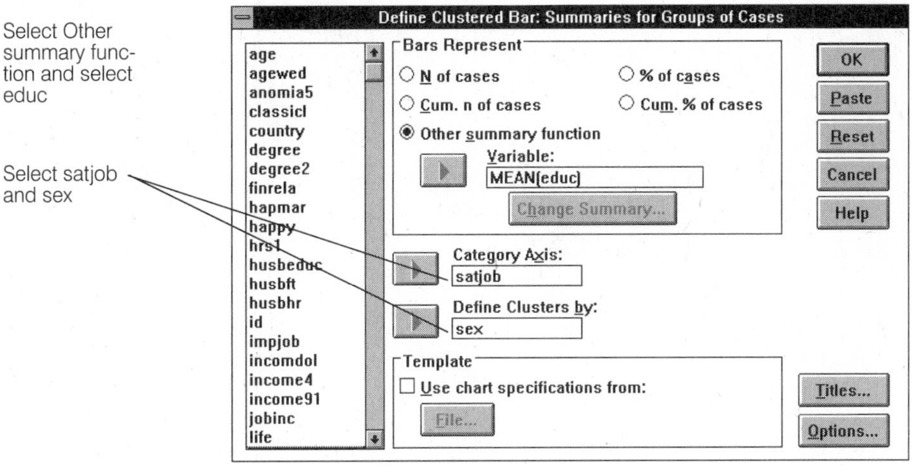

▶ In the Bars Represent group, select Other summary function and move *educ* into the Variable box.

MEAN(educ) appears in the Variable box. (The default summary function is to show the mean for the selected variable. You can change the summary function by selecting Change Summary as described in "Changing the Summary Statistic" on p. 534.)

▶ Move *satjob* into the Category Axis box.

▶ Move *sex* into the Define Clusters by box.

▶ Click on OK.

The resulting chart is shown in Figure A.3. To modify the chart, see "Modifying Charts" on p. 536.

Figure A.3 Clustered bar chart summarizing groups of cases

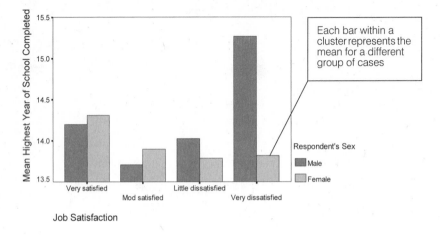

Data Summary Options

Most chart types have a dialog box similar to Figure A.1, where you specify the chart type and data structure for the chart you want. Choosing the right chart type icon is usually easy—just click on the icon that looks most like the chart you want. The data summary option can be a little trickier; as you read the descriptions below, think about how your data are organized:

Summaries for groups of cases. Displays a summary statistic for different groups of cases. For example, in Figure A.3, a single variable—*educ*—is summarized. Each bar within a cluster represents the mean for a different group of cases.

Summaries of separate variables. Displays summary statistics for different variables. In Figure A.5, several variables are summarized. Each bar within a cluster represents the mean of a separate variable.

Values of individual cases. Displays the actual values of a variable for different cases. No summary statistic (such as mean) is represented—rather, each bar represents the actual value of a case.

Click on the Help button in any initial chart dialog box for more specific information and examples for each chart type. It may take a bit of trial and error, but don't worry too much. If you get the wrong chart the first time, just go back to the Graphs menu and try again.

Creating a Chart Comparing Several Variables

The previous example describes how to create a chart comparing groups of cases. In this example, you will create a chart in which several different variables are grouped into clusters by selecting Summaries of separate variables (rather than Summaries for groups of cases) in the Bar Charts dialog box.

▶ Open the *country.sav* data file.

▶ From the menus choose:

  Graphs
    Bar...

This reopens the Bar Charts dialog box, as shown in Figure A.1.

▶ Click on the Clustered icon if it is not already selected.

▶ Click on Summaries of separate variables.

▶ Click on Define.

This opens the Define Clustered Bar Summaries of Separate Variables dialog box, as shown in Figure A.4. (You'll notice that this dialog box is similar but not identical to the one shown in Figure A.2.)

Figure A.4   Define Clustered Bar Summaries of Separate Variables dialog box

Select lifeexpf and lifeexpm

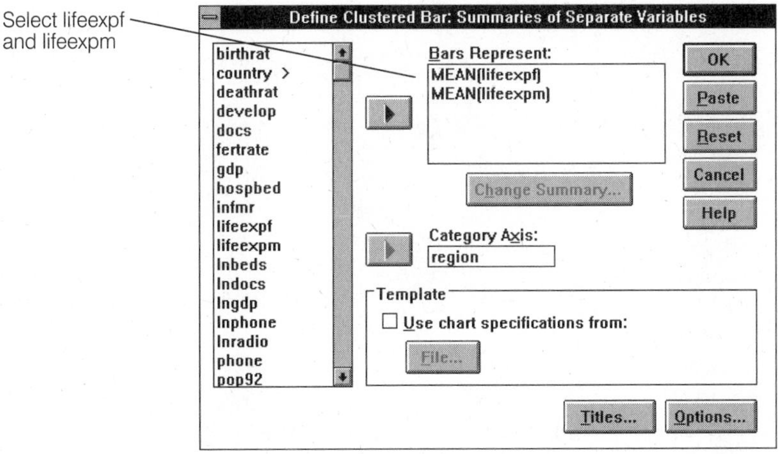

▶ Move the variables *lifeexpf* and *lifeexpm* into the Bars Represent group.

MEAN(lifeexpf) and MEAN(lifeexpm) appear in the list. (Mean is the default summary function. You can change the summary function by selecting Change Summary as described in "Changing the Summary Statistic" on p. 534.)

▶ Move *region* into the Category Axis box.

▶ Click on OK to create the chart.

Figure A.5 Clustered bar chart summarizing separate variables

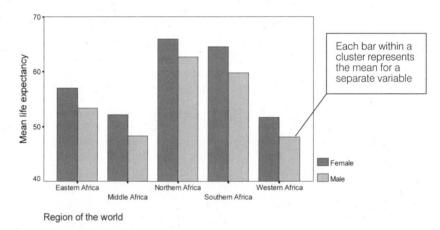

Creating a Chart Comparing Cases

You can also create a clustered bar chart that compares values of individual cases. For example, rather than showing the mean male and female life expectancies in different regions in Figure A.5, you might want to display values for several countries. (For this example, we'll use Select Cases on the Data menu to select the first five countries in the *country.sav* file.)

Bear in mind that the variables you select should be measured on comparable scales. In addition, since there will be a cluster of bars for each case, charts based on values of individual cases are not useful for large data files.

▶ Open the *country.sav* data file.

▶ Use Select Cases to restrict the analysis to the first five cases in the data file (see "Case Selection" on p. 559 in Appendix B).

▶ From the menus choose:

Graphs
  Bar...

This reopens the Bar Charts dialog box, as shown in Figure A.1.

▶ Click on the Clustered bar chart icon if it is not already selected.

▶ Click on Values of individual cases.

▶ Click on Define.

This opens the Define Clustered Bar Values of Individual Cases dialog box, as shown in Figure A.6.

Figure A.6 Define Clustered Bar Values of Individual Cases dialog box

Select lifeexpf
and lifeexpm

Select variable
and select
country

▶ Move the variables *lifeexpf* and *lifeexpm* into the Bars Represent group.

▶ Under Category Labels, select Variable and move *country* into the box.

▶ Click on OK to create the chart, as shown in Figure A.7.

Figure A.7 Clustered bar chart showing values of individual cases

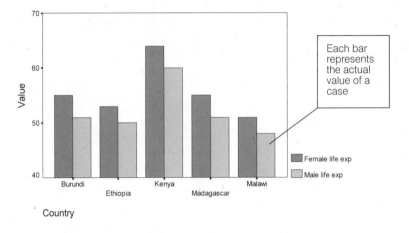

Changing the Summary Statistic

Many charts include an option to select a summary statistic. The default statistic is to display the mean, but you can choose from many different statistics.

Before you can change the summary statistic, you must specify a variable to be summarized.

▶ Select Other summary statistic and select a variable to be summarized. (See Figure A.2 and Figure A.4.)

▶ To change the summary statistic for a variable, select the variable (or variables) whose summary you want to change in the variable list under Bars Represent.

▶ Click on Change Summary.

This opens the Summary Function dialog box, as shown in Figure A.8.

Figure A.8 Summary Function dialog box

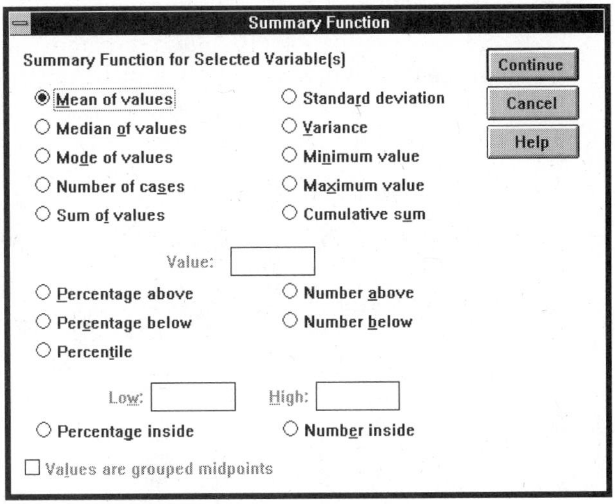

▶ Select the desired summary function and click on Continue.

Options in Creating Charts

Most chart-definition dialog boxes contain a Titles button, an Options button, and a Template control group.

- **Titles.** Opens the Titles dialog box, where you can enter a title, subtitle, and footnote for the chart. You can also change the titles and footnote in the Chart Editor after creating the chart.

- **Options.** Opens the Options dialog box, where you can control the way that missing values are processed in the creation of the chart.

To apply a template after creating the chart, use the Apply Chart Template command on the File menu.

- **Template.** Allows you to select an existing SPSS chart file, from which formatting specifications for the new chart will be copied as closely as possible. Select the check box in the Template group, then click the File button and choose an SPSS chart file saved on disk to serve as a template for the new chart.

Modifying Charts

When you create a chart directly from the Graphs menu, it opens in the SPSS Chart Carousel, as shown in Figure A.9. Think of the Carousel as a holding tank for newly created charts: you can browse through the charts in the Carousel, print them, or save them to disk. However, to modify a chart, you must move it out of the Carousel into a chart window.

Figure A.9 Chart Carousel

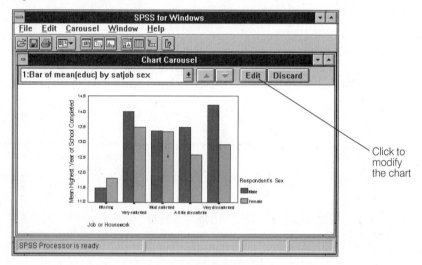

▶ To modify a chart that is currently displayed in the Chart Carousel, click on the Edit button.

This moves the chart into a chart window. The menu bar and toolbar change to offer options for modifying charts.

Modifying Chart Options

Each chart type has an Options dialog box, which contains options unique to that chart type. For example, the Scatterplot Options dialog box allows you to add fit lines to your scatterplot, as described in Chapter 9. The Pie Options dialog box shown in Figure A.10 allows you to explode or collapse slices in your pie chart.

▶ To open the options dialog box for the active chart (in this case, a pie chart), from the menus choose:

Chart
  Options...

Figure A.10 Pie Options dialog box

Select to
collapse
categories,
as shown in
Figure 4.4

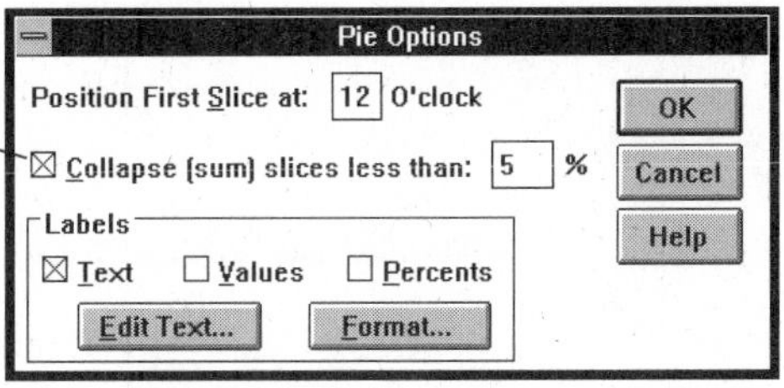

Hints on Editing Charts

Once you have moved your chart into a chart window, you can select chart objects to be modified by using the mouse or by choosing options from the menu bar and toolbar.

▶ Clicking once on an object (such as a bar or line) selects the object, allowing you to change attributes such as color or fill for that object. After selecting an object, modify the object using the Attributes menu or the toolbar.

▶ Double-clicking on an object generally brings up a dialog box that allows you to modify that object. For example, double-clicking on the scale axis will allow you to change scale, tick marks, and other characteristics for that axis.

▶ Clicking on Help in any dialog box will provide specific information about the options available in that dialog box.

Saving Chart Files

You can save a chart to disk as an SPSS chart file.

▶ To save a chart, activate it in the Chart Carousel or in its chart window and save it from the File menu.

Charts Used in This Book

The basic steps for creating a chart are similar, regardless of the chart type. Assuming you have worked through the examples above and understand the basic process of creating a chart, this section provides specific instructions to obtain a number of the charts discussed in this book.

Bar Charts

In a bar chart, the length of each bar represents a data value or statistic.

▶ To open the Bar Charts dialog box, from the menus choose:

Graphs
  Bar...

▶ To obtain the clustered bar chart in Figure 6.4, select the Clustered icon and Summaries for groups of cases in the Bar Charts dialog box, as described in "Creating a Chart Comparing Groups of Cases" on p. 528. Then select Other Summary Function and move *educ* into the Variable box. Move *satjob* into the Category Axis box, and move *sex* into Define Clusters by.

▶ To transpose the clustered bar chart in Figure 6.4, resulting in the chart in Figure 6.5, move the chart into a chart window and choose Transpose Data from the Series menu. (Alternatively, you follow the instructions for Figure 6.4, reversing the positions of *satjob* and *sex,* so that *sex* is selected for the Category axis and *satjob* is selected for Define Clusters by.)

▶ To obtain the clustered bar chart in Figure 8.5, select the Clustered icon and Summaries for groups of cases in the Bar Charts dialog box and click Define. Then select N of cases, move *income4* into the Category Axis box, and move *satjob* into Define Clusters by.

▶ To obtain the stacked bar chart in Figure 8.6, select the Stacked icon in the Bar Charts dialog box. Then select variables as described for Figure 8.5.

▶ To modify the stacked bar chart in Figure 8.6 to show a percentage scale as in Figure 8.7, move the chart into a chart window. Then select Options from the Chart menu, and select Change scale to 100% in the Stacked Bar Chart Options dialog box.

▶ To obtain the clustered bar chart in Figure 16.2, select the Clustered icon and Summaries for groups of cases in the Bar Charts dialog box and click Define. Then select Other Summary Function, move *hrs1* into the Variable box, move *degree* into the Category Axis box, and move *sex* into the Define Clusters by box.

Line and Area Charts

Line Charts and Area Charts are closely related to bar charts. All three chart types display counts, data values, or summary statistics for each discrete category of a categorical variable.

- The variable assigned to the Category Axis of a Line Chart or Area Chart should be measured on (at least) an ordinal scale, to justify the continuity implied by these chart types along the category axis.
- When a stacked area chart is based on Summaries of Different Variables or Values of Individual Cases, the variables or summaries should be on comparable scales, so that it makes sense to cumulate them.

Otherwise, the discussion of Bar Charts above applies in a straightforward way to Line and Area Charts.

▶ To open the Line Charts dialog box, from the menus choose:

Graphs
  Line...

▶ To obtain the multiple line chart in Figure 16.7, select the Multiple icon and Summaries for groups of cases in the Line Charts dialog box and click on Define. Then select Other Summary Function, move *hrs1* into the Variable box, move degree into the Category Axis box, and move *sex* into Define Lines by.

Pie Charts

Pie charts are discussed in Chapter 4.

Pie charts display data in a common, easily understood form. The Pie Charts dialog box offers the same data alternatives discussed above, allowing you to compare categories, variables, or individual data values. A pie chart implies that the summary statistics can be regarded as parts of a whole, so counts, percentages, and sums are the most commonly used statistics.

The Chart Editor lets you "explode" pie segments for emphasis or collapse the smallest segments into one. (See "Modifying Chart Options" on p. 536.)

▶ To open the Pie Charts dialog box, from the menus choose:

Graphs
  Pie...

▶ To obtain the pie chart shown in Figure 4.4, select Summaries for groups of cases in the Pie Charts dialog box. Then select N of cases as the Slices Represent alternative and move *wrkstat* into Define Slices by.

▶ To collapse the small categories shown in Figure 4.4 to obtain the chart shown in Figure 4.5, move the chart into a chart window, select Options from the Chart menu, and select Collapse (sum) slices less than 5%.

Boxplots

Boxplots are discussed in Chapter 7.

Boxplots are used to compare distributions. Each distribution is represented by a rectangular box whose length represents the variable's interquartile range, on a scale corresponding to the observed values of the variable. A line, or "whisker," extends from each end of the box to the variable's largest and smallest values, aside from those classed as outliers or extreme values. In SPSS, an **outlier** is a value that is more than one and one-half box lengths from the end of the box, while an **extreme value** is a value that is more than three box lengths from the end of the box. Outliers and extreme values are plotted individually and can be identified in the Chart Editor.

Boxplots are available from the Explore procedure (see Chapter 7), or from the Graphs menu.

▶ To open the Boxplots dialog box, from the menus choose:

Graphs
  Boxplot...

▶ To obtain the clustered boxplot in Figure 16.3, select the Clustered icon and Summaries for groups of cases in the Boxplots dialog box and click on Define. Then move *hrs1* into the Variable box, move *degree* into the Category Axis box, and move *sex* into Define Clusters by.

Case Labels

Like scatterplots, you can identify individual cases in boxplots. Simply specify a variable for Label Cases by in the dialog box in which you define options for the boxplot. You will then be able to identify the individually plotted cases on a boxplot. (See "Case Identification" on p. 173 in Chapter 9.)

Error Bar Charts

Error bar charts are discussed in Chapter 15.

Error bar charts are similar to boxplots but are usually used to compare confidence intervals or standard errors rather than the distributions. Each error bar is centered on the mean of a distribution and extends above and below to show a confidence interval or a specified number of standard errors or standard deviations.

▶ To open the Error Bar dialog box, from the menus choose:

Graphs
  Error Bar...

▶ To obtain the error bar chart in Figure 15.2, select the Simple icon and Summaries for groups of cases in the Error Bar dialog box and click on Define. Then move *hrs1* into the Variable box and move *degree* into the Category Axis box. Be sure that Confidence interval for mean is selected in the Bars Represent group.

Histograms

Histograms are discussed in Chapter 4 and Chapter 7.

A histogram displays the distribution of a single variable. It resembles a simple bar chart, but each bar represents the number of cases falling into a range of values for the variable.

You can request histograms from the Frequencies procedure or the Explore procedure, or you can obtain them directly from the Graphs menu.

Normal Probability Plots

Normal probability plots are discussed in Chapter 7 and Chapter 22.

Normal probability plots are used to check whether distributions of variables follow the normal distribution. They are essentially scatterplots of a variable's distribution against a normal distribution. If the data are a sample from a normal distribution, points will cluster along a straight (diagonal) line. SPSS offers two types of normal probability plots:

Normal Q-Q. The Q-Q (quantile-quantile) plot shows the variable's observed values on the *x*-axis, and the corresponding predicted values from a standard normal distribution on the *y*-axis.

Normal P-P. The P-P (proportion-proportion) plot shows the observed cumulative proportion of cases on the *x*-axis, and the predicted cumulative proportion of the normal distribution on the *y*-axis.

Detrended normal plot. A detrended normal probability plot uses the difference between the cases's observed value and its predicted value, rather than the predicted value itself, for the *y*-axis. If the sample is from a normal distribution, the points are randomly scattered around a horizontal line through 0. SPSS always produces detrended plots to accompany normal probability plots.

The Explore procedure offers Q-Q plots. The Linear Regression procedure offers P-P plots. Both types are available directly from the Graphs menu.

▶ To open the Normal Q-Q Plots dialog box, from the menus choose:

Graphs
  Normal Q-Q...

See Appendix B for instructions on how to compute a new variable.

▶ To obtain the normal Q-Q plot in Figure 13.5, compute a variable *diff* equal to the difference between the pre-race and post-race measurements. In the Normal Q-Q dialog box, move *diff* into the Variables box.

▶ To obtain the normal Q-Q plots in Figure 22.3 and Figure 22.4, you must run the regression described in that chapter and save the studentized residuals as a new variable as described in "Linear Regression Save: Creating New Variables" on p. 411 in Chapter 20. Then move *sre_1* (the studentized residuals variable saved by the regression) into the Variables box.

Transforming and Selecting Data

SPSS includes a powerful set of facilities for transforming data values and selecting which cases should be analyzed. This appendix covers two general types of data manipulation: data transformation and case selection.

Data transformation procedures change the actual values of your variables or create new variables. For example, you can create a new variable that contains the natural log of an existing variable. **Case selection** procedures do not change data values but restrict the number of cases used in the analysis. For example, you can restrict your analysis to people who are married or who are holding full-time jobs.

SPSS also provides a number of advanced data manipulation utilities that are not used in this book and are not discussed here. These utilities are described, however, in the online Help system.

Data Files

The data files used in the chapters and in the exercises are distributed on diskette to instructors who adopt this book for classroom use. Others can purchase the data files from the publisher.

Data Transformations

Often you need to make modifications to your data before you can perform your analysis. For small changes, such as the urbanization of Bhutan in Chapter 9, it is easy to enter the corrected value into the Data Editor. But suppose you want to take the natural log of several variables, each with 1500 cases, as you do for the analysis in Chapter 23? SPSS provides data transformation facilities to handle such tasks easily and accurately.

Data transformations affect the values of existing variables or create new variables. Transformations affect only the working data file; the changes do not become permanent unless you save the working data file to your disk.

Transformations at a Glance

This appendix describes the following transformations, available using the SPSS Transform menu:

Compute. Compute calculates data values according to a precise expression. With this option, you can do anything from set a variable to 0 for all cases to calculate an elaborate expression involving the values of other variables. You can assign the computed values to a new variable, or you can assign them to an existing variable (replacing the current values). You can also request that the computation be carried out selectively based on a conditional expression.

Recode. Recode assigns discrete values to a variable, based solely on the present values of the variable being recoded. You can assign the recoded values to the variable being recoded, or you can assign them to a new variable. You can also request that the computation be carried out selectively based on a conditional expression.

Automatic Recode. Automatic recode assigns successive integer codes—1, 2, 3, and so on—to a new variable, based on the existing codes of another variable. This saves you the effort of specifying how the recoding should be carried out.

The following options are also available on the Transform menu but are not discussed in this book. These transformations are described in the online Help system.

Random Number Seed. Lets you reproduce the pseudo-random numbers generated by SPSS for sampling and certain functions in the transformation language.

Count. Creates a new variable that counts for each case the number of times certain specified values occur in other variables. You can count, for example, the number of times that values of 1 or 2 occurs in a group of existing variables.

Rank Cases. Creates rank scores, which show each case's rank among all the cases in the file according to the values of a particular variable.

Create Time Series. Creates new time series, containing functions such as the differences between successive cases, in a time series data file.

Replace Missing Values. Supplies nonmissing values to replace missing values, according to any of several functions that might provide plausible values.

Run Pending Transformations. Forces SPSS to execute transformations that are pending as a result of the Transform & Merge Options setting. (See "Delaying Processing of Transformations" below.)

Saving Changes

Bear in mind when transforming your data that you are only changing the working data file.

▶ To make the changes permanent, save the working data file to your hard disk.

▶ To discard the changes, exit SPSS (or open a new data file) without saving the working data file.

Delaying Processing of Transformations

SPSS normally executes transformation commands as soon as you request them. However, since transformations can take several minutes to execute for a very large data file, there are times when you want to enter a dozen or more transformation commands one after another and then let the computer process them all at once.

▶ To prevent SPSS from processing transformations immediately, from the menus choose:

Edit
  Preferences...

This opens the Preferences dialog box, as shown in Figure B.1.

Figure B.1 Preferences dialog box

Select Calculate values before used

Preferences		
Session Journal C:\WINDOWS\TEMP\SPSS.JNL ☒ Record syntax in journal ⦿ Append ○ Overwrite [File...] **Toolbar Buttons** ⦿ Small ○ Large Special Workspace Memory Limit: [512] K bytes ☐ Open a syntax window at startup to run SPSS command syntax	**Transformation & Merge Options** ○ Calculate values immediately ⦿ Calculate values before used **Display Order for Variable Lists** ⦿ Alphabetical ○ File **Display Format for New Variables** Width: [8] Decimal Places: [2]	[OK] [Reset] [Cancel] [Help]
	[Graphics...] [Custom Currency...] [Output...]	

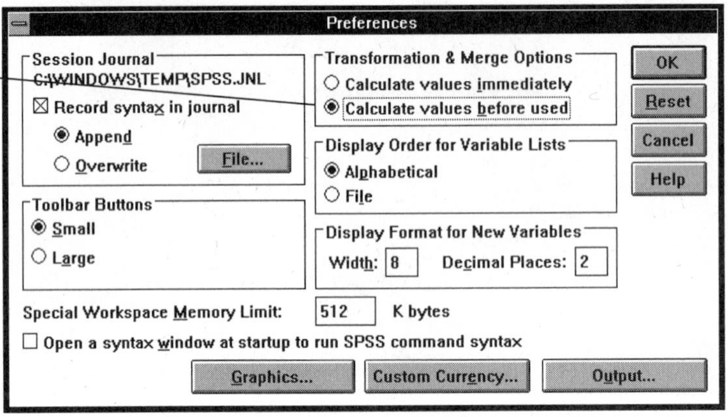

▶ Set Transform & Merge Options to Calculate values before used and click on OK.

With this setting, SPSS does not execute Compute and Recode transformations until you tell it to. In the meantime, the status bar displays the message Transformations pending and the results of transformations are not yet visible.

▶ To execute pending transformations, run a procedure that requires SPSS to use the data or choose Run Pending Transformations from the Transform menu.

When transformations are pending, the Data Editor will not allow you to make certain changes to your working data file.

Recoding Values

Recoding is done with a series of specifications, of the form, "If the old value is this, assign a new value of that." A case's existing value is checked against each of these specifications until one of them matches. Then the new value is assigned, and SPSS moves on to process the next case.

There are two Recode commands: Recode into Same Variables and Recode into Different Variables. The former changes the values of variables based solely on their existing values, while the latter creates new variables with values that depend only on the existing values of single variables.

- A case is never changed by more than one of a group of recode specifications.
- If a case doesn't match any of the recode specifications, its value remains unchanged (if recoding into same variable) or becomes system-missing (if recoding into a new variable).

Example: Recoding Age into Age Categories

This example recodes the variable *age* (age in years) into a new variable that contains age in one of three categories: 14 through 29, 30 through 49, and 50 or older.

▶ Open the *salary.sav* data file.

▶ From the menus choose:

Transform
  Recode ▶
    Into Different Variables...

This opens the Recode into Different Variables dialog box, as shown in Figure B.2.

Figure B.2   Recode into Different Variables dialog box

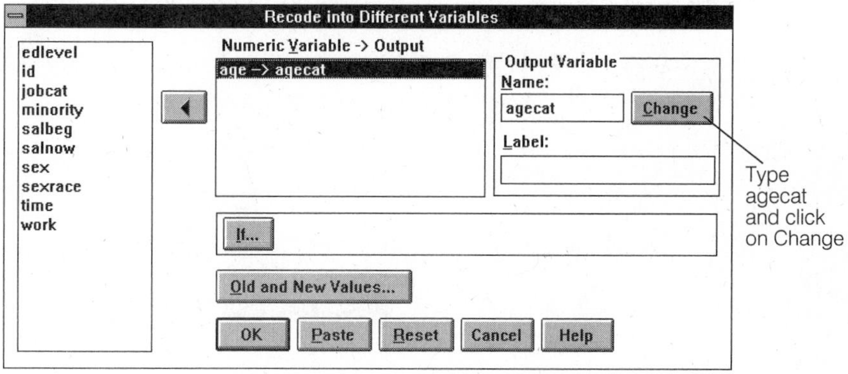

Move *age* into the Input Variable -> Output Variable list. The name of the list changes to reflect that a numeric variable has been selected, as shown in Figure B.2.

▶ In the Output Variable box, type *agecat* for the output variable and click on Change.

This adds agecat to the Numeric Variable -> Output list. A new variable *agecat* will be created, which contains the recoded values of *age*.

▶ Click on Old and New Values.

This opens the Old and New Values dialog box, as shown in Figure B.3.

Figure B.3   Old and New Values dialog box

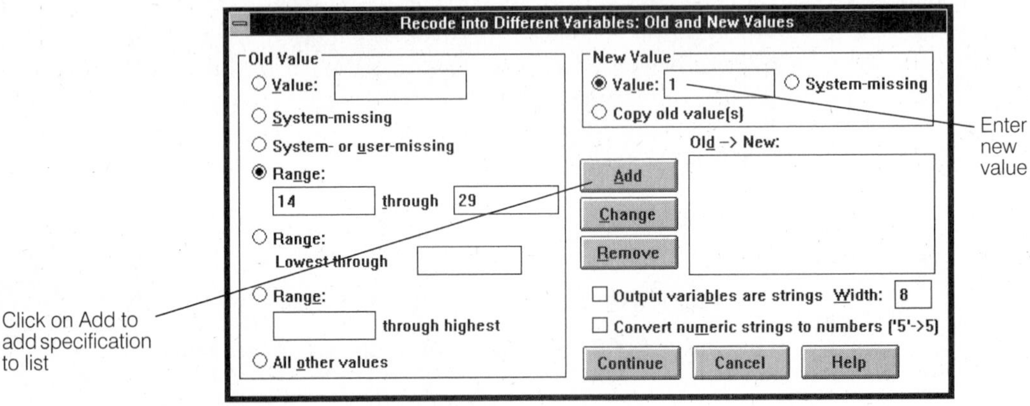

▶ In the Old Value group, select the first Range alternative.

▶ Type 14 in the first range box and 29 in the second range box.

▶ Type 1 in the New Value box.

▶ Click on Add.

The specification 14 thru 29 -> 1 is added to the Old -> New list. All ages between 14 and 29 will be coded 1 in the new *agecat* variable.

▶ Click again on Range. Type 30 in the first range box and 49 in the second range box.

▶ Type 2 in the New Value box and click on Add.

▶ Click on Range: through highest and type 50 in the box.

▶ Type 3 in the New Value box and click on Add.

That should take care of all age groups in this file. But what if someone is coded with an age less than 14? Since the file contains data about adults who work for a bank, that would surely be a coding mistake, but it could happen. It's best to be safe.

▶ In the Old Values box, click on All other values.

▶ In the New Value box, click on System-missing and click on Add one more time.

Figure B.4 Completed Old and New Values dialog box

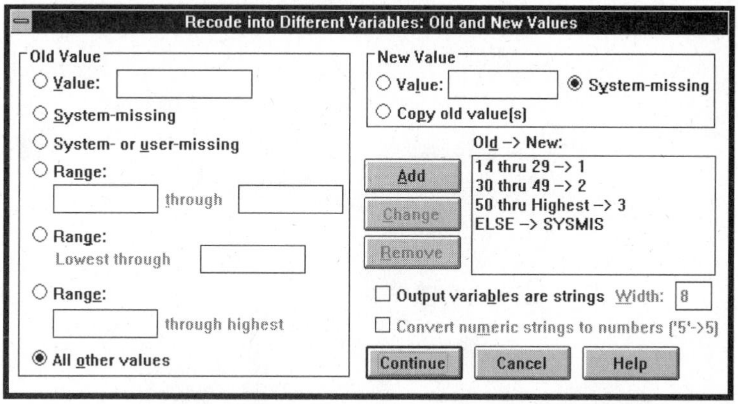

The Old and New Values dialog box should now look like Figure B.4. If it doesn't—if one of your specifications is incorrect—click on the incorrect specification in the Old -> New list, make the needed correction, and click on Change.

▶ Click on Continue to return to the Recode into Different Variables dialog box. Then click on OK to execute the transformation.

You have now changed the working data file; however, you don't want to make these changes a permanent part of the *salary.sav* data file.

▶ To avoid saving changes to the *salary.sav* data file, exit SPSS *without* saving changes or clear the Data Editor by selecting New from the File menu.

Computing Variables

The Compute Variable dialog box assigns the result of a single expression to a "target variable" for each case. The target variable can be a new variable or an existing variable (in which case the existing values will be overwritten). For example, you can compute standard scores for a variable, as described in the first example below. A great number of functions are available, so expressions can be quite complex.

▶ To open the Compute Variable dialog box, as shown in Figure B.5, from the menus choose:

Transform
  Compute...

Figure B.5   Compute Variable dialog box

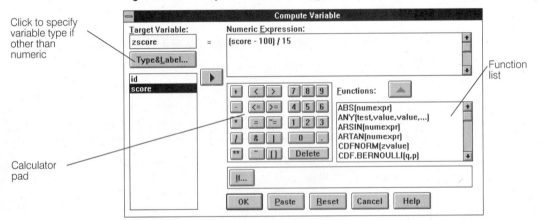

Unlike a spreadsheet, SPSS does not remember the formula used to compute data values or automatically update them. (In the example mentioned above, if you go back and change the values for the variable *score*, the *zscore* values will not be automatically recalculated to reflect the change.)

The Calculator Pad

The calculator pad allows you to paste operators and functions into your formula. You don't have to use the calculator pad: you can click anywhere in the Numeric Expression box and start typing. Often that's the simplest and quickest way to build an expression. The visual controls in the calculator pad are there to remind you of the possibilities and to reduce the likelihood that you won't remember how to spell one of the many functions available in SPSS.

To use the calculator pad, just click on buttons to paste symbols and operators at the insertion point. Use the mouse to move the insertion point.

To paste a function, select it in the scrolling list and click on the [▲] button. You must then fill in the arguments, which are the values that the function operates on.

A few basic calculator pad operators are described in Table B.1. The Help system contains a more detailed description of the calculator pad, with definitions of all the functions.

See "Example: Cumulative Distribution Function" on p. 553 for an example of using functions in an expression.

Table B.1 Calculator pad operators

*	Multiply
/	Divide
**	Raise to power
+	Add
–	Subtract

Example: Computing Z Scores

Suppose you have a sample of IQ scores, and you wish to calculate standard scores (Z scores) for the sample. Assuming that in the population IQ scores have a mean of 100 and a standard deviation of 15 (as was long assumed to be true), the formula is

$$z\text{score} = (\text{score} - 100)/15$$

To compute standard scores for a variable according to this formula:

▶ Open the *iq.sav* data file.

This file contains IQ scores for a hypothetical group of students.

▶ From the menus choose:

Transform
  Compute...

This opens the Compute Variable dialog box, as shown in Figure B.6.

Figure B.6 Compute Variable dialog box

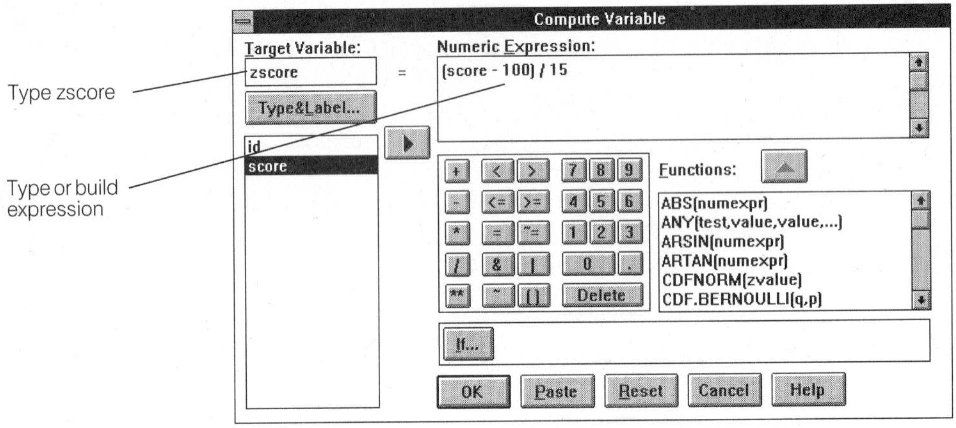

You can simply type the expression `(score-100)/15` directly in the Numeric Expression box or build it using the calculator pad, as follows:

▶ Click in the Target Variable box and type `zscore`.

▶ Click in the Numeric Expression box.

▶ Select score in the variable list and click on ▶.

The variable name *score* is pasted into the expression at the insertion point.

▶ Enter –100.

▶ Select the entire expression score –100 and click on the ( ) button.

The expression now reads (score –100).

▶ Enter /15.

The expression now reads (score –100)/15.

▶ Click on OK.

SPSS computes *Z* scores for all cases in the working data file.

Since zscore is a numeric variable, you don't have to click the Type & Label button.

Example: Cumulative Distribution Function

You can calculate the proportion of the population with Z scores greater in absolute value than each of the Z scores in your sample, as discussed in question 10 in the exercises for Chapter 11. Assuming the variable *zscore* contains the Z scores for your sample, the formula is

$$\text{twotailp} = 2 * (1 - \text{cdfnorm}(\text{abs}(\text{zscore})))$$

▶ If you want to attempt this example, you can substitute any variable that contains Z scores for the *zscore* variable named in the formula above. (You can use the Descriptives procedure to save Z scores for any variable, as described in Chapter 5.)

▶ From the menus choose:

Transform
  Compute...

This opens the Compute Variable dialog box.

▶ Type `twotailp` in the Target Variable box.

Figure B.7 Compute Variable dialog box

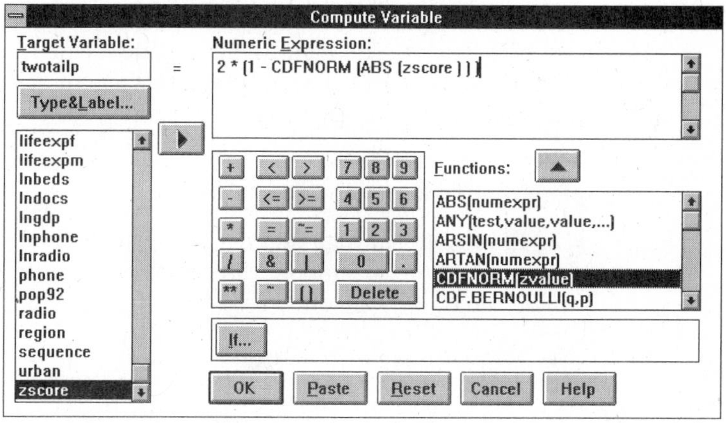

You can simply type the expression `2*(1-CDFNORM(ABS(zscore)))`, as shown in Figure B.7, or build the expression as follows:

▶ Enter `2*(1-)`.

▶ With the cursor inside the parenthesis, select CDFNORM(zvalue) in the Functions list and click on ⬛.

The CDFNORM function is pasted into the formula at the insertion point. The expression now reads 2 * (1– CDFNORM(?)), with the question mark selected. You must replace the question mark with an argument for the CDFNORM function.

▶ Select ABS(numexpr) in the Functions list and click on ⬛.

The expression now reads 2 * (1– CDFNORM (ABS(?))). Once again, the question mark is selected; you must now supply an argument for the ABS function.

▶ Select *zscore* in the variable list and click on ⬛.

The variable *zscore* is now pasted in as the argument for the ABS function. The expression is now complete.

▶ Click on OK.

SPSS computes the proportions for all cases in the working data file.

Automatic Recoding

Automatic Recode is particularly useful as a way of converting a string variable into a numeric variable.

SPSS's Recode facility is quite useful but requires you to enter detailed specifications. The Automatic Recode facility needs no specifications. It simply converts all the codes of a current variable into new codes— 1, 2, 3, and so on—for a new variable.

Example: Creating Numeric Country Codes

In the *country.sav* data file, the string variable *country* contains the name of each country. Suppose you want to create numeric country codes. You can do this as follows:

▶ From the menus choose:

Transform
  Automatic Recode...

This opens the Automatic Recode dialog box, as shown in Figure B.8.

Figure B.8   Automatic Recode dialog box

Type name for new variable and click on New Name

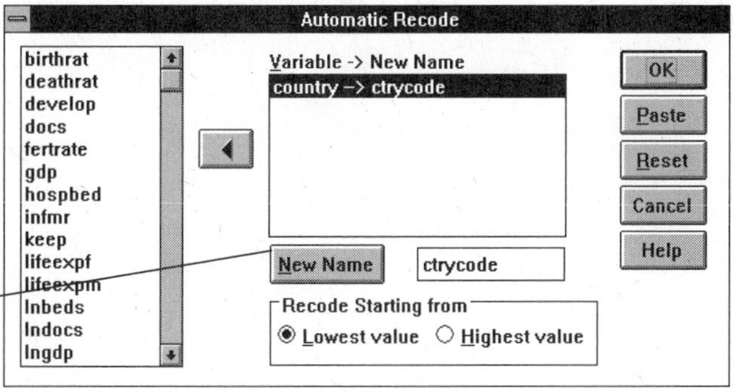

▶ Select *country* in the variable list and move it into the Variable -> New Name list.

▶ Type `ctrycode` in the New Name box and click on New Name.

▶ Click on OK.

SPSS creates the new variable *ctrycode*, which contains a unique numeric code for each country. The codes are assigned in sequence; the first country will have a code of 1, the second 2, and so on. If there were several cases for the same country, they would all be assigned the same code value.

Since the original variable *country* does not have value labels, the actual values of *country* (Afghanistan, Albania, Algeria, and so on) are used as value labels for the new variable *ctrycode*.

Conditional Transformations

If you want to transform the values of only some cases, depending on their data values, you need a **conditional transformation**, one that is carried out only if a logical condition is true. For example, you might want to transform *only* cases for people who are full-time workers.

The Compute Variable dialog box, both Recode dialog boxes, and the Count dialog box (not shown) allow you to specify such a logical condition.

▶ To specify a logical condition for a transformation, click on If in the Compute Variable, Recode, or Count dialog box.

This opens a dialog box where you can specify a logical condition. For example, the Compute Variable If Cases dialog box is shown in Figure B.9.

Figure B.9   Compute Variable If Cases dialog box

Select to specify a logical condition

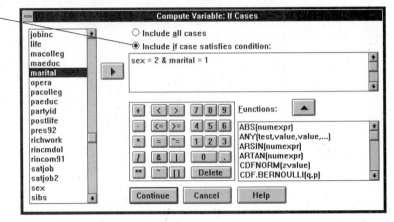

See "The Calculator Pad" on p. 550.

This dialog box contains the familiar Calculator Pad. Here you use it to build a logical condition, one that is either true or false for a case, depending on the case's data values. Table B.2 describes some operators that are particularly useful in building logical conditions.

Table B.2   Operators useful in logical expressions

<	Less than
>	Greater than
<=	Less than or equal to
>=	Greater than or equal to
=	Equal to
~=	Not equal to
&	And
|	Or
~	Not

The logical expression sex = 2 & marital = 1, for example, is true only for those cases in which *both* conditions are met: the variable *sex* must equal 2 *and* the variable *marital* must equal 1. The logical expression sex = 2 | marital = 1, by contrast, is true if either of the conditions is met.

Example: Wife's Employment Status

The General Social Survey contains employment status questions for the respondent and for the respondent's spouse. The respondent could be either husband or wife, depending on who was interviewed. This means that for each household, the wife's work status could be coded in either the variable *wrkstat* (if the wife was interviewed) *or* in the spouse's work status variable *spwrksta* (if the husband was interviewed). To create a variable containing, for all married couples, the wife's employment status, you might proceed as follows:

▶ To open the Compute Variable dialog box (see Figure B.10), from the menus choose:

Transform
  Compute...

Figure B.10 Compute Variable dialog box

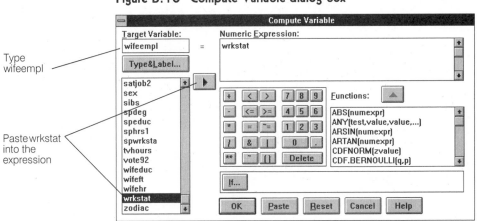

▶ In the Compute Variable dialog box, type `wifeempl` into the Target Variable box.

▶ Select *wrkstat* in the variable list and press ▶ to move it into the Numeric Expression box.

The new variable *wifeempl* will have the same value as the variable *wrkstat*. However, you must specify that this expression will only be evaluated for cases where the respondent is a married woman.

▶ Click on If.

This opens the Compute Variable If Cases dialog box, as shown in Figure B.11.

Figure B.11 Compute Variable If Cases dialog box

Select Include if case satisfies condition

Enter expression

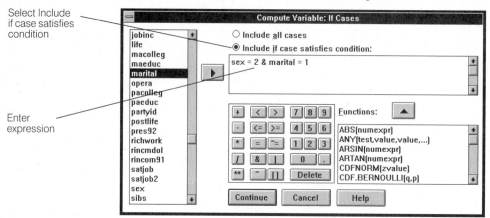

▶ Select Include if case satisfies condition.

▶ Using either the calculator pad or the keyboard, enter the condition `sex = 2 & marital = 1`.

This condition specifies that the new value should be computed only for cases for whom the value of the variable *sex* equals 2 (the code for female) *and* for whom the value of *marital* equals 1 (married). For cases that do not meet this condition, the new variable *wifeempl* will be equal to the system-missing value.

▶ Click on Continue to return to the Compute Variables dialog box. Then click on OK.

This creates a new variable *wifeempl*, which is equal to *wrkstat* for married women. For cases where the respondent is not married, or is a man, the value of *wifeempl* is not defined (system-missing).

At this point, you're halfway there. But what about respondents who are married men? In that case the wife's employment status would be coded in the variable *spwrksta*, which contains the work status of the respondent's spouse.

▶ Open the Compute Variable dialog box again.

▶ Delete *wrkstat* from the Numeric Expression box.

▶ Select the variable *spwrksta* and paste it into the Numeric Expression box.

▶ Click on If.

The logical expression still reads sex = 2 & marital = 1.

▶ Delete the 2 and type 1 in its place.

The expression now reads sex = 1 & marital = 1.

▶ Click on Continue and then click on OK.

This sets *wifeempl* equal to *spwrksta* for married men. To summarize, the first transformation creates a new variable *wifeempl*, which is equal to *wrkstat* for married women and not defined for others. The second conditional transformation sets *wifeempl* equal to *spwrksta* for married men. The end result is a variable equal to wife's employment status for all married couples. For unmarried respondents, neither transformation is executed and *wifeempl* is never changed. Since it's a new variable, it is assigned the system-missing value for the unmarried respondents.

Case Selection

Sometimes you want to analyze only part of your cases. For example, some of the analyses described in this book look only at full-time workers or only at college graduates.

The Select Cases dialog box allows you to restrict your analysis to a specific group of cases. There are a number of options for selecting cases:

- You can choose cases according to a logical condition based on their data values.
- You can select a random sample of the cases in your file.
- You can select a range of cases according to their order in the file.
- You can select those cases that are marked with a non-zero value for a "filter variable."

▶ From the menus choose:

Data
  Select Cases...

This opens the Select Cases dialog box, as shown in Figure B.12.

Figure B.12 Select Cases dialog box

Select If condition is satisfied

Specify temporary or permanent selection

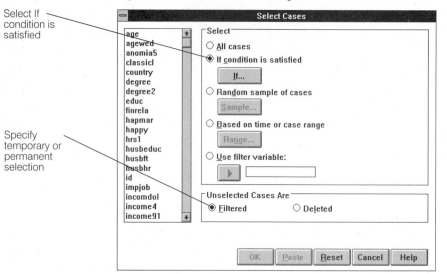

Temporary or Permanent Selection

The Select Cases dialog box offers a choice between filtering cases (selecting temporarily) or deleting cases (selecting permanently). The distinction between temporary and permanent case selection is important to understand.

- When you **filter** cases, or select a temporary subset, the unselected cases remain in the working data file. You can regain all the original cases at any time.

- When you **delete** cases, or select a permanent subset, SPSS deletes them forever from your working data file. If you save the working data file, replacing the copy on your disk, the deleted cases are gone forever from that file, too. This can be useful because it allows you to save a smaller data file.

If you haven't saved the working data file, you can often "undo" a permanent case selection by reopening the original data file. If you have saved the working data file there is no way to get back cases that have been deleted, unless you have a backup copy of the data file.

Example: Selecting Full-Time Employees

Many of the analyses in this book that use the GSS data restrict the analysis to full-time workers. In the *gss.sav* file, respondents who are employed full time are coded 1 for the variable *wrkstat*. To select full-time employees:

▶ From the menus choose:

Data
  Select Cases...

▶ Select If condition is satisfied alternative in the Select Cases dialog box (see Figure B.12).

▶ Select Filtered in the Unselected Cases Are group.

This assures that the unselected cases will remain in the working data file if you want to use them in future analyses.

▶ Click on If.

This opens the Select Cases If dialog box, as shown in Figure B.13. This dialog box, which strongly resembles the Compute Variable If Cases dialog box shown in Figure B.9, allows you to specify a conditional expression.

Figure B.13 Select Cases If dialog box

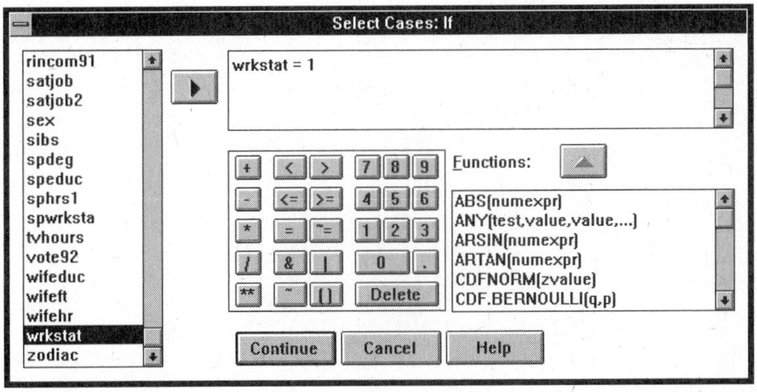

▶ Enter the expression wrkstat = 1.

▶ Click on Continue to return to the Select Cases dialog box.

▶ Click on OK.

Cases for people who work full time are now selected. In the Data Editor, unselected cases are indicated by a slash mark over the row number.

▶ To turn off case selection, open the Select Cases dialog box again and select All cases.

Example: Selecting College Graduates

In the *gss.sav* data file, the variable *degree* indicates the highest degree earned by each respondent. Four-year college graduates are coded 3 (for bachelor's degree) or 4 (for advanced degree). To select people with bachelor's or advanced degrees:

▶ Open the Select Cases dialog box as described above.

▶ Select Filtered in the Unselected Cases Are group.

▶ Select If condition is satisfied and click on If.

▶ Enter **degree** >= 3 in the Numeric Expression box.

This expression specifies that cases should be selected "if degree is greater than or equal to 3."

▶ Click on Continue to return to the Select Cases dialog box and click on OK.

Other Selection Methods

Other options available in the Select Cases dialog box include:

Random sample. Sometimes you want a random subset of cases. You have no particular criterion for choosing which cases to process, but you don't want the whole data file.

Based on time or case range. Under some circumstances, it is desirable to select a range of cases according to the order of cases, as displayed in the Data Editor. This can be useful for time series data files.

Use filter variable. A filter variable is simply a variable that indicates whether or not a particular case should be selected. Cases for which the specified filter variable has a valid non-zero value are retained. Cases for which it is 0 or missing are dropped.

The t Distribution

t Value	0.0	0.25	0.50	0.75	1.00	1.25
df	Two-tailed Probability					
1	1.0000	.8440	.7048	.5903	.5000	.4296
2	1.0000	.8259	.6667	.5315	.4226	.3377
3	1.0000	.8187	.6514	.5077	.3910	.2999
4	1.0000	.8149	.6433	.4950	.3739	.2794
5	1.0000	.8125	.6383	.4870	.3632	.2666
6	1.0000	.8109	.6349	.4816	.3559	.2578
7	1.0000	.8098	.6324	.4777	.3506	.2515
8	1.0000	.8089	.6305	.4747	.3466	.2466
9	1.0000	.8082	.6291	.4724	.3434	.2428
10	1.0000	.8076	.6279	.4705	.3409	.2398
11	1.0000	.8072	.6269	.4690	.3388	.2372
12	1.0000	.8068	.6261	.4677	.3370	.2351
13	1.0000	.8065	.6254	.4666	.3356	.2333
14	1.0000	.8062	.6248	.4657	.3343	.2318
15	1.0000	.8060	.6243	.4649	.3332	.2305
16	1.0000	.8058	.6239	.4641	.3322	.2293
17	1.0000	.8056	.6235	.4635	.3313	.2282
18	1.0000	.8054	.6231	.4629	.3306	.2273
19	1.0000	.8053	.6228	.4624	.3299	.2265
20	1.0000	.8051	.6225	.4620	.3293	.2257
22	1.0000	.8049	.6220	.4612	.3282	.2244
24	1.0000	.8047	.6216	.4605	.3273	.2234
26	1.0000	.8046	.6213	.4600	.3265	.2224
28	1.0000	.8044	.6210	.4595	.3259	.2216
30	1.0000	.8043	.6207	.4591	.3253	.2210
35	1.0000	.8040	.6202	.4583	.3242	.2196
40	1.0000	.8039	.6198	.4576	.3233	.2186
45	1.0000	.8037	.6195	.4572	.3227	.2178
50	1.0000	.8036	.6193	.4568	.3221	.2171
∞	1.0000	.8026	.6171	.4533	.3173	.2113

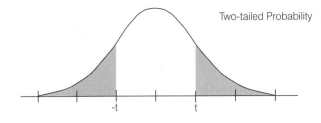

Two-tailed Probability

1.50	1.75	2.00	2.25	2.50	2.75	3.00	t Value
			Two-tailed Probability*				df
.3743	.3305	.2952	.2662	.2422	.2220	.2048	1
.2724	.2222	.1835	.1534	.1296	.1107	.0955	2
.2306	.1784	.1393	.1099	.0877	.0707	.0577	3
.2080	.1550	.1161	.0876	.0668	.0514	.0399	4
.1939	.1405	.1019	.0743	.0545	.0403	.0301	5
.1843	.1307	.0924	.0654	.0465	.0333	.0240	6
.1773	.1236	.0856	.0592	.0410	.0285	.0199	7
.1720	.1182	.0805	.0546	.0369	.0251	.0171	8
.1679	.1140	.0766	.0510	.0339	.0225	.0150	9
.1645	.1107	.0734	.0482	.0314	.0205	.0133	10
.1618	.1079	.0708	.0459	.0295	.0189	.0121	11
.1595	.1056	.0687	.0440	.0279	.0176	.0111	12
.1575	.1037	.0668	.0424	.0266	.0165	.0102	13
.1558	.1020	.0653	.0411	.0255	.0156	.0096	14
.1544	.1005	.0639	.0399	.0245	.0149	.0090	15
.1531	.0993	.0628	.0389	.0237	.0142	.0085	16
.1520	.0981	.0617	.0380	.0229	.0137	.0081	17
.1510	.0971	.0608	.0372	.0223	.0132	.0077	18
.1500	.0963	.0600	.0365	.0217	.0127	.0074	19
.1492	.0954	.0593	.0359	.0212	.0123	.0071	20
.1478	.0941	.0580	.0348	.0204	.0117	.0066	22
.1467	.0929	.0569	.0339	.0197	.0111	.0062	24
.1457	.0919	.0560	.0331	.0191	.0107	.0059	26
.1448	.0911	.0553	.0325	.0186	.0103	.0056	28
.1441	.0903	.0546	.0319	.0181	.0100	.0054	30
.1426	.0889	.0533	.0308	.0173	.0094	.0049	35
.1415	.0878	.0523	.0300	.0166	.0089	.0046	40
.1406	.0869	.0516	.0294	.0161	.0086	.0044	45
.1399	.0863	.0509	.0289	.0157	.0083	.0042	50
.1336	.0801	.0455	.0244	.0124	.0060	.0027	∞

*For one-tailed probablity, divide by 2

Areas under the Normal Curve

One-tailed

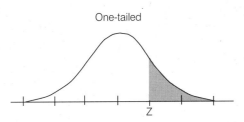

Two-tailed

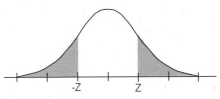

Z Scores	Probability		Z Scores	Probability	
	One-tailed	Two-tailed		One-tailed	Two-tailed
.0	.50000	1.00000	1.96	.02500	.05000
.1	.46017	.92034	2.0	.02275	.04550
.2	.42074	.84148	2.1	.01786	.03573
.3	.38209	.76418	2.2	.01390	.02781
.4	.34458	.68916	2.3	.01072	.02145
.5	.30854	.61708	2.4	.00820	.01640
.6	.27425	.54851	2.5	.00621	.01242
.7	.24196	.48393	2.6	.00466	.00932
.8	.21186	.42371	2.7	.00347	.00693
.9	.18406	.36812	2.8	.00256	.00511
1.0	.15866	.31731	2.9	.00187	.00373
1.1	.13567	.27133	3.0	.00135	.00270
1.2	.11507	.23014	3.1	.00097	.00194
1.3	.09680	.19360	3.2	.00069	.00137
1.4	.08076	.16151	3.3	.00048	.00097
1.5	.06681	.13361	3.4	.00034	.00067
1.6	.05480	.10960	3.5	.00023	.00047
1.7	.04457	.08913	3.6	.00016	.00032
1.8	.03593	.07186	3.7	.00011	.00022
1.9	.02872	.05743	3.8	.00007	.00014

Z Scores	Probability	
	One-tailed	Two-tailed
3.9	.00005	.00010
4.0	.00003	.00006
4.1	.00002	.00004

Z Scores	Probability	
	One-tailed	Two-tailed
4.2	.00001	.00003
4.3	.00001	.00002
4.4	.00001	.00001

Descriptions of Data Files

gss.sav	1500 randomly selected cases from the 1993 General Social Survey. Some variables have been recoded or otherwise modified. Cases were dropped due to case number limitations for the student version of SPSS. See Davis and Smith (1993).
gssft.sav	Only full-time employees (*wrkstat*=1) and a subset of variables from *gss.sav*.
country.sav	Demographic information for 122 countries. Most of the data are from 1992. See *The World Almanac and Book of Facts* (1994).
cntry15.sav	A random sample of 15 countries from *country.sav*.
buying.sav	Information about buying behavior for 100 married couples. One of the goals of the study was to examine husband and wife agreement in product purchases (Davis & Ragsdale, 1983).
electric.sav	A sample of 240 men from the Western Electric Study. Half of the men experienced a cardiac event and half did not. The Western Electric Study was a prospective study of factors related to the incidence of coronary heart disease. The procedures according to which participants were selected, examined, and followed are described in Paul et al. (1963).
endorph.sav	Beta endorphin levels before and after a half marathon run for 11 men. See Dale et al. (1987).
salary.sav	Information about 474 employees hired by a Midwestern bank between 1969 and 1971. The bank was subsequently involved in EEO litigation. For additional information, see Roberts (1979, 1980).

renal.sav   Contains medical data on 84 patients, all undergoing cardiac surgery. Forty-two patients experienced acute renal failure; the other 42 did not. The study is described in Corwin et al. (1989).

schools.sav   Demographic and performance data for 64 Chicago high schools for 1993 and 1994. See the *Chicago Sun-Times* (1993, 1994).

Bibliography

Cedercreutz, C. 1978. Hypnotic treatment of 100 cases of migraine. In: *Hypnosis at Its Bicentennial*, F. H. Frankel and H. S. Zamansky, eds. New York: Plenum.

Chicago Sun Times. 1993. Demographic and performance data for 64 Chicago high schools, November 16.

_____. 1994. Demographic and performance data for 64 Chicago high schools, October 27.

Corwin, H. L., S. M. Sprague, G. A. DeLaria, and M. J. Norušis. 1989. Acute renal failure associated with cardiac operations. *Journal of Thoracic and Cardiovascular Surgery*, 98:6, 1107-1112.

Dale, G., J. A. Fleetwood, A. Weddell, and R. D. Ellis. 1987. β-endorphin: A factor in "fun run" collapse? *British Medical Journal*, 294: 1004.

Davis, H., and E. Ragsdale. 1983. Unpublished working paper. Graduate School of Business, University of Chicago.

Davis, J. A., and T. W. Smith. 1972–1993. General Social Surveys. Chicago: National Opinion Research Center.

Neter, J., W. Wasserman, and M. Kutner. 1985. *Applied linear statistical models*. 2nd ed. Homewood, Ill.: Richard D. Irwin, Inc.

Paul, O., et al. 1963. A longitudinal study of coronary heart disease. *Circulation*, 28: 20–31.

Roberts, H. V. 1979. An analysis of employee compensation. *Report 7946*. Center for Mathematical Studies in Business and Economics, University of Chicago.

_____. 1980. Statistical bases in the measurement of employment discrimination. In: *Comparable Worth: Issues and Alternatives*, E. R. Livernash, ed. Washington, D.C.: Equal Employment Advisory Council.

Robey, B., S. O. Rutstein, and L. Morris. 1993. The fertility decline in developing countries. *Scientific American*, 269:6, 60–67.

Santelmann, N. 1991. The FYI CEO cholesterol level contest. *Forbes*, 147: 39–40.

Stevens, S. S. 1946. On the theory of scales of measurement. *Science*, 103: 677–680.

The World Almanac and Book of Facts. 1994. R. Famighetti, ed. Mahwah, N.J.: Funk & Wagnalls.

Velleman, P., and L. Wilkinson. 1993. Nominal, ordinal, interval, and ratio typologies are misleading. *The American Statistician*, 47:1, 65–72.

Index